*Bear Manor Media*
Presents

# Hold That Ghost

Including the Original Shooting Script

## By Ron Palumbo

Foreword by Robert Rinaldo

Series Editor
Philip J. Riley

UNIVERSAL FILMSCRIPT SERIES
FIRST EDITION


**Published by**
**BearManor Media**
**P.O. Box 71426**
**Albany, GA 31708**
**E-mail: books@benohmart.com**
**Phone: 580-252-3547**

The purpose of this series is the preservation of the art of writing for the screen. Rare books have been a source of enjoyment and an investment for the serious collector, and even in limited printings there were usually a few thousand produced. Scripts, however, numbered only fifty at most, and we are proud to present them in their original form. Some are final shooting scripts and some are earlier drafts, so that students, libraries, archives and film-lovers might, for the first time, study them in their original form. In producing these volumes, we hope that the unique art of screenplay writing will be preserved for future generations.

The opinions expressed in this series are those of the individual authors and not the publisher.

Front cover poster courtesy of Bob Furmanek.
Back cover art courtesy of Ron Palumbo.

Manufactured in the
United States of America

*To two great teams:*
*Bud and Lou, and Bob and Fred*

# Contents

# Acknowledgements

*H*old That Ghost was Abbott and Costello's second and, as it turned out, third starring film. As most fans know, it was shot immediately after their first, *Buck Privates,* temporarily shelved while the boys made *In The Navy,* and then put back into work to add musical numbers, new scenes, and revisions to existing scenes. It's hard to say if the original version would have been better than the one we know. But this volume, with the original screenplay, revisions script, and over 200 photographs, gives us the best opportunity to compare them. The first part of the book traces the original production, which was called "Oh, Charlie," and unfolds in shooting order. This is followed by the second round of filming and what ultimately became *Hold That Ghost.*

Obviously this picture was more complicated than most to trace. I would again like to express my deepest gratitude to Bob Furmanek, my collaborator on *Abbott and Costello in Hollywood* and other projects. His research for that book once again provided the sturdy foundation for another. Thank you, Bob.

My thanks to the late Phil Riley for creating the MagicImage Filmscript series, and advocating an Abbott and Costello branch.

Thank you to Ben Ohmart and Bear Manor for adopting MagicImage and his unfailing support.

I remain greatly indebted to the Abbott and Costello families: the late Bud Abbott, Jr.; Vickie Abbott Wheeler and Don Wheeler for giving us unprecedented access to Bud's scrapbook; Paddy Costello Humphreys for permitting unlimited access to Lou's scrapbook; and an extra special thanks to Chris Costello for donating hours of interviews she conducted with Betty (Mrs. Bud) Abbott, Maxene Andrews, Robert Arthur, Pat Costello, Alex Gottlieb, Arthur Lubin for her book, *Lou's On First.*

I have also drawn from interviews conducted for *Abbott and Costello in Hollywood* with Arthur Lubin, Robert Lees, Patty Andrews, Pat Costello, and Norman Abbott. In supplementing that research, I had the pleasure of interviewing Elwood Bredell's granddaughter, Cheryl; the late Dann Cahn, whose father, Phil, edited many Abbott and Costello hits, including *Hold That Ghost*; Richard Carlson's son, Hank; and Fred Rinaldo's son, Robert. I also referred to an interview with Robert Lees conducted by Jim Mulholland for *Abbott & Costello Quarterly.* Jim also alerted me to Richard Carlson's homage to Lou Costello in an episode of *Burke's Law.* Thanks, Jim.

I am grateful to Tom and Dorothy Fahn for their invaluable help with research in Los Angeles while I was in New York. Thanks, guys. I am also indebted to Michael Ribak at NBC Universal, Ron Borst, Bill Honor, and Jonathan Reichman.

Many thanks to the staffs of the Academy of Motion Picture Arts and Sciences Margaret Herrick Library (Los Angeles) and the Billy Rose Theater Collection of the New York Public Library at Lincoln Center (New York) over the years. A special thanks to Ned Comstock at the USC Cinematic Arts Library in Los Angeles. Anyone who writes about film knows how invaluable Ned is.

Most importantly, this book, or any of my projects, would be not be possible without the patience, love, and support of my wife, Karen, and our daughter, Vienna.

*—Ron Palumbo*

# Foreword
## by Robert Rinaldo

My old friend Pierre Rissient, the French cinema legend known as Mr. Cannes Film Festival, always called me the "Son of Abbott and Costello." In a *Crazy House* kind of way there was an element of truth to that.

My father, Frederic I. Rinaldo, and his writing collaborator, Robert Lees, wrote the best, most iconic Abbott and Costello movies, beginning with *Hold That Ghost*. For better or for worse, Abbott and Costello always shadowed my life.

From my earliest days I remember driving with my father in our brand new Oldsmobile 88 to the main gate at Universal Studios, where the security guard would give us a sharp salute as the gate slid open. We would drive on the lot to my father's plush office where he and his partner would write their scripts.

On the screen, Abbott and Costello played two everyday guys who tried to find their way through life. Whenever they came to a fork in the road, they always picked the wrong road. I believe this simple truth accounted for their enormous success. The vast majority of the people who struggled every day found that through Abbott and Costello they could laugh at their own condition and the dilemmas that they faced in their lives.

It is here where the intersection of my father's beliefs cross with the characters in the film. My father, to the bone, was a patrician, born into a well-to-do Upper West Side New York family, a graduate of Dartmouth and would-be Harvard Law School student. Because of the experiences of his life—the Great Depression, the worldwide rise of fascism, and world war—he would become a member of the Communist Party, a founder of the Screen Writers Guild and, in 1951, a blacklisted screenwriter. That transformation was truly astounding, and my father (Bobby Lees, too) literally became a common man, a champion of the working class and of the people. You could say that he was the perfect writer for Abbott and Costello because he truly understood what made the duo tick—not in a political sense but in the life struggles of the average person.

When Ron Palumbo first interviewed me about my father and those Abbott and Costello movies, I had to tell him that for me the story was not so much about Abbott and Costello as it was about the Hollywood Blacklist. It was a jarring juxtaposition: two successful Hollywood comedy writers cast down, literally overnight, into this unbelievable nightmare. What my father loved to do more than anything else was to make people laugh. The blacklist took that away from him and it took it away from you.

I believe that this revelation gave the subject matter a new dimension. It not only put Abbott and Costello into a broader context but also brought my father out from the shadows to bestow on him the full credit he deserves in the history of Hollywood and his truly historic stance as a great American.

The Hollywood studios never conceded that there was a blacklist because it was totally illegal. You didn't get a letter or a phone call. The studio gate told you if you were blacklisted or not. For years it opened for my father. One day when he drove to the studio to return to work, the gate did not open. For my father it would never open again.

# Abbott and Costello Meet Universal

Bud Abbott (1897-1974) and Lou Costello (1906-1959) first crossed paths in burlesque in January 1933, when each was employed by the Minsky brothers. The boys didn't formally team up, however, until three years later.

They had taken distinctly different paths in burlesque. Bud's father, Harry, had been an advance man or road manager for shows on the preeminent burlesque circuit, the Columbia wheel, from about 1902 to 1925. ("Wheel" shows rotated through three to four dozen affiliated theaters over a nine month season.) The Abbott children followed suit and entered burlesque when it was family entertainment. Bud worked his way up from ticket taker to treasurer, road manager, producer, and finally performer by 1924. By then Bud and his wife, Betty, a talented performer in her own right, had joined a mass exodus of performers to the boisterous Mutual wheel.

Lou Costello became a burlesque comic out of necessity. He had spent two years trying to break into Hollywood as an actor and was headed back East in 1929 when his bankroll ran out. He joined a tiny burlesque stock company at the Empress Theater in St. Joseph, Missouri. After several months he returned home and was signed by Mutual for the fall season.

Mutual collapsed two years later during the depths of the Great Depression. It was supplanted by stock burlesque, where performers remained in the same theater for weeks or months. The most famous purveyors of stock burlesque were the four Minsky brothers, who operated several theaters in New York. Their showplace was the Republic Theater on 42nd Street. (Today it is the New Victory.) Bud and Lou worked with other partners for the Minskys and other stock burlesque impresarios. Their decisive encounter was in 1935 at the Eltinge Theater, across the street from the Republic. (It is now a multiplex.)

On April 30, 1937, not long after their first anniversary as a team, Abbott and Costello were in the show "Tease-a-Long-Way to Strip-er-ary" at the Star Theater in Brooklyn when Mayor Fiorello LaGuardia ordered the city's fourteen burlesque theaters closed. It was the boys' last performance in burlesque. Fortunately their future agent, Eddie Sherman, had booked them for a second summer with the Steel Pier Minstrels in Atlantic City.

For the first half of the 20th century, Atlantic City was America's greatest seaside resort, and the Steel Pier the "Showplace of the Nation." For fifty cents, customers had access to all of the shows and attractions, including vaudeville, movies, big bands, a haunted house, a water circus, an opera company, and the famous diving horse. On weekends the Pier was so busy it was open from 8 a.m. to 2 a.m.

By this time Abbott and Costello's "Who's On First?" and army "Drill" routines were well-developed. They were adapted from older wordplay and slapstick bits and refined to suit the boys' rapid-fire style. After the Steel Pier, Abbott and Costello signed with a traveling vaudeville unit called "Hollywood Bandwagon." The show opened on September 23 at the Paramount Theater in Springfield, Mass., and played east coast and Midwest theaters. According to Variety, "Who's On First?" was the big hit of the show.

When "Hollywood Bandwagon" was in Milwaukee, Bud and Lou performed their signature routine

*Left to right: Bud in a Sunday school photo, circa 1907; Lou on a Paterson basketball team, circa 1915; both men on the Mutual burlesque wheel: Bud in "Social Maids" in 1928, and Lou in "Best Show in Town" in 1929.*

at a banquet for the National Association of Professional Baseball Leagues. The audience included baseball writers, officials, and legendary commissioner Kenesaw Landis.

"Hollywood Bandwagon" played Baltimore's Hippodrome Theater, one of America's premier vaudeville houses, in January 1938. Bob Rappaport, whose father, Izzy, managed the venue, told *Baltimore Style* in 2004: "My father said he'd never seen anything like it, [they were] so outstanding." Betty Abbott recalled, "Bud and Lou went over so big, Mr. Rappaport phoned Eddie Sherman, who also booked for the Hippodrome, and said, 'Eddie, you better grab these guys, they're great!' And Eddie said, 'I don't want them. They're a couple of burlesque actors.' I was in Mr. Rappaport's office when that happened. I told that story to Eddie Sherman and he denied it. He said, 'Oh, no. I never said that.' But [Eddie] got them away from Leddy and Smith, [the producers of 'Hollywood Bandwagon']."

Sherman booked the team into the Strand, an enormous vaudeville theater on Fulton Street in Brooklyn. (It is now the BRIC Arts Media House.) *Variety* reviewed the act: "Received okay here, in rather homespun presentation..."

The following week, on January 24, 1938, Abbott and Costello officially signed with Sherman; he remained their manager until Bud's death in 1974. Sherman invited Sam Weisbord of the William Morris Agency to see the team at the Strand. Weisbord recalled, "I thought they were great. I was the favorite agent of the Kate Smith Hour. I booked almost everybody on that radio show. I told Ted Collins, her manager and producer, that there are two comedians who I think are just absolutely marvelous. I brought Bud and Lou up to his office and they did the act. Ted thought they were good, but he was very, very concerned that they were too visual for radio. I did all I could to sell them. Finally—and I remember this as clear as anything—I said, 'Ted, you'll go down in recorded history as the man who had an opportunity to buy Abbott and Costello and didn't.'"

A month later the boys were booked in a stage show at Loew's State in New York. The star of the show, which included a dog and pony act, tap dancers and a chorus line, was a young and pre-*Wizard of Oz* Judy Garland. *Variety* called Judy "an undeniable smash," while Abbott and Costello, performing the "Drill Routine," evoked a "not bad" from the trade paper.

Henny Youngman, then a regular on Kate Smith's show, claimed that he also urged Collins to see Bud and Lou. (Youngman had been called to Hollywood for a screen test and wanted to offer Collins a replacement while he was away.) Collins agreed to give the team a shot on February 3 for $350. In their first appearance the boys did their "Mudder/Fodder" crosstalk, but their voices sounded alike over the air. This may have detracted from the effectiveness of the bit since, as Lou put it, "the listeners couldn't tell who was asking and who was answering." The similarity was never discovered on stage, Lou said, probably because "I shout and jump around so much." Even so,

*The boys do the Drill routine in "Hollywood Bandwagon" at the Oriental Theater in Chicago in November 1937. The soldier next to Lou is acrobat and dancer Vic Parks who, coincidentally, will become Costello's stunt double in the 1950s.*

at least two radio columnists were impressed. The *Pittsburgh Press* wrote, "So far, 1938 has produced the zaniest comedy team we have ever heard in the way of new radio talent. We speak of Abbot [sic] and Costello, who got their tryout on Kate Smith's program Thursday night. If you heard them and didn't like them, your funny bone is in need of an operation, a transfusion and a few other things." The radio critic for the *Los Angeles Times* advised, "Keep an ear on these lads—they are headline-bound as sure as your born."

Collins asked the team to return the following week, and Costello adopted an exaggerated falsetto to distinguish his voice. The boys didn't miss a turn on the program after that and stayed for 99 weeks.

Naturally Abbott and Costello wanted to use "Who's On First?" on the program but Collins didn't think it was funny. Bud and Lou recalled that experience in a 1956 interview. Lou said, "We started to [audition] the routine and we got as far as the outfield before he stopped us." Bud added, "He said, 'If you do that, you'll never do another radio show again.'"

They finally convinced Collins by claiming it was the only thing left in their repertoire. Rather than let the boys skip a week, Collins relented, and on March 24, 1938, a national radio audience heard "Who's On First?" for the very first time. It was an instant smash. Even *Variety* was impressed: "Bud Abbott and Lou Costello are building steadily. Their fast *vis-à-vis* style of patter isn't new in radio, but less practiced than many other methods. And they do keep out of the hysterical pitches that mar many other comedians. Pair

went into the trunk and exhumed a bit they must have done in show biz over ten years ago. Routine was the fast 'baseball bit,' about 'Who's on first, what's on second, I don't know's on third.' They actually put it over."

But the team really was running low on material. Not many burlesque bits were purely verbal or clean enough for radio. A week later, John Grant, an old acquaintance from Mutual and Minsky's, was hired as their writer. Grant had been in Toronto producing burlesque and vaudeville shows. It was a remarkably creative association that lasted seventeen years.

At the end of June *Variety* reported that MGM had given the boys a screen test for the film *Honolulu,* starring Eleanor Powell and Robert Young. However, George Burns and Gracie Allen were ultimately cast.

That summer Bud and Lou returned to the Steel Pier as headliners. By October, the boys were headling at the prestigious Roxy Theater. *Variety* noted, "A&C have traveled fast and far…this year. Their stuff now pars with their strong radio impression, the two-man combo feeding the customers a highly impressive total of laughs." Still, the trade paper misidentified Bud as the comic and Lou as the straight man.

In November the team branched out with their first nightclub gig at Billy Rose's Casa Manana, followed by an engagement at another club, the Versailles. Director Henry Koster, who helmed the Deanna Durbin films at Universal, saw Abbott and Costello at either the Casa Manana or Versailles and recommended to his studio bosses.

The team reportedly received a film offer around Thanksgiving. They turned this down (and another in 1940) because of their commitment to Kate Smith and because the offers were single shots. Lou explained, "We don't want to make *a* picture; we want to keep on making them. We'll wait for the right story to come along."

In 1939 producer Harry Kaufman approached them about a Broadway show he was preparing called "Streets Of Paris." Kaufman's other show, "Hellzapoppin'" with Olsen and Johnson, was a huge hit. Kaufman and Olsen and Johnson would produce the new show, to star veteran burlesque comic Bobby Clark.

"Streets of Paris" opened at the Broadhurst Theater on June 19, 1939. Legendary *New York Times* theater critic Brooks Atkinson welcomed "the hilarious team of Lou Costello and Bud Abbott, who carry laughter to the point of helpless groaning…Both men work themselves up into a state of excitement that is wonderful to behold."

The show ran for 274 performances, until February, 1940. The boys' future producer at Universal, Alex Gottlieb, said he saw them in "Streets of Paris" and "laughed my fool head off."

The William Morris agency, meanwhile, was working on a deal with MGM for the team to do a couple of routines in the musical *Ziegfeld Girl* for $17,500. Around this time Matty Fox, a Universal vice president, called Eddie Sherman to inquire about the boys. The studio was preparing the screen version of *The Boys From Syracuse* and the Ritz Brothers had quit, complaining that roles were not big enough. Bud and Lou may have been considered as replacements. In any case, the boys attended the film's July 1940 premiere in Syracuse, New York.

Soon after, they made a deal with Universal to appear in an upcoming musical for $35,000. Eddie Sherman reasoned that Bud and Lou would have a better chance of being noticed at the smaller studio. MGM was notorious for signing talent and then having it sit idle. By the time MGM released *Ziegfeld Girl* in April 1941, Abbott and Costello were working on their fourth film at Universal.

The musical was *One Night in the Tropics*, with songs by the legendary Jerome Kern. The cast included Allan Jones, Robert Cummings, Nancy Kelly, and Peggy Moran. Shooting began on August 26, 1940, with A. Edward Sutherland directing. *One Night in the Tropics* had been in development for months when word came down from the front office to integrate the two burlesque comics into the script. John Grant went with them to Hollywood and suggested routines that might be shoehorned into the film's dizzy plot. Even though Bud and Lou performed several of their best bits (including an abbreviated "Who's On First?"), and the soundtrack featured five Kern songs, the picture was a mess.

When *Tropics* wrapped on September 30, Bud and Lou thought they were finished with Universal and perhaps motion pictures. Lou's brother, Pat, recalled, "After we saw [a screening of] *One Night in the Tropics*, we thought that it was the end of Abbott and Costello's movie career." Co-star Peggy Moran laughed, "Bob Cummings and I always referred to it as 'One Night in the Flopics.'"

With his bags packed for new vaudeville tour, Lou, along with his brother, Pat, drove out to Universal City one last time. Pat recalled, "We went back to the studio because Lou wanted to go around and thank everybody and say good-bye to the people we had met."

Lou explained in 1954, "I once had been a stunt man, carpenter and extra in the movies, and I knew I wanted to stay in the movies. I had nothing to lose, so I went over to see Matty Fox at Universal." Fox (1911-1964), a former theater chain executive and nephew of studio president Nate Blumberg, was then a Universal vice president. An industry innovator, Fox was later the first to syndicate old movies to the new medium of television and pioneered subscription TV in the 1960s.

Pat Costello recalled, "Lou said, 'Pat you stay in the car, I'll go in and say good-bye, and then we'll go.' I said fine, and I stayed in the car."

Lou continued, "I said, 'Matty, I just came over to say goodbye before I go over to Paramount.' Matty got up from his chair and said, 'What are you going to do over at Paramount?'"

What followed was the most important ad-lib of Lou Costello's career.

"I told him they wanted to see me about some story ideas I had for Abbott and Costello," Lou said. "Fox got interested right away and said Universal would like to hear the ideas. This caught me off guard because I had no story ideas and in fact I didn't even know anyone at Paramount. So I enacted two old burlesque routines that Abbott and I had done many times. Matty held his sides laughing. He called in the other top studio brass. I had a bunch of laughers, so I really gave out with the routines."

Lou somehow managed to present the "Drill" and

*Left: Bud and Lou considered the Kate Smith radio show their biggest break in show business.*
*Right: With Universal's reigning boxoffice star, Deanna Durbin, in 1940. She'd be dethroned in a few months.*

"Moving Candle" bits on his own.

Pat recalled, "Well, Lou finally came out, and he was as white as a ghost! I had never seen him so rattled. I said, 'Lou, what's the matter?'

"He said, 'We've got to get a hold of Bud right away—we've got to find Abbott!' I said, 'What for?'

He said, 'They want us to do two more pictures!'

"I said, 'What?!'

"He said, 'They want us to do two more pictures!'"

Lou continued, "[Universal] not only signed us, but they bought the routines as original stories."

The "Drill" formed the centerpiece of *Buck Privates,* and the "Moving Candle" inspired *Hold That Ghost.* In retrospect, both were sound, commercial ideas. The "Drill" was particularly timely. After the Nazis captured Paris that June, a Gallup Poll found that 64% of Americans approved of a peacetime draft to shore up our own frail military. After much wrangling, Congress on September 14 passed the Selective Service and Training Act. The bill required sixteen million men between the ages of 21 and 35 to register for the draft. In a few weeks, on October 29, a lottery would select 800,000 of those men to be inducted and trained for a year.

Such a sweeping national event would certainly capture Hollywood's attention, and by November 18, the day that the first draftees were inducted, the *New York Times* reported that six studios were prepping conscription comedies, including *Buck Privates* with Abbott and Costello and *Caught in the Draft* with Bob Hope.

Prospects were also bright for the team's spooky "Moving Candle" bit. *The Cat and The Canary* (1939) and *The Ghost Breakers* (1940), two recent old dark house comedies starring Bob Hope and Paulette Goddard, had been hits. (Ironically, Universal, which made the landmark silent version of *The Cat and The Canary* in 1927, planned a remake in 1938 but sold the rights to Paramount, which tailored it for Hope and Martha Raye. Raye was replaced by Paulette Goddard.) *Motion Picture Daily* called Hope's version, "A wedding of laugh and thrill so neatly contrived as to equal, virtually, a new film formula, inducing shrieks of terror and shrieks of laughter." *The Ghost Breakers* received similar glowing reviews. *Variety* declared it "solid comedy entertainment that will generate plenty of laughs and roll up some hefty b.o. figures along the way." Wanda Hale, critic for the *New York Daily News,* predicted, "...look for [Hope and Goddard] in a whole bunch of comedy-mysteries in the future..." They might have been except for a film Hope made in the interim, *Road to Zanzibar,* with Bing Crosby and Dorothy Lamour, that launched an even more lucrative series.

Thus Lou Costello dropped two timely, bankable ideas in Universal's lap. A few days after the national draft lottery, Bud and Lou arrived at Universal's New York headquarters at 1250 Sixth Avenue to negotiate their film contract. The studio started off by offering the team a contract for four pictures a year, at $35,000 per picture. The bidding rose to $40,000 or $45,000 per picture, but Eddie Sherman instead asked for ten percent of the profits. "I had a crazy idea about it because I thought those pictures would be great," Sherman explained. "Now, Abbott and Costello were adding this up in their heads, and saw maybe $40,000 more a year if we took a higher salary per picture. Lou called me out into the hall. I said, 'Look, Lou, take the deal I suggest. I think those pictures will make you a hell of a lot of money percentage-wise. I'll make you a deal right now. If you don't make at least the $10,000 difference on each picture, you don't have to pay my commission.' Lou said, 'If you feel that strongly about it, I've got to go along with you.'

"Universal was tickled to death to take the percentage deal rather than pay the extra money," Sherman continued. "As it turned out, the *least* Abbott and Costello made on any of the first four pictures was $250,000—their percentage amounted to that much. So it was almost a difference of $1 million a year."

On November 6, 1940, Bud and Lou signed their second contract with Universal. The deal called for two pictures—*Buck Privates* and *Oh, Charlie*—over a period of twelve weeks. They would receive $35,000 per picture plus ten percent of the gross over 170% of the production cost. For example, if a film cost $250,000 to make, the team's profit participation kicked in after the film earned its first $425,000. Later, if the studio wished to exercise its option and keep the team, the boys would get $3,500 per week the first year, for no more than four pictures per year, with salary increases each year for up to seven years. They couldn't have known it then, but with extensions, re-negotiations, and raises, this contract would last fourteen years.

When Universal signed Abbott and Costello the studio was on its way to its best year since 1926. For the fiscal year ending October 31, 1940, the studio posted a profit of nearly $2.4 million—double that of 1939—and enjoyed its second consecutive year in the black after four straight years of losses.

The turnaround might be credited to Universal's latest management team. President Nate Blumberg and head of production Cliff Work replaced Robert Cochrane and Charles R. Rogers on January 1, 1938. Cochrane and Rogers had replaced Universal's founder, Carl Laemmle Sr., and his son, Carl Jr., in 1936 after they defaulted on a loan and lost control of the studio. Under Blumberg and his staff, Universal went from a loss of $1 million in 1938 to a net profit of $2.2 million in 1940.

Before joining Universal, Blumberg (1894-1960) was the vice president and general manager of RKO's theater chains. Work (1891-1963) was his West Coast division manager. They brought in other former theater managers to produce films and run the studio. Screenwriter Edmund L. Hartmann (1911-2003) recalled, "The studio executives were all theater exhibitors, owners, and operators. They knew nothing about the technique of making movies, but they knew what to put on the marquee to bring in a crowd. So they would assign contract people to do something in a picture that had nothing to do with the story at all— just to be able to use the person's name on a marquee. And they never talked about movies; you could talk about football, you could talk about horse racing. But if you talked about movies, they looked at you like you were some kind of nut."

It was not at all uncommon for ex-exhibitors to wind up running studios. Louis B. Mayer's career began when he transformed a rundown theater in Massachusetts. Paramount's Y. Frank Freeman started in the deep South. Jack and Albert Warner got their start in Ohio and Pennsylvania. Sam Katz, A. M. Botsford, and Lou Edelman were with Publix, Paramount's theater chain, before becoming producers at MGM, Paramount, and Warner Bros., respectively. At Universal, a nine-man executive committee made every decision related to production. In daily meetings that started at 8:30 a.m. and ran about half an hour, they discussed films in production, scripts, casting, contracts, talent, and so on.

But Universal had something more influential on its bottom line than just new management. It had box office gold in teenage songstress Deanna Durbin. Between 1937 and 1940, Durbin's eight hit musicals grossed over $16 million. The infusion of cash allowed Blumberg and Work to increase production from 47 films in 1938 to 55 in 1940 and expand the studio's talent roster.

Cliff Work assigned Milton Feld, an executive producer on the lot, to oversee the two Abbott and Costello films. Feld wound up supervising all of the boys' films at Universal from 1941 through 1945.

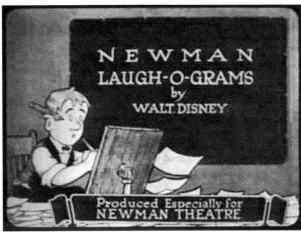

*Long before he became the executive producer of the Abbott and Costello films, Milton Feld (right, circa 1919), managed the largest theaters in Kansas City. In 1921 Feld hired a young animator named Walt Disney to create cartoons for his show-place theater.*

Milton also had experience on both ends of the movie business. Born in Kansas City on November 17, 1892, he started as an usher in a small neighborhood theater, and by the age of nineteen was Universal's branch manager in Kansas City. After serving stateside as a Quartermaster in World War I, Feld was hired by Kansas City's leading showman, Frank L. Newman, to run the city's first elegant theater, the Royal.

In 1919 Newman built Kansas City's grandest movie palace, the eponymous Newman Theater, at a cost of $400,000. He was inspired by the Balaban & Katz theater chain in Chicago. Created by Barney and A.J. Balaban and their brother-in-law, Sam Katz, these opulent theaters were designed to draw crowds regardless of what film was playing. The Newman Theater had similar amenities, including air conditioning, a large mezzanine promenade between the first floor and balcony, a nursery for children, and various lounges. A young Thomas Hart Benton painted many of the murals that decorated the interior. The orchestra pit accommodated a thirty-five piece orchestra, and up to fifty musicians on special occasions. Every year on the anniversary of the Royal's opening, a week-long celebration was held with special stage acts, most of them from out of town.

Feld soon became the managing director of Newman's three theaters in Kansas City. He not only selected the films but gained a reputation for producing and staging the accompanying live shows. Feld also edited newsreels to make them consistently engaging. He replaced stories that he knew were distasteful or not relevant to his audience with footage of celebrities from *Screen Snapshots* newsreels. Trade publications such as *Exhibitor's Herald* and *Exhibitor's Trade Review* often quoted Feld about methods to

promote films with stage shows or local merchant tie-ins.

He also hired a fledgling local animator named Walt Disney to provide his seminal *Laugh-O-Gram* cartoons to the Newman Theater and create special titles for coming attractions, holidays, and anniversary shows. One cartoon even addressed manners inside a theater, showing patrons who read the title cards aloud getting whacked on the head by a mallet or dropped down a chute to the street. The cartoons did not earn a profit, but they made Disney a local celebrity and were invaluable learning experiences.

Independent theater chains like Newman's sprang up in and around large cities in the 1920s. Meanwhile, vertical integration—that is, controlling production, distribution, and exhibition—became the imperative in the movie industry. Two studios, Warner Bros. and Paramount-Famous Players-Lasky, assembled their own theater chains, while three theater chains—Fox, Loew's and Radio-Keith-Orpheum—created their own studios (Fox, MGM and RKO).

In 1925 the Balaban & Katz chain merged with Paramount-Famous Players-Lasky, and the new chain was named Publix. Paramount's founder, Adolph Zukor, brought Sam Katz to New York to run the theater division and directed him to buy up independent theaters and theater chains. Newman's three theaters in Kansas City were among Katz's many acquisitions; the Newman was eventually renamed the Paramount.

Katz sent Frank Newman and Milton Feld to Los Angeles to manage and produce stage shows for Publix's Rialto, Metropolitan, and Million Dollar theaters. Two years later, Katz brought Feld to New York to be one of five regional managers. Feld oversaw theaters in the southwest and Midwest before he was put in charge of the prime markets of Metropolitan New York (including the flagship Paramount Theater in Times Square), Los Angeles, and Buffalo (then the country's thirteenth largest city).

By 1930 Publix had two thousand theaters nationwide. The chain was so important that the parent company was renamed Paramount-Publix. But even the biggest studio and theater chain was not immune to the great Depression. Movie attendance fell forty percent from 1929 to 1932, and nearly one in five theaters closed. Still, Zukor pushed obsessively to acquire more theaters. In order to buy out independent owners, he offered them company stock redeemable at a fixed price on a fixed date. Although Paramount-Publix's stock tumbled during the Depression, the company was still obligated to redeem the stock at the higher guaranteed prices. Additionally, Zukor was slow in adopting talking pictures and spent a fortune hastily converting both the studio and its theaters to sound. Profits fell from $18 million in 1930 to $6 million in 1931.

When Paramount signed Bing Crosby for a series of features in 1932, the studio consulted with Milton Feld. Crosby was then the country's leading vocalist; he was featured in ten of the top fifty songs in 1931. "In these anxious times," *Photoplay* wrote, "the company intends to make as few commercial mistakes as possible with their pet songbird. Milton Feld…has been assigned to bring the theater point of view to the Crosby set."

But by the end of 1932 the studio was $121 million in the red and bankruptcy was imminent. Sam Katz, along with divisional directors Milton Feld, David Chatkin, and Harry Katz (Sam's brother), quit. Sam Katz went into production at MGM; he is often credited with signing Judy Garland for *The Wizard of Oz* (1939). Feld, Chatkin, and Harry Katz acquired ten theaters in Ohio and formed a chain they named Monarch Theaters.

Meanwhile, a board of directors consisting of bankers, lawyers, and realtors tried to keep Paramount-Publix solvent. The company emerged from bankruptcy as Paramount Pictures with Barney Balaban, the Chicago theater chain owner, as president. Adoph Zukor was made chairman and removed from any decision-making.

In the fall of 1934, Milton Feld married Shirley Vogel, a New Yorker, in Jackson, Missouri. Monarch announced plans to produce its own films but the idea never panned out. Feld resigned, and late in 1935

he joined 20th Century-Fox as part of Darryl F. Zanuck's staff. The following summer Feld became an associate producer under Sol Wurtzel who, as head of Fox's second-tier productions, was known as "The Keeper of the B's."

In his book *Moving Pictures,* screenwriter Budd Schulberg described Wurtzel as "a prototype of what outsiders thought a Hollywood producer should be. A burly cloak-and-suiter who had never read a book and who had his scenarios synopsized for him by more literate assistants." Schulberg quoted Wurtzel: "I don't give a shit about art. It's a business, and anybody who doesn't think so oughta get out of it!"

It's not surprising, then, that Wurtzel (1881-1958) started as a bookkeeper at New York's Fulton Fish Market. In 1912 he joined a film distribution firm founded by theater chain pioneer William Fox (Wilhelm Fried). Wurtzel was hired to keep track of studio prints, but because he knew shorthand he soon became Fox's personal secretary. In 1917 Wurtzel was dispatched to Hollywood to oversee Fox's West Coast studio facility. Since Wurtzel knew nothing about making movies, he dutifully carry out Fox's instructions and sent copious updates back to New York by mail or telegram. With stars like Theda Bara, Tom Mix, and Buck Jones, and directors including Raoul Walsh, Frank Borzage, John Ford, Howard Hawks, and F. W. Murnau, Fox prospered.

In 1928 and 1929 Fox borrowed heavily to upgrade production, expand theater operations, and promote its Movietone sound-on-film system. Fox also financed a hostile take-over bid for Loew's and MGM. But in 1929 William Fox was nearly killed in a car accident; the federal government prepared an antitrust suit over the Loew's take-over; and, of course, the stock market crashed. Fox was ousted in 1930 and replaced by one of his creditors, Harley Clarke. But nothing could stem the effects of the Depression. Like Paramount-Publix, Fox went into receivership in 1933.

Sol Wurtzel, meanwhile, survived and thrived. During the Depression he spent $100,000 to build a mansion in Bel-Air. He was promoted to producer in 1933 and supervised several Will Rogers and Spencer Tracy vehicles, as well as Shirley Temple's star-making hit, *Bright Eyes* (1934).

Things were about to change, however. Darryl F. Zanuck quit his job as production chief at Warner Bros. and partnered with Joseph Schenck to create an independent production company, 20th Century Pictures. In their first two years they turned out twenty

*Milton Feld produced several films at 20th Century-Fox, including these two with Joan Davis.*

films that were released by United Artists. When efforts to form a partnership with United Artists were squelched by two of its cofounders, Charlie Chaplin and Mary Pickford, Schenck and Zanuck made a deal with bankrupt Fox. In May 1935 they formed 20th Century-Fox. Zanuck took and kept complete control of the studio until 1970.

With Zanuck's arrival Wurtzel was reassigned to Fox's B-unit, which was housed on a separate lot. His group turned out as many B films as Zanuck's A unit. These included the Charlie Chan, Mr. Moto, and Michael Shayne detective pictures; the Jones Family domestic comedies; and the Jane Withers musicals. Wurtzel firmly believed that these films would be profitable no matter how little time or money was spent on them. Comedian and Fox contractee Harry Ritz summed it up: "Things have gone from bad to Wurtzel."

Milton Feld's first production under Wurtzel was a Claire Trevor programmer, *Career Woman* (1936). Trevor, at Fox since 1932, made several films a year. "I worked like a demon, and I knew it was a job," she told the *Los Angeles Times* in 1995. "Saturday night, you never could plan on going out to dinner because we'd break for dinner for one hour and work till 1, 2, 3, 4 or 5 in the morning." Trevor was Oscar-nominated for her performance in *Dead End* (1937), and later won for *Key Largo* (1948).

Feld produced two more Trevor films in 1937, *Time Out for Romance* and *Big Town Girl*, as well as *Midnight Taxi*, *Born Reckless*, and *Sing and Be Happy*.

Two of these, *Time Out for Romance* and *Sing and Be Happy*, featured gangly comedienne Joan Davis.

Universal hired Feld in July 1938 as an executive producer. Director Arthur Lubin explained, "There were five or six executive producers [at Universal]. They were responsible to Cliff Work, whose job was to keep the pictures under budget and on schedule. Each executive producer had a few associate producers under them."

Dann Cahn, whose father, Phil, edited several Abbott and Costello films, said, "Milton Feld was more concerned with the overall budget and would approve casting and certain things. He also executive-produced other pictures at the same time." Among others, Feld supervised the Sherlock Holmes films.

Universal had recently made deals with outside stars. These included Constance Bennett, Edgar Bergen, Jackie Cooper, Adolphe Menjou, George Murphy, and Irene Dunne. The studio also arranged to borrow Jimmy Stewart, Robert Montgomery, and Robert Young from MGM. A month after Feld arrived, Universal negotiated a cooperative picture deal with Bing Crosby, whose Paramount contract permitted him one outside film per year. Feld produced Crosby's two Universal pictures, *East Side of Heaven* (1939) and *If I Had My Way* (1940).

Associate producers under Feld were responsible for day to day production. When Abbott and Costello were signed, Feld promoted a press agent turned screenwriter named Alex Gottlieb to associate producer to oversee *Buck Privates*. Gottlieb (1906-1988)

*Left to right: Executive producer Milton Feld and the asssociate producers under him: Alex Gottlieb, Burt Kelly, and Glenn Tryon. Gottlieb produced seven Abbott and Costello films at Universal, while Kelly and Tryon shared credit on* Hold That Ghost. *Tryon also produced the team's third service comedy,* Keep 'Em Flying *(1941).*

knew Feld from New York. He ultimately produced seven Abbott and Costello films at Universal, their two independent color films, and the initial episodes of the team's television series.

Another associate producer under Feld was a 42-year old Brooklyn native named Burt Kelly. Born on October 6, 1898, Kelly enjoyed the theater from an early age. In 1911, the *Brooklyn Daily Eagle* polled its readers about their theatrical tastes. Kelly, then twelve years old, responded, "I do not like to look at distressing situations, but I am sometimes moved. I like to laugh at funny situations, provided they are not silly. I like to listen to good music, but not operas. Realness in the plays of to-day is lacking. Because I am young is not any reason that I do not go to the theater, as I have gone many times.—*Burt Kelly, 269 Dean Street.*"

Kelly began his career as an assistant manager, and later a manager, of a theatrical troupe in Pennsylvania. After serving two years in World War I he joined the booking department of the Publix theater chain. He purchased short subjects and was in charge of installing sound equipment in theaters. When Paramount-Publix faltered in 1931, Kelly took a job as executive assistant to the founder of Educational Pictures, Earle W. Hammonds.

As the name implies, Educational was originally established to make films for schools. Starting in the 1920s, however, it rivaled Mack Sennett and Hal Roach for its output of slapstick two-reelers. Its stable of comics included Roscoe "Fatty" Arbuckle, Al St. John, Lupino Lane, Lige Conley, Lloyd Hamilton, and Felix the Cat. (In the early 1930s, Educational released shorts with Buster Keaton, Harry Langdon, and Andy Clyde, as well as Mack Sennett's early talking comedies.)

A subsidiary of Educational, Tiffany Productions, had loftier ambitions. Actress Mae Murray, known as "The Girl with the Bee-Stung Lips," and her third husband, director Robert Z. Leonard, quit Universal at the peak of her popularity to form Tiffany. The couple made eight melodramas featuring over-the-top performances and ostentatious costumes designed by Murray. (She was an inspiration for Norma Desmond in *Sunset Boulevard.*)

Murray and Leonard divorced in 1925. John M. Stahl, a founding member of the Motion Picture Academy and part of the team that established MGM, became the director of Tiffany. He renamed it Tiffany-Stahl Productions and released seventy silent and sound features. Perhaps his most notable production was *Journey's End* (1930), directed by James Whale a year before he made *Frankenstein.*

Tiffany ran into financial trouble and began producing cheap westerns starring Bob Steele and Ken Maynard and short subjects like *The Talking Chimp* series (the ancestor of TV's *Lancelot Link, Secret Chimp*). Stahl quit, briefly returned to MGM, then signed with Universal, where he directed *Imitation of Life* (1934), a Best Picture nominee, and *Magnificent Obsession* (1935).

Burt Kelly was sent to Hollywood to manage what was left of Tiffany. Sam Bichoff, who had his own small production company, became Kelly's production manager, but the studio declared bankruptcy in 1932. MGM later purchased Tiffany's film negative library and set it on fire for the burning of Atlanta sequence in *Gone with the Wind* (1939).

Kelly, Bischoff, and William Saal, an associate

from Paramount and Tiffany, formed KBS Productions. The trio picked up where Tiffany left off with Ken Maynard westerns as well as dramas like George Abbott's *Those We Love* (1932); Eugene O'Neill's *The Constant Woman* (1933); *The Death Kiss* (1933) with Bela Lugosi; the Sherlock Holmes mystery *A Study in Scarlet* (1933); and *Deluge* (1933), the first disaster film to show the destruction of New York City.

KBS lasted until late 1933, when Bischoff was hired away to supervise feature film production at Columbia Pictures. Kelly joined Universal for two months then quit to form Select Productions with William Saal. They planned to shoot twelve features at the old Biograph Studios in the Bronx, but only made three. The first, *Woman in the Dark*, starring Fay Wray, was from a short story and screenplay by Dashiell Hammett.

Select also released four action films starring a pre-*Hopalong Cassidy* William Boyd. These were helmed by Sam Newfield, the most prolific feature film director of the sound era. Kelly produced two other Newfield films, *Undercover Men* (1934) and *Thoroughbred* (1935). Kelly's wife, Adrienne Doré, was the leading lady in *Undercover Men*. She was a former Miss Los Angeles and first runner-up in the 1925 Miss America Pageant.

Select and other Poverty Row studios were soon absorbed by Republic Pictures, and Kelly became an associate producer there. He produced *Navy Born* (1936) with William Gargan and Claire Dodd; *The President's Mystery* (1936) with Henry Wilcoxon; and *Affairs of Cappy Ricks* (1937) with Walter Brennan in a rare starring role.

Kelly's next move was back to Universal. This time he stayed for three years and produced about a dozen films, including *The House of the Seven Gables* (1940). Nearly all of his productions were shot by cinematographer Elwood Bredell, and four were directed by Arthur Lubin.

Kelly had just started production of *The Invisible Woman*, starring John Barrymore and Virginia Bruce, when he was assigned to produce the second Abbott and Costello picture, "Oh, Charlie." Two young freelance screenwriters, Robert Lees and Fred Rinaldo, worked on the screenplay for *The Invisible Woman* and had just completed another script for Kelly, a horror spoof called *The Black Cat*. They were the logical choice to write an old dark house comedy for Abbott and Costello.

Robert Lees recalled, "Burt Kelly was a very nice guy and very bright. He was one of those real old Broadway guys who had all these wonderful clichés. If our script was taking too long to set up the story, he'd say, 'You're taking too long to dust off the iron apples.' You see, in those days, all these stage plays would open with the butler and the maid. They'd set the scene and tell you the whole plot. They'd say, 'Oh, the boss sure got in late last night. I wonder if he's going to marry that girl.' And while they were setting the scene, they'd be dusting off the iron apples on a table. So if we were 'dusting off the iron apples,' we were not getting into the story fast enough. Burt had a lot of lines like that."

In his book *Hollywood Exile, or How I Learned to Love the Blacklist*, the prolific screenwriter Bernard Gordon recalled working for Kelly on a cheap melodrama at Columbia in 1948. "He was a handsome, white-haired man who seemed old to us though he probably wasn't more than fifty," Gordon wrote. "But he was an old-timer in the sense that he'd held down production and executive jobs at various major studios and had come from a theatrical background. That background explained his first comment. After reading what we considered the first act, he complained, 'You're still dusting off iron apples.' ... Kelly meant: get moving, get into the story, stop stalling. His other complaint came at the end of the script: 'No, no, no. They're outside cranking up the Fords,' which meant: you're losing the audience, they've already left the theater, finish the picture."

Kelly's production of *The House of the Seven Gables* differed dramatically from Nathaniel Hawthorne's novel in several ways. Kelly explained the superficial changes in his own vernacular: "I think our best bet is to fabricate a heart thing between the man and the woman, and then young them up as characters. In the original, we can't believe the heart thing. Too much gray wash in the hair. But if we young them up, we've got something."

Once "Oh, Charlie" was under way, Kelly planned to shoot *The Black Cat* (1941) on a similar budget. Casting issues, however, delayed the start until February 17. The players included Basil Rathbone, Hugh Herbert, Bela Lugosi, and Gale Sondergaard. Richard Carlson was also originally cast, but was reassigned to "Oh, Charlie." Broderick Crawford took his role in *The Black Cat*.

# "Ghost" Writers

"I guess I was a comedy writer from the word go," said Robert Lees. The youngest of three children in a middle-class Jewish family in San Francisco, Lees was born on July 10, 1912. "We were an old San Francisco family," he recalled. "My mother and father were born there. I think I had a grandparent there.

"My father was a wholesaler in the ready-to-wear business. He had jobbing houses across the country. We were fairly well off back then. Then the Depression came. He stayed in the Los Angeles office. I was going to go to Berkeley but I came to Los Angeles and went to UCLA. I was only there until midterms in my freshman year, then went to help in the office. He had some connections at MGM and suggested that maybe I get some money doing 'extra' work."

Lees acquired a taste for show business while acting in school plays. He became an extra in 1930 and worked his way up to bit parts. In 1932 he played a bellboy in *Grand Hotel*; a boatman in the Greta Garbo-Erich Von Stroheim film *As You Desire Me;* and a servant carrying the trains of the emperor's daughter in *Rasputin and the Empress.* He also danced in the Clark Gable-Joan Crawford picture *Dancing Lady* (1933), which also marked the first time Fred Astaire danced on film.

In 1934, hoping to get speaking parts, Lees wrote a screen test for himself. "The studio thought my acting was lousy but felt that the test was well-written," he laughed. "Metro had a Junior Writers Department and they decided I could be a junior writer. There was a story that Louis B. Mayer said, 'What are we going to

do when all the old writers die?' Somebody said, 'We should start a junior writers department.' That's where I met Fred Rinaldo."

Frederic Irwin Rinaldo was born on September 27, 1913 on Manhattan's Upper West Side. "Dad always had a New York accent, or at least you knew he was from the East Coast," Fred's son, Robert, recalled. "My father's family were Italian bankers who moved to Poland. His father, Benjamin, immigrated to the U.S. and had a very successful ribbon and velvet business in New York. He went to Europe on buying trips every year. Occasionally the whole family went, too. We have 16mm home movies of one trip in the 1920s. Not many people at that time had movie cameras."

Fred went to Dartmouth and majored in English literature. "The people who are great writers have photographic memories," Robert explained. "He could recite long passages from Shakespeare, or poems, that were just embedded in his head. His brain was a library." Rinaldo was accepted to Harvard Law School but then the Depression hit and he couldn't afford to go. "So he followed his first love, writing," Robert said. "I'm sure it was not a hard decision since it was always something he wanted to do. He loved to make people laugh. That's why he was a comedy writer. He had a roommate at Dartmouth named Maurice Rapf, whose father, Harry, was a producer and one of the founders of MGM. He got them into the Junior Writers Program there. That's where dad met Bob Lees."

Lees said, "Fred knew how to write and spell, and I knew what went on on a soundstage. We were earning $50 a week, which was a helluva lot of money in those

Fred Rinaldo (left)
and Robert Lees (right).
(Courtesy of Bob Rinaldo)

days, but to the studio wasn't that much."

In *Lion of Hollywood: The Life and Legend of Louis B. Mayer*, author Scott Eyman described the Junior Writers Program: "The system was structured more or less on the mentor system, with the program headed by Richard Schayer, an amiable writer left over from the silent days who acted as a surrogate father. The group could encompass as many as twelve or as few as five or six writers per year. They shared offices, ate together, looked at movies, and were given old scripts to read, usually scripts that hadn't been made, on the off chance that a fresh young mind might be able to come up with a solution to the problems that had stifled production."

During the Depression, in an effort to secure fair wages, better working conditions and, significantly, proper credit for their work, screenwriters formed the Screen Writers Guild. This union, like most others, met violent opposition from the studios. (The battle between Hollywood labor and management led screenwriter Albert Hackett to quip, "Louis B. Mayer created more communists than Karl Marx.") Lees and Rinaldo were founding members of the SWG. Lees joined the American Communist Party in the mid-1930s and recruited Fred Rinaldo. Sixty years later Lees explained that he had been a "San Francisco Republican," but that the Communists in the entertainment industry "were making such sense that I figured, what the devil, maybe that's where I should be. And that's how I became a member..."

Early in 1935 Rinaldo and Lees learned about an opportunity in MGM's short subjects department. "We heard that Pete Smith wanted to do a short called 'Chain Letter Dimes.'" Smith had been the head of MGM's publicity department. In 1931 he was pressed into service writing and narrating a series of sports highlight shorts. The scope gradually expanded to factual short subjects. As the films became more popular, Smith focused on them full time. He produced and narrated 150 shorts between 1931 and 1955 and received an honorary Academy Award in 1954.

During 1935 the "Prosperity Club," or "Send a Dime" chain letter, was big news all over the world. It originated in Denver. Six names were listed at the top of the letter. Recipients were asked to send a dime to the first person on the list, scratch that name out, add their own name at the bottom, and send the letter on to five friends. After five such progressions, your name would, presumably, reach the top of the list, and you would receive 15,625 dimes, or $1,562.50 (over $27,000 today). Within weeks, millions of copies had clogged post offices throughout the country. Within a few months, over a billion copies were sent worldwide. Federal authorities sought the mastermind for prosecution but never found him.

Lees continued, "So Fred and I stayed up all night and wrote something and went to present it to the head of the shorts department. Chic Sales, a very well known comedian with a hick character, was in the waiting room and asked us what we were there for. We said 'Chain Letter Dimes.' He was there for the same thing. He said, 'Do you mind if I see it?' So we showed

*Lees and Rinaldo co-wrote shorts for Robert Benchley (1889-1945) and the Pete Smith series. The Benchley short* How to Sleep, *and a Smith short,* Penny Wisdom, *both won Academy Awards.*

it to him and he said 'Do you mind if I take it inside [to the producer]?' Then we heard them laughing inside. They never did our script, but that's how we got into shorts."

The short subjects department was a studio within the studio; it turned out about seventy films per year. "Metro did wonderful things with their shorts," Lees recalled. "Everyone under contract, if they weren't doing anything, had to work. So we had some of the greatest cameramen, editors, everything." It was an invaluable training ground for writers and directors, as well as new talent such as Jimmy Stewart, Judy Garland, and Robert Taylor.

Lees and Rinaldo's first screenplay credits were for the sober "Crime Does Not Pay" series, which produced five or six shorts a year between 1935 and 1948. The young team wrote *Hit and Run Driver* (1935) and *The Perfect Set-Up* (1936). Then they were assigned to the Robert Benchley and Pete Smith shorts.

Benchley, a prolific humorist and critic for *Vanity Fair* and *The New Yorker,* had made satiric shorts at Universal and RKO. MGM signed him to write and perform in a short inspired by a study on sleep commissioned by a mattress company. The film, *How to Sleep,* won Best Short Subject at the 8th Academy Awards in 1935. (Lees and Rinaldo worked on it

without credit.) This prompted the studio to launch a series with Benchley. Lees and Rinaldo collaborated on his very next films, *How to Train a Dog* and *How to Behave* (1936) as well as *How to Be a Detective* (1936), *How to Start the Day* (1937), *A Night at the Movies* (1937, which was nominated for an Academy Award), *An Evening Alone* (1938), *Music Made Simple* (1938), and *An Hour for Lunch* (1939).

Lees told Scott Eyman: "Robert Benchley always considered himself to be first and foremost a critic of the New York stage. He'd say, 'I want go back to New York for the fall. If you want any shorts done, send the boys and we'll shoot a couple at Astoria [Studios in Queens]. So Fred and I would go to New York, to a suite at the Algonquin. The Royalton, where Benchley lived, was across the street. We were given carte blanche to see anything that Pete Smith or the other producers could use, and we saw wonderful plays at Metro's expense."

Their first Pete Smith short was *Penny Wisdom* (1937), featuring *Los Angeles Examiner* culinary columnist Prudence Penny. It won an Academy Award for Best Short Subject, Color. Their other Smith shorts were *Decathlon Champion: The Story of Glenn Morris* (1937); *Candid Cameramaniacs* (1937); *The Story of Dr. George Washington Carver* (directed by Fred

Zinneman, 1938); *Follow the Arrow* (1938), with marksman Howard Hill; *Weather Wizards* (1939, directed by Fred Zinneman); and *Let's Talk Turkey* (1939). In all, Less and Rinaldo did about three dozen shorts at MGM.

In 1937 Fred married Marie Halff. Their son, Robert, recalled, "My father met my mother when she was an extra at MGM. She was a rarity; she was born in Los Angeles. Back then, it was a much smaller place and everybody was involved in the film industry in some way or other for some period in their lives." In addition to Robert, who was named after Robert Lees, Fred and Marie had two daughters, Ann and Judith.

Lees and Rinaldo scripted longer form films, including a weak MGM Miniature musical, *It's in The Stars* (1938). The following year, Lees married Jean Abel. They had a son, Richard, and a daughter, Katherine.

Given their politics, two short films the pair wrote are intriguing. *Prophet Without Honor* (1939) was a biography of Matthew Fontaine Maury (1806-1873), an American Naval officer who charted the ocean's currents and revolutionized travel by cutting sailing times by weeks or months on long voyages. He determined the location for the first transatlantic cable and was also a pioneer in meteorology. Maury Hall at Annapolis is named in his honor, and his birthday is a school holiday in Virginia. But Maury's work was largely forgotten because he was branded a traitor for supporting the South during the Civil War. *Prophet Without Honor* was nominated for an Oscar.

The second film, *The Flag Speaks,* was a nineteen-minute Technicolor short made at the behest of the American Legion. In the late 1930s there were renewed calls for patriotism, good citizenship, and respect for the flag. This new Americanism was triggered by the war in Europe and concern that immigrants might remain loyal to their native countries. A new holiday, "I Am an American Day," was created on May 19, 1940. President Roosevelt called on everyone, especially new citizens, to pause and reflect on the rights and obligations "of all patriotic and home-loving Americans." In *America's Forgotten Holiday: May Day and Nationalism, 1867-1960,* Donna T. Haverty-Stacke writes: "…Americans from all walks of life, including organized workers, answered Roosevelt's call…by celebrating in great outdoor meetings with mass recitations of the Pledge of Allegiance. This new civic event became a focal point for the shaping of wartime, postwar, and Cold War Americanism."

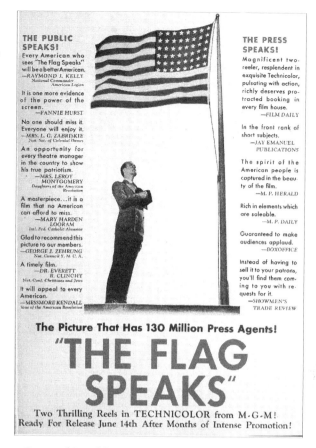

*Lees and Rinaldo wrote a patriotic history of the flag.*

Flag Day, June 14, 1940, therefore took on a new urgency. (That same day, the Nazis captured Paris and unfurled the swastika atop the Eiffel Tower.) *The Flag Speaks* told the history of the flag through re-enactments and offered instructions on flag etiquette. It closed with the singing of "America the Beautiful." *Boxoffice* noted, "Embarrassingly vigorous patriotism has been soft-toned in this film. In any case, it's guaranteed to make audiences applaud." It was shown in theaters and schools in the 1940s and 1950s.

The film's premiere at Grauman's Chinese Theater on February 18, 1940, was accompanied by a parade of 2,000 members of the American Legion and other patriotic groups and the National Guard. Citations were presented to Louis B. Mayer and Walter Wanger. Lees and Rinaldo were probably amused when Los Angeles Mayor Fletcher Bowron declared, "Hollywood is not a hotbed of Communism, but a hotbed of patriotism."

The writing duo began to edge away from documentary shorts. They wrote an unproduced, feature-length adaptation of the Sinclair Lewis story "The Willow Walk," about a trusted teller who concocts an elaborate scheme to embezzle money from his bank.

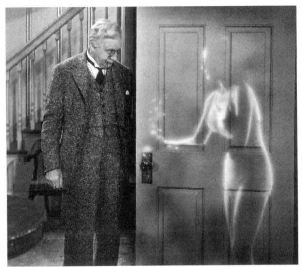

*Lees and Rinaldo's first feature film credits were* Street of Memories *(1940), with Lynne Roberts and John McGuire; and* The Invisible Woman *(1940), with John Barrymore and Virginia Bruce.*

They also worked on adapting the 1927 Broadway show "Good News" for Judy Garland and Mickey Rooney as a follow-up to *Babes in Arms* (1939). Louis B. Mayer, however, suggested capitalizing on the swing music craze instead, and producer Arthur Freed developed *Strike Up the Band* (1940).

Lees and Rinaldo's first feature film was not made at MGM, however. Lees recalled, "Our producer in the shorts department, Jack Chertok, wanted to move up to produce full-length films. He wanted to see if we could come up with something. Fred and I wrote our first original screenplay, 'Tomorrow Never Comes.' It was 'Grapes of Wrath' set in the city, really. This was 1938; we were still in the Depression. We wanted to make a statement that if a man was out of work, he wasn't necessarily a bum." In their story, an amnesia victim drifts into a small town in search of work. He falls for an attractive waitress and is befriended by a sympathetic tramp with whom he sells oranges on the street. A blow on the head restores his memory; he is the son of a wealthy manufacturer in Chicago.

Lees continued, "Lucien Hubbard, a producer at Metro who'd made *Wings* (1927), read it and wanted to do it very badly. But Louis B. Mayer said it wasn't politically propitious for MGM. In 1940 Hubbard went to 20th Century-Fox. Darryl Zanuck asked him what he wanted to do and Hubbard told him, 'I want to do a picture I read at Metro.' So they bought our script from Metro—which we got nothing for. Zanuck also thought it was a good script and said to Hubbard, 'If you want produce it, it'll be a B picture. If I produce it, it'll be an A picture and you'll be associate

producer.' Well, the idiot did it himself, and it was a bad B picture with unknown actors and a terrible title, *Street of Memories* (1940)."

*Los Angeles Times* critic Edwin Schallert called it "a commendable piece of work," but *Variety* dismissed it as "a laboratory experiment for some new talent on the studio roster" that "unsuccessfully tries to put over an 'arty' and psychological preachment while losing sight of basic audience requirements for entertainment purposes."

Lees said, "I think it wound up on the bottom of a bill with Hoot Gibson. It was the biggest disappointment of our entire lives. But now we had a feature credit, and that made a difference."

In the spring of 1940 their agent got them a gig at Universal. "We were never under contract to Universal other than a picture-to-picture contract," Lees explained. "*The Invisible Woman* was the first picture we did at Universal. Sometimes the producers, like Burt Kelly or later Robert Arthur, did several pictures and would call your agent and say I want them back."

Shooting had just begun on *The Invisible Woman* when Burt Kelly was tapped to produce "Oh, Charlie." He wanted Lees and Rinaldo again. The pair had just finished working for Kelly on *The Black Cat*, an old dark house spoof "suggested by" the Edgar Allan Poe short story. Lees recalled, "Burt liked us and he was producing "Oh, Charlie," so that's how we got our first Abbott and Costello assignment. In fact, I think he was going to do *Buck Privates* and we got involved with that picture, too. I can't recall what we did, but we didn't get any credit on it."

# "Oooh, Spooky Joint!"

**R**obert Lees explained, "As I recall, the whole reason for the haunted house thing was that they wanted to use the 'Moving Candle' routine. That was something that they did in burlesque." John Grant, the boys' writer, provided an eight-page script of haunted house bits that include the routine (see Chapter 8), while Lees and Rinaldo crafted the story context. Lees continued, "But *Hold That Ghost* started with a very strong idea—which was Fred's—that there's this gangster who's so distrustful of those around him, he wills everything to whoever is with him when he dies. And, of course, that's where we had Abbott and Costello come in."

*Hold That Ghost* is often grouped with haunted house comedies, but there is nothing supernatural in the film, unlike *The Time of Their Lives* (1946), where Costello plays a ghost from the American Revolution. More accurately, *Hold That Ghost* belongs to the "old dark house" and "explained supernatural" genres.

In old dark house stories, bad weather, car trouble, or the reading of a will prompt a group of people to stay overnight in an creepy old house with sinister servants, sliding panels, hidden rooms, clutching hands, and mysterious doings. Although it did not create the genre, the category gets its name from the 1932 Universal film directed by James Whale.

The "explained supernatural" goes back much further, to the Gothic novels of Ann Radcliffe (1764–1823). In her tales *The Mysteries of Udolpho* (1794) and *The Italian* (1797), seemingly supernatural phenomena are revealed to be part of a hoax or criminal conspiracy: a decaying body is really made of wax; a haunted room where faces appear in a mirror and from which a servant disappears is built over a cavern hideout of bandits, with access via a trap door, and so on.

Radcliffe did not invent the "explained supernatural" either, but she became the highest paid and most emulated author of the period. Academics have branded her work as the "female Gothic." It relies on suspense and terror rather than horror, imagined evils over real physical threats. The real danger to intelligent women, scholars suggest, is not the supernatural, but men attempting to steal their property or restrict their freedom. The Gothic castle is seen as a metaphor for domestic confinement. Radcliffe legitimized the Gothic genre and influenced Mary Shelley, the Brontë sisters, and Jane Austen, who played with gothic clichés in *Northanger Abbey* (1803). Radcliffe also anticipated the psychological novel and inspired radical feminist writers like Mary Wollstonecraft.

The "explained supernatural," minus its feminist subtext, became popular with mystery writers, playwrights, and early screenwriters. Sherlock Holmes, the personification of rational thought, finds real-world explanations for supernatural events in "The Hound of the Baskervilles," "The Adventure of the Sussex Vampire," and "The Devil's Foot." Later detective stories freely borrowed Gothic plots.

Early silent movies also featured haunted houses with fake spirits. In *The Haunted House* (1911), a would-be buyer stages ghostly pranks in order to purchase a house at cheaper price. In *The Haunted House* (1913), the town beauty proclaims that she will marry the first man to spend the night in an alleged haunted house. To weed out the weakest suitors she poses as a ghost, but it turns out the house is secretly occupied by opium smugglers, who capture her. In *The Haunted House* (1917), a young woman befriends a wounded young bank robber hiding in a deserted mansion. She pretends to be a ghost to frighten away his pursuers. In *The Ghost House* (1917), the long-empty Atwell home is haunted by the gardener, who heads a band of thieves using the place as a hideout. In *The Haunted Bedroom* (1919), a female reporter investigates the disappearance of a man at a haunted estate. She confronts a ghost who turns out to be the missing man, a wanted international forger. In *The Haunted House* (1921), Winifred Allen masquerades as a ghost to keep people away from her western retreat. In *The Ghost in the Garret* (1921), Dorothy Gish is framed for stealing pearls from her aunt and uncle, and follows the real thief to his gang's hideout in a haunted house. Gish then pretends to be a ghost to terrorize the gang, retrieve the pearls, and clear her name.

Broadway saw its share of old dark house and explained supernatural melodramas and farces. One of the earliest was "The Ghost Breaker," by Paul Dickey and his brother in law, Charles W. Goddard. It debuted in 1913. A man who is on the run after avenging his father's death meets a Spanish princess whose ancestral castle is haunted. He agrees to rid the place of ghosts and help her locate a hidden treasure inside. They discover that a neighbor, who hoped to find the treasure and marry the princess, hired the "ghosts." Although the play was a flop, Paramount bought the screen rights and filmed it four times.

In 1920 another mystery, "The Bat," opened on Broadway. Unlike "The Ghost Breaker," however, it was a huge hit and ran for nearly two years. Mary Robert Rhinehart and Avery Hopwood adapted the story from her 1908 bestseller, "The Circular Staircase." In this thriller, Cornelia Van Gorder rents the summer home of a bank president who was reported killed in Colorado. Most of the servants believe that the place is haunted, but she refuses to move. She learns that $1 million was either stolen or embezzled from the dead man's bank. Some suspect that the banker took the money, hid it in the house and, far from being dead, will return to retrieve it. Four others are also after the money: a teller wrongfully accused of stealing it; a detective; a doctor friend of the missing banker; and The Bat, an agile masked criminal who has long eluded the police. (This character, added for the play, inspired Bob Kane to create Batman.)

"The Bat" was adapted to film in 1926, 1930 and 1959. D. W. Griffith was interested in filming it but balked at paying $150,000 for the movie rights. Instead, he wrote his own old dark house film, *One Exciting Night* (1922). In his picture, a gang of bootleggers search for money hidden inside a house. Two murders are committed and all of the guests are suspected.

Phony hauntings were often tied to conditional wills. In the silent films *Haunting Shadows* (1920) and *The House of the Tolling Bell* (1920), a wealthy man fakes his own death to test the character of his heirs, who must live in his purportedly haunted house for a year or forfeit the estate. In other instances, a disgruntled relative does the haunting to discredit the rightful heir. In *The Courageous Fool* (1925), an uncle's will requires three heirs to stay in a haunted house for seven days. After a series of nightly frights, the bogus ghosts are unmasked. In *The Haunted Range* (1926), Ken Maynard will inherit a spooky ranch provided that within six months he solves its mystery. He discovers that the "haunting" is a ruse for cattle rustling.

The most famous entry in this subgenre was the "The Cat and the Canary," which opened on Broadway in 1922 and overlapped with the run of "The Bat." A group of heirs gather exactly twenty years after the death of a reclusive millionaire for the reading of his will. The will stipulates that his niece inherit his fortune if she is judged sane after spending the night in his haunted mansion. Otherwise, the fortune falls to another relative whose name is known only to the attorney. At least one relative is therefore motivated to either drive the girl insane or kill her. Before the attorney can reveal the identity of the secondary heir, a clawed hand pulls him inside a secret door in a bookcase. Later, while the niece sleeps, the same hand emerges from the wall behind her bed and snatches the family jewels from around her neck. During a search of the bedroom the attorney's body falls out from behind a secret panel, then goes missing. The stalker may be a homicidal maniac who has escaped from a nearby asylum, but is revealed to be the secondary heir, her cousin Charles.

The glut of old dark house mysteries on Broadway intrigued and annoyed two writers. Owen Davis won the Pulitzer Prize for Drama in 1923 and later wrote "Jezebel" and the comedy "The Nervous Wreck," which was the basis for Eddie Cantor's *Whoopee* (1930) and Danny Kaye's *Up in Arms* (1944). He penned a fast-paced spoof of the mystery genre in 1924 called "The Haunted House." *Variety* reported, "The first act...piles up so many laughs it seems impossible [for the author

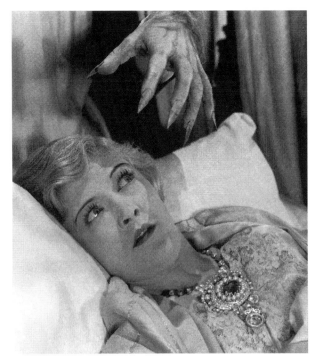

*Laura La Plante in Paul Leni's seminal old dark house thriller,* The Cat and the Canary *(1927), and Gloria Stuart in James Whale's* The Old Dark House *(1932). Stuart later appeared in* Titanic *(1997).*

to sustain them]. But this is accomplished, the laughter holding out voluminously until the final curtain." Unfortunately, a 1928 film version with Chester Conklin not only altered Davis' material, but is also lost.

Another writer, Ralph Spence, was the leading title writer for silent films. He also wrote material for the Ziegfeld Follies, Earl Carroll's Vanities and, later, Wheeler and Woolsey. Spence dashed off his own spoof, "The Gorilla," in three nights to win a bet. "For a long time I have been laughing at these mystery plays around town," Spence explained to the *New York Herald*. "I could not take them seriously so I decided the only thing to do was write a mystery deeper than any of them. After having conceived this mystery, I kid the audience and let them know it was all in fun." (Spence was sued for plagiarism but settled for only a tiny fraction of what "The Gorilla" earned him.)

When "The Gorilla" opened in 1925, publicity boasted that it "Out-bats 'The Bat'! Out-cats 'The Cat and the Canary'! Out-warns 'The Last Warning.'" Spence wrote a play within a play that revolved around a master criminal who sends a letter with the handprint of a gorilla to his victims before he strikes. In addition to all the trappings of the genre—secret panels, screams, gunfire, and lights that go out suddenly—there are two inept, wisecracking detectives and, by coincidence, a real escaped gorilla. (At one point the "gorilla" leaps into the theater audience.)

Spence named his gorilla Poe, an allusion to Edgar Allan Poe's classic "The Murders in the Rue Morgue," where the culprit is an orangutan. The opening night audience cheered the cast and author for five minutes after the final curtain, but the *New York Times* critic found the new play "only moderately entertaining." *Variety* correctly predicted that it wouldn't last long in New York but was a cinch to clean up on the road. It closed after just fifteen performances, but eight road companies toured America and Europe with great success. Bids for the film rights set a record, and movie versions were made in 1927, 1930, and 1939 (with the Ritz Brothers and Bela Lugosi). There were also the inevitable imitations. If you wondered why comedians inexplicably ran across apes in haunted houses, blame "The Gorilla."

By the late 1920s the popularity of these mysteries waned on Broadway, probably because they were now saturating the movies. "The Ghost Breaker" was filmed for the second time in 1922. The first film version of "The Bat" appeared in 1926, followed by *The Cat and the Canary* in 1927. (In a reverse, another old dark house mystery centered on a will, *Easy Pickings* [1927], was written for the screen, then adapted for the stage.)

*The Cat and the Canary* was a pivotal entry in the genre and considered the cornerstone of Universal's school of horror. Émigré director Paul Leni

*Bob Hope and Paulette Goddard in the hit remake of* The Cat and the Canary *(1939). Hope called it "the turning point of my film career." They were reunited the following year in* The Ghost Breakers, *a third remake based on the play.*

memorably blended German expressionism with black comedy and influenced the screen versions of *The Gorilla* (1927) and *The Haunted House* (1928). Hitchcock later cited it as an influence on *Psycho* (1960).

Leni's film also inspired James Whale's production of *The Old Dark House* (1932). Loosely adapted from J.B. Priestley's 1927 novel, "Benighted," the film stars Boris Karloff, Melvyn Douglas, Gloria Stuart, and Charles Laughton. Although there is no will or hidden fortune to attract them, a group of travelers, seeking shelter from a pounding rainstorm in a remote area of Wales, are admitted to the foreboding Femm mansion. The family includes Horace Femm, who claims to be a fugitive; his religious, malevolent sister, Rebecca; and brother Saul, a pyromaniac who is released from his room by the mute butler, Morgan. *Variety* called it a "somewhat inane picture," but all nine New York newspapers gave it positive reviews.

While there was dark humor in both Leni's and Whale's films, a comedic take on the genre started earlier. In *Haunted Spook* (1920), Mildred Davis will inherit a southern plantation provided she lives there for a year with her new husband, Harold Lloyd. To drive the couple away, her dastardly uncle makes the house appear to be haunted. In *The Haunted House* (1921), bank teller Buster Keaton is framed for a robbery and holes up in a creepy house used by

counterfeiters as a hideout. They dress up as ghosts and goblins to convince people the place is haunted. To complicate matters, a third-rate theatrical troupe, also in scary costumes, takes cover from an irate audience in the same house. In *Au Secours* (*"Help!"* 1924), comedian Max Linder accepts a bet that he cannot remain in a haunted castle from 11 p.m. to midnight without calling for help. He encounters nightmarish visions, but they are pranks staged by the owner to pay upkeep on the castle.

After silent and sound versions of *The Cat and the Canary, The Bat,* and *The Gorilla* reached wider audiences on screen, comedians began to borrow some of their tropes as well. *The Laurel-Hardy Murder Case* (1930) spoofs *The Cat and The Canary,* with Stan as an heir to the estate of Ebenezer Laurel. In *Detectives Wanted* (1930), another comedy team, Clark and McCullough, cleaned out a supposedly haunted house. Eventually, nearly every film series or comedian had at least one entry set in a supposedly haunted house, including the Bowery Boys' *Spooks Run Wild* (1941) and *Ghosts on the Loose* (1943); *Mexican Spitfire Sees a Ghost* (1942); and *Henry Aldrich Haunts a House* (1943). *Gildersleeve's Ghost* (1944) not only featured ghosts of his ancestors, but also a mad scientist, an escaped gorilla, and an intermittently invisible showgirl. Later, Don Knotts made *The Ghost and Mr. Chicken* (1966) as well as *The Private Eyes* (1980) with

Tim Conway. Gene Wilder and Gilda Radner played radio murder mystery writers in a spooky mansion in *Haunted Honeymoon* (1986). The supernatural hoax was a fixture of the Scooby-Doo cartoons. Fittingly, Robert Lees provided the story for a 1983 episode of *The New Scooby and Scrappy Doo Show* called "Scoobygeist."

Of course, some old dark houses were home to genuine horrors. *The Monster* (1925), with Lon Chaney, is a hybrid of the old dark house and an early mad scientist movie. But, as Douglas Gomery points out in his essay, "The Economics of the Horror Film," Hollywood could not establish the horror film as a consistently popular genre until *Dracula* became a sensation in 1931. It was soon followed by *Frankenstein* (1931), *The Mummy* (1932), *The Black Cat* (1934), and *Bride of Frankenstein* (1935).

After a brief lull, comedic old dark house films made a comeback starting with *The Cat and the Canary* (1939) with Bob Hope and Paulette Goddard, and their follow up, *The Ghost Breakers* (1940). Although the ghosts in *The Ghost Breakers* were fake, there was the significant addition of a "real" zombie. *New York Times* critic Bosley Crowther wrote, "It looks as though Paramount has really discovered something: it has found the fabled formula for making an audience shriek with laughter and fright at one and (as the barkers say) the simultaneous time." The *New Yorker* thought, "The amalgam of farce and horror is very successful." This version was the basis for *Scared Stiff* (1953) with Martin and Lewis.

Hope's character in *The Cat and the Canary* is a radio actor who has performed in melodramas and murder mysteries. As the film's sinister events unfold, he references the clichés of the genres. This may have been an inspiration for Camille Brewster in *Hold That Ghost*. She is a radio screamer who can't help recalling episodes of her show.

Another inspiration for Camille may have been a diminutive utility actress who was a fixture on the Universal lot: Sara Swartz (1906-1949), who dubbed the screams for the leading ladies in the studio's horror films. Universal's founder, Carl Laemmle, discovered Sara playing child roles in a Denver theater and suggested she come to Hollywood. Her grandfather was from the same German town, Laubheim, as Laemmle, and Sara reportedly gave Laemmle the nickname "Uncle Carl," which was known throughout the industry. According to legend, the eleven-year-old actress was working at Universal in 1917 when a major fire broke out. She rushed into a burning editing room and saved a valuable film. Laemmle decreed that her name appear on the studio's casting lists for the rest of her life. Swartz dispelled that story, but until her death, she worked in over 2,000 films at Universal in bit parts or crowd scenes. She often worked in more than one film per day.

Her unique vocal talent was discovered during the filming of *Waterloo Bridge* (1931). The women in a crowd scene were instructed to scream during an air raid. "Either I was a little louder, or a little better than the rest," Sara explained. "Anyway, James Whale singled me out, and I have been screaming in pictures ever since. Short or long, loud or soft, it's $25 a scream." Her shrieks can be heard in *Dracula*, the Frankenstein films, *Murders in the Rue Morgue, Flesh and Fantasy,* 1943's *Phantom of the Opera, Man in the Iron Mask,* and many others. She dubbed screams for Mae Clarke, Irene Dunne, and Susanna Foster and was loaned out to other studios, including Paramount for *The Uninvited* (1944).

Swartz likely dubbed Joan Davis' howls in *Hold That Ghost*. Evelyn Ankers, however, did not require Sara's services. Evelyn proved that she could shriek with the best of them every night in the 1940 Broadway mystery "Ladies in Retirement." The magazine *Hollywood* wrote, "Miss Ankers has that on her conscience as a matter of fact, and lowers her eyes somewhat guiltily whenever she sees [Sara] on the Universal lot. 'I hope she isn't mad at me,' Evelyn said."

Evelyn explained, "I'm proud of my scream. I developed it when I made six mystery pictures in England and was always terrified."

It is ironic that Camille laments being exploited for her scream when that is what happened to Ankers. Robert Lees and Fred Rinaldo could not have known that Evelyn would be in the film; their first draft was written before Universal signed her.

Between 1941 and 1951, Lees and Rinaldo were credited on seven Abbott and Costello films, although they worked on more. Lees explained, "Here's how we worked," Lees explained. "I would come up with the storylines very quickly. I think if Fred were left on his own he would have come up with stories but it would have taken longer. On the other hand, Fred was much faster with dialogue. So we'd finally knock out the treatment so we were both satisfied with it. If we didn't like the way it was, we didn't tell the other guy 'fix it.' We fixed it until the other guy said it was okay. We would go back and

*John Grant not only contributed dialogue and routines to the Abbott and Costello screenplays, but he was always on the set to tweak scenes. Here he discusses slapping technique on the set of* Hit The Ice *(1943), which was also scripted by Lees and Rinaldo. Marc Lawrence is directly behind Lou.*

forth until we both agreed. Two-thirds of the story would be mine, and two-thirds of the dialogue would be Fred's. I really learned to write dialogue from Fred."

"Oh, Charlie" was the first time that Lees and Rinaldo "collaborated" with the boys' writer, John Grant. "We weren't happy with John Grant," Lees confessed. "He had nothing to do with the stories, but he'd write so much dialogue that he'd get a screen credit. Fred and I were screenwriters, not gag writers. The problem was, we wanted to write stories that held up, had character, and developed. And we would write what we would consider Abbott and Costello routines which were verbal or physical. Sometimes we felt that John Grant would take perfectly good dialogue that was advancing the script and turn it into one of those things they had done a thousand times before. And they'd put it in just because it was Grant. They were more sure of their routines or more sure of John's stuff."

Screenwriter Edmund L. Hartmann, who also worked on several of the team's films, said, "John's job was to take a finished script and go through it and see where they could inject these comedy routines from burlesque, because that is the only thing that Lou would willingly do. They were very resistant to using new material, especially Lou."

In explaining their affection for repeating gags that have stood the test of time, Bud said, seriously, "That's how we know they're funny. They have lived.

Only bad jokes die young."

Grant also contributed ideas during filming. "They usually kept him on the set to jazz up scenes that had no reason being jazzed up in the first place," Lees said. Norman Abbott, Bud's nephew, explained, "John worked on the set all the time, which was a boon to the director, because I tell you, when you have the writer next to you on the set who comes up with stuff all the time, it's like pure gold. That's what John did. They had so many years with him, he was like a member of the family."

Arthur Lubin asserted, "John Grant was greatly responsible for the success of the writing of [the] five pictures [I did with them]."

Furthermore, the boys were always improvising. "They were from burlesque and they were used to [having an audience]," Lees said. "So if there was a little scene that was just advancing the plot, Costello would trip over his foot, or do a routine—because he could *not* not get a laugh. And, because they were really saving the studio's neck, the director was never in a position to say, 'Cut it out Lou, it's only going to be on the screen for a second, let's just go through it.' They would not control him. Sometimes Costello would read a line during the rehearsal that would get laughs from the crew. But after the third or fourth take, nobody laughed because everyone knew the joke. So Costello would ad-lib to see if he could get a laugh on something else."

In an interview with the *Philadelphia Inquirer*, the

boys explained that after reading a dozen pages of *Buck Privates* they gave up reading screenplays because, as Lou explained, "Whenever we were on, all it said was 'Spot for Abbott and Costello.'" Bud added, "So now, we just tell 'em to keep the cameras turning, and throw away what they don't like. That hammock scene in *In the Navy*. Did you think it was funny? Well, all we had to go on was, 'Costello tries to get in the hammock and can't.' See what we mean?"

The screenplay and the final cut of the film also had to be approved by Hollywood's self-regulating censor board, the Production Code Administration (PCA). Production Code guidelines, which spelled out what was permissible or unacceptable on screen, were applied to almost every film produced in the United States from 1930 to 1968. Since the Supreme Court had decided unanimously in 1915 that free speech did not extend to motion pictures, one motivating factor in Hollywood adopting the Code was to avoid direct government intervention. The Code was also popularly known as the Hays Code, after Will H. Hays, the president of the Motion Picture Producers and Distributors of America (MPPDA). The goal of the MPPDA was to rehabilitate the immoral image of the movie colony and industry. Hays appointed Joseph Breen, a journalist and an "influential layperson" in the Catholic community, to enforce the Code from 1934 to 1954. Arthur Lubin later mused, "Wouldn't Breen turn over in his grave if he knew what was happening now?"

Lees and Rinaldo apparently had an easier time developing their story than Alex Gottlieb had with *Buck Privates*. Their twenty-nine-page treatment for "Oh, Charlie" (called "Don't Look Now" in its earliest stages) was delivered on October 26, even before the first treatment of *Buck Privates*. It is close to the final shooting script but lacks input from John Grant.

Their story begins with the boys operating a gas station and parking lot in Los Angeles. They open with their "Ethyl" routine, and Costello adroitly parks a car in a tight space. Then the notorious gangster Moose Matson drives up in a hurry. As the boys service his car, Costello discovers pistols and bullets in the back seat. When the cops spot Matson, the mobster steps on the gas before Abbott and Costello are clear of the vehicle. The police give chase and open fire. Matson and Costello trade places in the car so that Costello drives and Matson shoots at the cops. Suddenly, Matson is mortally wounded, and

Costello performs a remarkable feat of driving which completely baffles the pursuing police. (This stunt was eventually eliminated.) The boys pull over. Moose calls out the names of various members of his gang. When he realizes that none of them are around and that he is dying in the presence of two strangers, he breaks into a bitter, ironic laugh. With his last breath he pulls his last will and testament out from his coat.

In probate court, Abbott and Costello learn that since they were with Moose at his demise, they are his sole heirs. No actual cash has been discovered; Moose always said that he kept his money "in his head." Perhaps the legendary hidden treasure of the notorious bootlegger and racketeer Dutch Schultz was an inspiration here. In 1935 Schultz and three henchmen were gunned down in a Newark restaurant. Schultz lived for twenty-four hours, during which time he gave a long, delirious "confession." Many speculated that a clue to the location of the fortune was hidden in his enigmatic last words, but it has never been found.

Moose's only material possession is the Forrester's Club, a roadhouse tavern outside of Seattle which served as a speakeasy and gambling joint, but has been abandoned for years. Costello wants to drop the whole thing but Abbott sees an opportunity to better themselves. As they leave court, Charlie Smith, a sinister but dapper member of Moose's gang, tails them.

The boys see a personal ad in the newspaper for a bus service. On a cold gray morning, they meet the driver of this wildcat jitney on a Main Street corner. (As in *Buck Privates*, Costello is laden with the team's luggage.) The shifty-eyed driver shows an unusual interest in his passengers' bags. Already waiting is Martha Davis, a disillusioned radio actress whose sole job so far has been the opening scream on the "Tales of Terror" program. (It's probably no coincidence that her name is an amalgam of Martha Raye and Joan Davis.) Martha takes an immediate shine to Costello. Smith is the next passenger to arrive. (It's unclear in this version how he knew the boys' travel plans.) He calls himself John Smith and is vague about his business.

The last two members of the party are in the drug store. Norma Lynd, a pretty girl, is on her way to a waitressing job in the East. (Why she takes a bus headed north to Seattle is not explained.) Ordering breakfast, she tells the soda jerk that she wants her toast without butter. A pleasant-looking man at the counter remarks that she should eat butter. As a hyperthyroid-extensor type, she needs the dextrose

*Clutching hands reach out from secret panels in* The Cat and the Canary *(the 1927 version, far left, and the 1939 version with Paulette Goddard) and in* Hold That Ghost. *Production Code censors warned Universal that some local censors frequently deleted scenes and sounds of characters being choked.*

butter contains. Norma replies coolly that she doesn't like butter. The man lists traits she exhibits, and she confirms them. He's a doctor, and he can tell a lot by general primary characteristics. He introduces himself as Dick Jackson. (The doctor's first name is never revealed in the film.) The bus driver enters the drug store to collect the couple, who are pleasantly surprised to learn that they will be traveling together.

The group starts their journey with Jackson, Norma and Smith in the back seat, and Abbott, Martha and Costello on the jump seat. While Dr. Jackson is engrossed in a medical book, Smith immediately goes on the make for Norma. Martha goes to work on Costello while Abbott eggs her on. Up front, the driver glances covetously at Dr. Jackson's bag of instruments. As they pass a farm, Abbott and Costello do their "Herd of Cows" routine. Night finds them traveling through a rain-drenched countryside. The passengers have lapsed into weary silence. Norma dozes uncomfortably between Smith and Dr. Jackson. When her head starts to sag towards Smith's shoulder, she catches herself and leans instead on the doctor.

The driver pulls into a gas station to ask directions to Moose's tavern. At first the attendant cannot remember any such place, then his memory clicks. The old tavern is on a road nobody uses anymore since the new highway was built. This is quite a blow to the boys, but they purchase groceries in a little store next to the gas station, where a deaf proprietor provides them with a comedy routine.

The old highway is bogged down in heavy mud. Finally they pull up before the weather-beaten "Forrester's Club." It reminds Martha of the setting for one of her radio programs, "The Death of the Five Legged Cat," but almost everything reminds Martha of one of her programs. Considering the weather conditions, the driver thinks that they should all take shelter until morning. But while they open the front door, the driver peels off with the group's luggage. Smith casually explains that wildcat busses often resort to such thievery. Fortunately, Costello has the groceries.

The interior of the roadhouse includes a dining room, dance floor, a large fireplace, and a bandstand. Tables and chairs are piled in a corner. Around the room are hunting trophies, including a large moose head over the fireplace. Norma and Dr. Jackson build a fire, but Smith thinks there must be a furnace and heads for the cellar. Abbott, Costello and Martha begin to prepare dinner. Costello discovers a water pump out on the porch, but the water has a horrible taste. Perhaps it just needs to be boiled.

Dr. Jackson and Norma set up tables and chairs by the fire. Norma finds their situation rather romantic. The Doctor, however, expresses his interest in her in purely medical terms. If she would only eat more butter and drink more milk, she could be a perfect physical specimen. Norma is amused and exasperated.

Down in the cellar, Smith is not interested in the furnace. Instead he feverishly searches for something. Abbott, Costello and Martha return to the dining room with dinner. They call to Smith to come up and join them; he replies that he will be right up. Smith crosses to the furnace and opens the grate. Before he can move or cry out, a pair of brutal, hairy hands reach out from inside the furnace and clutch at his throat. Smith's eyes pop out and his face contorts with horror. He drops his flashlight, and in the dimness we see him being dragged into the furnace. (Smith's fate

*The bodies of the attorney and Charlie Smith drop out of hiding places in master bedrooms and then vanish in*
The Cat and the Canary *and* Hold That Ghost. *Lees and Rinaldo made Smith's body a running gag.*

mirrors that of the attorney in *The Cat and the Canary.* The lawyer is grabbed from behind by the neck, and his body turns up falling face first from a hidden panel in the master bedroom. Later on it disappears from the bedroom. Lees and Rinaldo repeated this hide-and-seek with Smith's body for laughs.)

Upstairs, Abbott calls to Smith again. He and the others are puzzled when there is no answer, but assume he'll be up shortly. They sit down to eat. Martha, by this time, is definitely interested in Costello, but Costello claims he enjoys his bachelorhood. Abbott goes into a routine about the virtues of married life.

Martha discovers an old Victrola in the corner of the dining room. She puts on a warped record and insists on dancing with Costello. They start a comedy-dance routine. Their fun is interrupted when Norma remembers that Smith is still missing. They decide to look for him. On the side of the mantelpiece hangs a lantern. As the Doctor lifts it, a secret panel slides open, revealing a barroom which has not been used since Prohibition. The group enters and looks around when Martha suddenly points and tries to scream. On the floor is a fresh carnation—the one Smith has been wearing. There seems to be no other entrance or exit to the room other than the secret panel.

The group rushes to the cellar steps. The Doctor suggests that the three men should go down and the girls should stay by the fire. In the cellar they conduct a futile search for Smith by lantern and candlelight. As Costello pauses in front of the furnace, a pair of evil eyes peers out at him through the grate. A puff of breath blows out Costello's candle. Costello does a "take," and crosses to Abbott just in time to elude the same burly hands that grabbed Smith. Costello

trembles so hard that he can barely hold his candle for Abbott to relight it. He claims that somebody blew out the flame, but Abbott insists that it was only a draft.

The Doctor finds a pit just big enough for a body in the corner of the cellar. As the men examine this, they are startled by a scream from one of the girls upstairs and rush to the rescue. Norma and Martha had started upstairs but saw a pair of eyes peering down at them from the landing. The men discover that the eyes belong to an owl perched in a niche on the landing. Norma feels a little ashamed that she was so easily frightened. The Doctor reassures her that they are all nervous and exhausted. They should all go to bed and investigate further in the morning. Before they head upstairs they return to the kitchen and draw several pitchers of water to use in washing up.

Upstairs, there is a long narrow hall with a series of rooms on each side. The girls take the first room, and the Doctor will use the room opposite them. Abbott and Costello go down the hall and open the next door. There is a gaping hole in the roof; rain pours in and spatters in the boys' faces. They hastily close the door and try the room across the hall. It's a suite: two bedrooms rooms connected by a bathroom.

Abbott returns to the first room. Costello takes off his coat and hangs it on a hat rack next to the bathroom door. He enters the bathroom to wash his face before retiring. What he does not know is that his coat tripped a lever which turns the bedroom into a gambling den. The bed disappears into the wall, pivoting into view a crap table; the chandelier lowers from the ceiling to make a roulette wheel; and the bureau turns into a Chuck-a-Luck table. (Also known as Birdcage, Chuck-a-Luck is played with three dice and is more of a carnival game than a casino game). Costello finishes washing up, once again commenting about the horrible water. He returns to his bedroom and does a double take at the metamorphosis. He dashes to the wash basin, douses more water in his face, rubs his eyes and returns for another look. His eyes are not deceiving him. He snatches his coat off the rack and rushes into Abbott's room. With his coat off the lever, however, the bedroom swiftly returns to normal.

Costello tries to explain this to Abbott, who, of course, is skeptical. He leads Costello to his room to find everything in order. Abbott accuses Costello of letting his nerves run away with him, but Costello insists that he saw what he saw. Abbott offers to take this room and let Costello have his room. Costello returns to Abbott's room and hangs his coat up on another rack. He suddenly remembers that he left his tie in the first bedroom and goes back to get it. When he returns, he finds this room is now filled with gambling equipment. Frightened, he grabs his coat, again releasing the lever, and rushes to get Abbott. By the time the boys get back to this room, the gambling den has transformed back to a bedroom.

Thoroughly annoyed, Abbott orders Costello to stop this silly business and get into bed. Abbott returns to his room and finds Costello's coat on the floor. He picks it up, brings it to Costello's room, brusquely hangs it on the hat rack, closes the door, and leaves. To Costello's horror the room begins to change around him—his bed starts to tilt up and disappear into the wall. With a horrified yell, he jumps out just in time and rushes back into Abbott's bedroom, taking his coat with him. He drags Abbott forcefully out of bed to the other room, where once again all appears normal.

This is too much for Costello. He decides to find another room. This is a master bedroom, lined in heavy velvet drapes with a four-poster bed. (Moose's bedroom in the film.) Costello takes a childish delight in this luxury. He calls Abbott to come and have a look. Next to the bed is a heavy bell cord. Costello wonders whether it will ring in the kitchen or if it is disconnected. He pulls it; it isn't a bell cord, but a drawstring for the drapes beside the bed. The drapes part to reveal a door. (In the final shooting scrip this sequence in Matson's bedroom comes before the Changing Room.) Abbott tells him to open the door, but he refuses because he's seen this sort of thing in the movies: you open that door and a bound and gagged body falls out. If Abbott wants it opened, he can open it himself. So Abbott opens the door and reveals an empty clothes closet. Abbott looks sternly at Costello. Isn't he ashamed of himself now? He slams the closet door in annoyance, but the slam shakes loose a body which has been propped up behind the drapes. It keels over onto the floor in classic style. It's Charlie Smith. Costello does a weak "I want my Mama" and faints into Abbott's arms. Abbott carries him into the hall and yells for the Doc.

The Doctor and the girls rush out of their rooms. Abbott indicates the body inside to the Doc, who goes in to examine it. When Martha sees Costello out cold she rushes to get him a glass of water. (In an early draft of the screenplay, Martha faints when she thinks Costello has been murdered. Norma wakes Martha, and Chuck repeatedly slaps Ferdie to rouse him. Costello, apparently enjoying the slaps, exclaims, "Do it again, I like it!" This references Jean Harlow's famous response when Chester Morris slaps her in *Red Headed Woman* [1932]. The film made Harlow a star but was one of the movies that led directly to the enforcement of the Production Code.)

The Doctor pronounces Smith dead. Down in the dining room the group discusses their options. The Doctor is all for leaving immediately to get the police. Suddenly there is a heavy knock on the front door. Two burly men carrying powerful flashlights claim that they are the police. They want to know what is going on in this long deserted joint. Abbott explains that he and Costello are the new owners. The policemen plant the idea that Charlie Smith's ghost haunts the tavern. The Doctor rejects such superstitious nonsense and takes them upstairs to Smith's body, but it is gone. The policemen decide to search the house, starting with the cellar. The Doctor suggests that the group go to bed, but first he wants a glass of milk. (Lees and Rinaldo suggest planting some doubt about the Doctor in the audience's minds at this point; casting Carlson, who was revealed to be the villain in *The Ghost Breakers*, supported this suspicion.)

In the cellar, the policemen cross directly to the furnace and tap on the door. The furnace swings aside to reveal a long passageway. Out step six men. The eight men proceed to converse in guarded tones. The two "policemen" relate that two of the intruders upstairs claim that they now own the joint and that they intend to keep it. These men are the surviving members of Moose's gang and won't be cheated out of his loot. One gangster suggests disposing of the intruders the same way they did with Smith. One of the policemen, who seems to be the leader, disagrees. Smith was a double-crossing rat who tried to beat them to the money and deserved what he got. He has a better plan for handling the innocent dopes upstairs. They will divide into two groups. One group will look for Moose's dough. The second group will scare off Abbott and Costello and their companions. This subterfuge dates back to one of the two hundred or so stock comedy routines, or *lazzi*, associated with the *commedia dell'arte* of the Renaissance. (Like later performers in burlesque, the actors in *commedia dell'arte* troupes memorized these bits, and certain performers became identified with specific sketches.) In "The Lazzo of the Multiple Thieves," various characters pose as a devil, a ghost, and policemen to scare one another out of a gold necklace.

Norma finds Dr. Jackson testing the tavern's water with makeshift equipment. She tries to get him to pay attention to her, but Jackson is too absorbed in his work. The "detectives" emerge from the cellar and gather the others by the fireplace. They inform the group that they have not found a trace of Smith's body. Once again they relate how this tavern has long been considered haunted. It was the scene of several gang murders, and to this day the souls of lost gunmen wander down the corridors shooting it out. The police say that the safest thing for them would be to leave immediately. That's all Costello needs to hear, but Abbott thinks they are better off staying put now that the police are around. Dr. Jackson agrees and leads the way upstairs. The "policemen" promise to keep watch for the rest of the night.

Once the others are out of sight, however, the gangsters assigned to find the money start hunting all around the tavern. Upstairs, the second group of gangsters starts to work scaring off the newcomers. While Norma and Martha prepare for bed, a weird face peers in through the window, ducking out of sight whenever either girl glances that way. The girls come dangerously close to the window several times, with Norma finally actually opening it. The wind gusts so strongly that she closes it immediately.

Meanwhile, in his room, Costello prepares for bed. He folds his clothes very neatly over a chair, turns down his bed, and straightens a wrinkle or two in his pillow. Finally he places his shoes out in the corridor as though he expects they will be shined for him over night. His door suddenly slams behind him, bumping Costello out into the hall. (In the film he answers a knock on the door.) Costello turns the knob but the door refuses to budge. He pushes harder. The door opens several inches and then is obviously pushed closed from the other side. Costello gulps, "Locked…" He hurries down the hall to get Abbott. Meanwhile, inside Costello's room, the gangsters turn the place upside down looking for the loot.

Out in the hall, Abbott returns with Costello to investigate the locked door. He turns the handle and the door opens easily. When he sees the chaotic condition of the room, Abbott berates Costello for being a pig. This leads to an "I'm a bad boy" from Costello.

In the girls' room the window flies open and a dagger flashes across the room and quivers on the headboard of the bed, pinning a note which warns them to beware. Martha tries to scream, but can't. Norma's call brings the Doctor and Abbott and Costello to their room. Dr. Jackson is now convinced that somebody is trying to scare them out of the house. The two detectives, also drawn by the scream, agree and promise to be extra vigilant.

The group return to their individual rooms. Abbott calms Costello by pointing out that the police are going to handle everything. Costello prepares for sleep. As he leans over to blow out his candle, a mysterious puff of breath beats him to it. Costello keeps his courage up by repeating Abbott's statement, "The police will take care of everything." The words are barely out of his mouth when a tall figure in a monk's robe and cowling materializes from the wall and starts towards Costello's bed. (Monks, good and bad, figured in several early Gothic novels.) Costello is paralyzed with fright. Just as the figure approaches his bed, however, a panel in the wall slides open, a scrawny arm holding a long bladed knife appears and stabs the back of the hooded figure which crumples to the floor with a gasp. Before Costello can gather his wits, his bedroom door flies open and the detectives enter. They go straight to the fallen monk, look sternly at Costello and say, "This man is dead." They pick up the body and carry it from the room, slamming the door behind them. Costello, left alone, tries to reassure himself with Abbott's last remarks. He tries to go back to sleep when the same hooded figure reappears and starts toward his bed. The same panel slides open and the knife is plunged into the monk's back. As he crumples to the floor the bedroom door flies open, the detectives enter and go through the same routine. They leave a bewildered Costello trying to figure the whole thing out. (Perhaps the old "Crazy House" routine could have worked here.)

The girls also find it difficult to sleep. Martha decides she needs some warm milk. She goes down into the kitchen to heat some up. The gangsters downstairs quickly take cover as she approaches.

Costello, meanwhile, has almost fallen asleep when a drop of water falls from the ceiling and hits his nose. A steady stream follows. He tries to move out from under it but the raindrops follow him from one side of the bed to the other. Frustrated, he sits up. A section of the roof falls in and drenches him. He jumps out of bed, dashes out the door, down the hall and into Abbott's room where he jumps into bed beside his friend. When Abbott realizes that Costello is soaking wet he gives him a thoroughly disgusted look.

Downstairs, the gangsters grow impatient waiting for Martha to heat up her milk. They fix it so she won't wander around anymore. When Martha heads upstairs with the boiled milk, a ghostlike figure in a long sheet starts to follow upstairs step for step. Martha becomes conscious of the ghost's squeaking shoes and stops walking. (In the final screenplay and film, she walks downstairs with the ghost following behind her.) The ghost stops in time with her. Martha wiggles her toes but her shoes seem well broken in. She takes another step; the ghost squeaks after her. Martha then takes two more quick steps and starts to take a third but keeps her foot suspended. The ghost takes all three steps with a particularly long squeak on the last one. The routine builds along these lines until finally Martha forces herself to turn and look. When she sees the ghost she throws back her head and lets out that scream that is all the screams of the "Tales of Terror" program rolled into one. It even seems to build in intensity. The "ghost" runs away in fright. (In the final script and film he runs into Ferdie's room.) The gangsters cower in the cellar, holding their ears. Owls leave the attic and rats scurry from the cellar. Dishes crack in the kitchen and bottles tumble from the bar in the barroom. The occupants of the bedrooms upstairs come rushing downstairs to where Martha is at last quiet. The two detectives, however, are nowhere to be seen. When Martha explains about the ghost, everyone agrees that it would be foolish to stay any longer. They will leave and return in the morning. The question is, where can they go? Costello comes forward with a road map. He and the Doctor start to examine the map while the others go upstairs to gather their clothes. Costello, however, does not want Abbott to leave him. Abbott says that he will be within calling distance and that if anything happens he just has to yell, "Oh Abbott!" We now go into the "Oh, Charlie" routine. (Of course Costello was not paired with the Doctor, but with Martha/Camille.)

After the "Oh, Charlie" routine, the Doctor wonders whether the eerie events could possibly be connected to Moose's hidden fortune. Abbott doubts this because Moose said he kept the money in his head. Costello points to the moose head above the fireplace and wonders if that is where the money is. Abbott tries to explain that is merely a figure of speech, which only leads to an argument over other figures of speech. Finally, in exasperation, Abbott tells Costello to get up and see for himself if there's any money in the moose head. Costello climbs up and reaches his hand into the moose's mouth. He calls down to Abbott that the moose has a green tongue. Abbott replies that it's probably fungus. As he obliviously flicks greenback after greenback out of the moose's mouth, Costello complains to Abbott that the moose's tongue is peeling. He reaches deep inside the mouth and struggles to pull something out. It is a big wad of money. Costello drops it down to Abbott and remarks that whoever stuffed this animal sure did a rotten job. He reaches his arm all the way in the moose's mouth, feels around, then admits that Abbott was right: there's nothing in the moose's head. Abbott meanwhile has counted the money, which he now shows to Costello.

The girls return to the dining room with their hats and coats. Everybody is excited about the money when the gangsters appear in the doorways on either side of them. With guns drawn, they step forward to relieve Costello of the loot. Suddenly Costello makes a wild dash for freedom. He heads up the stairs to the second floor with the gangsters chasing behind him, while Abbott, the Doctor and the girls try to impede them. Costello ducks into his bedroom and, in trying to cut through to the bathroom, accidentally trips the lever on the hat rack. The room transforms into the gambling den just as the gangsters rush in. The lowering chandelier knocks one cold; the overturning bed trips up another. Costello cuts through to Abbott's bedroom and out into the hall again, with other gangsters in pursuit. He ducks into Moose's bedroom. The gangsters follow him in but find the room empty. There is a suspicious rustling behind the heavy drapes. One of the gangsters pulls his gun and orders Costello to come out. When he doesn't, the gangster fires into the drapes. Charlie Smith's body tumbles out onto the floor. Costello appears from another section of the drapes and bolts out of the room. He tears down the stairs and runs right into the two detectives. Relieved, Costello demands to know where they have been all this time. Then, as the gangsters race down the stairs, Costello quickly hands the money to the detectives and ducks behind them. To the surprise of the boys, Norma, and Martha, the detectives and the gangsters greet each other.

The gangsters tie Abbott, Costello and Martha together and are about to truss up Norma and the Doctor when the panel to the barroom slides open. Two very tough looking mugs, dressed in prison garb, enter and train their guns on the whole group. The first gang is surprised to see them; they thought this group was still in jail. The newcomers broke out when they heard Moose died. They figured there would be a scramble for the treasure and see that they arrived just in time. One of the detectives says hopefully that there's enough dough for everyone. But the toughest convict sneers that there probably is hardly enough for two. He orders his henchman to relieve the detectives of the money. The henchman hands the wad to his partner, only to find that the tough con doesn't intend to share. He orders the henchman to join the other gangsters, who stand helplessly with arms up.

The tough con takes Norma along as a hostage and backs out into the barroom. When he gets behind the bar he throws a lever which closes the sliding panel. At the same time a staircase behind the bar opens. It leads down to a passage from the furnace to an exit in the woods where his getaway car is parked. As he starts down the stairs Norma grabs his gun arm and starts to wrestle with it. Dr. Jackson takes advantage of this distraction and rushes through the sliding panel before it closes. The other gangsters break for the cellar stairs hoping to cut the escaped convict off.

The escaped con forces Norma ahead of him as he ducks down the passage. The Doctor rushes after. The con bolts the furnace door so that the gangsters are delayed. The Doctor catches the convict at the exit of the passage. His gun is empty and the two men engage in a short but fierce battle. The Doctor lands a lucky haymaker which flattens his opponent. The other gangsters, meanwhile, break through the furnace door and rush down the passage. The Doctor grabs Norma quickly and hides with her in the nearby weeds. The gangsters rush up to the unconscious convict, gather the money and are about to continue down the road when they spot a police car pulling up near the entrance of the passage. The gangsters beat a hasty retreat back to the tavern through the tunnel. (This

sequence, with Norma as a hostage and Dr. Jackson rescuing her, never made it into the final script.)

Meanwhile Martha, Abbott, and Costello are still tied back to back. They try to hop toward the kitchen where they hope to find a knife, but they trip and fall. They find it impossible to get to their feet, so are forced to roll one over the other like a huge, awkward barrel. They manage to squirm loose just as the gangsters return to the dining room.

By this time Abbott and Costello are infuriated: the money belongs to them. Near the Victrola, Costello seizes a pile of phonograph records and starts to skim them rapidly in the gangsters' direction. The gangsters duck for cover. The thug with the money makes a wild dash for the front door. Abbott however, grabs a chair and slides it across the slippery floor, tripping the man up. The money falls out of the thug's hands and skids right into Martha's hands. Another gangster raises his gun to shoot her, but Costello knocks the weapon out of his hand with a phonograph record. Martha dashes for the front door. Just as she opens it the real police enter. They grab her and carry her back into the room with them. The gangsters are quickly corralled. The police examine the money and pronounce it counterfeit. This is a terrible blow to Abbott and Costello. (In the final script, the police say they learned about the stranded group after capturing Hoskins. The police are not in the final film, however, and were replaced by Ferdie's clever heroics.)

Dr. Jackson and Norma return to the dining room as the police herd the gangsters out. Abbott and Costello glumly suppose it's back to the gas station for them now. But the Doctor has made an interesting discovery. He tells them to follow him. At the end of the passage where he and Norma hid, he points out several bubbling springs. He tells them to taste it. Costello takes one taste and pronounces it twice as bad as the water in the kitchen. The Doctor explains that the warm springs have affected the kitchen well water. Although it tastes terrible, it seems to have the ingredients for curative water. The boys have a possible gold mine in a future health resort.

The Abbott and Costello Rest Home is now an established success under the medical supervision of Dr. Jackson and his nurse-wife Norma. Martha has a job as room clerk. The boys also have a new gas station adjacent to their refurbished tavern. The boys do a final routine, which ends with them putting some of their healthy water in the motor of an old, wheezing jalopy and changing its sound to a powerful roar.

# Behind the Camera

irector Arthur Lubin was perplexed when he was assigned to *Buck Privates.* "I was honest," Lubin recalled. "I said, 'I'm sorry, but I just don't feel I'm the right director for this project. I'm not a dance director.' They all looked at me with puzzled expressions. One of the men said, 'Dancing? What do you mean?' I replied, 'There's a troupe at the Figueroa Theater called the [Merriel] Abbott Dancers. Isn't that who we're talking about?' Everybody laughed. Then they explained who Abbott and Costello were."

*Buck Privates,* of course, was a huge commercial and critical success. It's difficult to compare film grosses from that era because *Variety* did not begin issuing year-end figures for box-office rental grosses until 1946. Before then, *Showman's Trade Review* polled theater managers to determined "Hollywood's Twenty-Five Leading Productions" of the year. The caveat here is that theater managers tended to vote for the films that made *them* the most money. *Buck Privates* was voted the second "leading production" of 1941, behind MGM's *Men of Boys Town* and ahead of Bob Hope's *Caught in the Draft.*

Lubin perfectly balanced the comedy, music and story in *Buck Privates,* and most critics—particularly those from the trade papers—readily acknowledged his role in the success of the film. Lubin, however, was modest about his contributions. "*Buck Privates* was a very, very funny show and, actually, it was very little credit to the director," he said. "It consisted mainly of fabulous gags that these two wonderful guys knew from years and years of being in burlesque." Asked what he thought his contribution was to the Abbott and Costello films, Lubin replied, "I think I was very

good for them in this respect: not in their routines, but in trying to give them some class. Whenever they got rude or crude, I'd try to soften it, to keep a balance of refinement against the earthiness of some of the routines."

Lubin was born Arthur William Lubovsky in Los Angeles on July 25, 1899. Comedian Harold Lloyd, a family friend, recommended the boy for a scholarship to the San Diego School of Expression. After briefly serving in the navy as a radio landsman, he graduated from the drama school of Carnegie Tech in 1922. He soon began acting on Broadway. One of his earliest roles was in *The Red Poppy* with another newcomer, Bela Lugosi. Lubin recalled helping the Hungarian actor learn his lines phonetically. Lubin later directed Lugosi and Boris Karloff at Universal in *The Black Cat* (1940).

Lubin also began producing and directing theater in New York and Los Angeles. These productions included *This One Man,* starring Paul Muni; *When the Bough Breaks,* starring Pauline Fredericks; and *Her Man of Wax,* starring Lenore Ulric. In 1926, Lubin and his fellow actors were arrested in Los Angeles for putting on what was then considered an obscene play: Eugene O'Neill's *Desire Under the Elms.*

Lubin entered silent films during this period. In the 1925 Universal drama *His People* (retitled *Proud Heart*), he played Morris, an ambitious Jewish law student who, ashamed of his humble family background, pretends to be an orphan after falling in love with a judge's daughter. *The New York Times* wrote: "Arthur Lubin deserves great credit for his work as Morris." Lubin also played King Louis XIII in *Bardelys the*

*Magnificent* (1926); coincidentally, Lou Costello may have been a stunt performer in the film.

In a brief profile in *Picture-Play* magazine, Lubin said he saw himself as "a character juvenile," believing that "the leading man of the screen has no glowing future. At best, he is secondary to a feminine star, with the privilege of sharing a few beautiful close-ups. The character actor, however, has no limit. Why can there not be a greater number of youthful Chaneys, Beerys, and Torrences?"

But Lubin was less successful in films than he had been in the theater. "Whatever personality I had on the stage certainly wasn't photogenic," he later confessed. He joined MGM on the production end. "I was lucky enough to be chosen with Henry Hathaway as a protégé of Paul Bern," he said. (Bern was an assistant to the legendary producer Irving Thalberg. In 1932, shortly after his marriage to Jean Harlow, Bern famously committed suicide, although some believed he was murdered by his ex-wife.)

Lubin moved to Paramount, where his first big break was becoming an assistant to the revered producer William LeBaron (1883-1958). Before entering the film business LeBaron had written ten Broadway shows and was the managing editor of *Colliers* magazine. By 1929 he was head of production at RKO, where he established the popular comedy team of Wheeler and Woolsey. At Paramount he oversaw the Mae West films and brought his friend W. C. Fields over from RKO and produced his comedies as well. It must have been a valuable experience for Lubin to observe LeBaron' affinity for comedians and their creative processes. Lubin worked on the production end of two West pictures, *Night After Night* (1932) and *She Done Him Wrong* (1933), as well as Kate Smith's *Hello, Everybody* (1933), and *Hot Saturday* (1932) with Cary Grant in his first role as a leading man.

In 1934 Lubin directed his first feature, *A Successful Failure* (1934), at Monogram, followed by *The Great God Gold* (1935). He joined Universal in 1936. "I was the first director signed by Universal when Charlie Rogers and a new production team came in 1936," Lubin explained. "That was due to his assistant, who knew of my work directing on the stage in New York and out here, and the little reputation I had with Monogram and Republic in making pictures quickly. I don't think Charlie Rogers was at Universal more than two years. Most of the pictures he made were not very good, and then new management came in, a group of theater managers. Nate Blumberg became

*Arthur Lubin had been a serious actor and directed low-budget melodramas before directing Abbott and Costello.*

the president of the studio, but I remained under contract to Universal almost thirty years, through the various regimes that took over the studio."

Lubin's first credit at Universal was *Yellowstone* (1936). The following year he directed John Wayne in four action pictures. "Duke was a joy to work with," Lubin recalled. "We became close personal friends. But after our last picture together, he left Universal still waiting to hit the big time." That came two years later with John Ford's *Stagecoach* (1939).

Over the next three years Lubin helmed numerous mystery and gangster films including *Prison Break, Midnight Intruder, Secrets of a Nurse, The Big Guy, Big Town Czar, Call a Messenger, Risky Business, I'm Nobody's Sweetheart Now,* and *Meet the Wildcat.* By the time he was tapped for *Buck Privates* he had over thirty film credits. Yet the studio never considered Lubin for its prestige productions. Speaking about this period in his career, he reflected, "I was very happy. I was working regularly, and I had a lovely office at Universal. It was a small studio, and everyone was charming, both Mr. Rogers and later Mr. Blumberg and Cliff Work. I went on directing these B pictures until I got a break with Abbott and Costello."

With his background in B-movie melodrama, why was Lubin chosen to helm the first film by two burlesque comics? Screenwriter Edmund L. Hartmann said, "He was the last guy in the world you would figure would be working with Abbott and Costello."

Lubin explained, "I've never considered myself a great director. I consider myself a good director. Producers liked me because I am not temperamental. I got along well with the actors and the production department. I bring it in on schedule and on budget, but I enjoyed my work. So I had a reputation of doing pictures quickly and bringing them in on schedule."

Lubin's selection confirms that the studio put the budget ahead of art. "They warned me they didn't want to spend much money on *Buck Privates*," he said. "I don't think Universal had much faith in the outcome of the picture. They weren't sure how the audience would take the gags." So Lubin was shocked when the studio assigned him to the team's second film before he had finished *Buck Privates*. Lubin recalled, "They said they would like to start another one immediately. I said, 'Even before you've seen this?' They said, 'Yes, we're certain of this.' So they gave me $5,000 as a bonus [about $85,000 today]."

Bud's nephew, director Norman Abbott, explained, "Arthur Lubin was a very sweet, kind man. He handled the boys very well. He always had John Grant by his side. Even with all the tumult, Arthur was very strong and very solid. Why not go with the same people? The rapport was good, he handled them well, they liked him. They were social with him. They made his career."


Universal's production manager, Martin Murphy, assigned the other principal members of Lubin's crew, including cinematographer Elwood Bredell, art director Harold MacArthur, and film editor Philip Cahn.

Bredell was a perfect choice for a haunted house comedy. Earlier in 1940 he shot *Black Friday* for Lubin. He had just finished lensing *Man Made Monster,* Lon Chaney Jr.'s first role in the genre, and Lees and Rinaldo's most recent effort, *The Invisible Woman.*

Bredell was born on December 24, 1902 in Indianapolis—not, as some sources claim, in London. "To this day, I have no idea where that 'Englishman' stuff comes from," his granddaughter, Cheryl, said. His birth name was Jesse B. Bredell Jr., after his father. His mother, Mary ("May") Palmer Nields, was a stage performer. Just weeks after Elwood was born, May and Jesse Sr. split up; the boy never knew his father. After the death of her third husband, May and Jesse Jr. migrated to California. She met Vaughn "Val" Paul, a busy actor who appeared in over one hundred silent films between 1913 and 1922. They married in 1914, and May gave birth to Vaughn Jr. in 1916. Although her sons were born fourteen years apart, Jesse Jr. and Vaughn Jr. were very close.

Val provided entree into the movie business for both boys. As a teen, Jesse Jr. acted in six silent films. Of his performance in *Southern Justice* (1917), *Variety* wrote, "Bredell is so natural...that one wants to adopt him as being a diamond in the rough from the minute he quits his only home and strikes out for himself. This Bredell makes this boyish role genuinely human and not once does he step out of the character."

In the early 1920s Val shifted behind the camera and directed several Harry Carey westerns for R-C (Robertson-Cole) Pictures, the forerunner of RKO. At the time, Charlie Rogers was the general manager of distribution for R-C. Rogers moved to First National (before it was absorbed by Warner Bros.), then RKO, Paramount, and Universal in various executive capacities. Val followed as his production manager at each studio. Val produced Arthur Lubin's first Universal film, *Yellowstone* (1936). When Rogers was ousted from Universal in 1938, Val resigned and returned to independent production with Rogers as well as Edward Small. Martin Murphy, a veteran of the old Laemmle era, succeeded Val as Universal's studio manager.

Jesse Bredell, meanwhile, outgrew his film roles. He took a job as a studio lab technician while he cultivated a talent for photography. In 1923 he married his childhood sweetheart, Gertrude Stone. The couple raised two children, Jacqueline and Elwood Jr.

From about 1929-34, Bredell worked as a still photographer at RKO and Paramount, coinciding with his stepfather's tenures at those studios. Some of his portraits and landscapes were published in *International Photographer* and *Cinematographic Annual.* By then he was using the name Elwood Bailey Bredell. "We have no idea where the name Elwood came from," Cheryl confessed.

At Paramount, Bredell apprenticed under veteran cinematographers Charles Lang and Arthur C. Miller. Lang was nominated for eighteen Academy Awards, and won for *A Farewell to Arms* (1932). Miller later won for *How Green Was My Valley* (1941), *The Song*

ELLWOOD J. DELL
*Juveniles*
*Future Release*
*"Paint and Powder"—Hunt Stromberg*
Personal Management of
Lawrence J. Farrell

GL adstone 3435          GR anit 430

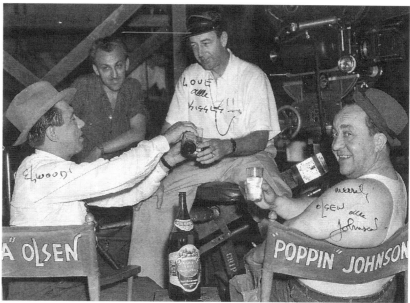

*Left: Elwood Bredell as Ellwood Dell, a young actor. Right: Cinematographer Elwood Bredell (visor) cooling off with* Hellzapoppin' *stars Olsen and Johnson and an unidentified crew member. (Courtesy of Cheryl Bredell.)*

*of Bernadette* (1944), and *Anna and the King of Siam* (1947). Val brought Bredell to Universal in 1936 and he continued his training under the studio's best cinematographer, Joseph Valentine. Bredell was promoted to cinematographer the next year, and when Val produced *Reckless Living* (1938), Elwood was the cameraman.

Vaughn Jr. also gravitated to the movie industry. He worked in production at Paramount and Warner Bros. before joining Val and Elwood at Universal. He reportedly started in the mailroom and advanced to second assistant director on the first Deanna Durbin film, *Three Smart Girls* (1936). Durbin, who was not quite fifteen at the time, soon became the studio's biggest star. She and Vaughn, who was twenty, fell in love, and he was promoted to first assistant director. They were engaged during production of *Nice Girl?* (1940), and Vaughn was promoted to associate producer. The couple married in April 1941, with Elwood as Best Man and actresses Helen Parrish and Anne Gwynne as Maids of Honor.

Three months earlier, Elwood served his wife, Gertrude, with divorce papers. "It must have been difficult for Gertrude to raise two young children while Elwood was shooting movie star stills and pin-up girls," Cheryl Bredell said. "We don't know what happened between them." Gertrude died in 1943 and Elwood never remarried.

In 1942, amid rumors that his marriage to Deanna Durbin was crumbling, Vaughn left Universal for RKO. He and Durbin divorced at the end of 1943. Elwood, however, continued to work on Deanna's films. He shot her last few musicals, and her first serious roles as a torch singer in *Christmas Holiday* (1944) and as a murder witness in *Lady on a Train* (1945).

Arthur Lubin knew Bredell from their days at Paramount when Bredell shot stills for Mae West's *She Done Him Wrong* (1933) and Lubin was a production assistant. At Universal they collaborated on seven films between 1938 and 1940, including *Black Friday* with Karloff and Lugosi. In *Horror Film: Creating and Marketing Fear,* author Steffen Hantke wrote: "Perhaps the most significant element of *Black Friday* is its cinematography by Elwood 'Woody' Bredell...His cinematography during a hospital scene establishes a visual pattern that he would return to in his later noir films: surgeon Karloff prepares a brain transplant in the shadowy hospital room where a gangster lies paralyzed. Bredell uses light bulbs mounted on the wall above each bed as his on-screen lighting source, creating arches of light that cast harshly juxtaposed semi-circular shadows on the top of the frame. As Karloff moves throughout the scene, he drifts in and out of the shadows, his face becoming completely silhouetted at times as he arranges the gruesome operation to follow. This visual pattern of half-seen faces draped in shadows is repeated later in the film, and would be repeated often in Bredell's later work."

Bredell's camera, however, ran out of film halfway through a heavily publicized scene where Lugosi

*Bredell's shot in* Hold That Ghost *(1941) anticipates another in the film noir classic* The Killers *(1946).*

imagines he is suffocating (his performance was supposedly aided by off-screen hypnosis). Greg Mank, in *Bela Lugosi and Boris Karloff: The Expanded Story of a Haunting Collaboration,* wrote, "Perhaps this is why the sequence fails to come alive in the film."

That same year Bredell shot *The Mummy's Hand,* the first in the cycle after Karloff's original. "Bredell typically never lets the viewer get a clear look at the Mummy," Hantke continues, "choosing instead to drape his face with the darkness and have him move in and out of the shadows, adding a further degree of terror to his menacing presence."

In addition to some Durbin musicals, Bredell's credits include *Argentine Nights* (1940) with the Ritz Brothers and the Andrews Sisters; *South of Tahiti* (1941) with Maria Montez; *Hellzapoppin'* (1942) with Olsen and Johnson; and *Eagle Squadron* (1942, again for Lubin). But it was his work on horror and mystery films that prepared him for his pioneering work in Hollywood's next genre, film noir.

Of particular note is Bredell's cinematography for Robert Siodmak's *Phantom Lady* (1944) and *The Killers* (1946), widely considered to be the archetypes of the genre. Incredibly, Bredell was not nominated for an Academy Award for either film. In *Weimar Cinema and After: Germany's Historical Imaginary,* Thomas Elsaesser quotes Siodmak: "Upon my insisting, [Universal] gave me Woody Bredell as cinematographer. I told him about my friend, Eugen Schüfftan, with whom I'd made *Menschen am Sonntag* (1930) and *Mollenard* (1938), and who was a great admirer of Rembrandt. The theory that the eye instinctively moves away from the brightest point and seeks out the darkest seemed to impress Bredell. He began to study Rembrandt's paintings."

In an article in *American Cinematographer,* Bredell said he relished "taking a crack at a show where nothing had to be beautiful." He cut back drastically on lighting for night scenes and avoided fill light in others. As for Ava Gardner's unearthly good looks, Siodmak wanted all of her close-ups done without make-up, making her, according to Bredell, "the first adult actress who had ever agreed to be filmed without make-up. All we did was rub a little Vaseline into her skin for a sheen effect." Bredell said he lit her singing scene with only the lamps on the nightclub tables.

That year Universal merged with International Pictures. William Goetz, a founder of International, became head of production and he hastily eliminated the studio's low-budget B movies, serials, horror, and "Arabian Nights" genres. After a decade at Universal, Bredell moved to Warner Brothers, where his first production was Michael Curtiz's initial film noir, *The Unsuspected* (1947). John Reid wrote in *Memorable Films of the Forties,* "While the picture abounds in menacing shadows and reflections, velvety blacks and fearfully bright whites, it must be said that all the images throughout are most attractively lit...Bredell invests the sets and costumes with such a rich sheen and gloss as to make every frame a pleasure."

Curtiz called on Bredell for a Technicolor opus, *Romance on the High Seas* (1948), starring Doris Day and produced by Alex Gottlieb. Bredell's only previous experience with color was as the camera operator on Deanna Durbin's *Can't Help Singing* (1944); the great W. Howard Greene was the cinematographer. But he took the assignment in stride and shot two more: the Errol Flynn swashbuckler *Adventures of Don Juan* (1948), and *The Inspector General* (1949) with Danny Kaye. *Don Juan* director Vincent Sherman, quoted in

*Errol Flynn: The Life and Career,* by Thomas McNulty, was impressed by how quickly Bredell worked. "I asked him how he did things so fast and he said that with black and white you have to do modeling, but with color, the colors themselves do the modeling for you. All you have to do is put flat light on it and the colors jump out." In his review of the film, Bosley Crowther of the *New York Times* described Bredell's lighting and color photography as "technically superb." (Peverell Marley, Cecil B. DeMille's cinematographer, shot some scenes when Bredell was temporarily sidelined by the flu.)

Bredell finished his feature film career with an independent pulp noir, *Female Jungle* (1956), starring Lawrence Tierney and Jayne Mansfield in her film debut. Unlike many of his contemporaries, Bredell showed little interest in series television. "He did some television work," granddaughter Cheryl explained, "but we don't know if it involved shows or commercials. Elwood didn't like doing TV, and mom definitely got the idea that he preferred black and white to color films. It would appear that he was financially able to retire early if the work didn't suit him."

Although he lost a small fortune in 1954 when a disreputable jeweler made off with his mother's diamonds, Bredell had substantial real estate holdings. "We know of at least four apartment complexes he owned, one of which he built as well," Cheryl recalled. "My dad, Elwood Jr., lived in and managed one of these on Hollywood Boulevard; Shelley Winters was a tenant. Supposedly, Elwood Sr. sold that complex so the historic Temple Israel synagogue could be built on the site."

An avid fisherman, Bredell kept a cabin cruiser moored near his apartment in Newport Beach, Calif. "I was pretty young, and don't remember much about him," Cheryl explained. She grew up in New Mexico and Colorado. "Dad took us back to California almost every summer, but rarely did such trips include a visit with 'Papa Woody' or Aunt Jackie. There was never any animosity; they just weren't a close-knit family, I guess. My grandfather was cordial enough to let us kids play on his boat, but he was also kind of reserved. His apartment was cold and dark, and never seemed to change. I remember looking through the same magazines and eating the same hard candy that had been on the coffee table years before. It was as if time had just stopped in his world."

Elwood Bredell died on February 26, 1969. He was 66. A fitting epitaph may be the compliment paid by famed Warner Bros. editor George Amy, who said Bredell could "light a football stadium with a single match."

The sets were designed by Harold H. MacArthur (1893-1980), who generally worked on the studio's low-budget productions and serials, including *Flash Gordon.* He started at Universal in 1939 and designed for several Abbott and Costello pictures, including *It Ain't Hay, Hit the Ice,* and *The Naughty Nineties.* In 1947 he moved to Columbia, where he finished out his career in 1951. MacArthur was supervised at Universal by Jack Otterson (1881-1975), who had been a prominent New York architect before migrating to Hollywood during the Depression. Otterson started at Fox in 1932 and joined Universal in 1936. The following year he replaced Charles D. Hall as the studio's Supervising Art Director. (Hall had designed the sets for Universal's most iconic horror films, such as *The Hunchback of Notre Dame* (1923), *The Phantom of the Opera* (1925), *Frankenstein, Bride of Frankenstein, The Old Dark House,* and many others.) Before his semi-retirement in 1943, Otterson was nominated for Academy Awards for *The Magnificent Brute* (1936), *Mad About Music* (1938), *First Love* (1939), *The Boys from Syracuse* (1940), *Flame of New Orleans* (1941), *The Spoilers* (1942), and *Arabian Nights* (1942).

Film editor Philip Cahn (1894-1984) had cut four of Lubin's previous films, including *Black Friday* (1940) and *Buck Privates* (1941). A founding member of Film Editors' Local 776 and a charter member of the American Cinema Editors (A.C.E.), Cahn started at Universal in the late 1920s. He edited one of Universal's biggest hits, *Imitation of Life* (1934), but mostly worked on the studio's run-of-the-mill fare.

His son, Dann Cahn, explained, "My dad would get the previous day's dailies around eight o'clock in the morning. (Back then they were called the 'rushes.') His assistant would sync up the sound and the picture tracks, and right before or right after lunch, my dad would run the dailies for the producer and the production heads. Then, when they finished shooting at night, he'd run the dailies again for the director and get his thoughts. Then his assistant would break everything down and my dad would go to work cutting together a sequence, sometimes having gotten input from the director, sometimes not, depending on what

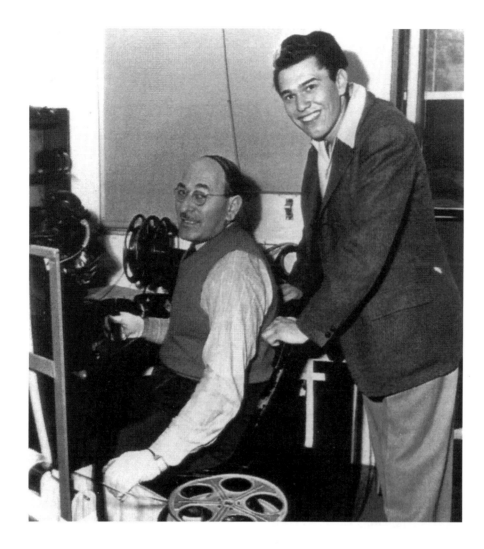

*Editor Philip Cahn at work in 1941 and his son, Dann, who later edited* I Love Lucy. *(Courtesy of Dann Cahn.)*

their relationship was and how much trust the director had in the editor."

Arthur Lubin recalled, "I no sooner finished an Abbott and Costello [picture] when I was pushed immediately into another one. In fact, I had so little time to see the dailies, unless it was way late at night. They were rushing to get as much as they could quickly. We made one right after the other. They would let you see the first cut and that was it. You made your suggestions and you never saw it again."

Cahn wound up cutting all five of Lubin's Abbott and Costello films and two important later A&C films, *In Society* (1944) and *The Time of Their Lives* (1946). He also edited two A-pictures, *Eagle Squadron* and *Arabian Nights,* for producer Walter Wanger in 1942. Many of his credits are in the horror genre, however, and include *The Mummy's Hand* (1940), *House of Frankenstein* (1944), *House of Horrors* (1946), *The Brute Man* (1946), *The Lost Continent* (1951) and *Bela Lugosi Meets a Brooklyn Gorilla* (1952).

Cahn also worked as a producer-director in Universal's B unit. In the 1950s he moved into television, and was most proud of his long association with Loretta Young and her TV series.

Cahn's son, Dann, began his apprenticeship as an editor at Universal in 1941, and even appeared as a sailor in the "Sons of Neptune" routine in *In The Navy.* He served in the First Motion Picture Unit during the war. Dann later edited *I Love Lucy* and became head of post-production at Desliu. He worked with Alex Gottlieb in 1955 when Alex produced the TV series *Dear Phoebe,* starring Peter Lawford. In 1978 Dann edited the TV movie *Bud & Lou,* which cast Harvey Korman and Buddy Hackett as Abbott and Costello. Editing is clearly in the family genes, because Dann's son, Dan, is also an editor, and is a Board member and past president of the Guild his grandfather helped found.

# "I Wasn't Cut Out to Be a Glamor Girl"

anny Brice was once asked who her choice was to portray her on stage or in film. "There's one dame that could play me," she replied. "That's Joan Davis."

Davis was not only one of the greatest slapstick performers of either gender but a comedienne who pioneered self-deprecating humor. Her comic persona of a gawky, man-hungry bachelorette delighted moviegoers in the 1930s and made her the highest paid comedienne on radio in the 1940s. She starred in, produced, and wielded sole creative control over her 1950s TV sitcom when no other woman did.

Joan was born in St. Paul, Minnesota, on June 29, 1912. (She was Abbott and Costello's fifth female co-star from Minnesota, following the three Andrews Sisters and Jane Frazee in *Buck Privates*.) Most biographies give her real name as Madonna Josephine Davis. But in *Joan Davis: America's Queen of Film, Radio and Television Comedy*, author David Tucker discovered that the name on her birth certificate was Josephine Donna Davis.

Her father, LeRoy, was a train dispatcher. Her mother, Nina, spearheaded Joan's career. Nina told an interviewer in 1953, "Joan gets her dramatic talent from me. Just because I wasn't on the stage doesn't mean I'm not as big a ham as the rest of them. I had to have a lot of faith in little Joanie's future on the stage to convince my husband I should give her a chance to perform. Aside from the fact that I'm her mother, no one could be more interested in her success than I. I take Joanie from the age of three and encourage her, travel with her, do without home life of my own for

years to give her the break I believe she deserves, and what do the columnists say? 'Miss Davis comes from a non-professional family.' If treading the boards all these years doesn't make me a professional, what does?"

Joan told the Associated Press in 1938, "The whole thing started when Mom began letting me sing and speak pieces in church when I was three. By the time I was seven I was sure (and Dad was willing to be convinced) that I was ready for my 'debut.'"

She entered a local amateur show and did a straight song that was met with laughs. "The trouble was, I was awkward," she continued, "and there was no use trying to pretty me up. My folks were smart enough to capitalize on my shortcomings. I've been deliberately awkward since." Joan entered every amateur talent show she could find. "I'd won 27 straight prizes as an amateur," she explained, "and after I copped an all-star championship in Seattle, we decided that it was about time to cash in on it."

She toured the Pantages circuit as "The Toy Comedienne." The chain, founded in 1902 by Greek immigrant Alexander Pantages with a single nickelodeon in Seattle, at its height included 84 theatres in the United States and Canada. While playing Los Angeles, she supposedly turned down an offer to join the *Our Gang* Comedies, which were launched in 1922. In New York, she ran afoul the state's child labor laws. "When we went to the theater the manager looked at Dad and said, 'Say, what is this, a midget?' and Dad said 'Well, sort of.' The manager said 'This is bad; I don't think you can get away with it.' But I had come to New York

to do my set and I wasn't going to leave without trying. I put on a pair of high-heeled shoes, the first I'd ever worn, and tried to do the first show. But it was murder. I couldn't stand up on high heels. The manager wouldn't let me go on again."

She attended school between jobs. "I was crazy for an audience," Joan later recalled. "I still attended school but worked nights and summers. It seemed perfectly natural to go to school and work. My attitude toward other kids was, 'What, you're not working? Pooh!'"

At Mechanic Arts High School she joined the debating and tracks teams, as well as the student council. She left school in 1927 to join a nautical-themed revue, "Hughie Clark's Jazz Boat." She toured with the show for two years as "Josephine Davis." *Variety* caught the revue in New York and dismissed it as "so-so…for the family trade." But Joan was cited: "Josephine Davis, comedienne of promise, was the individual highlight." She had incorporated a stuttering song along with her eccentric dances.

Joan returned to high school and according to some accounts was class valedictorian. At graduation she supposedly had to resist the urge to do her speech for laughs. "I had to play it straight," she remembered.

"Toughest assignment I've ever had." All the touring had a price, however: her high school sweetheart moved on.

When she outgrew kid parts she tried to be a singer. "I tried singing sweet, serious songs, but I kept getting giggles that I wasn't trying for," she explained. "So I gave up and went in for 'hokey' comedy. I had to admit that I wasn't cut out to be a glamour girl, and decided I'd have to play it for laughs."

After high school she decided to go to Broadway. "My parents and I talked it over and they reluctantly agreed that at last I was old enough to take care of myself and could go alone. After all, I had bookings, I had an agent—I was a real career woman. I took a room at the Century Hotel [on West 46th Street] in New York City. Two days later there was a knock on the door: Mother. My parents had talked it over again." She toured the country playing amusement parks, camps, and lodge halls. "I've played theaters so small," she cracked, "that if you took a bow the perspiration would drop off your chin into the balcony."

Joan briefly teamed with comedian Ben Blue (1901-1975). "That nearly killed me," she recalled. "We did a burlesque adagio dance with a big, flashy set. There was a flight of 32 steps and I did a leap from the top into Ben's arms. Only, half the time he'd let me jump and then turn around and start talking to the audience while I landed flat on my face. After the act, Blue would look on the floor, and if there wasn't any blood, it was no good. What a guy!"

In March 1931, Joan's agents introduced her to another client, comedian Serenus "Si" Wills (1896-1977), who was looking for a female partner. (Their agents also represented Howard, Fine & Howard—the seminal Three Stooges act.)

Wills, who was fifteen years older than Joan, had been part of two good vaudeville comedy teams in the 1920s. In 1925, *Variety* reported that he and another comic married the Darling Sisters, a song and dance act, in a double ceremony. The marriage, if there even was one, apparently didn't last long. By 1928 Wills was working solo to tepid reviews. In 1930, *Variety* described his act as a "familiar type of single gagger, best appreciated by neighborhood audiences. Gab lacks a solid punch. Goes in for some comedy instrument playing on what looks like…a small oboe and sounds like a bagpipe. Also does hoke crystal [ball] gazing, looking into a gray balloon while repeating and answering comedy questions."

Wills did comedy bits in a couple of two-reel musicals for Pathé. In one short he was paired with Bob Carney, who had been in burlesque. Pathé signed them to write and star in a handful of comedy shorts together. After completing the films, both comedians returned to vaudeville—Wills as a solo, and Carney reunited with a soubrette he had worked with in burlesque named Jean Carr. Both acts toured on the same bill. Perhaps Si began considering a female partner after working with Carney & Jean.

Joan recalled, "Si was a comedian looking for a straight woman and I was a comedienne looking for a straight man. When we started rehearsing I said: 'Say, which one of us is the straight man in this act,' and Si said: I don't know.' It turned out that he became the straight man."

A later profile of Joan in *Silver Screen* described the act: "Wills opened the act with jokes—Joan dashed onstage for a rapid comedy crossfire. Followed songs and dances by both with a finish that had Wills as a burlesque crystal gazer using a silver balloon as a crystal ball. Out among the audience, collecting questions, Joan would pounce on a respectable looking old lady and ask Wills what the customer was thinking. He would surreptitiously break the balloon with his left hand and scornfully ask the old lady if she was sure her

*Above: Joan and Si Wills, her partner and husband.*
*Below: Trade ad for the team's first tour in 1931.*

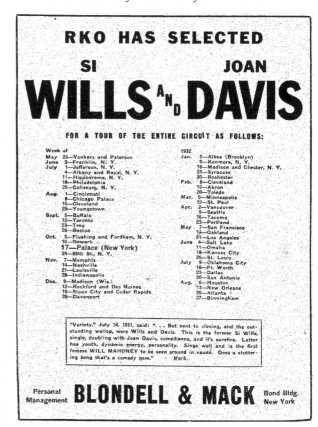

question was clean."

When they played New York that July, both trade papers had good things to say. *Variety* wrote, "Wills has a real find in the girl. She is funny and helps him to make this a good attempt to get away from [his] moth-eaten single [act]. Wills has taken some of his former single stuff and blended it into a fast moving mixed comedy turn that stands up. The old crystal bit is much funnier now than formerly and the mugging [is okay]. This act with a few minor cuts of mossy gags

Joan's film debut in the Mack Sennett short Way Up Thar (1935), with Buster Keaton's mother, Myra.

will be ready to shoot." *Billboard* thought "…Miss Davis is outstanding with her clowning. She is a shapely miss, going in for rough knock-abouts and warbling. Strong comedy combo, both when soloing and in duo."

Not only did the act click, but so did Si and Joan. He proposed to her only two weeks after they met. They were married in Chicago on August 12, 1931, and honeymooned on the road. The act was still called Wills & Davis, but she began using the name Joan professionally. (There was an older vaudevillian named Josephine Davis.)

While Joan was athletic and coordinated, her physical shtick was occasionally hazardous. "I have fallen on every stage in the United States and Canada," she said, "and I have never found a soft one." The worst splinter she every got "was from a stage in Grand Rapids, Michigan…[It] broke off in me and I'll never forget what a time a doctor had getting it out. He tried a couple of times and I was actually too tough to cut! He had to get out a little whetstone and sharpen his knife! I had hysterics, which was as good as an anesthetic."

In 1932 Wills & Davis were booked at the Mecca of vaudeville, the Palace Theatre in New York. Joan later recalled, "I was almost paralyzed, I was so scared, even through the applause, even though we were a hit." *Variety* reported, "Miss Davis works her audience up to a highly appreciative point, finally threatening to hold up the show with her dancing. She goes into some swell spills…Wills stands by playing the guitar and singing. He contributes much to the act, working gags, mugging and in other ways strengthening the

response, but it's Miss Davis who makes the act big."

Vaudeville, however, was dying; in November even the Palace began showing films. There were so few bookings that it cost the Willses more to travel than to stay home. Another consideration was the birth of their daughter, Beverly, in 1933. "It was because of her that we decided to give up the stage and try motion pictures so that she might have a real home," Joan explained. "Taking a youngster on tour isn't all that it's cracked up to be." Still, Beverly had a taste of show business at a young age. "She toured with us in vaudeville," Joan said. "Barbara Stanwyck carried her on the stage when she was five weeks old in Boston, in a sketch. She trouped with us until she was school age. She had started copying my routines from the time she could walk, just by watching."

Si and Joan bought a house in Beverly Hills but breaking into films was not easy. "Do you think anybody'd ever heard of us?" Joan said. "Not a soul. Our experience and success didn't mean a thing." She explained how she landed her first movie. "In 1934, Hughie Cummings, a pal of Si's, wrote a movie short… that seemed tailor-made for me. He brought his boss, Mack Sennett, out to our house to see me…I clowned like mad, and the stooges we'd been careful to ask in howled and rolled on the floor in delight. Sennett admitted I was funny, but said that I was too old."

The next day Joan went to Sennett's office dressed more youthfully in a shorter skirt with her hair in curls and a bow. "I had everything but a yo-yo," Joan quipped. It changed Sennett's mind. He put her in a hillbilly two-reeler, *Way Up Thar* (1935). Joan sang three songs including "That's Why I Stutter," and reprised a bit from vaudeville where she carried a teetering stack of plates. She later recalled the long hours of filming: "It [took] a day and a half, including all night. Buster Keaton's mother [Myra] played my mother in it. I was so worn out before I was through. I told Si: 'If this is the movies, get me out of them. I've aged so since yesterday that I won't match up in the rushes.'"

Joan appeared in a feature, Paramount's *Millions in the Air* (1935), as a favor to director Ray McCarey. She sang "You Tell Her Because I Stutter." Neither *Variety* nor *Billboard* mentioned her in their reviews, but the *New York Times* singled her out: "Joan Davis…puts over a comic song extremely well…"

RKO signed her but used her in only one film, *Bunker Bean* (1936), as a zany telephone operator. (Lucille Ball, still an ingénue, had a bigger role as a

*Joan, daughter Beverly, and husband Si in 1945.*

receptionist.) Joan's contract was terminated by mutual consent after four months and Wills and Davis went back out on the road. The act still received good reviews, but their material was wearing thin. *Variety* wrote, "Joan Davis is a surefire comedienne, but she is handicapped by shabby material."

When they returned to Hollywood Joan lobbied for a screen test at 20th Century-Fox. Her timing was perfect. Not only had the studio announced a slate of musicals, but it also needed an answer to Martha Raye, who had become a hit at Paramount in *Rhythm on the Range* (1936). The studio tossed Joan into eleven films in her first year. She sang, danced, mugged, cracked wise and took spectacular pratfalls in supporting roles of various sizes.

Joan once said that a comic in movies had it harder than an actor. Directors have definite ideas on how to play a dramatic scene, but with a comedian, the director says, in effect, "All right, action. Be funny." Since a comedian's only audience is the studio crew, he or she has no idea if the gags are working. Her own technique was to recall the response of the average vaudeville audience and time her antics accordingly. "I guess it's something like blind flying for an aviator," she said. "You rely on experience and hope for the best. But…a movie comedian doesn't know how things have gone until he sees and hears the scene screened for an audience."

She played the leader of an all girl orchestra and sang "I'm Olga from the Volga" and "My Swiss Hilly Billy" in *Thin Ice* (1937). A reviewer for *Family Circle* wrote: "Her two song numbers…wowed the preview audience, this time made up exclusively of the press and of motion picture people, who (particularly the latter) are the movies' severest critics. They see many, many pictures, and a film just has to be good or boredom sits obviously on their shoulders. Which makes it all the more significant that Miss Davis drew a large round of applause from them."

The *Brooklyn Daily Eagle* called her "indescribably funny… Mere words do not quite catch the quality of Miss Davis's brand of humor. Superficially it is slapstick but on second consideration it appears to be a super-sophisticated distillation of the most elegant type of humor. The comedienne goes directly to the heart of her material in an almost savage manner without once sacrificing method to mugging. You'll have to compare Miss Davis with the obvious Miss Raye to see how good she is."

As this critic observed, Joan was a nuanced performer. "Gags have to have a reason," she once explained, "and then they're ten times as funny. You can't fall down without reason, either. Falls are funny, too, if you're doing a comedy dance. But just walking along the street and tripping over your feet wouldn't be laughable." She also said, "I studied the technique of every stage and screen comedian, analyzing the slightest differences. I prefer the sympathetic type of comedy that carries the element of surprise. I make my comedy seem accidental and I like to have my audiences think, 'Poor girl, she tries so hard and everything goes wrong.'"

Joan collaborated with Si on her physical bits and wisecracks in these films. She said, "Even with 'hokum' comedy, which looks so natural, you need to study and study. One little slip of the finger, one slightly different expression on the face may make all the difference between getting a laugh or shrug."

Milton Feld, who, in a few years, would oversee the Abbott and Costello films at Universal, produced two of Joan's early pictures, *Time Out for Romance* and *Sing and Be Happy.* In *Sing and Be Happy,* Joan played a window washer. "A rather sloppy one," she recalled. "And while walking with a pail of sudsy water in my hand, both feet skidded out from under me and it seemed like I hit the ceiling, only it was my back that suffered and I went to the hospital for eight days."

When she returned to work, her first priority was to reshoot the scene. "If I don't do it the very first thing, I'll lose my nerve and it'll have me licked," she explained. She did it in one take. In a bit that foreshadows a gag in *Hold That Ghost,* Joan and co-star Chick Chandler play tic tac toe on windows they should be washing. When she loses, Joan says, "Oh, you won again! Well, Post Office is my game!"

Malcolm Phillips wrote in *Picturegoer,* "The, to me, inexplicable success of Martha Raye has brought the screen colony out in a rash of eccentric comediennes. Of them all (and that includes miss Raye, too) by far the best and in my opinion the greatest feminine comedy find for years is Joan Davis. She is the girl who does the comedy rumba dance in *Wake Up And Live.* Don't miss her in *Lovely To Look At.* She's a riot."

In *My Lucky Star* (1938), her second Sonja Henie musical, Joan was paired with Buddy Ebsen. During their duet "Could You Pass in Love?," Buddy was supposed to lift her over his head. "I guess I didn't know my own strength," Joan recalled, "because as Buddy gave a heave, I braced myself. We ended in a heap, with Buddy on top. He weighs a lot more than I, and the result was somewhat painful for me." She couldn't straighten up, and spent over six weeks in the hospital. She was still limping months later. Joan cracked, "I've been in the hospital so many times, I'm thinking of making a down payment on an ambulance."

Perhaps because of these injuries her output slowed considerably. After appearing in eleven films in 1937 alone, she made only four per year from 1938 through 1940. Although Darryl F. Zanuck told the press, "Before [1938] is out, Ms. Davis will have won number-one ranking as a comedienne," she was still relegated to comic relief. A review of *Life Begins at College* (1937) in the *Los Angeles Examiner* was typical of all her Fox efforts: "Joan Davis doesn't have a very big role…but she makes every moment count, and her songs and dances are hilarious."

In 1939 Joan and Si did another stage tour. *Variety* thought the act was more entertaining years ago, since Joan had abandoned much of her trademark slapstick and instead offered an "…overlong, dull medley of her picture songs." Wills did his vintage psychic bit "entailing the oldest gags around. It shows poor preparation and the audience didn't overlook it opening night. Only a few applauded."

Her last picture under her Fox contract was a murder mystery farce, *For Beauty's Sake* (1941). Shepard Traube, who helmed Lees and Rinaldo's first feature, *Street of Memories,* directed it. The film was made in 1940 but held back for eleven months, possibly because it was so bad. "After keeping it on the shelf for about a year," *Showmen's Trade Review* wrote, "the studio finally got up enough courage to release this one… It might have been better had they left it on the shelf." *Variety* wrote: "Ineptly written, directed and played, its comedy falls flat and the pace makes the 62 minutes' running time seem longer."

Squandered again in a small role in a bad film, Joan decided to leave 20th Century-Fox to freelance. "In my heart," she said at the time, "I feel I am so much more than a screwball." (*Variety* reported on January 5, 1941, that she signed with Fox again, but this appears to be for one film, her third Sonja Henie musical, *Sun Valley Serenade.* The picture began shooting in late March.)

Joan's gamble paid off. Milton Feld cast her in "Oh, Charlie" with Abbott and Costello. (Considering the delay in its release, however, Joan may have had a feeling of déjà vu.) Not only was it the biggest hit she'd ever appear in, but Joan also scored heavily in the picture.

Her role in *Sun Valley Serenade,* on the other hand, amounted to a cameo. She complained to a reporter that her ballet swan-dance and several other bits she performed on the ice were left on the cutting room floor to shorten the picture. The PCA reportedly objected to certain lyrics in her number, "I'm Lena, the Ballerina." However, lyrics had to be approved before they were filmed, so it is unlikely that Joan's number was cut for that reason.

When Universal recalled her for revisions to "Oh, Charlie," Joan had just started another film, *Two Latins from Manhattan,* at Columbia. Director Charles Barton, who had a two-week shooting schedule, worked around Joan for a day or two.

In August, while *Hold That Ghost* was packing audiences in theaters, Joan did a guest spot on Rudy Vallee's radio show. Like Abbott and Costello, there was some doubt whether her comedy would translate to radio. But Joan was a hit singing a few bars of the Jerome Kern ballad "Jim," then going into a monologue describing Jim as lazy and worthless. She was invited back for thirteen consecutive weeks. In November, she took part in a haunted house sketch that was a takeoff on *Hold That Ghost.* She became a regular the following spring, and Columbia and RKO offered her two-picture deals. She later said, "I practically parlayed 'My Jim' into a six-figure income."

Just as her career gained momentum, however, Joan and Si decided on a trial separation in October 1941; they got back together after just ten days. A few months later they bought a new home in Bel-Air for $26,500. Reportedly the house was used for exteriors in *The Philadelphia Story* (1941).

Thanks to Joan, Vallee's show climbed to No. 12 in the ratings, his highest ranking in seven years and just behind the Abbott and Costello radio program which had launched that fall. When Vallee was called up for military service in 1943, the program was retooled for Joan. ("It was her show anyway," Vallee told a columnist.) Her salary jumped from $1500 to $2500 a week, but the network and sponsor apparently doubted her ability to carry the show. It was retitled *The Sealtest Village Store* and Jack Haley, who was in *Wake Up and Live* and *Hold That Co-Ed* with Joan, was added as her co-star. Si was hired as a writer and daughter Beverly joined the cast as Joan's little sister.

Joan, Mischa Auer, and Marcy McGuire played themselves in a Kay Kyser musical, *Around The World* (1943). Davis has a wordplay mix-up with McGuire, who does not understand that a ring Joan has is Auer's, not "ours." Joan asides, "Boy, how Abbott and Costello could kick this around!"

Meanwhile, her radio show's ratings continued to rise and reached No. 7 in 1944, just ahead of the Abbott and Costello program. American Tobacco made a bid for Davis, offering twice her current fee, but she declined out of loyalty to Sealtest.

Things weren't sunny behind the scenes, however. *Variety* reported that producer Tom McAvity left the

*Joan with Eddie Cantor. The pair began an offscreen relationship when they made* Show Business *(1944).*

show "after a series of tiffs with Miss Davis." In Jordan R. Young's *The Laugh Crafters: Comedy Writing in Radio and TV's Golden Age,* staff writer Bob Weiskopf recalled Joan as "a difficult lady...We were there all night to get six jokes. 'Cause she would laugh like hell; two minutes later she'd say, 'I think we can do better than that.' Drove me crazy."

Eddie Cantor tapped Joan to co-star in *Show Business* (1944) at RKO. They also began a relationship. In *Banjo Eyes: Eddie Cantor And The Birth Of Modern Stardom,* co-star Constance Moore told author Herbert G. Goldman, "Eddie and Joan were mad for each other. It's hard to say exactly when their relationship began, but it soon became obvious...We tried to pretend they were studying the script, but there was very little doubt they were having a physical relationship. They spent so much time in his trailer."

In 1945, with her radio ratings consistently in the top ten, *Variety* reminded the industry, "Up until very recently Kate Smith was the lone femme headlining a nighttime commercial series, and for a long time it was thought she was the only gal strong enough to headline a top network production. However, after Rudy Vallee exited the Sealtest show, Joan Davis, teamed with Jack Haley, took over and in a remarkably short time, all things considered, Hooper survey figures disclosed that she was a definite click."

That year, RKO starred Joan and Haley in *George White's Scandals.* Daughter Beverly played Joan as a

*Joan plays cigarette girl to Bud and Lou at a Hollywood event in the early 1950s.*

child in a flashback. Meanwhile, her radio show peaked at No. 3 in the ratings, behind Bob Hope and *Fibber McGee and Molly.* Two other sponsors, Campbell Soup and United Drug (Rexall), bid for Joan's services. United won with an offer of $1 million a year. But while United had a star, neither NBC nor CBS had an open slot in their prime time schedules.

Joan's agents at William Morris decided to let United's option lapse and pursue a sponsor with an existing show willing to pay the same fee. George Burns and Gracie Allen, also William Morris clients, were unhappy with their sponsor, Swan Soap, a Lever Bros. product. When it became clear that Lever was courting Joan, Burns asked out of their contract. Davis' new show, *Joanie's Tea Room,* took over Burns and Allen's Monday night slot on CBS. The $1 million contract made Joan the highest paid comedienne in history up to that time and gave her creative control over the show with her own production company, Joan Davis Enterprises. Si also performed on the show.

Davis signed deals with Universal and RKO for her own low-budget comedies. Her fee reached $50,000 per picture. At Universal, Joan made *She Gets Her Man* (1945), playing the daughter of a former police chief who takes over to find a killer, and *She Wrote the Book* (1946), which cast her as a shy college math professor who is asked to pose as the author of a steamy best-seller, "Forever Lulu" (a takeoff on the 1944 novel *Forever Amber,* which was banned in fourteen states). A bump on the head causes Joan to imagine that she really *is* Lulu. Lou Costello, who was filming *Here Come the Co-Eds* (1945) at the time, visited the set of *She Gets Her Man* and had a photo taken with Joan.

In 1946 the nation's radio columnists voted Joan "America's Queen of Comedy" for the third consecutive year. But Joan suffered professional and personal setbacks the following year. She re-united with Eddie Cantor for the film *If You Knew Susie* (released in 1948), but their relationship had cooled. Cantor's biographer wrote, "Cantor and Davis, who had seemed like soul mates for four years, were never close again." Her radio ratings tumbled out of the top twenty, and Swan Soap dropped her halfway through a four-year contract. CBS picked up her program as a network-sustained vehicle, and the weekly budget was pared down to $12,000 from $17,000. In December, Joan filed for divorce from Si, charging mental cruelty for his abusive criticism of her show (which he helped write). There were rumors that they would reconcile, but the divorce became final a year later. Si got their home in Malibu while Joan kept the house in Bel-Air.

In 1948 she announced her engagement to Danny Ellman, president of the Chicago-Fort Dearborn Lumber Company, but after a year and a half Joan called it off. "I think Danny is a swell fellow," she said, "and we'll continue to be the best of friends, but it just wasn't meant to be that we should get married."

Davis continued on radio until 1950 when, like most radio stars, she set her sights on television. In a barebones pilot for CBS, "Let's Join Joanie," she played a man-hungry salesgirl with a crush on her rooming house neighbor. No sponsors stepped up. Joan then signed with NBC, and there was talk of her joining the roster of hosts on the *Colgate Comedy Hour.* While she and NBC looked for the right TV format, she made her final film, *Harem Girl* (1952), at Columbia.

In the interim, *I Love Lucy* became a national phenomenon. Joan's new NBC sitcom, *I Married Joan,* produced by Joan Davis Enterprises, followed a similar format—the scatterbrained housewife with an indulgent husband. Joan told the *Chicago Daily Tribune* that she turned down producers who wanted to transfer her self-deprecating bachelorette character to television. She explained, "You must not forget that [this show] is going into living rooms where the atmosphere is relaxed. Viewers don't want to be shocked out of their chairs. The man-chasing, screaming, and 'Love that boy' Joan Davis is not for television. In television I finally get my man." She later told the *Los Angeles Times* that her show was "patterned after believable situations that might be found in any home. The producers feel that with this homey formula the series can go on indefinitely. And that's all right with me." She even invited viewers to submit real-life anecdotes that might be fodder for future episodes.

*I Married Joan* debuted exactly one year to the day after *I Love Lucy*. *Variety* liked the show, which "has hit on a format for comedienne Joan Davis who registers solidly as the scatterbrained but thoroughly appealing wife of Jim Backus. Miss Davis manages not to overact in situations that must be tempting for her to do just that."

Fairly or unfairly, Joan's show suffered the inevitable comparisons with Lucy's. Not only did the title, *I Married Joan*, echo *I Love Lucy*, but both were filmed at General Services Studios until Desilu moved out in 1953. *TV Guide* called it "a show with more than a faint resemblance to *I Love Lucy*." These swipes galled Davis, who resented Ball's seemingly newfound success as a physical comedienne when Joan had been at it since childhood. Jim Backus, who played Joan's spouse, Judge Bradley J. Stevens, wrote in his memoir, "Lucille Ball was to Joan Davis what Moriarity was to Sherlock Holmes."

One can only imagine how Joan felt when she lost the Emmy to Lucy in 1953, or when *I Love Lucy* became a perennial Emmy nominee and frequent winner while she and her show were ignored. In spite (or perhaps because) of these knocks, an announcer introduced Joan's program was each week as "America's favorite comedy show," and its star "America's queen of comedy." Based on the ratings and public perception, both statements were no longer true.

In addition to owning the show, Davis earned $7,500 per week salary. But there was the inevitable drama behind the scenes. Producer Dick Mack, who had been with Davis for twelve years, left after just the fourth episode. Joan snagged director Marc Daniels, who left *I Love Lucy* after a salary dispute, as well as *Lucy*'s production manager, Al Simon.

Producing and starring in a weekly TV series was far more grueling than radio or films. (To avoid more stress, Joan's show was not filmed in front of a live audience like *I Love Lucy*.) A fan magazine reported Joan "crying from sheer nervous exhaustion," then composing herself before production was held up.

*Joan and daughter Beverly on the set of her sitcom. Beverly played Joan's sister on the show.*

"Darn, in TV, you don't even have time to be a woman!" she was quoted as saying ruefully. A *TV Guide* reporter observed that Joan "tends to tighten up on the set, is occasionally moody and at times downright depressed. But she bounces back the minute the camera starts to roll." Joan told columnist Sheila Graham, "When I think how wonderful it was in vaudeville—all you needed was a new routine every two years. Now I have to learn fifty pages of new dialogue every week …We shoot the whole show on [Friday]—on set at 9 a.m., and sometimes we don't finish until past midnight."

At the end of the first season, Joan's sponsor, General Electric, reportedly sought a replacement series. A few weeks later, however, GE renewed its sponsorship for $1.2 million. Joan cut her output from 39 episodes to 33 in the second season, and Beverly joined the cast, again playing her sister. Davis quipped, "Beverly, I always promised you a sister, but I had no idea she would turn out to be me." Off screen, Beverly was friends with a young actor named James Dean. Joan threw him out of her house at least once. Jim Backus later played Dean's father in *Rebel Without a Cause* (1955).

*I Married Joan* was the first sitcom directed by John Rich, who later won Emmys for *The Dick Van Dyke*

*Jim Backus places a chimpanzee who has just inherited $500,000 in Joan's care. Davis and Lou Costello were both bitten by chimps on their TV series.*

*Show* and *All in the Family*. In his memoir, *Wake Up the Snake,* Rich recalled filming his second episode with Joan. After a week of rehearsals and tweaks, the director was about to say "Action" when Joan called him over. She said, "John, I don't think this bit is funny." Rich was dumbfounded. "After five days of rehearsals," he wrote, "I thought we had solved all the flaws in the script. In the crushing silence that descended, all I could think to say was, 'It's been funny all week.'

"'No,' she countered, 'I don't think it's funny. Come up here and show me how to make it funny.'

"This was an outrageous request and it sent a shiver of fear down my spine. Time seemed to stand still as I reviewed the situation in my mind… I said, with some force, 'Show you? For Chrissake, if I could *show* you, I'd be standing where you are, making $30,000 a week. *You* show me, and I'll tell you if it's funny.'

"Everybody on stage began to applaud. Apparently this was an old cruel trick Joan played on unsuspecting directors…Joan Davis was a great physical comedienne, and no mere male could act out a humorous shtick better than she could. Directors who were thus humiliated never got invited back. Somehow my forceful response helped me earn employment for the next thirty episodes."

Rich continued, "I learned a lot about comedy from that talented but tortured woman who cursed like a longshoreman. She was given to extreme moods and sometimes bitter outbursts. I heard her ask the writers one day, 'Why can't our scripts have some of that fucking whimsy?' I'm not sure it was whimsical, but one episode required Joan to bathe a young chimpanzee in the kitchen sink. During the action, soap got into the monkey's eyes and he bit Joan on the hand. She exploded in pain and innovative invective. Filming was over for the day, and our star went to the hospital for precautionary shots.

"She recovered completely but the chimp died."

Among the show's new writers was Sherwood Schwartz, who had written for Bob Hope and later created *Gilligan's Island* and *The Brady Bunch*. In an interview for the Archive of American Television, Schwartz recalled, "Joan had enormous respect for writers—*too* much. She wouldn't do a scene unless a writer was on the [set] to make changes in the scene if she were uncomfortable. There were only three writers. Since one writer had to be on the stage all week long, what we would do was block out the show, divide it in half, and one writer would take the first half, another writer would take the second half, and the third writer had to be on the set. You think that's an easy job, being on the set? At any moment she'd swing around and say, 'Give me a better line.' With no time to prepare and no time to think, you have to give her a better line. Well, we dreaded it, but we each had to face it every third week. We called it 'Our Week in the Barrel.' I don't know what she thought writers were, but that's what I meant by too much respect."

The show never cracked the Top Ten. It faced stiff competition from *Arthur Godfrey and His Friends* on CBS and only gained ground after Godfrey famously fired singer Julius LaRosa late in the second season. At that time, *I Married Joan* peaked at number twenty-five. In Joan's third season, ABC scheduled *Disneyland* against her and Godfrey. *Disneyland* was an instant hit and drew roughly double Godfrey's audience and three times as many viewers as Joan's show. Davis asked out of her TV contract after thirty episodes that season, citing exhaustion. Industry cynics pointed out, "Joan Davis got 'fatigue' right after *Disneyland* dipped her rating past the danger point." Backus, writing in *TV Guide* years later, admitted, "Mr. Disney came on and our rating went down and so we were canceled." Joan cracked: "Imagine that, killed by a mouse."

But Joan was worn out, too. (Bob Hope also claimed to be fatigued and announced a hiatus from TV.) For a year she restricted her workload to guest spots on variety shows. Joan reportedly sold her interest in *I Married Joan* for $1.2 million, although other sources state she retained 50% interest in the show. In 1956, *I Married Joan* became the first TV sitcom to be reprised in daily afternoon reruns—and on its former network, NBC, no less. The ratings stunned the industry and started a trend on NBC and CBS of programming old sitcoms on weekday afternoons. Joan also exacted a measure of revenge against Disney: her reruns outdrew *The Mickey Mouse Club* in cities in which they directly competed, including New York. After running on NBC, *I Married Joan* was syndicated to local stations with similar success.

Joan was reported to be considering a Fanny Brice biopic. (Phillip Rapp, who wrote and directed episodes of *I Married Joan*, created Brice's Baby Snooks character.) She also signed a development deal with ABC. Her pilot was a fictionalized version of Joan's life, with Beverly finally playing her daughter. When it failed to sell, the rights reverted to Joan and NBC considered making it a summer replacement series.

Joan's personal life continued to make news. She sued a drug store chain for $100,000 over the instructions on her prescription for a stomach ailment. She became so ill that she collapsed on the set and was bedridden for a week, halting production. In 1955 she sued the Elizabeth Arden salon in Waikiki for $150,000 when the hairdresser allowed bleach to get in her eye. She settled for $20,000. In 1957, at age 44, she began a relationship with a 30-year safety engineer, Harvey Stock Jr. "He's been proposing to me almost since the first day we met," she told reporters. "I suppose we're going to be ribbed because of the differences in age, but I don't think that will make any real difference because we're in love." The relationship ended badly two years later when Davis filed assault charges, claiming Stock rabbit punched her during an argument. She later dropped the charges but broke off their engagement.

Nothing came of recycling her ABC pilot, but in 1958 Phillip Rapp created a new pilot for NBC called "Joan of Arkansas." Joan was cast as a dental hygienist selected by a computer glitch as the ideal astronaut candidate. This show also failed to interest any sponsors. Joan tried once more in 1960 with a pilot in which she ran an answering service and meddled in her clients' affairs. Again, there were no takers.

Like Lou Costello, a lifetime spent knocking herself out for laughs took its toll on Joan. She developed a heart ailment and spent her last years in seclusion. Jim Backus last saw Davis in the summer of 1960 when she attended his nightclub act accompanied by a nurse.

A month later Joan was in her Bel-Air home watching the Olympics on television when two boys knocked on her door and alerted her that the second story of her house was on fire. They helped her to safety, but the blaze, which was caused by an electrical appliance, destroyed a portion of Joan's home as well as her furs, clothing, jewelry and memorabilia.

Less than a year later, on May 23, 1961, Joan complained of chest pains and was rushed to a Palm Springs hospital by her mother. She died early the next morning, a few weeks short of her 49th birthday. At the time, Jim Backus called her "the greatest female comedy talent we've had," and said, rightly, "she wasn't appreciated as much as she should have been."

Joan's estate was estimated at $1 million. Her ex-husband, Si, produced a will from 1941 that left everything to him. Beverly contested it and found a handwritten will from 1956 that divided most of Joan's estate between Beverly and Beverly's five-year old son from her first marriage. In the end, Si got Joan's Palm Springs home, one of her businesses, a car, and $52,000. Beverly said, "I still love my father and I'm glad the matter is over."

In the summer of 1962, Beverly appeared in a revue, "Chip Off the Old Block," with other second-generation talents including Lou Costello's daughter, Carole; Harold Lloyd Jr.; Mickey Rooney Jr.; and Preston Foster's daughter, Stephanie. *Variety* called it "very entertaining" and "a cinch" to end up in Las Vegas. It didn't. (Another line-up, including Costello, Rooney Jr., Foster, and Ted Lewis, Jr.—actually his nephew—played the Chase Club in St. Louis in 1964.)

In 1963 Beverly fell asleep in bed with a lit cigarette. She, her two young sons, and Joan's mother all perished in the fire. In the space of just a few years, Joan Davis and her family all were lost.

In 1964 Louella Parsons reported that Si Wills had teamed up with Bill Bacher to write Joan's story. Their screenplay was titled "Laugh, Clown, Cry."

Late in her life, Joan reflected, "If show business has been good to me, it has also robbed me of many things. I'd have liked a college education, the chance to travel, and time for friends. Show business cost me my first beaux, and it eventually cost me my marriage.

"And I've been afraid all along that I just wouldn't be funny or pretty enough for the long-time big-time. I've kept going on a mixture of gall, guts, and gumption. Faith, too—I've hung onto faith until now I realize every heartbreak has been a stepping stone."

# The Supporting Cast

Richard Carlson was Bud and Lou's sixth co-star from Minnesota. He was born Richard Dutoit Carlson in Albert Lea on April 29, 1912. The youngest of four children, Carlson's attorney father moved the family to Minneapolis when Carlson was six. He attended Washburn High School, was elected senior class president, and voted "Most Imperious." He acted in two student productions and wrote, directed, and starred in a third.

Carlson graduated from the University of Minnesota with a Masters in English, *summa cum laude* and Phi Beta Kappa. "I thought then I'd like to teach," he told the *New York Times* in 1954. "The academic life seemed appealing. So I took my M.A. degree, my Phi Beta Kappa key, and $2,500 in scholarship cash and opened my own repertory theater in St. Paul!" He had written a number of sketches and one-act comedies for amateur groups. The venture was short lived, however, but it set Carlson's path.

He flipped a coin to decide between Hollywood and Broadway, and Hollywood won. Although he didn't know anyone in Los Angeles, he had a letter of introduction to critic and screenwriter Arthur Sheekman, who had worked on *Monkey Business* (1931), *Horse Feathers* (1932), and *Duck Soup* (1933). Sheekman was married to actress Gloria Stuart, who had appeared in *The Old Dark House* (1932) and later gained fame for *Titanic* (1997). The couple sent Carlson to her alma mater, the Pasadena Playhouse, to see its director, Morris Ankrum. Ankrum, who appears in *Ride 'Em Cowboy* (1942), put Carlson to work. In 1935 he played Prince Hal in "Henry IV, Part 2," and was

spotted by an MGM scout. He was cast as the on-camera host of one of the *Crime Does Not Pay* shorts, "Desert Death," but it did not lead to a contract.

Carlson decided to try his luck in New York where an old friend was now one of George Abbott's stage managers. He invited Carlson to the theater where Abbott was rehearsing the road company of "Three Men on a Horse." Carlson was cast in a small role and toured with the show for months.

Carlson made his Broadway debut in 1937 in "Now You've Done It," written by "Harvey" playwright Mary Coyle Chase. It was a flop. That summer he worked opposite a gifted physical comedienne, Imogene Coca, in the musical comedy "Calling All Men" at the Cape Playhouse in Massachusetts. Coca (1908-2001), who came from a theatrical family, received rave reviews. Carlson's work rated a profile in the *Baltimore Sun*: "Most promising among [Raymond] Moore's permanent company [at the Cape Playhouse] now is young Richard Carlson, who has barely a quarter of a century under his belt, but a Phi Beta Kappa key over it and an auspicious versatility for theater work...Offstage he acts as if he had never been on the other side of the footlights and talks of Kant and chemistry and John L. Lewis and football. Sometimes he talks of the historical play he has just written. He has Broadway and Hollywood offers for both his play and himself."

That fall Carlson was cast in "The Ghost of Yankee Doodle" on Broadway. Written by Sidney Howard and starring Ethel Barrymore, it was a prescient debate over U.S. neutrality in the looming war. *Billboard* wrote, "Richard Carlson proves again, as he did in his

*Richard Carlson in his first feature film,* The Young in Heart (1938), *with Douglas Fairbanks, Jr., and Janet Gaynor.*

one previous appearance, that he is probably the most promising juvenile on the stage today…"

Meanwhile, his own play, "Western Waters," about a Massachusetts family that travels down the Ohio River on a flat boat in 1800, found a producer and opened at Christmas. The production, which Carlson also directed, featured Van Heflin and Thomas Gomez. Brooks Atkinson wrote in the *New York Times:* "…Mr. Carlson has thrown together a rude smattering of history, some Paul Bunyan or Carl Carmer yarning and quite a likely helping of bawdy; and, serving as his own director, he has bedeviled a troupe of actors into shouting it at the top of their lungs." *Variety* thought the "play has possibilities for picture material on the strength of its folklore atmosphere, but would require extensive adaptation." The show closed after seven performances, but the 25-year old Carlson had added playwright and director to his resumé.

Four months later, while appearing in another play with Ethel Barrymore, "Whiteoaks," Carlson was signed by producer David O. Selznick to a writer-actor-director contract. (Sidney Howard, who was working for Selznick on the screenplay for *Gone With the Wind*, recommended him.) The contract permitted Carlson to work half the year in films and half the year in the theater. Barrymore induced the producers of "Whiteoaks" to let Carlson out of the show to appear in his first feature film, *The Young in Heart.* In 1953 he told the *Saturday Evening Post* that it was his favorite role: "I really liked everything about this part—the script, the

dialogue, even wearing a kilt with a dinner jacket. And I especially enjoyed [my character's] rude Scottish honesty and the natural comedy it spawned."

When the film wrapped, Selznick loaned him out for *The Duke of West Point* with Louis Hayward, Tom Brown and Alan Curtis. Carlson also tested for the roles of Hindley Earnshaw in *Wuthering Heights* and Ashley Wilkes in *Gone With the Wind.* He was at a disadvantage for the latter. "I'm one of the few people who never read the book," he said.

Carlson was thoroughly taken with Hollywood this time around. He told the *New York Herald Tribune,* "To my mind it is the ultimate in collaboration. The writer is on the set ready to advise the director if necessary, and sometimes he almost acts as a director himself. The actors may suggest changes in the script, and often lines are altered or written in. I enjoy acting in pictures more than I thought I would. In fact, I think I like it better than acting on the stage. However, it's more difficult, for one can't rehearse for pictures as one can for a play."

*The Young in Heart* and *The Duke of West Point* were both released late in 1938. By then Carlson was back in New York rehearsing the musical "Stars in Your Eyes," a satire of Hollywood starring Jimmy Durante and Ethel Merman. Carlson played a young screenwriter. *Variety* wrote, "Richard Carlson upholds the promise he showed in the 'Young in Heart' film and surprises with a fairly good [singing] voice. He's set for bigger things."

While this show was running, Carlson tested for the prized role of Joe Bonaparte in the film adaptation of "Golden Boy." The search for a lead actor rivaled that of Scarlett O'Hara in *Gone With the Wind*. Louella Parsons wrote, "You can take it from me that the chances of Carlson playing the title role are 99½% in his favor..." A week later, however, 20-year old William Holden was coincidentally spotted in an actress's test footage and cast instead. The role made him a star. It was a disappointment to Carlson, and his next roles in three flimsy college comedies were no consolation.

Selznick loaned him to Walter Wanger for *Winter Carnival* opposite Ann Sheridan, who had recently been dubbed "The Oomph Girl." Wanger's publicity agent fabricated a Sheridan-Carlson romance for the gossip columns, but by then he was engaged to Mona Mayfield, a Houston debutante and model whom he'd met in New York. They were married in Las Vegas before *Winter Carnival* wrapped.

The young couple's honeymoon was postponed, however, while Carlson quickly made *These Glamour Girls* and *Dancing Co-Ed* with Lana Turner at MGM, and the Baby Sandy opus *Little Accident* at Universal. There were rumors he would return to Broadway in "Journey's End," or co-star with Vivien Leigh in *Waterloo Bridge*. He finished 1939 at RKO in a mediocre fantasy-romance, *Beyond Tomorrow*, with Jean Parker. Production was held up while Carlson recovered from an appendectomy. Meanwhile he optimistically adapted his play, "Western Waters," for the screen.

Carlson began 1940 at Paramount in *The Ghost Breakers*, Bob Hope and Paulette Goddard's follow-up to their previous hit, *The Cat and the Canary* (1939). Always innocuous in his previous roles, Carlson turns out to be the villain.

His next assignment was at Columbia where he played Thomas Jefferson in *The Howards of Virginia*. The film, which starred Cary Grant and Martha Scott, was partially shot on location at Colonial Williamsburg, which had recently been restored.

That spring Carlson signed a term contract with RKO. He was cast in lead roles in *Too Many Girls* (another college musical) and *No, No, Nanette.* The studio also showed interest in his new play about national preparedness, with the understanding that he'd direct and star if it ever became a film.

His co-star and love interest in *Too Many Girls* was Lucille Ball. The film was directed by George Abbott, who gave Carlson his break in the touring company of "Three Men on a Horse." Abbott produced "Too Many Girls" on Broadway and brought cast members Eddie Bracken and Desi Arnaz to Hollywood for the film. Lucy and Desi met on the RKO lot before production began; he immediately broke off his engagement to a dancer and Lucy ended her relationship with director Alexander Hall. They eloped a few months later.

Carlson was slated to do another film with Lucy, *A Guy and Girl and Gob,* for director Harold Lloyd. But Carlson hadn't finished *No, No, Nanette,* in which he played a pin-up artist competing against Broadway producer Victor Mature for Anna Neagle.

In November Carlson returned to Universal for a supporting role in *Back Street* with Margaret Sullavan and Charles Boyer. One of Universal's prestige pictures of 1941, it was in release when "Oh, Charlie" was shooting. Milton Feld was the executive producer of *Back Street* and he thought of Carlson when he began casting "Oh, Charlie." Meanwhile, Mona Carlson was pregnant with the couple's first child.

Evelyn Ankers and Abbott and Costello were the only performers in "Oh, Charlie" under contract to Universal; the others were either on loan or freelancers. Evelyn would appear in more than two dozen films in her seven years at the studio, while Abbott and Costello starred in 28 over fourteen years. Evelyn and the boys both "met" almost all of Universal's monsters.

The daughter of a British mining engineer, Evelyn was born in Valparaiso, Chile, on August 17, 1918. According to a profile in the *New York Herald-Tribune,* it was an adventurous and sometimes dangerous childhood: "Her mother was tangled up in three Mexican revolutions; she remembers the day when her father was shot through the stomach by a disgruntled worker whom he had discharged in Colombia; remembers, too, that on another occasion he had his horse shot under him by the henchmen of a rascally rubber magnate; and she herself had been whisked all over South

*Evelyn's first lead role was in the British film* Murder in the Family *(1938). Jessica Tandy and Roddy McDowall were also in the cast.*

America by the time she was ten."

She was ten and living in Colombia when she made her stage debut in the title role of a religious play, "La Hija de la Dolores" ("The Daughter of Dolores"). Evelyn spoke fluent Spanish.

The family returned to England, where her father eventually deserted the family and her mother pressed Evelyn into a theatrical career. According to Richard Denning in Greg Mank's *Women in Horror Films, 1940s,* "Evie grew up under so many difficulties as a girl. She learned to survive through grit and determination…Evie became one of those child actresses whom the mother kept pushing and pushing—Evie *never* really liked the business. Her mother was not only excited about her career, she became dependent on her career…"

In London she trained in drama and dance at, among other places, the Tacchomo School of Music and Dramatic Art. Her dream was to become a ballerina. In May 1932 she and other Tacchomo dancers performed in a show called "Frito Misto." She danced on the very first live broadcast on British television in 1934. Evelyn also reportedly won several beauty contests and was the youngest person in the United Kingdom to qualify as a professional ballroom dancer.

Producer Alexander Korda signed her and seasoned her with small roles in the films *Rembrandt* (1936) with Charles Laughton and Elsa Lanchester; *Land Without Music,* with Jimmy Durante; *Fire Over England,* with Flora Robson, Laurence Olivier and Vivien Leigh; *Knight Without Armour* with Marlene Dietrich; and *Over The Moon* with Merle Oberon. "You'd have to look close to see me in the Korda pictures," Evelyn told *Hollywood* magazine in 1942.

She left Korda's aegis and trained at the Royal Academy of Dramatic Art. In 1937 she landed a stage role

*Evelyn on Broadway with Flora Robson in "Ladies in Retirement" in 1940. Ankers played a lady-in-waiting to Robson's Elizabeth I in* Fire Over England *(1937).*

in a comedy-melodrama, "Bats in the Belfry," with Vivien Leigh. Her next crop of film roles was meatier, and included her first lead in *Murder in the Family* (1938). Her other credits that year included *The Villiers Diamond, The Claydon Treasure Mystery, Second Thoughts,* and *Coming of Age.* Evelyn reportedly was considered for the female lead in *Goodbye Mr. Chips* (1939) but lost out to Greer Garson.

Evelyn returned to Buenos Aires in 1939 to star in the film *Ultimo Viajo (Last Journey).* The picture was made in Spanish and English. After the film she toured Argentina and Chile and hosted and sang on her own hour-long radio show. "I might have stayed to make another picture," she explained to *Hollywood,* "but European war rumors alarmed me and I sailed for England, pausing [there] only long enough to get my mother on a boat to New York. It was a lucky thing. Right after we sailed war was declared."

On the September day when Great Britain declared war on Germany, Evelyn and her mother sailed for New York on a Holland-America liner. Their ship reached New York on the same day as two British liners. Normally the arrival of three liners wasn't news, but a few weeks earlier the *Athenia* became the first British ship sunk by Germany during World War II.

The *New York Times* reported that the liners zigzagged across the Atlantic and that "most of their 1,831 passengers, at least those on the British vessels, lived in constant fear that they would share the fate of those who sailed on the *Athenia.*" Evelyn was mentioned among the notable passengers. A U-boat stopped their ship on its second day out until its registry was confirmed and allowed to sail on.

Broadway producer Gilbert Miller cast Evelyn in "Ladies in Retirement." The play is based on a real crime about a housekeeper who kills her employer to save her two visiting sisters from a mental institution. Miller read a review of the London production that suggested that Flora Robson would be perfect for the lead role. Robson, in Hollywood at the time, was signed and received rave reviews. Ankers' role as the maid required a blood-curdling scream at the climax. During the show's Toronto tryouts, *Variety* called the play "a marrow-chilling murder yarn," and added, "Evelyn Ankers, as the maid, played for non-comedy, is even in tempo, but rises to one screaming exit in the last scene that had the audience limp."

"Ladies in Retirement" opened at the Henry Miller Theater on March 26, 1940. *Variety* said it "steadily piles up interest to a genuinely stirring climax," and thought Robson stood out in an excellent cast. *Billboard* called Evelyn's performance "beautiful, breathtakingly right…" The critic for the *New York Sun* wrote, "[T]here are moments when it brings you back to the chills and the tremors of such hardy moneymakers as 'The Bat' and 'The Cat and the Canary'… Evelyn Ankers is an attractive maid and screams beautifully at the end."

On April 19, Robson and other cast members did an excerpt from "Ladies in Retirement" on the Kate Smith radio program. Abbott and Costello were still regulars on the show; had Ankers appeared, Bud and Lou would have met their future co-star nearly a year earlier.

While the play was running on Broadway, *Variety* reported that MGM optioned Evelyn for a screen test. The show closed after 151 performances on August 3, 1940 and opened in Los Angeles five days later. (Columbia Pictures adapted it for film in 1941 with Ida Lupino in the lead role and Evelyn Keyes as the maid.)

While Ankers was in Hollywood, 20th Century-Fox, Warners, and Universal courted her. Perhaps because her earlier films were made by its British subsidiary, she signed with Fox. Her first assignment was *Scotland Yard,* opposite George Sanders. According to the *Hollywood Reporter,* however, Sanders refused to play the role because his character turned out to be the head of a Nazi spy ring in England. Sanders was suspended and replaced by John Loder. Evelyn lost her role because the studio decided she was not well known enough. Nancy Kelly, who had recently finished *One Night in the Tropics* (1940) with Abbott and Costello, replaced her.

Evelyn made one of her first appearances in a gossip column in December. Jimmy Fidler reported, "[Director] Alexander Hall, who was about to wed Lucille Ball before Desi Arnaz, is mending his heart with Evelyn Ankers." Hall soon helmed *Here Comes Mr. Jordan* (1941), which was nominated for seven Academy Awards, including Best Picture and Best Director.

Evelyn's scream no doubt intrigued Universal, now the undisputed home of horror films. The studio gave her a screen test that was directed by Henry Koster, who helmed the popular Deanna Durbin films. On January 3, 1941, the *New York Times* reported that she had signed a long-term contract with the studio. *Variety* carried the same news on January 8. Evelyn's first Hollywood film would be "Oh, Charlie."

*Lawrence with an uncharacteristic smile.*

"Being a tough guy is easy," Marc Lawrence wrote in his memoir, *Long Time No See.* "You just give them this hard look and yell, 'Hey, you! Get over here!,' and nobody bothers you."

For more than sixty years Lawrence played a thug or bad guy in nearly 200 films. His pockmarked face, icy stare and brooding manner made him a natural for those roles. "Ed Sullivan put together a whole newspaper column about tough guys," Lawrence told Anthony Slide in *Actors on Red Alert,* "and he said the only man who could come on the screen without make-up was Marc Lawrence."

In 1998 he told the *Chicago Tribune,* "I had this effect on people. I remember walking along the street and seeing Eddie Cantor's name up on one of the theaters, so I stopped by the ticket seller and asked him, 'When does Eddie go on?' He looked at me and went pale and said, 'You-you-you-you're the guy in that picture up the street!' He was petrified of me. So I went and watched that movie again and thought to myself, 'Christ almighty, what an ugly bastard!' Holes in my face, black eyes that pierce right through you. Here I thought I looked like Ronald Colman, and the ticket seller was right."

He was born Max Goldsmith on February 17, 1910 in the Bronx. "I grew up in the Bronx near Claremont Parkway and Third Avenue, where my dad was a builder," he told the *Chicago Tribune.* "He put up gambling houses for Arnold Rothstein." Rothstein, a kingpin of the Jewish mob, transformed organized crime into a big business and, by all accounts, fixed the 1919 World Series.

Lawrence planned to become a doctor but acted in plays through high school. "I was the best actor in our school," he explained. "I could memorize faster than anyone, and my old uncle in the Yiddish theater, Jachiel Goldsmith, said I had 'stage guts,' so I guess he inspired me." Jachiel worked with Paul Muni in the Yiddish theater. "They were buddies," Lawrence recalled. "My uncle said, 'When you get through college, I'll take care of your career.' But he died in my sophomore year. He was 39."

After two years at City College, Lawrence was accepted into Eva Le Gallienne's renowned Civic Repertory Theater. "Miss Le G.," as generations of theater people called her, abandoned her career as a Broadway star in 1926 to found the company. She staged classics at popular prices for six seasons. Other novices in her repertory included Burgess Meredith, John Garfield, J. Edward Bromberg and Howard Da Silva. Lawrence and

*Lawrence in 1938's Criminals of the Air, with a brunette Rita Cansino, whose last name was changed to Hayworth before the film was released.*

Garfield became friends and worked together in a number of plays, including some with the left-wing Group Theatre, which was founded in 1931 by Cheryl Crawford, Lee Strasberg and Harold Clurman.

In 1930 James Cagney and Edward G. Robinson scored in the films *Public Enemy* and *Little Caesar.* They inspired Lawrence "like kids today hear music and they want to play the music," he explained. The following year Lawrence and a friend hopped a freight train to try their luck in Hollywood.

"I was fond of *The Last Mile* [John Wexley's 1930 Broadway play about death row inmates]," Lawrence told Lee Server in *Film Comment.* "I used to read part of that play in a presentation I did on a little stage when I got to Los Angeles. This agent saw me and thought I was crazy or had some talent. He sent me to Paramount to try for this prison scene in *If I Had a Million* (1932)." The film follows eight complete strangers who each receive $1 million from a dying businessman. "I was in the story that starred Gene Raymond, who was lousy in it. I went to the director [James Cruze]—this is the nerve I had back then—and asked him to get Raymond off the picture," Lawrence laughed.

In 1935 Lawrence appeared in the Group Theater's Los Angeles production of Clifford Odets' "Waiting for Lefty." The play is about a union meeting of cab drivers contemplating a strike. The "Lefty" in the title is Lefty Costello (yes, really), a character who never appears

but is a symbol for a left-wing radical. The cabbies are reluctant to act until he arrives. When they learn that Lefty has been murdered, however, they decide to strike. Lawrence received good reviews, and more casting and film directors took notice.

Although he wasn't "Lefty" in that production, he soon began playing a series of thugs named Lefty in the films *Dr. Socrates* (1935, with Paul Muni), *Invisible Stripes* (1939), *The Man Who Talked Too Much* (1940), and *Lady Scarface* (1941). Lawrence recalled, "Jack Warner once threw a fit in a screening room. He said I played every goddamn guy named Lefty in every Warner Bros. picture they released!"

In 1937 Lawrence was cast in *San Quentin* with Humphrey Bogart. In *Film Comment* he recalled, "[Bogie] used to be very worried about his lisp; he'd injured his lip and that's why he had this strange style of speech…and he wanted me to tell him if I heard him start lisping his lines…I'm this young kid in this fucking gangster thing, trying to be a tough guy, and the guy says, 'Watch my lisp!' Ha!"

Around this time Lawrence joined the Communist Party. "What did we know then?" Lawrence said in 1994. "They passed out forms and said, 'Sign your name for hope and humanity.' I was all for hope and humanity, so I signed my name. I went to about five or six meetings. When I got bored at home, I'd go to a meeting. That's just about it as far as I was concerned."

His career as a Hollywood gangster flourished and he averaged about a dozen films per year from 1935 through 1939. "The same part, over and over, same wardrobe," he said. "I wasn't a tough guy in life. I was an actor! But I fell in love with the character I played. I began to think I was that guy…"

His work was so convincing that real-life gangster Johnny Roselli, who helped organized crime control Hollywood and the Las Vegas Strip, gave Lawrence his seal of approval. At a screening of one of Lawrence's films, Roselli told Harry Cohn, the head of Columbia Pictures, "You know that kid up there, he's pretty good. Acts like the real thing. He could be one of the Mob." Lawrence said, "Cohn always liked me, because he loved gangsters."

Real gangsters were flattered by the portrayals of James Cagney, Edward G. Robinson, and Marc Lawrence. "They loved it," Lawrence told *Film Comment*. "'Hey look fellas, that's us! Pretty good!' Copied the gestures, the clothes. The time I met Lucky Luciano in Italy, I swear to God, I thought he was imitating me. He had that 'dead look.' Eyes looking at you cold, without blinking."

Lawrence knew Bugsy Siegel, who was a member of the same club in Beverly Hills, and New York Mafia chieftain Albert Anastasia, who once agreed to finance a movie.

While "Oh, Charlie" was in production, two films Lawrence made late in 1940 were released: *Tall, Dark and Handsome,* a gangster comedy for 20th

*Lawrence in his second Charlie Chan film,*
Charlie Chan and the Wax Museum (1939).

Century-Fox, and Paramount's *The Monster and the Girl,* about an ape with a human brain.

His salary was usually modest. "I made $750, sometimes $1,000 a week, seldom more."

# "Oh, Charlie"

en days after he wrapped *Buck Privates,* Arthur Lubin rolled film on "Oh, Charlie." It was a particularly busy time at Universal; seven productions were shooting, including *Flame of New Orleans* with Marlene Dietrich; *The Lady from Cheyenne* with Loretta Young; *Model Wife* with Joan Blondell and her husband, Dick Powell; and the Buck Jones serial *Riders of Death Valley.* "Oh, Charlie" was among the cheapest, budgeted at $190,000 on a twenty day schedule. *Buck Privates* also had a twenty day schedule, but on a $233,000 budget. *Flame of New Orleans*, by contrast, was allocated $817,000.

Daily Production Reports, which log every scene, camera set-up and "take" during filming, no longer exist for "Oh, Charlie," but we can still piece together a rough schedule using notes from the studio's executive committee meetings. In daily conferences that started at 8:30 a.m. and ran about half an hour, a nine-man board discussed the films in production, scripts, casting, contracts, talent, and so on.

"Oh, Charlie" began production at 8:30 a.m. on Tuesday, January 21. Franklin D. Roosevelt was inaugurated as President for an unprecedented third term the previous day.

There are many reasons why movies are not shot in sequence. Lubin could not begin with the film's opening gas station exteriors because a suitable service station location had not been found. In addition, it was the wettest winter in Southern California in forty-eight years and exterior filming was a headache for every studio. Bad weather had caused *Buck Privates* to run four days over schedule.

Instead, Lubin started with an interior sequence where the boys buy groceries in a general store enroute to the tavern (Scenes 90-95). This included Abbott and Costello's "Herd of Cows," "Duck in the Icebox," and "Mudder/Fodder" crosstalk. It became customary for the boys to start a film with a familiar routine. For their first film, *One Night in the Tropics* (1940), director Edward Sutherland initiated A&C with "Who's On First?," and Lubin began with the "Dice" game on the first day of *Buck Privates.*

Although Lubin once worked as an usher in a San Diego burlesque theater, he was unfamiliar with these stock comedy routines, so he would ask Bud and Lou to demonstrate. "When we came to their scenes in the script I'd say, 'Well, boys, let me see it first.' I would rehearse with them and would ask them not to give me everything but just to show me where they were going to go," he explained. "Then from that I would say, 'We'll take a close-up here, and a two-shot here,' and we'd shoot it. I never interfered, because no one could direct their routines as well as they."

Still, Lubin had to adapt. "I found it very difficult to direct them at first," he recalled. "They were naive as far as filmmaking was concerned. They played to the people on the set instead of the camera. They were used to having a live audience and missed getting laughs. But they learned quickly and we had a lot of fun on that picture."

Lubin had seen the boys in action for the first time and realized that he had to stay alert. There was no guarantee that the rehearsal would match the performance for the camera, or that any two takes would be

*On the way to their new property, Chuck and Ferdie stop off to buy groceries at a general store.*
*This sequence, filmed on the first day of production, was cut from the finished film.*

exactly the same. "They were always coming up with things," Lubin said. "A lot of the things were spontaneous, and I think you had to be very open minded. Bud was probably the finest straight man in the business. Lou had a tendency to run off into something else, and Bud would bring him right back into the scene. That's why they were such a very, very good team. Most comedians are jealous of each other. Bud wasn't. Bud knew that he was a good straight man and he didn't get any laughs, and the only way that he was good was in holding Lou in abeyance." He added, "I would say that most of their ad-libs, if they did not get too dirty, were very funny."

Standard movie-making practice required

shooting a scene from three different camera angles—first in a wide shot, then in close-ups for each of the principal characters. The dialogue and action in each shot had to match so that the sequence, when edited together, appeared seamless. Repeating a scene for various camera angles was routine for actors, but not for burlesque comics. Dann Cahn, whose father, Phil, edited the team's first five pictures, recalled, "My dad used to complain that they never did anything the same way twice. The script girl couldn't control them. That made it hard for my dad to cut scenes together—it was hard to match Lou's position or dialogue from shot to shot. And that made the editing look bad."

In addition to continuity, Lubin had another

*The storekeeper (Spencer Charters) gives the boys some bad news about the location of the Forrester's Club. This sequence was also cut from the film.*

*Moose Matson's attorney, Bannister (Russell Hicks), shows the boys a sketch of the property they've inherited from the late gangster. This was also cut from the finished film, and Bannister was later changed from a lawyer to Moose's "top man."*

worry whenever Bud and Lou strayed from the script. "The only thing that was difficult when they added things was, it took a little more time out of your day's work, and you had to watch that very carefully," Lubin explained. "Each day was budgeted for so many hours, particularly with the crew. Now, Lou and Bud were on a straight salary for the whole picture, no matter how long it took. But the crew is usually on an eight to ten hour schedule, and they would have to be paid overtime. The production manager, Martin Murphy, who supervised all the films in production, would confer with my assistant director and ask, 'How many pages [of the script] did you do?' They didn't ask how *good* did you do, but how many *pages* did you shoot. Then they'd come in and say, 'Look, Lubin, there's a half-hour left and you can only do two more pages. You're behind. What are you going to do about it?' It would drive you mad."

Lubin had a strategy. "I would do all of my homework at home at night so when I came on the set I knew exactly what I wanted for the day. And when the day's work was finished, I would give the first set-up to the cameraman, so that when I came on the set in the morning it was already lit and he knew what I was going to do."

Lubin did not have the luxury on either *Buck Privates* or "Oh, Charlie" of shooting Abbott and Costello's scenes simultaneously with more than one camera; it was too expensive. In these early films, whenever a shot cuts to a different angle, it's a completely different take. Later on, as the budgets

increased, Lubin was able to add a second camera. "Lou never did a scene the same way twice, so I shot all their scenes with two or three cameras simultaneously so as not to lose any of his reactions," Lubin explained. "This actually saved time and money, because they were always well-prepared when they walked on a set."

The general store sequence was later cut, but the routines were salvaged in other films. "Herd of Cows" was repeated in *Ride 'Em Cowboy* (1942), while "Mudder/Fodder" was used in better contexts in *It Ain't Hay* (1943) and *The Noose Hangs High* (1948).

Losing the general store sequence presented a continuity problem, however. When the group arrives at the tavern, Ferdie carries groceries that are used to make soup. Without the general store scenes, the groceries appeared from nowhere. This was solved during re-takes. When the boys arrive at Hoskins' bus, Ferdie carries a box of groceries (Re-67), which he quickly stows inside the vehicle.

Bud and Lou finished their first day at 4:15 p.m. Lubin then shot some tests of Evelyn Ankers and Joan Davis until 6:30. The next morning began on the probate court set for the reading of Sidney "Moose" Matson's will (Scs. 53-68). In the original script, Charlie Smith discreetly slips into the back of the courtroom and quietly observes the proceedings. This was the only time that the attorney, Bannister, appeared in the original screenplay. There was no indication that he is disreputable or knows Charlie Smith. That would come later in re-takes at the nightclub. To avoid

*Scenes in probate court (Scs. 53-68) were later cut and replaced with one where Bannister reads Moose's will in his office. Right: Ferdie and Chuck are nearly rubbed out. The gunmen in the car (below) do not match anyone in Moose's gang, and appear to be wearing fezzes. This was a stock shot, possibly from* Dark Streets of Cairo *(1941).*

criticism from members of the bar, Bannister was not identified as an attorney but as Moose's "top man."

Bannister is played by Russell Hicks (1895-1957), who recently appeared as J. Frothingham Waterbury, the fast-talking phony stock salesman, in the W. C. Fields classic *The Bank Dick* (1940). Often seen as a military officer, attorney, judge or executive, Hicks had an uncredited role as a rodeo announcer in *Ride 'Em Cowboy* (1942) and played the president of Appleby Motors in *Buck Privates Come Home* (1947). He can also be seen as the manager of the Copper Club in *The Noose Hangs High* (1949).

Late in the afternoon Lubin moved to the back lot and worked on exteriors until 8:30 p.m. Since sunset was at 5:15 p.m., booster lights were required. This may have been the drive-by shooting as Chuck and Ferdie exit the courthouse (Sc. 68-A). The original script never reveals who fires at them. The medium wide shot of two men shooting from a sedan is a stock shot; the gunmen are wearing fezzes. The scene inside the sedan, showing Charlie Smith and four other gang members, was added during re-takes (Re-66).

Thursday, January 23, marked the first day on the picture for co-stars Joan Davis, Evelyn Ankers, and Richard Carlson. Like their characters, they first gathered by Harry Hoskins' bus. In the original screenplay Smith did not arrange the boys' bus ride; he was just another passenger. (How he knew their travel plans is unclear.) He introduces himself as "John Smith" (Sc. 74), which prompts some corny wisecracks from Ferdie. This sequence also had to be re-shot, since Bannister introduced the boys to Smith in his office and Smith organized their bus ride. Smith knows Harry

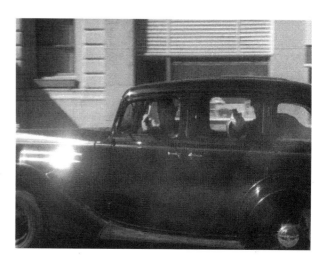

Hoskins, too. In fact, he is annoyed that Hoskins has accepted other passengers.

Hoskins is played by Milton Parsons (1904-1980), whose gaunt appearance and lugubrious voice usually landed him roles as undertakers, reverends, or hotel clerks. Parsons appeared in over 160 films and television shows. He made two other films with the boys. He played the coroner in *Who Done It?* (1942) and the Crystal Gazer in *Lost in a Harem* (1944). His other credits include *The Secret Life of Walter Mitty* (1947), *Dick Tracy Meets Gruesome* (1947), and *Haunted Palace* (1963).

Hoskins acts untrustworthy. When the boys ask, "Are you Harry Hoskins?," he replies, evasively, "Who are you?" (Sc. 70.) Wildcat buses were unregulated, uninsured, and sometimes unscrupulous. They sprang up around 1920 to cover routes and customers not served by legitimate bus or rail lines. Typically they were eight-passenger sedans used by traveling salespeople, transients, and employment agencies to

*In the script, Norma orders breakfast using diner slang, indicating to the soda jerk (Shemp Howard) that she has had experience as a waitress. Although* Daily Variety *reported that Shemp was recalled in May with the rest of the cast, there is no other indication that this sequence was reshot.*

send clients to jobs. Bus operators advertised in newspapers or solicited passengers on the street or through hotel clerks, who received a commission. But dishonest drivers dropped off passengers for connecting service that did not exist, or left fares stranded in out-of-the-way places. Some drivers coerced riders for extra money along the route. These buses were the bane of authorized companies. In 1935 a Congressional bill regulating trucks and buses also outlawed wildcat buses. But a 1939 report by the California Railroad Commission found that wildcat buses "had developed into a flourishing business" within the state despite attempts by authorities and private companies to quash them. California's two largest bus lines, Pacific Greyhound and Santa Fe Trailways, pressured the railroad commission to put the wildcatters out of business in 1942, but they returned during the war as Americans were encouraged to share rides.

When bad weather forced the production indoors, Abbott, Costello, and Joan Davis were dismissed, and Lubin worked with Ankers, Carlson, Shemp Howard, and Harry Hayden on the interior drug store set (Scs. 75-80) until 9:45 p.m. From the script we learn that Norma is a waitress heading East for a new job and, perhaps, a new life. At the end of the sequence the script calls for Hoskins to enter and collect the couple for the bus trip. In the film, however, the doctor realizes he is late and dashes out the door.

The soda jerk is played by once and future Stooge Shemp Howard. Born Samuel Horowitz in 1895, Shemp was an original member of the trio in the early 1920s along with his brother, Moe, and Larry Fine. Shemp left the act in 1932 and was replaced by younger brother Jerome (Curly). After Curly was sidelined by a stroke in 1946, Shemp returned to the fold until his own untimely death in 1955. This was the second of his five appearances in Abbott and Costello films. He recently worked in *Buck Privates* (when Lou sang "When Private Brown Becomes a Captain,") and will appear in *In The Navy* (1941), *It Ain't Hay* (1943), and *Africa Screams* (1949).

Mr. Jenkins is played by Harry Hayden (1882-1955), who recently appeared with Laurel and Hardy in *Saps at Sea* (1940) as Mr. Sharp, the horn factory owner. A familiar face in Preston Sturges films, Hayden also worked on stage and in films with his wife, actress Lelia Bliss. They ran the Bliss-Hayden Miniature Theatre in Beverly Hills, whose alumni include Veronica Lake, Doris Day, Debbie Reynolds, and Marilyn Monroe. It is now the site of the Beverly Hills Playhouse. Hayden appears as the diner counterman in the opening of *The Killers* (1946). He later played a murder suspect in *Abbott and Costello Meet the Killer, Boris Karloff* (1949).

The next day, Friday, began on the process stage with scenes inside Hoskins' bus. There are more of these scenes in the script than in the film, including one leading up to the stop at the general store (Sc. 87-89 and 97). The unit then returned to the back lot and continued filming scenes outside the bus. The highlight of the day was Camille's bone-jarring collision with Ferdie (Sc. 72-A). Joan Davis regularly took

Two of the era's best physical comedians meet with a bang. "Anyone who plays rough-and-tumble vaudeville comedy learns to break a fall," Joan once explained. The still on the right was taken when the scene was originally filmed in January. It was re-shot in May (above), along with the entire bus sequence. See Chapter 10 for a production still on this set.

*Camille demonstrates her blood-curdling scream from the "Tales of Terror" radio program. The still on the left is from the original shoot in January. Lou was ill that day and went home early. The scene was re-shot in May (below).*

spills in her stage act and in films, and Costello was a natural athlete who had a brief career as a Hollywood stunt man while trying to break into films. He told columnist Sheila Graham in 1941, "In all the time I stunted I had only one accident. That was when I jumped through the high window of a burning house wearing a wig for Dolores Del Rio [in *Trail of '98*]. I broke my ankle because I had to keep my eyes closed and couldn't watch my landing." (In production stills from that film, Costello appears on crutches and has a cast on his right leg.)

The collision between Camille and Ferdie was filmed again, however, in May during re-takes to accommodate script changes (Re-67). It is this later take that appears in the film. As the light faded, Lubin returned to the process stage to continue covering dialogue inside the bus.

On Saturday morning the cast and crew reported to the back lot to finish up the bus exteriors. Lou reported ill, however, and went home soon after shooting Camille's piercing radio scream. (This sequence was also re-shot in May [Re-68] due to script changes.) Although it is not specified what ailed Costello, a particularly virulent flu struck Hollywood in mid-December and sidelined 500 key personnel and hundreds of other workers. At Universal, seventy people were affected, including Deanna Durbin, Milton Feld, and cinematographer Joseph Valentine. The *Motion Picture Herald* reported on January 25 that the epidemic was "sweeping eastward at about fifty miles per day," resulting in school and theater closings. The latter concerned Hollywood the most: in some places the box office was off more than twenty percent.

With the bus exteriors completed, Lubin and the other cast members moved for the first time to the interior tavern sets and worked until 11:15 p.m. At

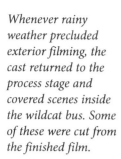
*Whenever rainy weather precluded exterior filming, the cast returned to the process stage and covered scenes inside the wildcat bus. Some of these were cut from the finished film.*

nearly fifteen hours, it was the longest day of the production. These scenes included Dr. Jackson and Norma lighting the fireplace (Sc. 116), and Norma and Camille frightened by an owl (Scs. 148-151). Camille is rendered speechless with fright, but Norma lets out a cry that rivals the radio actress' finest work. It was the first time Evelyn Ankers screamed in a Universal picture. Lubin may also have filmed the gang hatching their plan to scare off the boys and their guests. Of course, those scenes were eventually cut.

The following day, Sunday, was a day off, but a doctor recommended that Costello stay home on Monday, January 27, as well. Lubin worked with the rest of the cast on several interior sets, including Norma gingerly walking downstairs to find Dr. Jackson analyzing the water (Scs. 218-220). Scenes of Charlie Smith searching the cellar (Scs. 113, 120, 121) may have been taken, too.

That day in Tokyo, the Peruvian ambassador to Japan alerted the American ambassador, Joseph Grew, that the Japanese planned to attack Pearl Harbor. Grew, however, sent a cable to Washington downplaying the warning. Ten days earlier, Vice Admiral Patrick N. L. Bellinger, stationed in Hawaii, warned of Pearl Harbor's vulnerability. Ironically, it was Bellinger who sent out the first radio alert on December 7: "Air raid. Pearl Harbor—this is no drill."

A few days into filming "Oh, Charlie," Universal held a sneak preview of *Buck Privates* at the Academy Theater in Inglewood, an industrial suburb next to what is now Los Angeles International Airport. "There was a theater in Inglewood about an hour

from the studio where Universal often previewed its pictures," Dann Cahn recalled. "They're called 'sneak' previews because they were always secret, and were held some distance from Hollywood so that competing movie studios and the press would not see them until the executives were satisfied with the audience reaction. The laughs were so great that after the pre-

*Norma walks warily downstairs. Cinematographer Elwood Breddell achieved this stunning chiaroscuro with a small light built into the column of the candlestick.*

*The group watches as Harry Hoskins drives off and abandons them at the tavern. The sequence where Ferdie attempts to batter down the door is not in the script and was added on the set.*

view my dad had to extend the lengths of the cuts so that the audience could hear the dialogue that was drowned out in the laughs."

Following this initial screening, Alex Gottlieb was promoted from supervisor to associate producer and told to start immediately on a follow-up picture placing Abbott and Costello in the navy.

Lou reported for work on Tuesday morning but still did not feel well. Lubin covered more dialogue inside the bus. Although it's not known what specifically was filmed, it may have been the "Post Office" bit; Costello sounds nasal when he says, "Certainly I play games," possibly from the effects of his flu. This "Post Office" gag is not in the shooting script, and the Ohio censor board deleted Ferdie's rejoinder, "Not the way I play it!" Ryan Gosling and Emma Stone resurrected the joke in the period film *Gangster Squad* (2013). Gosling, a big Abbott and Costello fan, also deliberately duplicated Costello's sputtering scare take in *The Nice Guys* (2016).

Lubin also shot scenes of the group outside the tavern's front door (Scs. 103, 106 and 108), which included Ferdie's attempt to batter down the door and

*Two bits not in the script or the film: Camille's hand is caught in a mousetrap, and she faints from a potent onion. (The mousetrap can be glimpsed in the film in the kitchen scene, above right). Lou left early after shooting these scenes, and Lubin shot Dr. Jackson and Norma in the girls' bedroom and the "ghost" stalking Camille on the stairs.*

his exchange with Camille about her "mules." (*Mule*, from the French, is a backless and usually closed-toe style of shoe.) Costello left at 3:15 p.m., and Lubin switched the schedule around to cover scenes of Camille and Norma in their bedroom (Sc. 217 and Sc. 221. The company finished for the day at 6:55 p.m.

That night, January 28, Universal previewed a refined cut of *Buck Privates* at the Alexander Theater in Glendale, about fifteen minutes east of the studio. It is not clear if Bud and Lou attended the screening, but the studio bosses did, and they were euphoric over the audience reaction. Meanwhile, earlier that day, Alex Gottlieb and Arthur Horman, delivered a story outline for *They're In the Navy Now*.

Due mostly to Lou's illness, "Oh, Charlie" began to slip behind schedule. Costello reported to the tavern's kitchen set the following morning. The gags depicted

in these stills—Camille with her left hand caught in a mousetrap and fainting from an onion—were apparently added on the set, but do not appear in the film. Look carefully, however, for the mousetrap on her hand after Chuck strikes a match to light up the kitchen.

Between set-ups, Lubin and the boys no doubt pored over the first trade reviews of *Buck Privates*. They were glowing. *Daily Variety* wrote: "Universal has a winner in 'Buck Privates.' ... First, a big credit to Arthur Lubin, directing his first A-picture [sic]... He has this one in hand at all times, squeezes every bit of fun out of the quick-paced succession of close-knit gags and episodes, and generally demonstrates a skillfulness and understanding which qualifies him for continued assignments in the upper brackets. ...Bud Abbott and Lou Costello amply justify their stellar

rating, establish themselves among the best film comedians of the day, never failing to develop a gag or situation with precision and sure fire in getting the laughs, from giggles to bellies. Time after time at the preview, the comics were roundly applauded for their adroit clowning."

*The Hollywood Reporter* thought, "Abbott and Costello, with a set of new routines, are smash hits… This…is certain to set them solidly as film funsters of the first magnitude…In his direction, Arthur Lubin displayed a brilliant flare for comedy and the spiritual handling of intricate musical numbers, and gave the picture a tremendous vitality…"

Lou did not appear to be entirely recovered from the flu and was excused at 1:30 p.m. He stayed home the following day. Lubin continued to shoot around him, covering Norma and Dr. Jackson in the girls' bedroom (Sc. 262-263, where he deduces her exasperation with him with more dry logic than Mr. Spock), as well as Camille's stairway encounter with the "ghost" (Scs. 239-247) and her exaggerated description of its "fangs" (Sc. 256).

The ghost is the gangster Glum. He also hides in Ferdie's bed and creeps up behind Ferdie and Camille during the "Moving Candle" routine. Nestor Paiva (1905–1966) plays Glum. Swarthy and bald, with a good ear for dialects, Paiva played virtually every ethnicity in 400 films and television shows. He was born in Fresno, Calif., to Portuguese immigrant parents and graduated from the University of California at Berkeley, where he acted in college theatricals. From 1934 to 1945 Paiva played the villain in the Los Angeles production of "The Drunkard." (The 1844 melodrama was a local institution and ran for twenty-six years. Paiva briefly returned to the show in 1951.)

Paiva made his film debut in 1937. When he made *Oh, Charlie,* Paiva was a very recent newlywed: he married Maxine Searle, once Howard Hughes' secretary, on January 18, 1941 in Las Vegas. (Paiva also worked at the Lockheed Aircraft plant in Burbank.) They had two children. Paiva had just finished shooting *The Devil's Pipeline*, a Richard Arlen-Andy Devine programmer, before "Oh, Charlie." He then went into *Hold Back The Dawn*, starring Charles Boyer and Olivia de Havilland, at Paramount.

In 1943 he played "The Scorpion," the villain in *Don Winslow of the Coast Guard*, opposite his fellow "Oh, Charlie" gang members Don Terry and Edgar Dearing. Paiva worked with Richard Carlson again in Robert Siodmak's *Fly-By-Night* (1942), *A Millionaire for Christy* (1951), *Four Guns to the Border* (1954), and in an episode of *McKenzie's Raiders* (1959). He and Carlson also appeared together with Evelyn Ankers' husband, Richard Denning, in *The Creature From the Black Lagoon* (1954). Paiva was the only actor to reprise his role in the sequel, *Revenge of the Creature* (1955). In the 1950s he also played the innkeeper, Teo Gonzales, on *Zorro*.

That afternoon, at 5:35 p.m., an earthquake centered in Pasadena shook the region but caused no damage. Lubin wrapped for the day an hour later. Despite the story in the film's press book, Costello was not at the studio when the tremor occurred.

With Lou at home the following day, Lubin continued to work around him, possibly on scenes with Moose's gang.

Costello returned to the studio on Friday, January 31, and worked in more kitchen scenes (Scs. 112, 114, 115, 117 and 118), including an added bit where Camille and Chuck inadvertently batter Ferdie's head between cabinet doors. Lubin also covered a playful sequence in the dining room where the group pretends that the run-down tavern is a swanky nightclub (Scs. 123-126). In an earlier draft, this was tied to a dream dance sequence with Ferdie and Camille.

*Daily Variety*, meanwhile, reported that choreographer Nick Castle, who was under contract to 20th Century-Fox, would stage a musical number in "Oh, Charlie." This could only be Camille and Ferdie's dance.

On Saturday, Lou and Joan, both big boxing fans, no doubt discussed the previous night's heavyweight title fight at Madison Square Garden, where Joe Louis knocked out Red Burman to retain his crown.

Although it was estimated that Lubin was now two days behind schedule, the film's budget remained at $190,000.

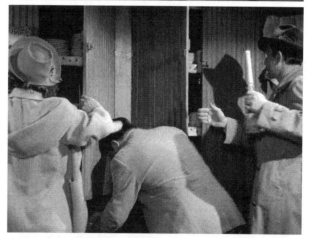

75

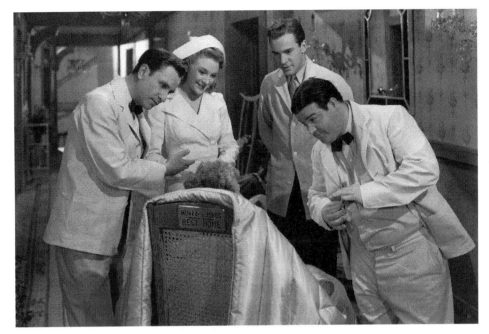

*In the original ending, the group assures a wealthy guest, Mrs. Giltedge, that's she's getting the best room in the resort (Moose's old bedroom). The plaque on her wheelchair reads "Murray & Jones Rest Home."*

On Monday the company began shooting the film's original ending (Scs. 323-326). At this point the tavern has been renovated and converted into a rest home. Moose's bedroom has been refurbished, but apparently no one bothered to check the closet. At the end of the day it was estimated that the picture was not two days behind schedule, but nearly four.

The following day was spent on the dining room set. Chuck orders Ferdie to call Smith up from the cellar. As written (Sc. 126), Ferdie calls feebly from the table, but in a memorable moment added on the set, he timorously hails Smith from the top of the stairs. Then the group eats unpalatable soup (Sc. 130). Camille cracks, "Just like mother used to make—it stinks!" The Breen Office warned that some political censor boards might delete the word "stinks." (It was cut in New Zealand.) Chuck speculates that the water "Might be poison," yet coerces Ferdie to taste it. Under duress, Ferdie confirms that the water is indeed the problem. This dialogue, and Ferdie's use of his necktie to reluctantly bring the glass to his mouth, were also added on set.

*The original film ended in Moose's bedroom, completely refurbished except for one gruesome detail. The dowager is played by Madge Crane (1875-1963), who made her film debut the previous year in the Bette Davis picture, All This, and Heaven Too.*

*A good view of the dining room set. Behind the cast is the fireplace, with the moose head centered above it. The table behind Lou will be used for the Moving Candle routine. Below, right: the necktie gag, added on the set.*

This was hard day on Marc Lawrence. Lubin shot three scenes with Charlie Smith's bound and gagged body in Moose's bedroom. Lawrence falls face first when Chuck and Ferdie explore the room (Sc. 165), and when the gangsters corner Ferdie with the money (Sc. 283). (Lawrence did a similar drop in *Sergeant Madden* [1939] after Alan Curtis shot him.) The Breen Office cautioned, "Scenes showing dead bodies falling into the camera are apt to be deleted by political [local] censor boards." In a hilarious added bit, Smith's body turns up in the closet when Ferdie ducks

*Smith's body turns up in Moose's bedroom three times. The center still showing Snake-Eyes (Frank Penny) holding a gun on Ferdie (center) is not representative of the actual scene. The closet gag (right) is not in the script.*

77

*After working inside Moose's bedroom, the cast shot scenes in the hallway. Camille and Ferdie trade faints when each thinks the other has been murdered. This differs from the script.*

inside during the chase. Working out of sequence in the bedroom, Lubin then shot Ferdie pulling the bell cord to first reveal the closet (Sc. 161), and Dr. Jackson examining Smith's body. The company then moved into the hallway for Scenes 168, 169, 171 and 172, including a fainting bit which was expanded on set.

Lou Costello's return to steady work may have pleased the studio, but it kept Evelyn Ankers as anxious as her character. In her foreword to the 1993 MagicImage volume on *The Wolf Man*, she recalled:

"My introduction to Universal Studios was worse than pledging for a college sorority. It was an Abbott and Costello picture entitled *Hold That Ghost.* In looking back I cannot, for the life of me, figure out how they ever got a picture finished. Once Lou Costello found out that I was English, from the English 'Theatre,' I spent most of my time checking my purse for mice and making sure that I had a solid wall behind me so that I wasn't squirted with a hose or swatted in a most uncomfortable spot through a canvas. They must have kept the local bakers very busy, for a typical vaudeville pie fight was soon a weekly event! They probably had pies written into their contract. At least the antics on *The Wolf Man* set were better than the 'vaudeville slapstick through the canvas' trick of Lou Costello. Did I say better? Let's say different. With Bud and Lou it was either the pies or a mouse in my purse, or when their friend

Jack Pierce, the makeup genius who made all the monsters in his magic laboratory, and his assistants would come down to the set for lunch there would inevitably be a food fight, or Lou would have Pierce make up something disgusting—which I won't go into detail on—and place it in my sandwich."

*Apparently there's nothing revolting in that sandwich. (Courtesy of Paddy Costello Humphreys and Chris Costello.)*

Evelyn's husband, Richard Denning, told Greg Mank: "Did Evie enjoy working with Abbott and Costello? No, they kept goosing her all the time. And that didn't go over too well—she was this almost 'stuffy' English girl, in one of her early films. Of course they were difficult to work with—and then Evie met an equal to them in Lon Chaney, Jr."

Arthur Lubin told Mank, "In those days, Evelyn Ankers had just what the moviegoers wanted to see—beauty, and gentleness. I did two pictures with her at Universal, *Hold That Ghost* and *Eagle Squadron*. She was a darling girl, always on time on the set—and she always looked well-groomed. Everybody loved her."

On Wednesday and Thursday the company worked on the dining room and secret barroom sets. This included Ferdie and Camille drying out by the fireplace after their soggy ballet; Chuck, Dr. Jackson, and Ferdie leaving the girls to search for Smith (Sc. 144); and the accidental discovery of the secret barroom (Scs. 136-143).

Thursday, February 6 was a 13½-hour day primarily devoted to the "Moving Candle" (Scs. 258-260). Like the "Drill" routine in *Buck Privates,* it was the film's centerpiece and was shot several times owing to its importance. Also remember that Lubin had only one camera, so any cut to a different angle or framing is from a different take. Between set-ups, Lubin may have switched off to other scenes, including Sc. 261, where Ferdie speculates that the cash is in the moose head, and Scs. 117-118, where Chuck

orders him to fetch water.

The "Moving Candle" is a hybrid of two classic medicine show afterpieces called "Ghosts in a Pawnshop" and "Over the River, Charlie." (An afterpiece was a final sketch featuring all of the performers from the different acts.) Traveling medicine shows date back to Renaissance Europe and appeared in the U.S. before 1772. Crowds were drawn by the entertainment while phony doctors touted miraculous elixirs or ointments. Medicine shows reached their peak in the late nineteenth century, particularly in the Midwest and rural South. They resembled small traveling circuses, complete with vaudeville-style acts, strong men, magic tricks (Harry Houdini was once part of a Midwest medicine show), freak shows, and Wild West themes. Between acts, the "Doctor" or

*The film's centerpiece, the Moving Candle, was shot several times for different camera angles. Between set-ups, Lubin covered other scenes, including one where Chuck orders Ferdie to fetch water (below).*

"Professor" would boast about his remedies, usually employing shills in the audience who offered "unsolicited" testimonials or were suddenly cured. This structure—entertainment interrupted by sales pitches—was later adopted by radio and television broadcasters.

According to theater historian Brooks McNamara, a mid-sized medicine show of the 1910s and early 1920s included a lecturer-manager, a sketch team (both of whom also worked solo), a song and dance man, a pianist, and a vestige of the 19th century minstrel show, the blackface comedian. The blackface comic served as chief comedian and master of ceremonies. He acted in sketches, played the banjo and cracked jokes with a straight man. Typically called Sambo or Jake, he dressed a lot like an early burlesque comic tramp—huge "slap shoes," oversized trousers held up by springy suspenders that made his pants wobble and bounce with every step, and a shirt or jacket in some gaudy color combination or outlandish pattern. His character was dumb, superstitious and cowardly. There was much cross-pollination between medicine shows, burlesque, and vaudeville because many performers moved through all three. As in burlesque, medicine show sketches were not formally written out but handed down orally in the tradition of the *commedia dell'arte*—loose outlines with ample room for creative improvisation and expansion.

The "moving candle" comes from "Ghost(s) in the Pawnshop," also known as "Pete in the Well." This famous sketch dates back to the early minstrel days. Michael B. Leavitt (1840-1935), a theatrical entrepreneur who is credited with the creation of the American burlesque form, recalled performing "Ghost in a Pawnshop" in 1859, and he wasn't the first.

In this sketch, the owner of a pawnshop discovers that his safe has been robbed. Jake, the comic, tattles on Pete, a dishonest co-worker. Pete is fired but vows to return that night to rob the shop. The owner and Jake wait up for him, and the owner unintentionally shoots Pete dead. He orders Jake to dispose of Pete's body in a nearby well (thus the sketch's title). After the usual comic fumbling with a uncooperative corpse, Jake manages to drag Pete away. When Jake returns, the pawnshop owner wants to take inventory. Jake sits at a table with a pencil and paper and, by candlelight,

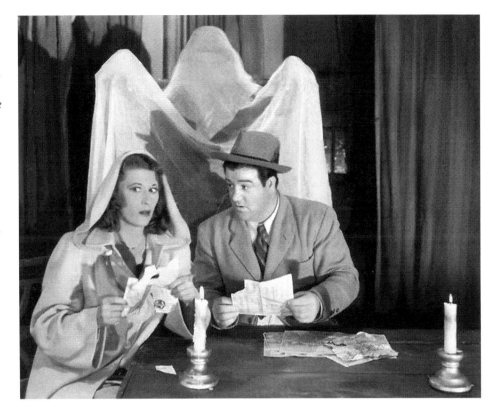

*Returning to the routine, Lubin covered the ending, a classic bit from the* commedia dell'arte *and medicine shows. The "ghost" (Nestor Paiva) creeps up behind Camille and Ferdie, slaps them, and stamps out the candles. The candles in these stills are not the ones rigged to move in the film. Before continuing with the routine, Lubin covered Ferdie wondering if the loot is in the moose head.*

prepares to write a list as the proprietor calls out the items from offstage. The candle on his table slowly grows taller, frightening Jake, who yells for the boss. Of course the boss returns too late to see the candle. He admonishes Jake and leaves the room to continue with the inventory. Now the candle slides across the table. Jake calls out again, but the owner misses that, too. Finally, Pete returns as a ghost and scares off the boss. He approaches Jake, who is too preoccupied with his list to notice him. Jake slowly realizes his predicament and runs away, but not before Pete's ghost hops on his back for the blackout.

Another version of this sketch took inspiration from a comic scene from the *commedia dell'arte*. In "The Lazzi of Fear," one character sneaks up behind another, who is slow to realize the genuine or bogus danger. In this version, the candle remained static; instead, Pete's ghost appeared behind Jake and touched his cheek, moved the inkwell, and blew out the candle. Between each action, Jake cried out for the owner, who returned, saw nothing, rebuked Jake, and exited. Elements of this version also appear in "Oh, Charlie" when the ghost stands behind Camille and Ferdie, slaps them, and stamps out the candles.

Ferdie's cry, "Oh, Chuck!," comes from another medicine show sketch, "Over the River, Charlie." ("Over the River, Charlie" is a well-known Appalachian folk song descended from an English folk song,

"Over the Water to Charlie," which was a favorite among colonists in the Carolinas more than 200 years ago.) Red Skelton performed "Oh, Charlie" in medicine shows as a kid. In one of many versions of this routine, a doctor sends Jake to retrieve a corpse for an autopsy. Jake returns with a body in a sack, but it is not the dead man. A suitor named Charlie, who plans to elope with the doctor's daughter, switched places with the corpse when Jake stopped to rest. To avoid arousing the doctor's suspicions, Charlie asks Jake to temporarily take his place as the "corpse" on the operating table. Jake frets that the doctor will perform the autopsy on *him*, but Charlie assures him that the doctor won't operate before morning. But, if anything

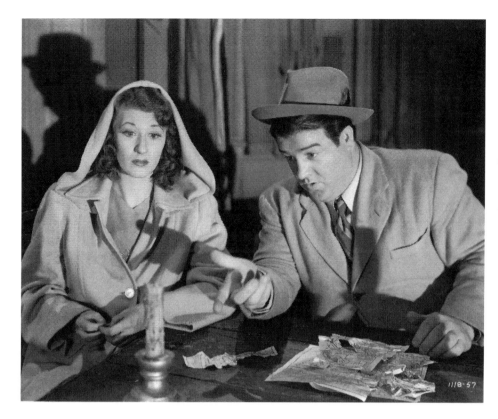

*Back to the "Moving Candle" routine, likely for coverage of the individual close-ups. In her close-up in the film, notice that Camille holds a map of Texas, but the Forrester's Club was supposedly located outside of Seattle.*

should happen, Charlie instructs Jake to call out, "Over the River, Charlie," and Charlie will come right back. Jake reluctantly obliges and lies trembling under a sheet on the operating table. As soon as Charlie exits, the doctor is heard offstage planning the autopsy in grisly detail. He punctuates each step by tossing a band saw, followed later by a meat cleaver, onto the stage. With each fearsome metallic crash, Jake cries out, "Over the River, Charlie!," and Charlie returns to calm him. During the autopsy, Jake comically avoids the surgeon's terrifying tools by squirming or flip-flopping around the table, and the young couple enter and announce their marriage.

A simpler version of the sketch was set down around 1900 by a prolific writer (or collector) of minstrel sketches named O. E. Young. Jake and his pal, Charlie, search for treasure in a haunted house. After Jake spots a knife-wielding ghost, he refuses to be left alone. Charlie, of course, sees nothing but reassures him, "I won't be far away. You just yell out, "Over the River, Charlie," and I'll be *right here."*

As newer versions of the sketch were developed, the line was truncated to "Oh, Charlie!," and any reference to the folk song was lost.

Many haunted house comedies can be traced back to the premise of another classic sketch, "Three O'Clock Train." Through a bet or a stipulation, someone must spend the night in a supposedly haunted house to claim money or the house itself. The sketch appears in a book published in 1894, but dates back to at least 1870. It is associated with George H. Coes (1828-1897) who, with Luke Schoolcraft, formed one of the most famous minstrel teams in history.

The comic is just passing through town but needs a place to spend the night before catching the three o'clock train the next day. The straight man offers to let him stay with him but explains that, according to his landlord, the house he rents is haunted. The straight man is not superstitious and has made a deal with the landlord: if he can last until midnight, the straight man can live there rent-free. The straight man offers the comic half of the house if he stays with him until midnight. The comic agrees. That night, while they wait, the straight man plays the banjo and sings verses of a song called "That's What They Call the Old Nightmare." (Coes played the banjo.) The creepy lyrics cue terrifying noises like clanging chains, shrieks, and ghostly wails from off stage. The comic trembles with fear, but the straight man hears none of it. This business is repeated until a ghost enters and scares off the straight man and then the comic.

Some tab show owners and vaudevillians complained to *Billboard* in 1918, 1921, and 1922 that "Over the River, Charlie," "Ghost in a Pawnshop," "Three O'Clock Train," and other medicine show standards should be retired. In 1930, a medicine show

82

*The "Moving Candle" runs seven minutes. In the original film, the routine was intercut with shots of a gang member manipulating the strings on the candles. This was re-edited when the gang was minimized in re-retakes.*

operator who ran shows from 1896 to 1912 told *Billboard* that he had seen "Over the River, Charlie" when he was a kid, and that it was still popular with young people in medicine show crowds in 1930. Another operator told *Billboard* in 1938 that so many medicine shows had recently played around Fort Worth, Texas, that "children recite 'Three O'Clock Train' and 'Over the River, Charlie' from memory."

Perhaps the earliest burlesque citation of "Oh, Charlie" is from 1922, when productions on different circuits staged the sketch. In "Radio Girls," a hit show on the Columbia wheel, comics Billy Gilbert and Bobby Wilson looked for lost pirate treasure in a gloomy, haunted cavern. *Variety* called it "one of the funniest comedy scenes ever witnessed in burlesque…Bobby Wilson, the second comedian, does tramp splendidly to Gilbert's unctuous eccentric half nance character." *Billboard* declared, "[N]ever have we seen [the 'Oh Charlie' bit] go over for as much laughter and applause." The show and the sketch received raves wherever it went.

At the same time, a Mutual burlesque show, "Playmates" (later renamed "Girls From the Follies"), also featured two comics, Sid Rogers and Jack "Mickey" McCabe, looking for lost pirate treasure, a playful skeleton, and the "Oh, Charlie!" bit. *Billboard* said they also garnered laughter and applause.

Billy Gilbert appeared in "Radio Girls" for two

years then, like many comics, moved to the Mutual circuit in 1924. In his show "Whiz Bang Babies," Gilbert did a haunted house sketch with moving candles and the cry, "Oh, Charlie!" *Variety* wrote: "'The Haunted House' remains the comedy high light. A pair of trick candles which move about weirdly, a couple of skeletons and other spine-tickling props are used for big laughs." Around 1917 Gilbert gave young Bud Abbott, then a ticket taker at a burlesque theater, his first taste of the stage.

In 1928 Abbott was in the Mutual show "Social Maids" with a haunted house sketch inspired by "Three O'Clock Train." The *Buffalo Evening News* reported: "One scene, which provokes mirth for over a quarter of an hour, is a dim-lit episode in a haunted castle, wherein Chuck Wilson, the comedian, unwillingly hears the tale of a miser and murder. A skeleton, two suits of armor and a revolving door enliven the narrative." This miser bit appears in an undated eight page script with the "Moving Candle" routine (see Chapter 8). It turned up later in the "Haunted House" episode of the Abbott and Costello television series, and on a live *Colgate Comedy Hour* in 1951. There were variations on the premise, but the miser version may be the best since the sound effects are cued by a spooky tale, not song lyrics.

According to Douglas Gilbert in *Lost Chords: The Diverting Story of American Popular Songs*, veteran

*Joan and Lou dance to the music of "The Blue Danube," composed in 1866 by Johann Strauss II.*

blackface vaudevillians Lew Simmons and Frank White may have been the first to combine "Ghosts in a Pawnshop" and "Three O'Clock Train." Simmons (1838-1911) was a great minstrel star after the Civil War. In 1870 he formed a minstrel company with Edwin Slocum and leased the Arch Street Opera House in Philadelphia (which later became the Trocadero, a burlesque house). President Grant celebrated his fiftieth birthday at a performance of Simmons and Slocum's Minstrels. Remarkably, Simmons also managed the 1886 Philadelphia Athletics to the pennant. He teamed with Frank White (1846-1910), another blackface comedian, in the 1890s. Of course we'll probably never know how similar Simmons and White's hybrid sketch was to Bud and Lou's.

Costello's brilliant pantomime brings the "Moving Candle" to life. He uses everything–bulging eyes, gasping breath, hand motions, etc., to convey sputtering fear. "The great thing about Costello," Robert Lees conceded, "was his total belief in the reality of the comic situation he was in…This is a must, in my opinion, for any successful actor, whether it be comedy or drama." Lou senses exactly how long to keep this up before giving birth to an audible "Oh, Chuck!" Bud also knows when to toss his partner a plum line like, "You have company here—you're not alone." To which Costello, glancing at Camille, can sarcastically crack, "No, not much."

The moving candles were obviously controlled by fine strings or wires, but who manipulated the wires? (In the script, it was a gangster in the cellar, Sc. 258-A.) In medicine shows and burlesque, someone was hidden under the table. The eight-page undated script indicates that Costello works the candles. But how? He clearly cannot use his hands, and foot pedals would be too complicated. It also seems like a lot for a comic to do—operate the candles *and* react. (Bud's nephew, the late Norman Abbott, did not recall how the effect was achieved.) Our own sense is that someone familiar with the bit—Grant or Bud—controlled the candles off camera, allowing Lou to do what he did best: react. In a live performance on their first *Colgate Comedy Hour* appearance, Bud, seated next to Costello, surreptitiously worked the candles with one hand under the table.

Next, Lubin shot Ferdie and Camille's comic dance (Sc. 131-135). "A lot of people think they just improvised that," Robert Lees said. "But it's in the script. Otherwise, how could they have built the set and had that rain puddle and everything?" It took nearly the whole day, until they wrapped at 7:30 p.m.

Lees and Rinaldo had suggested a more elaborate musical number back in November. With the Victrola playing, Camille ("Daisy" in the script) drags Ferdie onto the old tavern's dance floor for a comic jitterbug. She pretends that they are in a swanky nightclub and nods to imaginary celebrities, acknowledges a famous band-leader, and bumps into nonexistent couples. Ferdie, meanwhile, thinks she's nuts. Then he slips on the rain puddle and bangs his head on the floor. This starts a dream sequence. Camille, now dressed in an evening gown, helps Ferdie, who's wearing a tuxedo, to his feet in a crowded, ritzy club. Chuck, Norma, and the Doc are nearby, also dressed to the nines. The

script suggests using vocalist Maxine Sullivan (1911-1997), who had a hit in 1937 with a swing version of the Scottish folk song "Loch Lomond," and followed it with recordings of "Molly Malone," "It Was a Lover and His Lass," and "If I Had a Ribbon Bow," and "I Dream of Jeanie." Chuck takes the microphone and announces a dance specialty by Camille and Ferdie. They begin, but Ferdie falls and hits his head again. He wakes up where they left off in the old tavern.

The script indicates that a rain puddle has formed on the dance floor, but there is no specific direction other than, "We now have a comedy dance routine" (Sc. 132). Lees and Rinaldo's other concept for this sequence exploited the old Victrola's variable speed; Camille and Ferdie speed up or slow down their dancing accordingly.

Joan and Lou worked on their dance with choreographer Nick Castle. Born Nicholas Casaccio in Brooklyn in 1910, Castle began his Hollywood career in 1935 teaching tap to Fox star Dixie Dunbar. He collaborated with stars like Bill Bojangles Robinson, George Murphy, Ann Miller, Shirley Temple, and the Nicholas Brothers. Castle choreographed Joan Davis in several films, including *Love and Hisses* (1937),

*The dance remains one of the film's funniest sequences to this day. Note the bucket, waiting on the right edge of frame.*

Hold That Co-Ed (1938), Sally, Irene and Mary (1938), Josette (1938), My Lucky Star (1938), and Just Around the Corner (1938). He also choreographed the Andrews Sisters' numbers in Buck Privates. Several months later, Castle joined Universal under a term contract. His son, Nick Jr., is an actor, screenwriter, and director, known for playing Michael Myers in the original Halloween (1978) and co-writing Escape from New York with John Carpenter.

The bucket gag is not in the script. According to the press book, Joan's derriere had to be measured. A studio press release reads: "As everyone knows, there are buckets and buckets and it was quite essential that Miss Davis should fit in the container when she did her comedy fall without either losing too much skin or on the other hand, rattle around like a bean in a gourd. So the wardrobe department, flanked by an expert tinsmith, took the exact measurements, making due allowance for comfort of fit, and a special bucket was tailored to size. As a tribute to Costello's

*Lou charms his female co-stars. (Courtesy of Paddy Costello Humphreys and Chris Costello.)*

*Joan plays cards with the boys. "I used to love to play cards and I always lost," she once said. "Show business was full of people who hoped they'd get on the same bill with me because they could make two salaries— theirs and mine. And after one particularly tough season I ended up with no dough. I had been making very good money, too."*

marksmanship, he planted Miss Davis snugly in the bucket on the first try."

Publicity blurbs are often written before a film is completed, sometimes relying on an early draft of the screenplay. Joan falls into the bucket without any assistance from Lou. A thin cord or monofilament around Davis' hips plainly holds the pail in place.

*Photoplay* columnist Cal York reported: "...Joan Davis' familiar voice said over the phone, 'Come on over on the set. I'm getting measured for a bucket.' This was too much for old Cal's curiosity and, despite the pouring rain (yes, ma'am, it rained and rained out this way), we swam out to Universal and onto the Abbott and Costello set of 'Oh Charlie.' Believe it or not, Joan was getting her—er,—posterior measured for a bucket. It seems the star had to fall backwards in a scene into a bucket and the fit had to be exact."

Robert Lees recalled, "I remember being in the projection room looking at this dance scene. Joan Davis did a thing where she'd slide on her heels; it was an old routine of hers, and it's hysterical. Literally. And from the back of the [screening] room we hear a voice that is obviously Costello's saying, 'Who's the star of this film?' He felt he was being upstaged by Joan Davis and he wanted it cut out. But what he didn't realize yet was that  when he had a good comedienne to play off, it made him funnier, too."

Arthur Lubin said, "I thought Joan Davis added a great deal. She was almost as big a slapstick as Abbott and Costello."

Lees also told the authors of *Tender Comrades: A Backstory of the Hollywood Blacklist,* "Costello screwed up some scenes, or tried to screw them up, by objecting to her action and her lines. He was a fat little egotist. He couldn't stand the attention being drawn away from him, even if it made the movie funnier and better."

Lubin said, "There was no problem with co-stars; he (Lou) was a genial host."

According to Bob Thomas in *Bud & Lou,* Costello was jealous of co-star William Bendix in *Who Done It?* (1942). Lou reportedly told Alex Gottlieb not to cast "anyone who's funnier than me in one of my pictures." There's also an unattributed legend that Shemp Howard's "best stuff" was deliberately cut out of his Abbott and Costello films. (This may be confused with assertions that W. C. Fields trimmed Shemp's work in *The Bank Dick.*) Actors have always complained that their best moments wound up on the cutting room floor; conveniently, there's no way to disprove it. Longtime Stooges foil Emil Sitka said that Shemp only complained about the meager parts or unexceptional material he was given in Bud and Lou's pictures.

If he was insecure, Costello apparently never harbored grudges against these performers. In 1945, when she was a huge radio star, Joan Davis returned to Universal for a two-picture deal. There is a photograph of Costello visiting Davis on the set of her film *She Gets Her Man.* William Bendix later appeared in a

*Following the Moving Candle, Lubin covered Camille's terrifying description of what turns out to be an owl (Sc. 156). Right: Ferdie's hatcheck gag, added during filming.*

1947 short, *10,000 Kids and a Cop*, promoting the Lou Costello Jr. Youth Foundation, a facility the team built for poor kids in East Los Angeles. Shemp continued to turn up in Bud and Lou's films.

Many elements of Camille and Ferdie's choreography reappeared a decade later when Costello danced with statuesque actress Dorothy Ford in *Jack and the Beanstalk* (1952) and on the *Colgate Comedy Hour.* (*Showmen's Trade Review* reported in that Lou would dance with six-foot Glamazon Bunny Waters in *Abbott and Costello in Hollywood* [1945], but if he did, the scene was cut from the film.)

Although Lubin had now finished two crucial scenes, Universal's executive committee was still concerned by the slow progress of the production, which remained five days behind schedule.

On Friday, the director shot Camille's exaggerated description of the owl's fangs (Scs. 153-156); the arrival of the detectives (Scs. 173-175), who claim that the tavern is haunted; and their stealthy use of a secret passage behind the bar (Scs. 183-186). These cops, who are really other members of Matson's gang, are played by Don Terry and Edgar Dearing.

Terry's character is called Strangler. Terry was best

*After they discover Charlie Smith's body in the bedroom, the group is startled by knocking at the front door (Sc. 174).*

*Posing as detectives, two members of Matson's gang question the boys about their business in the old tavern (Sc. 175). They are played by Edgar Dearing (far left) and Don Terry, who later appeared together in the serial* Don Winslow of the Coast Guard *(1943). Terry played the title character and Dearing played Chief Petty Officer Ben Cobb.*

known for playing Naval Commander Don Winslow in the Universal serials *Don Winslow of the Navy* (1942) and *Don Winslow of the Coast Guard* (1943). The serials, which were based on a comic strip by Commander Frank V. Martinek, utilized the battleship sets constructed for Abbott and Costello's second service comedy, *In The Navy*. (Terry appeared in that film as well.)

Terry (1902–1988) was born Donald Prescott Loker in Natick, Mass. He was a stand out athlete at Norwich University, the oldest private military college in the United States. He left the school in his junior year to attend Harvard. According to some sources, he pitched on the university's baseball team, played right tackle on the football team, and played pro football with the Providence Steam Rollers. Other sources claim he was an Olympic boxer. Loker appeared in school plays and amateur theatricals but his movie break came by chance. During a vacation in California, he was spotted having lunch in a restaurant by Charles Francis Coe, who was adapting his novel, *Me, Gangster,* for director Raoul Walsh. Terry did a screen test that day and landed the lead role. In its review of the 1928 film, *Variety* called Terry "an engaging newcomer." Between 1928 and 1943, he acted in over thirty films and serials.

Early in 1940, Terry appeared on stage in Philadelphia in Clare Boothe Luce's comedy-melodrama "Margin for Error" for director Otto Preminger. That summer he worked in stock in Skowhegan, Maine, with Hume Cronyn. Among the plays produced was

"The Gorilla." Later in 1941 Terry married Katherine Bogdanovich. Her father, a Yugoslav immigrant, cofounded a cannery called the French Sardine Company in 1917. It grew rapidly, and by World War II supplied the U.S. army with more than half of its tuna output.

After making *White Savage* (1943) with Maria Montez (for director Arthur Lubin), Terry enlisted in the Naval Reserve. He was made Lieutenant Commander in the Pacific and spent nine months overseas with the Fifth Amphibious Force. In May 1944 he was awarded a commendatory ribbon for rescue operations as a volunteer landing boat officer. Terry received a medical discharge in 1945 and was set to resume the *Don Winslow* series but joined his father-in-law's company instead. The Navy sent him to Civil Government School and Japanese Language School. President Truman requested that he report to General MacArthur in Tokyo as his advisor on the rehabilitation of the Japanese fishing industry.

In 1953 the French Sardine Company became StarKist Foods. Terry served as an executive under his real name, Donald Loker. In 1959 he received another request from Washington to work with Thailand's Fishery Department. He was tapped for a similar project in Morocco in 1964. Loker retired in 1965 when StarKist merged with Heinz. He had spent twenty years as vice-president of Public and Labor Relations. In 2002, Del Monte bought StarKist, and in 2006 it was acquired by Dongwon Industries.

Loker became a noted philanthropist. He was

*After Chuck and Camille refute Ferdie's figures of speech, he sets out to prove that there is no money in the moose head. Chuck and Camille count the cash, which in the original script was counterfeit. Bud and Lou kept the moose head for good luck in their dressing room trailer.*

board chairman of the Donald P. Loker Cancer Treatment Center in Los Angeles, and founding member of the Southern California Cancer Center and the California Museum of Science and Industry Foundation. He and his wife were two of the nation's most active and generous supporters of higher education, medical care for the underserved, scientific research, and the arts. Her gifts to his alma mater, Harvard, totaled $27 million, and to hers, USC, topped $30 million. She died in 2008.

Edgar Dearing (1893–1974) plays Iron Dome. Since Iron Dome poses as a detective, who better to play on audience expectations than Hollywood's perennial policeman? Dearing's career began on the stage but was interrupted by World War I. He served as a motorcycle messenger attached to General Pershing in Europe. After the war he joined the Los Angeles Police Department as a motorcycle cop. He started moonlighting in films and even supplied his own bike and uniform. He made his film debut in Harold Lloyd's *Hot Water* (1924) and appeared in several Laurel and Hardy shorts including *On the Front Page* (1926) and *Two Tars* (1928). He played policemen, sheriffs, or guards in at least half of his 245 films, and was a motorcycle cop forty-five times. He was also the recruiting sergeant in Bob Hope's *Caught in the Draft* (1941).

Dearing played a cop in the Abbott and Costello films *One Night in The Tropics* (1940) and *In Society* (1944), and a studio guard in *Abbott and Costello in Hollywood* (1945). He also played Mike the Cop's (Gordon Jones) boss, Lieutenant Ryan, in an episode of the *Abbott and Costello Show*, "Bank Hold Up."

Saturday, February 8, was the second longest day of the production. Lubin shot for fourteen hours, until 10:35 p.m. This consisted of the business around the moose head, from the "figures of speech" dialogue (Scs. 261-262) to Ferdie's search and recovery of the loot (Scs. 268-273), and the confrontation with the gang (Sc. 275-278). Some of this was later re-shot owing to script changes, and in the original screenplay Moose's stash was counterfeit. The moose head wound up decorating Bud and Lou's thirty-foot dressing room trailer. A studio electrician rigged it with neon antlers that lit up whenever someone entered.

The next day, Lubin shot Ferdie's encounter with a recalcitrant water pump on the back porch and worked out of order on scenes with the gangsters and the group. The gangsters are played by Edward Pawley, Harry Wilson, Nestor Paiva, and Frank Penny.

*The other members of Moose's gang demand the loot. They are, left to right, Edward Pawley (Rosy), Nestor Paiva (Glum, in the background), Frank Penny (Snake Eyes), and Harry Wilson (High Collar).*

(Their unsuccessful attempt to rubout Chuck and Ferdie earlier in the film was added in re-takes.)

Pawley (1901-1988), who plays Rosy, starred in several well-known Broadway dramas including "Elmer Gantry" (1928). In "Two Seconds" (1931), he portrayed a condemned man who, as he dies in the electric chair, relives the events that led to his execution. (Edward G. Robinson starred in the 1932 film.) Pawley signed with Warner Bros. and appeared in over fifty films in a ten-year span. His best role was as Danny Leggett, the notorious criminal hunted by James Cagney in *G-Men* (1935). Leggett wore a gardenia in his buttonhole. This affectation was based on real-life Chicago mobster Dean O'Banion, who dabbled in flower arranging and always sported a white carnation or sprig of lily in his lapel. (In *Hold That Ghost*, Charlie Smith wears a carnation.)

Pawley befriended Cagney and appeared with him in three other films: *Angels With Dirty Faces* (1938), *The Oklahoma Kid* (1939), and *Each Dawn I Die* (1939). Pawley's brothers, William and Anthony, were also actors, and also appeared in *White Banners* and *Angels with Dirty Faces*. Before "Oh, Charlie," Pawley worked for Arthur Lubin in *Prison Break* (1938), *The Big Guy* (1939) and, most recently, *San Francisco Docks* (1940). After "Oh, Charlie," Pawley, Evelyn Ankers, and Shemp Howard were cast in the Dead End Kids programmer *Hit The Road* (1941).

In 1942, after making an impassioned speech about Communists in the movie industry, Pawley found himself shunned by several producers and directors. He returned to the New York stage where he starred with Gregory Peck in "The Willow and I." The following year Pawley replaced Edward G. Robinson as the crusading newspaper editor on the radio drama *Big Town*. He left the show in 1951 and retired to rural Virginia with his second wife, musical comedy star Helen Shipman (1899-1984). As early proponents of "back-to-nature" living, the Pawleys maintained an organic vegetable farm, raised champion goats, and ran a local grocery store. He also wrote poetry and was a part-time announcer at a

Glum (Nestor Paiva) appears to force Chuck to tie up the Doc, which differs from the scene as scripted (Sc. 296). Below: Ed Pawley as gangster Danny Legget in G Men *(1935), and Harry Wilson in* Go West *(1940).*

local radio station.

Harry Wilson (1897-1978) is called "Harry" in the film but "High Collar" in the script. He is instantly recognizable for his exaggerated facial features, the result of acromegaly, a pituitary disorder. (Another actor with a more severe case, Rondo Hatton, became a cult figure.) Speaking of his frightful mug, Wilson told columnist James Bacon, "It's my fortune. With a face like mine, you don't need an agent."

Wilson, a London-born American, sailed in the merchant marine and the U.S. Navy in World War I. After the war he became a professional wrestler and had a bit part in the Three Stooges' *Grips, Grunts and Groans* (1937). His film career was launched when he volunteered to jump forty feet into San Pedro harbor for a movie stunt. He continued to do stunts and became a longtime stand-in and double for Wallace Beery. This led to his casting as various henchmen, thugs, pirates, convicts, and brawlers in a few hundred

films and TV shows between 1928 and 1965. His most famous roles were as the Winkie Guard in *The Wizard of Oz* (1939); the female(!) monster in *Frankenstein's Daughter* (1958); and one of George Raft's henchman (along with Mike Mazurki) in *Some Like It Hot* (1959). Wilson's fearsome hands were also utilized in menacing close-ups in several films, including *Gone With the Wind* (1939) and possibly "Oh, Charlie." He appears in four other A&C films: *Pardon My Sarong* (1942), *Lost in a Harem* (1944), *Abbott and Costello Meet Captain Kidd* (1952), and *Abbott and Costello Meet Dr. Jekyll and Mr. Hyde* (1953). His granddaughter, Shauna Bloom, is an actress best known for her work as Red on *The Mentalist*.

Stout and frog-voiced Frank Penny plays Snake-Eyes. By the time they made "Oh, Charlie," Penny had known Bud Abbott for nearly twenty years. He appeared in a Mutual burlesque show, "Laughing Thru 1922," that was produced by Bud's cousin, Al Golden, who was also the show's straight man. Bud was the road manager. Penny was in "Broadway Flashes," a bare-bones tab show Bud mounted in 1924, as well as the last burlesque shows Bud produced before teaming with Costello. According to an article in *Collier's* magazine, Penny helped Bud financially in those early days. An undated clipping in Lou's scrapbook claims that Penny, who became a board member of the Burlesque Artists Association, managed the last theater the boys played before hitting the big time.

Penny was born Louis Frank Landsman in New

*In another deleted scene (Sc. 297), Chuck mumbles a string of insults under his breath, which Strangler (Don Terry) attributes to Ferdie. The gangster slaps Ferdie each time. When Camille protests, Strangler wags a threatening finger at her and she bites it. Glum (Nestor Paiva) looks on.*

York in 1894. Early in his career he worked as a black-face comic on the same vaudeville bill with Buster Keaton's family, The Three Keatons. During his time in burlesque Penny played Jewish and Dutch characters. When he headlined the 1924 Mutual show "Stolen Sweets," *Variety* wrote: "Penny is improving right along and will develop into a first-class comedian before the season finishes."

Penny married Mary "Mae" Santley, a burlesque soubrette, in the early 1920s, but she filed for divorce in 1929 after he was caught with another woman in a West Side theatrical hotel. From 1927 to 1929 he was part of a vaudeville musical comedy trio with his brother Harry Reed and Eddie Gold. They wore heavy make-up, played instruments, sang, and did moldy gags. After Penny went to Hollywood with Bud and Lou, Reed and Gold reunited and played clubs as the Barbary Coast Boys.

Penny lived in Bud's home in Encino and then in a guest house built on the grounds. He appeared in every A&C film from *One Night in the Tropics* (1940) to *Abbott and Costello in Hollywood* (1945). In *Buck Privates* (1941) he had the honor of introducing the Andrews Sisters when they perform "Boogie Woogie Bugle Boy." Penny also turned up in Arthur Lubin's drama, *Eagle Squadron* (1942); Olsen and Johnson's *Crazy House* (1943); *Kismet* (1944); and *The Dolly Sisters* (1945). He died while visiting family in the Bronx, and was survived by three brothers and four sisters.

Lubin filmed past 10 p.m. on Tuesday night to finish the fight with the gangsters and wrap the tavern dining room set. Most of this was eventually cut. Only a few scenes, like the chase with Ferdie (Sc. 276-280, 284, and 288), were kept in the film. Scenes 222-224 showed the gang congregating in the cellar and plotting to scare the boys away. We also learn that Strangler killed Charlie Smith. The Breen Office warned, "Care should be exercised to avoid any suggestion that Smith is being choked at this point. Political censor boards are especially sensitive with reference to choking scenes." The gang is also concerned about rival members who have escaped from jail and may be headed their way.

The phony detectives reappear during the chase, and Ferdie, after sliding down the bannister, trustingly hands them the loot (Sc. 290). They unmask themselves as members of Matson's gang and tie up Norma, Ferdie, Camille and Chuck (Scs. 292-297, 299

*Escaped convicts Lefty (Paul Fix, background) and Little Fink (Joe LaCava, kneeling) challenge rival gang members for Moose's stash (Scs. 300-310). This still, with Dr. Jackson holding a gun, doesn't quite match the action in the script.*

and 300). John Grant inserted two familiar Abbott and Costello bits in the script. One was a variation on the "Go On and Play the Radio" routine from *Buck Privates* (Sc. 297). Chuck mumbles several insults under his breath, which Strangler attributes to Ferdie. He slaps Ferdie each time. When Camille protests, Strangler wags a threatening finger at her and she bites it. Later, when Strangler is caught and bound, Ferdie believes he is helpless and taunts him. This was the boys' "Handcuff" gag, memorably reprised in *Who Done It?* (1942) with William Bendix.

Lees and Rinaldo also added an inside joke in Scene 297: Chuck warns Strangler, "Crime Doesn't Pay," a plug for the writing duo's earliest screenplays.

As expected, the fugitive gang members turn up to claim Moose's bankroll (Scs. 301-316). They are Lefty, Big Fink, and Little Fink.

Lefty was played by Paul Fix (1901-1983), a prolific character actor best-remembered as Marshal Micah Torrance on the television series *The Rifleman*. Fix was born in Dobbs Ferry, New York, where his father, a German immigrant, was the brew master at the Manilla-Anchor Brewery. The plant, which operated for fifty years, was in the midst of a foreclosure in 1917 when Fix's father died. Soon after, the boy lied about his age and joined the navy. He spent his service time state-side and made his first stage appearance in a Navy Relief production of Gilbert and Sullivan's "HMS Pinafore" in a female role.

Fix graduated to local productions in New York and broke into silent films in Hollywood in 1925. "In those days the movies didn't want actors, they wanted types," he recalled. "I had a face that could be an Indian in one scene, and you'd never recognize me playing one of the sheriff's posse or one of the bad guys in the next scene. So they got double work out of me for a single paycheck!"

He continued doing plays on the West Coast and appeared in twenty productions with Clark Gable. "Clark couldn't get into the movies then. Ears was too big. So he went on the stage," Fix explained. Then the talkies came in. "Oh, those days when actors found out they had to talk to work! I remember all the elocution studios that sprang up in Hollywood." Fix's voice and delivery got him typecast as a heavy for many years. "I was everything from a trigger man to a condemned killer in the electric chair," he said. Like Marc Lawrence, Fix also played gangsters named Lefty. He was Lefty in *Charlie Chan at the Racetrack* (1936), *Trail of the Vigilantes* (1940), and, of course, in "Oh, Charlie." He also played Lefty in the "Cheapskates" episode of the *Abbott and Costello Show.*

Fix befriended John Wayne and became Duke's acting coach. Fix explained, "My job, other than playing the role I was signed for, was to watch Wayne. We worked out a set of hand signals so I could tell him what he was doing wrong without the director knowing…Duke was not what you would call a natural

*Left to right: Paul Fix as Marshall Micah Torrence in* The Rifleman; *Joe LaCava in* Buck Privates; *Paul Newlan in* Abbott and Costello Meet Captain Kidd *(1952).*

actor, but he learned. And when he learned, he mastered one of the hardest things of all—to act natural. And he does it so well that a lot of people still don't know he's acting." Fix made thirty films with Wayne and co-wrote *Tall in the Saddle* (1944).

In fifty-six years, Fix appeared in 350 movies and television shows. He attributed his longevity to "not wanting to be a star. People around the business knew I would take any talking part and could deliver on the first take. I rarely made over $750 a week, but it was steady. Producers knew I'd go into a role at a moment's notice without squabbling about the salary. Also, I had friends at every studio. My idea was to keep working…and I did."

His many film credits include Bob Hope's *The Ghost Breakers* (1940) with Richard Carlson; Arthur Lubin's *Black Friday* (1940); *The Bad Seed* (1956); *Giant* (1956); *To Kill a Mockingbird* (1962); and *The Sons of Katie Elder* (1965). Fix played Dr. Mark Piper in the second pilot episode of *Star Trek*. When NBC picked up the series, he was replaced by DeForest Kelley as Dr. Leonard McCoy. Fix once said, "Television is just like the old B movies. I think, however, the B movies were better."

Joe LaCava (1908-1992) was Little Fink. LaCava was born in Paterson, New Jersey, and, according to his sister, Bea Altschuler, hitchhiked to California with Costello in 1927. Both men came back home after unsuccessful attempts to break into films. Years later, when Costello returned to Hollywood with Bud Abbott, LaCava and Lou's brother, Pat, served as the team's stand-ins and stunt doubles. They even roomed together. "Lou's sister, Marie, had a crush on Joe," Bea said, "and I think, confidentially, their family wanted to make a match. But Joe wasn't ready for that." When LaCava did wed, it was to another girl from Paterson, Mary McElwee. They were married 49 years when he died.

LaCava, who was a charter member of the Screen Actor's Guild, had bit parts in the team's early films—notably in the "Drill" routine in *Buck Privates* and the "Lemon Bit" in *In The Navy*. He worked uncredited in other A&C films and television episodes, including doubling for Bud in *Abbott and Costello Go To Mars* (1953).

LaCava later made a career playing waiters and croupiers; of his 84 film and TV credits he portrayed a waiter fifty-nine times, and croupier or roulette dealer fourteen times. According to Bea it was by choice: "He was comfortable doing them. He'd turn down other roles." His brother, Louis (1903-1992), was a make-up artist at MGM and worked on *The Wizard of Oz* (1939). Among his other credits are Roger Corman's *Tales of Terror* (1960), and the TV series *Death Valley Days*. Louis and Joe worked together on the films *Beyond a Reasonable Doubt* (1956), *Pay or Die* (1960), and an episode of the TV series *Honey West*. Louis died a few months after Joe.

Paul Newlan (1903-1973) played Big Fink. According to some sources, Newlan started acting in repertory companies, worked in vaudeville, played semi-pro baseball and basketball, then returned to acting. Tall and imposing, he was given the nickname "Tiny." Newlan played Pierrat Torterue, the official torturer who lashes Quasimodo (Charles Laughton) in *The Hunchback of Notre Dame* (1939). The two actors were later reunited in *Abbott and Costello Meet Captain Kidd* (1952). Newlan played the pub owner who inflicts further abuse on Laughton by sending Costello to wait on him. The following year Newlan was cast in the Columbia serial *The Great Adventures of Captain Kidd* (1953) as pirate Long Ben Avery, one of the few real pirates to retire with his treasure intact. Newlan had bit parts in three other films with Bud and Lou: he played a guard in *Lost in a Harem* (1944); Captain Chisholm in *Lost in Alaska* (1952); and a traffic cop in *Abbott and Costello Go to Mars* (1953). Meatier roles came to him on television. He was best

*Lubin often worked out of sequence. After Chuck, Ferdie and Camille manage to untie themselves, the group keeps Moose's gang at bay by flinging phonograph records at them (Scs. 315-320). Gangster fights with killings or woundings were prohibited by the Production Code. Censors suggested playing these scenes for comedy. Notice Costello's cigar, which does not appear on screen.*

*In the original script, the state police arrive, corral the gang, and reveal that Moose's money is counterfeit (Sc. 321). This scene, with Ferdie scaring off the gang with his own siren sound effect, was shot instead. Steve Allen later recalled that after seeing this gag, he would do his own siren call whenever he was stuck behind a slow-moving car.*

known for playing Captain Grey on the police series *M Squad* (1957-60), starring Lee Marvin. (*M Squad* was later spoofed as *Police Story.*) Newlan also portrayed General Prichard on *Twelve O'Clock High* (1964-66).

Lubin shot elements of the fight and chase out of order. The Breen Office cautioned Burt Kelly, "There is one element which we cannot approve. This is the business of the prolonged gangster fight in which, apparently, some men are killed or wounded. This constitutes a definite violation of the special regulations re: Crime in Motion Pictures. Material of this sort would, also, undoubtedly suffer widespread deletion by political censor boards. This could be approved if the shooting is materially lessened and their are no killings or woundings, but the whole business is treated for comedy."

Kelly assured them that it would be.

*After Ferdie's siren gag, Lubin shot earlier scenes with the cast looking for Charlie Smith's body in Moose's bedroom. (Scs. 176-182). The detectives reiterate that Smith is the ghost of gangster who was killed on the premises fifteen years earlier. There is a continuity gaffe between Scenes 182 and 187, where Ferdie exits Moose's bedroom without his hat but enters his suite with it on.*

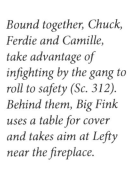

*Bound together, Chuck, Ferdie and Camille, take advantage of infighting by the gang to roll to safety (Sc. 312). Behind them, Big Fink uses a table for cover and takes aim at Lefty near the fireplace.*

Bud, Lou, and Joan endured an awkward sequence that required them to roll over one another through the rain puddle several times. Additionally, Costello's brother, Pat, who doubled him in the first ten Abbott and Costello films, was called on for a hazardous stunt. "I only did one stunt—where I go flying down the bannister with the bag of money," he recalled. "I rolled down the bannister on a flat board. The only thing was, I went down so fast the first time that I went flying off the bannister about fifteen feet and bounced into a wall on the other side of the room!" Perhaps Pat's mishap inspired an adjustment to the gag, where Ferdie flies head first into wall, not as the script has it (Sc. 289). Lou was rigged in a harness to safely "fly" through frame in a fleeting tighter shot.

On Wednesday, Lubin shot scenes in Ferdie's bedroom. A pair of menacing hands appear through a secret panel behind his bed, a reference to another

*Lou rigged for a close shot flying off the bannister (Sc. 289). His brother Pat did the hazardous part of the stunt. Below: the gangsters secretly ransacked Ferdie's bedroom, but Chuck blames him for the mess (Sc. 233). Bottom: after Camille is stalked by the ghost, the group finds its telltale sheet in Ferdie's bed.*

classic scene in *The Cat and the Canary.* Ferdie gets up to answer a strange knock (Sc. 226), but when he opens the door to investigate, he is locked out. He brings Chuck over, who finds the door unlocked (Sc. 232) and the room in shambles. (As Ferdie crosses the room to answer the knock, a secret panel starts to open before the scene cuts to him at the door. Shots of the gangsters entering, bracing the door and ransacking the room were deleted.) Chuck blames Ferdie for the mess and berates him.

Lubin then backtracked to an earlier sequence. After the "ghost" stalks Camille, he runs and hides in Ferdie's bed (Sc. 253). Ferdie calls to the others and the group discovers the ghost's telltale sheet on Ferdie's bed (Sc. 257).

The next day, February 13, the boys started on the Changing Room (Scs. 187-216). (More accurately, two bedrooms transform.) This was saved for later in the schedule to give John Fulton, the studio's special effects chief, time to design, build, and test it. This sequence required numerous takes to work on cue and it slowed Lubin up considerably; they didn't wrap until 9:45 p.m. Lubin likely also covered the gangsters getting caught up in the mechanisms during the chase (Sc. 285-287).

An inspiration for the Changing Room was a sequence in the Wheeler and Woolsey comedy *Peach O'Reno* (1931). The team play cut-rate attorneys who run a quickie divorce racket in Reno, then the new annulment capital of the world. Their office is methodically converted into a gambling joint at

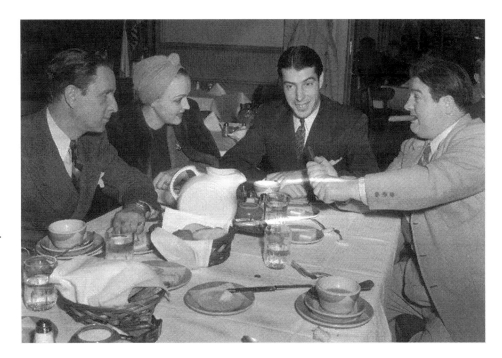

*Joe and Dorothy DiMaggio lunch with the boys in the studio restaurant as filming winds down. DiMaggio was famously holding out for a $7,500 raise before the start of the 1941 season. The Yankees gave him a $5,000 increase, to $37,500 (about $620,000 today). That year he would hit safely in 56 games, lead the Yankees to a world championship, and win the MVP award.*

night. Table tops open and roulette wheels come up; bookcases turn into a bar; and the largest book case swings around to reveal an orchestra. *Variety* wrote, "Trick sets in which a law office is transformed in a trice into a gambling joint and speakeasy looks like money. Sequence here is interesting and one of the best in the footage." It also got the biggest laughs.

Burt Wheeler and Robert Woolsey were vaudeville and Broadway comedians who broke into RKO musicals in 1929. Like Abbott and Costello, they began their own series of feature films with a service comedy, *Half Shot at Sunrise* (1930). Over the next eight years they made twenty-one films, a pace matched only by Bud and Lou ten years later. Similarly, Wheeler and Woolsey's films relied heavily on old vaudeville routines, which critics decried, but their studio made money grinding them out and had no incentive to change the formula. There were other uncanny parallels between the two teams. Like Lou, Burt was born in Paterson. Burt and his wife, like Bud

and Betty Abbott, had been a team on the stage. Both teams prematurely dissolved their partnerships but patched things up. And, like Lou, Bob fell ill at the height of the team's career and was confined to bed for a year.

The backgrounds and plots of Wheeler and Woolsey's films informed several Abbott and Costello films. This is no coincidence since Bud and Lou's producer, Alex Gottlieb, admitted, "I had gone through all the team pictures and made a list of all the backgrounds they had used. RKO had Wheeler and Woolsey, a comedy team that worked almost the same way as Bud and Lou did, only they weren't anywhere as good. Other studios had teams like that. I made a list of all the backgrounds they had used."

Wheeler and Woolsey's second staring film, *Hook, Line and Sinker* (1930), may have influenced *Hold That Ghost* (1941). In the former, co-star Dorothy Lee inherits a rundown hotel that W&W help turn into a swanky resort. Along the way they get mixed up with

*In one of several transformations, a desk in a law office becomes a roulette table in Wheeler and Woolsey's* Peach O'Reno.

gangsters who try to hide stolen loot there. In *The Nitwits* (1935), Wheeler and Woolsey run a cigar store in a midtown skyscraper. When a magazine publisher in the building is murdered, Bert and Bob attempt to solve the crime themselves. In *Who Done It?* (1942), Bud and Lou are soda jerks at Radio City. When the president of the network is murdered, Bud and Lou try to solve the crime themselves. MGM followed suit when it dusted off Wheeler and Woolsey's *Rio Rita* (1929) and retailored it for Abbott and Costello in 1942. A western dude ranch was the locale for Wheeler and Woolsey's *Girl Crazy* (1932) and Abbott and Costello's *Ride 'Em, Cowboy* (1942). *So This is Africa* predated Bud and Lou's *Africa Screams*. What's more, in *Cracked Nuts* (1932), Wheeler and Woolsey examine a map with towns named Which and What, also anticipating "Who's On First?"

Unlike the law offices in *Peach O'Reno,* the Changing Room in "Oh, Charlie" transforms mechanically. "That Changing Room scene was very, very carefully worked out," Robert Lees said. "We had to figure just what the props were. We knew that the chandelier would come down and be the roulette table. We knew the beds would turn over and be the crap tables. We knew all these things would happen. Now, they managed to work that out pretty well. But they could have done so much more with it but it called for a tremendous amount of rehearsal and they didn't have that rehearsal time, and they were never sure of these visual gags. They were more sure of John Grant's stuff, the play on words.

"But what we *never* expected—this was either the director or Costello—was how big a laugh there was in *anticipation.* Costello is dabbing water in his eyes, singing, and the audience already knows he is going to go back and go crazy because the room had changed. The audience was laughing all through that. As I say, [Fred and I] were not that hep as to what an audience was going to do. You've *got* to see comedies with an audience. They went *crazy* on this picture.

"When we first saw it [without an audience], I said to Fred, 'Jesus, this guy isn't funny. Damn it, if we were on the set we would do this, we'd do that.' And then, magically, Fred and I are laughing at the very things we said were terrible. Also, the timing changes. The [audience] laughter makes the thing play much faster. I remember when we were doing shorts at MGM and a scene dragged, we'd say, 'Why don't we cut?' And Dave Miller, the director, would say, 'Wait for the laugh. We have to stretch this.' And he was right."

*On Valentine's Day, Lubin wrapped scenes with Bud and Lou's co-stars, including the search of the cellar; a gag between Ferdie and Camille (Sc. 257); and the group exploring the upstairs bedrooms for the first time (Sc.157-159).*

Miller, who was also born in Paterson, directed Lees and Rinaldo's Oscar-winning "Pete Smith" short, *Penny Wisdom* (1937).

With the most challenging aspects of the Changing Room completed, Lubin's priority on Friday, Valentine's Day, was to finish up with the supporting cast. This included the search of the cellar (Sc. 145-147), with Ferdie's close call with Strangler's deadly hands (Sc. 146), and a weak gag at the end of Sc. 257 between Ferdie and Camille that was ultimately cut. Lubin also covered the group venturing upstairs and setting up the girls' bedroom (Scs. 157-159). In the script, Camille asks, "Norma—we're sleeping together, aren't we?" Norma replies, "By all means." However, in the film, Camille says, "Looks like we're going to sleep together—," which Ferdie answers with a provocative wolf whistle before Camille can say, "—huh, Norma?" Censors in Ohio deleted Camille's line, Ferdie on the bed, and his wolf whistle.

With the supporting cast wrapped, Lubin on Saturday intended to work with Bud and Lou on the back lot gas station set, but inclement weather forced them to work indoors and use rear-screen projection to fake the station.

This was the first day on the picture for William B. Davidson as Moose Matson. A former leading man in silent films, Davidson was born in Dobbs Ferry, New York (as was a member of his "Oh, Charlie" gang, Paul Fix) on June 16, 1888. He graduated with a law degree from Columbia University, where he also appeared in student theatricals. Some sources claim Davidson was a football star, but he did not have many opportunities on the gridiron. He played just a few games on Columbia's freshman team before many colleges banned football. Nineteen players died and 137 were seriously injured during the previous season. President Theodore Roosevelt urged reforms that ultimately saved the sport and gave birth to the modern game. Columbia reinstated football in 1914, five years after Davidson graduated.

By then he had made his first picture, *For the Honor of the Crew* (1914), in which he played a member of Columbia's rowing team. Thereafter he was prolific and quickly rose to leading man. He appeared

*William Davidson had been a leading man in silent films. His first days on "Oh, Charlie" were spent on a sound stage, where rear screen projection simulated the gas station.*

opposite Ethel Barrymore in four films and Theda Bara in three. Davidson supported other well-known actresses of the era such as Edna Goodrich, Mabel Taliaferro, Charlotte Walker, Olga Petrova, Viola Dana, and June Caprice.

Davidson migrated to Hollywood in 1924 and soon edged into character and villain roles. He appeared in over 300 films between 1915 and 1947, including *Monkey Business* with the Marxes; *I'm No Angel* with Mae West; *Scarface* (1930); *Hell's Angels* (1930); and *The Most Dangerous Game* (1932).

Early in his career Davidson married Mary Hellen Dorsey who, it turned out, loathed his profession. During a professional lull Davidson switched to selling insurance but soon accepted a film role over her strenuous objections. "No actor ever amounted to anything," she reportedly told him. They divorced in 1932. Two years later he married Helen Bolton, an

*The last scenes to be filmed on the tavern sets included more coverage of the Changing Room (left); Chuck and Ferdie finding Moose's bedroom (above right, Sc. 161); and Ferdie washing up before bed (bottom right, Scs. 192-3).*

*The opening scenes were filmed at the end of the production. Top left: the original opening shot. Some crew equipment is refelected in the car passing behind Chuck. Bottom right: The boys service Moose Matson's 1936 Buick Roadmaster.*

actress, who survived him.

Davidson was active in The Masquers Club and succeeded Frank Morgan as president. An avid golfer, he can also be seen in a couple of the instructional shorts of legendary golf pro Bobby Jones. He had recently worked for Arthur Lubin in *San Francisco Docks* (1940), and had concurrent bit roles in *Nice Girl?, The Lady from Cheyenne,* and *Man Made Monster* at Universal. He later appeared in three other Abbott and Costello films. He played Captain Richards in *In the Navy* (1941); the carnival owner, McGonigle, in *Keep 'Em Flying* (1941); and a butler in *In Society* (1944). His last films were *The Bachelor and the Bobby-Soxer* and *The Farmer's Daughter* (both 1947). Davidson died suddenly after surgery on September 28, 1947 in Santa Monica.

It had rained for six of the previous seven days, and the forecast called for more. Universal's executive committee considered shutting down the picture and shooting the opening exteriors when the weather was more promising. "Oh, Charlie" was again three days

over schedule, not only due to Lou's illness and rain, but also on-set additions and ad-libbed gags. The overage was estimated at $3,000.

On Monday, February 17, the boys shot connecting scenes for the Changing Room sequence in Chuck's bedroom and bathroom. The Breen Office cautioned, "There must be no undue exposure of Abbott's person where he undresses for bed. Care must be exercised to avoid vulgarity when Costello undresses for bed."

Lubin still had to cover the gas station exteriors; scenes inside Moose's automobile; and the police chase. On Tuesday, February 18, he finally got to work on the back lot's new service station set. It was built at cost of $3500 and used in other films, including *Pardon My Sarong* (1942). Although the weather threatened, it did not rain, and Lubin was able to cover much of the sequence. (A second unit was also out making chase shots for the rear screen backgrounds.)

In the first draft of the screenplay, Ferdie asks Chuck why ethyl is more expensive. Chuck replies,

*Bud, Lou, and William Davidson spent nearly two days shooting scenes inside the sedan. Top, left: Ferdie tests one of the revolvers. (The Breen Office warned, "The business of Ferdie putting the gun to his head and pulling the trigger may be deleted by some political censor boards.") Top, right: a police bullet undoes Ferdie's bowtie. Bottom, left: Ferdie wants his mama. Bottom, right: Mortally wounded, Moose takes out his will. His last words were eventually cut.*

"You can go farther with ethyl." The Breen Office ruled that his answer was unacceptable because of its suggestiveness.

The following day Lubin returned to the gas station set, but nearly an inch of rain forced him to dismiss the company 10:15 a.m. without rolling film. Thursday and Friday were literally wash-outs, with more than four inches of rain on Thursday and over an inch on Friday. Saturday, February 22, looked promising, and the company started on the back lot again, but more than an inch of rain drove them indoors once again. Lubin ended the day shooting process shots in and around Moose's sedan until nearly 8 p.m. The Breen Office warned, "It is important that there be no showing of machine guns or other illegal weapons in [Moose's] car."

The usual weather pattern continued on Monday, February 24: Lubin started outside but was chased indoors by rain. During the company move, Bud and Lou had lunch with the Hollywood correspondent for United Press, Frederick C. Othman. He reported that the team quarreled loudly over who was building the bigger swimming pool. "The argument…became so hot at the Universal Studio restaurant we thought maybe Mr. Abbott was going to take a poke at Mr. Costello. 'Oh no,' said he, 'I wouldn't swat the little runt; that's how we get our gags, fighting all the time.' As time went on they managed to tell the story of their careers, fighting fiercely over every point. Mr. Costello's the smart one, says he. Mr. Abbott has the brains of the pair, he reports."

The afternoon was spent on the process stage, filming the chase sequence from inside Moose's sedan. During the police pursuit, Ferdie whimpers, "I want my Mama." This was the English title of a popular song, "Mamãe Eu Quero," recorded by Carmen Miranda and performed in her film debut, *Down Argentine Way* (1940). Composed by Vicente Paiva and Jararaca, it is one of the most famous Brazilian songs of all time. The Andrews Sisters covered it in the fall of 1940 in a swing version with English lyrics by Al Stillman. But Bud Abbott surely knew "I want my Mama" as the catchphrase of burlesque comic Chuck Wilson, with whom he performed haunted house sketches in "Social Maids" in the late 1920s. Wilson even resembled Costello; he was short, plump and moon-faced.

Moose's threat, "I'm gonna fill them cops full of lead," (Sc. 36) was another red flag for the Breen Office: "[It] is highly censorable and we recommend it be changed to 'I'm gonna get their tires.'" Furthermore, Moose was prohibited from shooting much at all. Another Breen caveat stated, "Please have in mind the special regulations re: Crime in Motion Pictures, which prohibit the showing of gun battles between criminals and the police. With this thought in mind, Moose should not fire over two or three shots at the police, but the police may fire unlimited times at Moose." Matson is shot before he can fire at the cops. Once he is hit, the producers were warned, "Please avoid gruesomeness in Scene 46, where Moose is shot, and Scene 52 where he dies." Although his torso is well below the seat back, Moose is hit in the chest. Also, his line, "Pull over somewhere, will ya," is post-dubbed; Davidson's mouth does not move.

To the relief of his studio bosses, Lubin, finished principal photography at 6 p.m. on February 24. All that remained was the exterior police chase, which another director, John (Jack) Rawlins (1902–1997), would cover. But Rawlins had to cancel on Tuesday, Wednesday, and Thursday when nearly two inches of rain fell. He was then scheduled to direct *Mutiny in the Arctic* with Richard Arlen and Andy Devine.

It wasn't until March 6 that a third director, Ray Taylor, could take a crew out and shoot the pursuit. Taylor (1888–1952), who had been an assistant director to John Ford, joined Universal in the late 1920s. He rose to director, initially of one- and two-reelers, then features and serials. When talkies came in, Taylor was assigned to many of Universal's top westerns, and later one of its most popular serials, *Flash Gordon*. When serials died out Taylor went back to westerns. He eventually joined Producers Releasing Corp. (PRC) to helm C-grade westerns starring Lash La Rue. Taylor retired in 1949.

The chase was pared down from what Lees and

*Moose's car fishtails during the chase. This was a different 1936 Buick Roadmaster: the license plate is not the same as the one in the gas station.*

Rinaldo envisioned in the script. There is also a continuity error. Moose's car bears different license plates in the chase; the plate is black with yellow lettering and reads 36 Q 355. In the gas station the plate is mustard yellow with black lettering that reads 2W 926. California plates alternated yellow and black in even and odd years; these are different 1936 Buick Roadmasters. The prop department also masked the state name, which ran across the top of the plate.

"Oh, Charlie" was finally complete. It had been in work for thirty days, ten more than scheduled, and ran $3,000 over budget. Release was scheduled for May 30.

Bud and Lou played Ciro's on Sunset Boulevard on Sunday, March 9. The club had opened a year earlier and quickly became the place to be seen in Hollywood. The *Hollywood Reporter* wrote, "If Abbott and Costello did not lay 'em in the aisles it was only because [Ciro's] was so jammed there wasn't room to fall in an aisle. The boys were really hot!"

In New York the following week, they signed to appear as regulars on the Chase and Sanborn radio program with Edgar Bergen and Charlie McCarthy. Their first broadcast was on April 6, two days before production started on *In The Navy*.

Meanwhile, *Buck Privates*' stunning success would have an immediate impact on "Oh, Charlie."

# The "Oh Charlie" Routine

John Grant, the boys' writer, almost certainly provided the following undated eight-page script of the "Oh, Charlie" scene that inspired the film. This was for the benefit of the Production Code Adminstration as well as the studio.

It is a greatest hits of vintage haunted house routines that begins with a bit descended from an old minstrel sketch, "That's What They Call the Old Nightmare." Abbott tells an eerie tale about Moose's hidden treasure, a fierce gun battle, and Moose's ghost that is punctuated by frightening sound effects that only Costello hears. Abbott performed this scene in burlesque with comic Chuck Wilson, and later with Costello in the "Haunted House" episode of the team's TV series. In fact, most of the bits in this script were used in that episode.

This is followed by a segment where a ghost enters and stands behind Costello and Joan Davis and pulls pranks on them, and the "Moving Candle" routine. These gags sprang from a famous medicine show sketch, "Ghost in the Pawnshop," which may have taken some inspiration from "The Lazzi of Fear" of the Renaissance *commedia dell'arte*. (At the end of the script is a puzzling notation that Costello somehow works the candles. There is no other evidence that this is the case. Bud surreptitiously worked them with one hand under the table in a live performance on the *Colgate Comedy Hour*.)

The script ends with a hidden revolving panel gag that was better developed in *Abbott and Costello Meet Frankenstein* (1948) and the boys' TV episode.

Most of these bits did not fit with the story Lees and Rinaldo crafted for "Oh, Charlie," and so were not used in the film.

---

ABBOTT
(to Costello and
Daisy)
I found a blue print of this house. You and Daisy
study it and see if you can figure out where Moose hid
his money.


COSTELLO
What do you mean, hid his money?


ABBOTT
Moose was the head of a mob, but instead of splitting
his ill-gotten gains, he hid the money here. They say
he used to come here every night and count his money.

(CLINK OF COINS)


COSTELLO
Did you hear that?


ABBOTT
Did I hear what?


COSTELLO
Moose counting his money.


ABBOTT
Moose is dead and buried.


COSTELLO
Maybe he came back to collect his social security.
(to Daisy)
Did you hear him counting his money?


DAISY
Nooooo !


ABBOTT
One night Moose was sitting here, when there were footsteps outside.

(SOUND OF HEAVY FOOTSTEPS)


COSTELLO
(to Daisy)
You heard footsteps, didn't you?


DAISY
Nooooo !


COSTELLO
YOU heard footsteps, didn't you?

ABBOTT

That was mice.

COSTELLO

Mice?  They must be wearing skis.

ABBOTT

Quiet.  It was Moose's mob.  They had found his hideout.

COSTELLO

Why didn't he pull his hide in?

ABBOTT

Talk sense.  With a might crash, they broke the door down.

(SOUND OF CRASH)

COSTELLO
(to Daisy)
Now, don't tell me you didn't hear that!

DAISY

Nooooo!

COSTELLO
(to Daisy)
Whose side are you on?  ME OR THE GHOSTS?  Nobody hears
nothing.  There's money counting, feet walking, doors
breaking - and I'm the only one that hears it.

ABBOTT

Stop raving.  We don't want any of your frenzies.

COSTELLO

What frenzies?  I ain't gonna be frenzies with nobody.

ABBOTT

With the crash of the door, Moose drew his gun - bang,
bang, bang.

(SOUND OF THREE SHOTS)

COSTELLO
(starts to run,
Daisy grabs him)
Lemme go, LEMME GO!  If you want to ride, hop on, but
DON'T NEVER HANG ON...

ABBOTT

Now they dooooo saaaay!

COSTELLO

Come on, Abbott, don't give me that scary stuff.
(mocks Abbott)
They doooo saaaaay.  If you want to say it, say it fast,
like
(very fast)
They do say.

                    ABBOTT
They do say, that night Moose took a vow that if
anything happened to him, he would haunt this house.
Of course Moose's ghost may be only a rumor.


                    COSTELLO
I don't care if he's the landlord.

                    DAISY
                 (shivering)
A ghost can't hurt you.


                    COSTELLO
No - but he can make me hurt myself.


                    ABBOTT
Never mind that.  I want you to study that blue-print.
I'm going down to the cellar.  If you want me in a
hurry, just call "OH, ABBOTT" and I'll be right here.
                 (starts off)


                    COSTELLO
OH, ABBOTT!


                    ABBOTT
What's the matter.  I didn't even leave the room.


                    COSTELLO
Come on, what kept you?


                    ABBOTT
I told you, I didn't even leave the room.


                    COSTELLO
Listen when I call you.  Don't wait for OH, ABBOTT...
Get in here when you hear "OH".


                    ABBOTT
Stop this nonsense and study that blue-print.  I'm going
down to the cellar and look for Doc.
                 (exits)


                    COSTELLO
                 (to Daisy)
Are you scared?


                    DAISY

Nooooo!


                    COSTELLO
Me neither.  I would be silly if I was scared of a ghost.

(GHOSTLY WAIL)


                    COSTELLO
Boy, am I silly!

THEY SIT AT TABLE TO READ BLUE-PRINT.

                         DAISY
                        (coyly)
Cutie!

                         COSTELLO
                    (reading blue-print)
What?

                         DAISY
                        (coyly)
You and I are all alone, aren't we?

                         COSTELLO
I hope so.

                         DAISY
                    (whose back is
                     partly to Costello)
Wouldn't it be nice to have a pair of arms around you?

(DURING THIS SPEECH GHOST COMES BACK OF COSTELLO AND
 PUTS ARMS AROUND HIM)

                         COSTELLO
                    (pushing arms away)
Lady, this is no time for fol-de-rol.

                         DAISY
Gee, imagine a pair of arms holding you tight, and
squeezing you.

(GHOST'S ARMS XXXXXXX AGAIN GO AROUND COSTELLO, WHO
 PUSHES THEM AWAY)

                         COSTELLO
Stop putting your arms around me.  When I have to get
out of here, I don't wanna drag no woman with me.

                         DAISY
I didn't put my arms around you.

                         COSTELLO
Well, don't do it...
                    (does a take)
You didn't put your arms around me?

                         DAISY
No.  Did you want me to?

                         COSTELLO
                    (looks at her with disgust)
No.  When I command my feet to run, I don't want no
encumbrances.  Now, lemme study this blue-print.  Here's
the kitchen, and the hall, and the living room...

(DURING ABOVE SPEECH GHOST COMES IN AND KISSES
 DAISY ON CHEEK)

                              DAISY
                         (giggling)
Do it again.


                              COSTELLO
Do what again?


                              DAISY
Kiss me again.


                              COSTELLO
Did somebody kiss you?


                              DAISY
Yes!  Wasn't it you?


                              COSTELLO
Nooooo!
                         (they both look
                          around scared)
Maybe we better sit closer together.
                         (they sit closer)
Now, here's the kitchen, etc...

(BUSINESS OF CANDLE MOVING ACROSS TABLE)

                              COSTELLO
OH, ABBOTT!!  OH, ABBOTT!!


                              ABBOTT
                         (rushing in)
What's the matter?


                              COSTELLO
The candle went like this.
                         (shows him)


                              ABBOTT
That's only your imagination.
                         (to Daisy)
Did you see that candle go across?


                              DAISY
Nooooo!


                              COSTELLO
Where were you looking?


                              DAISY
                         (points to other candle)
There.


                              COSTELLO
Well, what were you looking there for?  This is the one.
                         (points to other candle)
Keep your eye on this one.

ABBOTT

Now stop this nonsense and study that blue-print. The
first thing you know Daisy will be getting scared.
(he exits)

COSTELLO
(starts reading blue-print)

The kitchen, etc.

(THIS TIME CANDLE GOES UP AND DOWN)

COSTELLO

OH, ABBOTT... OH, ABBOTT...

ABBOTT
(rushing in)

NOW, what's the matter?

COSTELLO
(breathlessly)

The candle... up and down.

ABBOTT

You mean to say the candle went up and down?

COSTELLO

Yes, sir.
(Abbott is about to
speak to Daisy)

Wait - don't ask her.
(to Daisy)

Didn't you see that candle go up and down?

DAISY

Nooooo !

COSTELLO

Where were you looking?

DAISY
(points to other candle)

There.

COSTELLO

What were you looking there for?

DAISY

You told me to.

COSTELLO

Well, don't believe me, I'm a liar.

ABBOTT

Costello, you've got to cut this out.  I have work
to do.
(he exits)

                              DAISY
Look, cutie, I'll watch one candle and you watch the
other.

                              COSTELLO
Okay -
                    (starts reading blue-pint)

(GHOST PUTS OUT BOTH CANDLES, THEN CAN'T FIND HIS WAY OUT)

                              COSTELLO
OH, ABBOTT... OH, ABBOTT...

                              ABBOTT
                    (rushing in)
What's the matter?

                              COSTELLO
Are my feet nailed to the floor?

                              ABBOTT
Certainly not.

                              COSTELLO
Then I must be paralyzed.

                              ABBOTT
What happened?

                              COSTELLO
A ghost came in and did a buck dance and put out the
lights.

                              DAISY
He don't even know the place he haunts.

                              ABBOTT
Costello, I've had enough of this.  Forget the blue-print,
and you two see if you can find a hiding place in the
wall.  If you find it, let me know.
                    (he exits)

                              COSTELLO
Okay.

(COSTELLO GOES TO ONE SIDE, DAISY STARTS FEELING OTHER
 WALL.  SHE TOUCHES PANEL.  AS SHE GOES THROUGH ONE SIDE,
THE GHOST GOES THROUGH THE OTHER.  COSTELLO SEES GHOST
AND GOES TO GRAB IT.  THE GHOST GOES QUICKLY THROUGH
PANEL AND COSTELLO GRABS DAISY COMING OUT.)

                              COSTELLO
OH, ABBOTT... OH, ABBOTT...

                              ABBOTT
                    (rushing in)
What is it now?

COSTELLO

I got the ghost.

(looks and sees it's Daisy)

ABBOTT

Costello, will you please look for that panel?
(exits)

COSTELLO
(to Daisy)
I'll look on this side, you look over there.
OTHER SIDE,
(FEELS FOR PANEL, GOES IN AND COMES OUT/FOLLOWED BY
GHOST)

COSTELLO

There's no ghost in there.
(Daisy is trying to signal him)
I don't believe there is such a thing as a ghost. Why
if I ever ran into that ghost, I'd haul off --
(turns and sees ghost)
OH, ABBOTT... OH, ABBOTT...
(runs through panel,
followed by ghost)

DAISY
(starts yelling)
OH, ABBOTT... OH, ABBOTT...

(COSTELLO'S VOICE IS HEARD BACK OF PANEL YELLING "OH, ABBOTT"

ABBOTT
(rushes in)
What is it?  What's the matter?

DAISY
(pointing to panel)
Cutie -- the ghost got Cutie.

ABBOTT

There's something screwy about this. Listen, Daisy, I'm
going in there to see what this is all about. Grab that
vase, and if any ghost comes through that panel, sock
it on the head.

(DAISY GRABS VASE. ABBOTT GOES THROUGH PANEL. AS HE
GOES IN ONE SIDE, GHOST COMES OUT OTHER AND DAISY HITS
IT OVER THE HEAD. GHOST FALLS AS ABBOTT COMES THRU PANEL)

ABBOTT

Good work... now we'll see who the ghost is!

(THEY TAKE OFF SHEET, DISLOCING IT'S COSTELLO)

The table used in this scene should be made so that candles
can cross each other and go up and down, worked by Costello.

# "Oh, Charlie":
# The Final Shooting Script

ollowing is a clean copy of Lees, Rinaldo and Grant's original screenplay, dated four days before the start of production.

All scripts are works in progress, often amended as scenes are rehearsed, blocked for the camera, and re-interpreted in the performance. Abbott and Costello preferred not to read a script, but get the gist of a scene from the director and ad-lib their dialogue. (Their routines, on the other hand, did not require a script.) Norman Abbott, Bud's nephew, recalled, "I remember the scripts would be sent to Bud's house, and I loved reading them. But they never looked at a script. They never really did their homework and studied like an actor should."

This pursuit of spontaneity came out of their burlesque training, where the classic routines were not written down but learned by watching other comics. This paradigm compelled the boys to improvise and therefore never do a scene exactly the same way twice. Additionally, John Grant was also on the set tweaking their scenes and adding new gags.

Directors learned to embrace the process. Jean Yarbrough, who directed the team's sitcom in the 1950s, confided, "If Lou has to stick to the letter of a script, he becomes mechanical. That's why it's necessary to keep a very loose rein on him so that the picture will benefit by the added laughs."

It fell to Bud to keep Lou on the rails. Arthur Lubin said, "I thought Lou would be lost without Bud, and Bud without Lou. I don't think there was ever a more wonderful 'feed' man. Lou would start to get away from the script and Bud could bring him right back to it, which was wonderful."

Perhaps Lou put it best when he once said, "I've got all my scripts at home in my den, bound in leather. Someday I'm going to read them."

*Bud Abbott* (signature)

*Lou Costello* (signature)

*Richard Carlson* (signature)

*Joan Davis* (signature)

*Evelyn Ankers* (signature)

*Marc Lea...* (signature)

*Arthur Lubin* (signature)

*William B. Sanoom* (signature)

"OH,   CHARLIE"

Screenplay

by

Robert Lees, Fred Rinaldo
and
John Grant

\*\*\*
\*\*
\*

REVISED FINAL

January 17, 1941

117

"OH, CHARLIE"

FADE IN:

1    MED. LONG - EXT. GAS STATION AND PARKING LOT - DAY

The station is of the small independent type that can
be found in the downtown section of Los Angeles.  The
Parking Lot is half full.  On SOUND TRACK are the noises
of fairly heavy traffic.

In f.g. a gas station attendant, CHUCK MURRAY (Abbott),
chalks the day's prices on a blackboard that stands near
the curb.

2    CLOSE - BLACKBOARD - OVER SHOULDER - CHUCK

He is busy chalking up the following sign:

                "8 GALS - $1.00"

3    MED. SHOT - CHUCK

He steps back and eyes the sign approvingly.  He is
dressed in routine white pants and shirt, with black
bow tie.

Approaching CAMERA from the gas pumps in b.g. is FERDINAND
JONES - (Costello).  He is rolling a tire, hitting it
with a wrench as a kid would play with a hoop.

4    MED. SHOT - FERDIE

He whistles "MERRILY WE ROLL ALONG", socking the tire in
rhythm to the tune.  CAMERA PANS him to CHUCK.  He stops
as he sees the sign.

                    FERDIE
                 (frowning)
            Hey, Chuck...

He takes a balloon from his pocket and attaches it to
the air hose.

                    CHUCK
              (putting finishing
               touches on sign)
            Don't bother me, Ferdie - I'm busy.
            And stop playing with that balloon.

                                        CONTINUED

4        CONTINUED

                              FERDIE
                    Yes, sir.

He sticks the balloon, still attached to the air hose,
into his jumper pocket.

                              FERDIE
                         (pointing to sign)
                    8 gals for a buck - that's pretty cheap,
                    isn't it?

                              CHUCK
                    Certainly not.  But that doesn't
                    Include Ethyl.

During this conversation the balloon inflates under
Ferdie's jumper, causing his chest to expand slowly.

                              FERDIE
                    Oh... Ethyl's more expensive, huh?

                              CHUCK
                    Always has been.

                              FERDIE
                    What has Ethyl got that none of the
                    others have got?

                              CHUCK
                    A higher octane rating...
                         (turning to him)
                    I'm surprised at you -- after all
                    the time you've worked on this job --
                    don't you know about Ethyl yet?

                              FERDIE
                    No, sir - I don't know any dirt about
                    any girls.

                              CHUCK
                         (annoyed)
                    Look - suppose somebody comes in and
                    asks for Ethyl - what would you do?

                              FERDIE
                    I'd tell them it's her day off.

                              CHUCK
                    Nonsense - you put Ethyl in their car.

                              FERDIE
                         (slowly burning)
                    I'd put Ethyl in the car!  I don't
                    even know the dame!
                                                        CONTINUED

4       CONTINUED - 2

                    CHUCK
          Talk sense!
                  (pointing)
          Ethyl's tanked right there in front
          of the station.

                    FERDIE
                  (angrily)
          Well - what do you want me to do --
          sober her up?


By this time the balloon has caused his chest to expand
terrifically.  Ferdie sees this and starts to cry.

                    FERDIE
          Chuck... Chuck...

                    CHUCK
                  (jerks air hose from
                   Ferdie's pocket and the
                   jumper slowly goes down)
          Now get busy and fix that tire.


5       MED. SHOT - CAR

It's a nice shiny convertible. As Chuck enters SCENE
he pulls out his pad of parking checks.

                    MAN
                  (indicating car)
          Be careful with it, Chief.  I just
          had it waxed.

                    CHUCK
          Absolutely.
                  (calling)
          Ferdie!


6       CLOSE SHOT - FERDIE

He has the tire over the air hose and is trying to pry
the casing loose from the rim.  At the moment he has an
iron wedge under the rim and is bending it against the
rubber with all his weight.

                    CHUCK'S VOICE
                  (continuing)
          ....Park this man's car.

                                        CONTINUED

6        CONTINUED

                              FERDIE
                          (holding iron)
                    Make up your mind!  Do you want
                    me to fix this tire or park that
                    car?

7        CLOSE - CHUCK

                              CHUCK
                    I want you to park this man's car.

8        CLOSE - FERDIE

                              FERDIE
                    Okay!

        Ferdie lets go of the tire iron which springs up and
        catches him neatly under the chin with a shimmering
        musical bong.  Ferdie shakes his head to clear the
        cobwebs.

                              FERDIE
                    But you don't have to get
                    tough about it....

        He exits shakily toward the automobile.


9        FULL - CAR

        While Chuck and the customer watch, Ferdie jabs the
        car in gear and with a loud roar backs in the direction
        of the parking lot.


10       PANNING SHOT - CAR (CAMERA UNDERCRANKED) HIGH SET-UP

        Ferdie takes a short cut by backing right thru the
        station, narrowly missing the gas pumps.  He whips around
        another parked auto and heads for a space between two cars
        that looks large enough for an Austin - maybe.


11       TWO SHOT - CHUCK AND CUSTOMER

        The customer can't bear to look.  He closes his eyes -
        Chuck holds his ears.


12       MED. - FERDIE AND CAR

        With a squeal of brakes the car skids miraculously into
        the narrow space and comes to a stop.

13      TWO SHOT - CHUCK AND CUSTOMER

        Chuck hands the man his parking check.  The man grabs it
        angrily and stalks away.

14      MED. SHOT - FERDIE AND CAR

        Ferdie now opens the door to get out.  The auto, however,
        is wedged in so tightly that there is no room for the door
        to open.  So Ferdie slides across the seat to the other
        door and finds he can't open that one, either. Chuck enters
        SCENE and watches Ferdie's performance with a wry expression.

15      MED. CLOSE - FERDIE IN CAR

                              FERDIE
                           (to Chuck)
                    Now don't worry - I can handle the
                    whole thing -
                              (cranks down window)
                    I just climb through the window into
                    the next car.

        Suiting action to words, Ferdie starts to climb through
        into the neighboring sedan.

16      CLOSE SHOT - OTHER CAR - OVER SHOULDER FERDIE

        A large dog which has been sleeping unnoticed in the
        back seat now springs into action with a savage growl...
        grabbing Ferdie's hand.

                              CHUCK
                    Stop sticking your hand in that
                    dog's mouth.

                              FERDIE
                    I'm not sticking it in, I'm trying
                    to get it out.

        He gets his hand loose and hastily retreats.

17      CLOSE SHOT - CHUCK

        He shakes his head disgustedly.

18      MED. SHOT - FERDIE - INT. CAR

        In jumping back he has hooked his belt on the catch that
        locks the folding top.

19      INSERT

        Belt hooked on catch.

20          CLOSE SHOT - FERDIE

            He struggles to free himself.

21          INSERT: DASHBOARD - CONVERTIBLE

            as Ferdie struggles his elbow strikes the button on the
            dashboard labeled: "TOP".  On SOUND TRACK there is the
            noise of churning gears.

22          MED. FULL - CONVERTIBLE

            The electrically operated top now lifts up from the wind-
            shield carrying the struggling Ferdie with it. Folding
            back, it deposits him in the rear seat.

23          MED. FULL - CHUCK

            He sighs wearily.  In b.g. a powerful-looking black sedan
            pulls up to the pumps.

24          CLOSE - DRIVER OF CAR

            He is a tough-looking hombre with a two days' growth of
            beard. This is none other than MOOSE MATSON, long wanted
            public enemy. He honks his horn savagely.

25          TWO SHOT - CHUCK AND FERDIE

            He struggles to free himself.

                              CHUCK
                    Now stop this fooling around and
                    help me with that customer.

            He exits.  Ferdie jumps heavily onto the front seat and,
            using it like a springboard, clears the front end of the
            convertible neatly.

26          MED. - GANGSTER'S CAR

            Chuck runs into SCENE.

                              CHUCK
                         (peppily)
                    Yes, sir...

                              MOOSE
                    Gimme ten gallons of gas.  And I'm
                    in a hurry.

                              CHUCK
                    You bet - check the oil?

                              FERDIE
                         (appearing at other window)
                    You want some oil?

                                                        CONTINUED

26        CONTINUED

                              CHUCK
                         (annoyed)
                    I just asked that.  You check the
                    water.

                              FERDIE
                    Right!

                              MOOSE
                         (protesting)
                    The water's okay.

                              CHUCK
                    It's all right, sir -- Super Service
                    courtesy.

26-A      MED. - FERDIE

          He lifts the car hood -- it comes down on his head with
          a bang.

26-B      MED. - GANGSTER'S CAR

                              MOOSE
                    Hurry up with that gas.

                              CHUCK
                    You bet.  You know we got a special
                    on.  With four quarts of Golden Nectar
                    oil we give you a pint of "DIE FLY".
                    It kills moths in rugs as well as
                    bugs and slugs.

                              MOOSE
                         (loudly)
                    Ten gallons of gas!

                              FERDIE
                         (still dazed by bump on head,
                          pops up at other window)
                    You want some oil?

                              MOOSE
                    NO!

                              CHUCK
                    Ferdie, you're taking up the man's
                    valuable time.  Vacuum the back seat.
                         (to Moose)
                    How about a set of tires?  Here's our
                    gift card.  When it's all punched, you
                    get a set of glassware - the little
                    lady will love it.

                                        CONTINUED

26-B    CONTINUED:

                            MOOSE
                I'm not married.


                            FERDIE
                        (from back seat)
                You want some oil?


                            MOOSE
                        (bitterly)
                No, I don't want dishes, tires,
                fly spray or grease--
                        (directly at Ferdie)
                and most of all-I don't want oil.


                            FERDIE
                Well, in case you want it- we got
                it.


        He ducks behind the back seat and continues to vacuum.


27      CLOSE - FERDIE - INT. BACK SEAT

        As he runs the vacuum cleaner over the upholstery it
        starts to wheeze a bit. Ferdie removes an obstruction
        from the mouth of the cleaner. It proves to be a gat.
        Not paying much attention, he places it on the seat
        and continues to clean. The cleaner coughs again and
        Ferdie removes another gun. Suddenly he does a delayed
        double take. He picks up one of the guns, looks around,
        then places the gun on his temple and pulls the trigger.
        It clicks- and he repeats this business.

                            FERDIE
                Empty!

        The gun explodes past his nose, shattering the window.


28      CLOSE - CHUCK AND MOOSE AT GAS TANK

        At SOUND of shot, they dash for the car.


29      MED. - POLICE CAR

        It jerks to a stop. The officers look off toward the
        gas station.

                            1ST POLICEMAN
                Hey! Isn't that Moose Matson?

        He swings the wheel.

30        SIDE ANGLE - MOOSE'S CAR

          Moose has jumped behind the wheel. He slams the door and
          grinds down on the starter. Chuck is trying to pull
          Ferdie up off the floor of the rear of the car. He is
          just pulling him up when Moose starts the car.


31        OMITTED


32        MED. FULL - MOOSE'S SEDAN

          With the throttle open, he heads for the street. Chuck
          is scooped up neatly by the open door. He is forced to
          jump on the running board to keep from being knocked down.

                              CHUCK
                    Hey!

          The sedan pulls out of scene and CAMERA HOLDS on the
          station while the police car roars past, then PANS to
          street where we can see the two cars speeding across the
          intersection.


33        INT. MOOSE'S SEDAN

          On the floor of the back seat Chuck and Ferdie untangle
          themselves.

                              CHUCK
                         (to Moose)
                    Hey-- what's the big idea?

          On SOUND TRACK there is the whine of the police siren.

                              FERDIE
                         (peering through
                          rear window)
                    Chuck--there's a white car
                    chasing us.

                              CHUCK
                    You mean a police car?

                              FERDIE
                    It ain't the ice cream man....


34        CLOSE - POLICE CAR

          The police open fire.

35      INT. SEDAN

The bullets start whining past the window. Ferdie sticks
his head up over the rear seat to take a look.


36      CLOSE-FERDIE

A bullet zips through the glass and neatly unties his
bow tie, leaving it to dangle in two black strings.
Ferdie 'takes' this and scrambles up to Moose, CAMERA
RETREATING AHEAD of him.

                        FERDIE
                  (shakily, in
                  Moose's ear)
            Hey, Mister-- stop this car. I
            wanta get out... I wanta go back
            to our gas station. I want...

                        MOOSE
                  (pulling Ferdie half
                  over the seat by his
                  shirt front)
            What is it you want?

                        FERDIE
                  (with a gulp)
            I WANT MY MAMA!

                        CHUCK
            Quiet, Ferdie. Another squawk out
            of you and he'll give you the business.

                        FERDIE
            I got my own business and I'm gonna
            make it my business to keep out of
            his business.

                        MOOSE
                  (commandingly)
            Get up here and drive. I'm gonna
            fill them cops full of lead.

                        FERDIE
                  (weakly)
            Me?

                        MOOSE
            Yeah...
                  (pointing his gun
                  to Chuck)
            And you get up here with him.

                                          CONTINUED:

36      CONTINUED:

        Moose pulls out the dashboard throttle. The men start
        changing places.


37      LONG SHOT- MOOSE'S SEDAN

        It sways drunkenly from one side of the street to the
        other.


38      INT. SEDAN

        Ferdie has one hand on the wheel and tries to balance him-
        self on the back of the seat. Moose and Chuck bump heads
        as they cross


39      LONG SHOT- CHASE-HIGH SETUP

        The cars are racing toward an intersection just as two
        street cars start across the street in opposite directions.
        The sedan plunges right thru the rapidly closing space
        between them without an inch to spare. The police car
        following a half-block behind goes right through the gap
        that opens up after the street cars have passed each other.
        Both cars look like cinch crack-ups.


40      INT. MOOSE'S SEDAN

        Ferdie is now at the wheel and Chuck sits tremblingly
        beside him.


41      EFFECT SHOT-STREET-CHUCK'S ANGLE
        Ferdie drives like a madman who's had one drink too many.


42      MED.- CHUCK

        He turns his eyes away from the view ahead and looks
        behind.


43      REAR OF CAR- CHUCK'S ANGLE

        Moose crouches in the rear seat exchanging shots with the
        police who can be glimpsed thru the shattered rear window.

                              MOOSE
                        (out of side of
                         mouth)
                Faster.

44      TWO SHOT- CHUCK AND FERDIE

        Chuck turns with a sick expression to Ferdie.

                              FERDIE
                    Faster? If I go any faster them
                    cops'll give us a ticket.


45      LONG SHOT- CHASE


46      INT. MOOSE'S SEDAN

        As Moose raises his gun to fire he is hit by the policeman's
        bullet. He drops to the floor of the sedan with a groan.


47      OVER SHOULDER SHOT-CHUCK AND FERDIE (PROCESS)

        At the sound of Moose's groan the boys turn their heads
        to look. Up ahead thru the windshield we can see that
        the car is approaching an underpass. The unattended car
        starts to swerve across the road toward the left wall of
        the underpass.


48      MED. LONG- UNDERPASS

        The sedan continues its swerve on two wheels, skids across
        the highway and jumps the curb.  It stalls halfway up the
        inclined retaining wall of the underpass. The police car
        speeding behind cannot stop and travels on thru.


49      MED.- SEDAN

        It now slides back down the incline and faces the opposite
        direction. Ferdie drives off in the direction from which
        he came.


50      CLOSE- MOOSE

        He raises his head with difficulty.

                              MOOSE
                            (gasping)
                    Pull over someplace....

51      MED.- CAR

It pulls to the curb. Chuck and Ferdie get out quickly, open the rear door and lift Moose out. They lay him on the ground.

52      MED.- GROUP

Moose's eyes are closed.

                    MOOSE
                  (weakly)
          Lefty, get a doctor.

                    CHUCK
          Lefty isn't here.

Moose opens his eyes and looks blearily about.

                    MOOSE
          Not here? Where's de rest of de
          mob?
                  (calling other
                   members of gang)
          Iron Dome!....Big Fink!... Little
          Fink?....

                    FERDIE
          There's nobody here but us gas
          station attendants.

                    MOOSE
                  (focussing on them)
          Just you two guys?
                  (as they nod)
          Oh-- that's rich--

He starts to laugh weakly. Chuck and Ferdie glance at each other, puzzled, then back at Moose. With his remain-ing strength the gangster reaches into his inside coat pocket and pulls out a legal-looking document.  He looks at it and laughs ironically. Suddenly he seems to deflate. His head rolls to one side. The hand holding the document slips to the ground. Moose is dead. CAMERA MOVES IN to hand holding document.
                                    LAP DISSOLVE TO:

53      INSERT-DOCUMENT ON TABLE

It's cover reads:

                "LAST WILL AND TESTAMENT
                         OF
                   SIDNEY MATSON"

                                        CONTINUED:

53        CONTINUED:

          A hand enters the scene and picks up the will. On SOUND
          TRACK there is the KNOCK of a gavel.


54        INT. PROBATE COURT- FULL SHOT- DAY

          The judge is just entering. A lawyer stands behind one
          table. Chuck and Ferdie huddle near him. The court clerk
          is knocking with the gavel.

                              CLERK
                    First Probate Court of Elk County
                    is now in session -- Hon. Judge
                    Finley, presiding.

          All sit as the judge takes the bench.

                              JUDGE
                         (to lawyer)
                    Are you the duly constituted attorney
                    for Sidney Matson, alias "Moose"
                    Matson, the deceased?

                              LAWYER
                    I am, Your Honor.

                              JUDGE
                    Have you caused all interested parties
                    to be properly notified?

                              LAWYER
                    I have, Your Honor.
                         (he nods toward
                         Chuck and Ferdie)

                              FERDIE
                         (starting to his feet)
                    Judge, I can explain everything....

                              CHUCK
                         (pulling him back)
                    Quiet.

                              JUDGE
                         (to lawyer)
                    You may read the will.

                              LAWYER
                         (hesitantly)
                    It's a rather curious document,
                    Your Honor.

                              JUDGE
                    I'll be the judge of that.

                                                      CONTINUED:

54        CONTINUED:

                              LAWYER
                    Yes, sir.

He clears his throat and prepares to read the will.


55        MED.- DOOR TO COURTROOM

It is pushed carefully open and the man whom we shall
know only as JOHN SMITH, sneaks in. Smith is an olive-
skinned, smooth-looking individual-- a careful dresser
who affects a carnation in his lapel. He takes a seat in
the rear of the courtroom and, keeping his hand over his
face, listens carefully to the reading of the will.


56        MED.- LAWYER

as he reads:


                              LAWYER
                    I, Sidney Matson, being of souund
                    mind and under no duress, do hereby
                    make this my last will and testament...

57        CLOSE- JUDGE

He nods absently as he listens to the lawyer's voice,

                         LAWYER'S VOICE
                    Whereas it is a universally accepted
                    fact that anybody who would associate
                    with me in the first place must be a rat...

The judge snaps out of his reverie, startled.


58        MED.- LAWYER

The lawyer shrugs apologetically, continues reading,

                              LAWYER
                            (continuing)
                    ... and whereas I can't tell my
                    friends from stoolies, leeches or
                    chiselers....


59        CLOSE-SMITH
                         LAWYER'S VOICE
                            (continuing)
                    ... and whereas it's impossible to
                    foresee who will turn yellow when
                    the going gets tough......

Smith winces a little.

60          MED. LAWYER AND JUDGE

                              LAWYER
                          (continuing)
                    Therefore, I hereby will and
                    bequeath all my earthly possess-
                    ions, share and share alike to.....


61          TWO SHOT - CHUCK AND FERDIE

                              LAWYER'S VOICE
                          (continuing)
                    ....all those who stick by me when,
                    in that final moment....


62          MED. LAWYER AND JUDGE

                              LAWYER
                    ... the coppers dim my lights.

          The lawyer clears his throat and looks rather
          embarrassed at the judge.

                              LAWYER
                    Signed, sealed, etcetera.

                              JUDGE
                          (wryly)
                    Is that all?

                              LAWYER
                    Yes, Your Honor.

                              JUDGE
                          (curiously)
                    Of what did this Mr. Matson's
                    property consist?

                              LAWYER
                          (riffling thru papers
                           and picking up one)
                    The only thing listed is a tavern --
                    The Foresters' Club on Highway 99,
                    in the Salmon River area.

                              JUDGE
                    No cash or securities?

63        CLOSE - LAWYER

                              LAWYER
                    Well, there must be a considerable
                    amount lying around someplace, Your
                    Honor, and I've had occasion several
                    times to ask Moose - Mr. Matson -
                    where he kept it, but all he'd ever
                    tell me was that the hiding place
                    for his cash was in his head.

64        MED. COURTROOM

                              JUDGE
                    I see.
                              (peering at Chuck
                               and Ferdie)
                    These are the beneficiaries, I presume?

                              FERDIE
                    Not guilty.

          Chuck slaps him.

                              LAWYER
                    They are, Judge.  I have the necessary
                    affidavits from two police officers.

          He hands them to the clerk.

                              JUDGE
                    In that case, since no charges of in-
                    competence or insanity have been
                    entered, and since I find that, con-
                    sidering the circumstances, this will
                    makes extraordinary sense, I admit to
                    probate.

          He rises and exits.

                              LAWYER
                    Thank you, Your Honor.

                              CLERK
                    Court adjourned.

65        MED. - SMITH

          He sneaks out.

66        MED. - LAWYER, CHUCK AND FERDIE

                              LAWYER
                              (as he puts papers
                               in briefcase)
                    Well, boys, that's that.
                                                    CONTINUED

66        CONTINUED

                         FERDIE
          Say, we got off easy, didn't we?
          Not even a fine.

                         CHUCK
          Ferdie, you still don't understand.
          We were the only people with Moose
          Matson at the time of his death.
          According to his will, we receive
          an inheritance.

                         FERDIE
                    (bewildered)
          An inheritance?

                         CHUCK
          Look - suppose I died and left you
          some money -- what would you call it?

                         FERDIE
          A miracle!

                         CHUCK
          Shut up.
                    (to lawyer)
          What is this Foresters' Club like?

He pulls a sheet of drawing paper from his brief case
and hands it to the boys.


67        INSERT:   DRAWING PAPER

The Foresters' Club is depicted in a typically flattering
architect's sketch.

                         CHUCK'S VOICE
          Say!  This is great!  We could
          really make something of a place
          like this.


68        MED. SHOT - GROUP

                         LAWYER
          Of course, it's been closed for a
          number of years.  It's -- er --
          usefulness diminished when pro-
          hibition was repealed.

                         CHUCK
          It was a speakeasy, huh?

                                                CONTINUED

68      CONTINUED

                        FERDIE
          What kind of place was it?

                        CHUCK
          Speakeasy!

                        FERDIE
                    (whispers)
          Okay - what kind of place was it?

                        CHUCK
                    (getting sore)
          I just told you - speakeasy!

                        FERDIE
                    (burning)
          I am speaking easy.  What do you
          want me to do.  Talk with my fingers?

                        CHUCK
          Be still.
                    (to lawyer)
          So it was a bootleg joint.

                        LAWYER
          Well, the front door is no stranger
          to a padlock.  But you'll find it
          fully furnished.

                        FERDIE
          Never mind that.  How much is it
          worth in a cash deal?

                        CHUCK
          Ferdie, I'm ashamed of you.  Do you
          want to be a gas station attendant
          the rest of your life?

                        FERDIE
          No, sir!  But I ain't goin' to no
          place that don't sound good --
          AND THIS DON'T SOUND GOOD.

                        CHUCK
          I suppose you realize what you are
          doing by refusing to operate this
          tavern.

                        FERDIE
          Yes, sir!

Chuck starts to tick off Ferdie's sins on his fingers.

                                        CONTINUED

68        CONTINUED - 2

                          CHUCK
                      (counting fingers)
              You're deliberately freezing a
              financial asset, slowing up the
              circulation of currency, depreciating
              property values, depleting the local
              and national treasuries, creating
              unemployment...

He has run out of fingers. Ferdie holds up one of his hands.

                          FERDIE
              Here, use these.

Chuck smacks his hand out of the way.

                          CHUCK
              Never mind that - if you don't
              want to go, I'll go alone.

                          FERDIE
              I'll go with you.  I don't wanna
              go, but I'll go.
                      (very sadly)
              You're the only pal I ever  had,
              outside of a dog - he even used to
              go to school with me - but at the
              end of the year, we parted.

                          CHUCK
              Why?

                          FERDIE
              The dog graduated.

                                          DISSOLVE TO:

68-A      MED. GROUP SHOT - EXT. COURT HOUSE

Chuck and Ferdie come out of Court House.  A car drives
by - and three shots come from its rear window. Chuck
ducks down.

                          CHUCK
                      (getting up)
              What was that?

                          FERDIE
              Backfire.

Chuck tries to speak, but can only point to Ferdie's hat.
Ferdie takes off his hat and sees three neat bullet holes.
He goes into a slow faint.

                                          DISSOLVE TO:

69     INSERT: NEWSPAPER

Transportation Column in Want Ad Section.  A finger goes
down the column and stops at one ad.  CAMERA MOVES IN to
frame ad.

                    "GOING EAST.  TAKE SIX (6)
                     Harry Hoskins - Wy. 8627"

                                        LAP DISSOLVE TO:

70     CLOSE SHOT - WINDSHIELD - WILDCAT TOURING CAR -
       EXT. DOWNTOWN STREET CORNER - DAY

A card, stuck under the windshield wiper reads:  "Harry
Hoskins - Transportation."  CAMERA RETREATS TO MED. SHOT
of car.  It is a dull gray morning, early.  The streets
are still deserted.  The driver, HARRY HOSKINS, is putting
suitcases in the little rack on the roof of his car.  He
is a shifty-eyed, Uriah Heep type.  In b.g. is a corner
drugstore.  CAMERA HOLDS on corner as Chuck, carrying a
light overnight bag comes into view.  He stops and looks
back around the corner.

                         CHUCK
                      (impatiently)
              Come on, Ferdie, come on.  Why
              do you always lag behind?

Ferdie staggers around the corner loaded down with suitcases.  CAMERA PANS the two men to Hoskins.

                         CHUCK
              Are you Harry Hoskins?

                        HOSKINS
                      (evasively)
              Who are you?

                         CHUCK
              I'm Chuck Murray.  This is Ferdie
              Jones.  We're supposed to pick
              up a ride here.

                        HOSKINS
                      (relaxing)
              Oh -- I'm Harry Hoskins all right.
                      (to Ferdie)
              Here, let me take those bags...
                      (as he lifts the first
                       one - pointedly)
              By the way, if there's anything of
              value in 'em, I can keep 'em up
              front with me.

                                        CONTINUED

70          CONTINUED

                              CHUCK
                    No.  There's nothing.

                              FERDIE
                    What do you mean, 'nothing'?  I got
                    valuables in my bag.

                              HOSKINS
                         (his eyes lighting up)
                    Jewelry?

                              FERDIE
                    My bubble gum!

          Chuck pushes Ferdie.  Hoskins starts to throw their
          Luggage onto the car.


71          MED. GROUP SHOT

          NORMA LIND, a pretty, heads-up sort of girl, enters SCENE.
          She carries one heavy suitcase.

                              NORMA
                    Mr. Hoskins?
                         (handing him her bag)
                    I'm Norma Lind.

                              HOSKINS
                         (as he takes bag)
                    Oh, hello, Miss....This is Mr. Chuck
                    Murray and Mr. Ferdie Jones.

                              NORMA
                    How do you do?

                              CHUCK
                    The pleasure is all mine.

                              FERDIE
                    Don't I get a little of it?

          He ducks as Chuck draws back his hand.  Norma has been
          regarding them with a suppressed smile.  She turns now to
          Hoskins, who has been loading her bag in the car.

                              NORMA
                    Driver, will I have time for some
                    Breakfast before we leave?

                              HOSKINS
                    I think so.  Two of my passengers
                    aren't here yet.

                                                         CONTINUED

71      CONTINUED

                        NORMA
            Well, I'll be in that drugstore
            whenever you're ready.
                    (smiling at Chuck
                     and Ferdie)
            Goodbye for now.
                    (she leaves)


72      MED. SHOT - CHUCK AND FERDIE

Looking approvingly after Norma.  Ferdie is completely dazed.

                        CHUCK
                    (indicating Norma)
            Looks like we're going to have some
            nice scenery on the trip.

He turns to speak - as Ferdie does a dead face fall.

72-A    LONG SHOT

Daisy comes through the street with grips, skidding
into pedestrians.  As she comes up to the car with a slide
her feet go into the air, hitting Ferdie's back.  Ferdie's
feet go into the air, and they both fall.

                        DAISY
            Hello.

(From the very start Daisy concentrates on Ferdie.)

                        FERDIE
            Chuck - more scenery.

                        DAISY
                    (getting up)
            Aren't you going to introduce me,
            Mr. Hoskins?

73      MED. GROUP SHOT

Hoskins comes over.

                        HOSKINS
            Oh -- I'm sorry, Miss.
                    (to the boys)
            This is Miss Brewster.

                        DAISY
            Daisy Brewster.

                        HOSKINS
                    (a bit proudly)
            Miss Brewster is a radio actress.

Daisy gives Ferdie a very superior look, intending to
impress him.                                    CONTINUED

73      CONTINUED

                              FERDIE
                         (unimpressed)
                    Radio actress.

                              DAISY
                    Oh, yes.  You must have heard me
                    on the air lots of times.  Listen...

She throws back her head and lets out a piercing SCREAM.

                              HOSKINS
                         (jumping)
                    Lady -- please!

                              DAISY
                         (breaking off sharply)
                    Recognize it?

                              FERDIE
                    Rigoletto?

                              CHUCK
                         (scornfully - to Ferdie)
                    No -- That's the scream that opens
                    the "Tales of Terror" program!
                         (to Daisy)
                    Right?

                              DAISY
                    That was the scream.  But no more.
                    After sixty programs I got mad!  I
                    told them I was an actress not a sound
                    effect.  So yesterday they said I
                    could have my big chance.  I was to
                    play the lead in "The Case of the
                    Frightened Lady."
                         (unconsciously starting
                          to act it out)
                    I'm missing.  The handsome detective
                    finds me unconscious in a cave.
                    Taking me in his arms, he says, "Lady
                    Faversham, speak to me.  Tell us who's
                    the ghost of Gruesome Manor?"....My
                    eyes open... I'm about to speak...

74      MED. GROUP SHOT

                              FERDIE
                         (breathlessly)
                    Well -- what do you say?

By way of reply, Daisy throws back her head and screams
sharply.  Ferdie jumps into Chuck's arms.

                                            CONTINUED

74        CONTINUED

                          DAISY
                  (breaking off abruptly)
          So I quit.

John Smith enters scene, his usual dapper self, the ever-
present flower in the buttonhole.  He looks like a man
working under pressure.  A cigarette is clamped between
his lips now -- and will be for the rest of our
aquaintance with him.  For Smith is a chain smoker,
lighting a new one off the butt of the old.  Incidentally,
he enters from the same direction as Chuck and Ferdie,
having followed them.

                          SMITH
                  (to Chuck and Ferdie)
          I'm looking for Harry Hoskins.

                          CHUCK
          That's him.

Smith crosses to Hoskins.
                          SMITH
                  (curtly)
          Smith.  John Smith.

                          HOSKINS
          Oh - yes, sir.
                  (taking his bag)
          Nice looking bag.  I'll keep it up
          front with me.  I'm glad you're on
          time, Mr. Smith.

                          CHUCK
          Got any of your brother's cough
          drops, Mr. Smith?
                  (laughs at his own witticism)

                          FERDIE
          John Smith, huh?  How's Pocohontas?
                  (laughs with Chuck)

Smith gives them a dead pan.

                          FERDIE
                  (aside to Chuck)
          I don't think that guy likes us.

                          HOSKINS
                  (to Smith)
          We can't go quite yet.  One passenger
          hasn't shown up, and the other lady is
          getting a bite to eat in the drugstore.

                          SMITH
          I'll wait in the car.

As he opens the door, it slams Ferdie in the face.
                                          CONTINUED

74        CONTINUED - 2

                              SMITH
                         (sarcastically)
                    Pardon me.

They look at each other - Ferdie doing a slow burn.

                                                     WIPE TO:


75        INT. DRUG STORE - AT SODA FOUNTAIN - MED. - NORMA,
          DR. JACKSON AND SODA JERK

An empty seat separates Norma and the Doctor.  He is an
intense young man with horn-rimmed glasses and a shock
of unruly hair.  He is absorbed in a book.  Norma is just
finishing her fried eggs.

                              SODA JERK
                         (to Norma)
                    Something to drink, lady?

                              NORMA
                         (off hand)
                    Draw one.

                              SODA JERK
                    Right...

He picks up coffee cup and saucer - as he turns to the
silex grill, he grins.

                              SODA JERK
                    You savvy the lingo, huh?

                              NORMA
                         (smiling)
                    I've been behind one of these
                    counters since they took down
                    the blue eagle signs.

                              SODA JERK
                    Work around here?

                              NORMA
                    Used to.  I'm heading East for
                    a new job.

                              DOC
                         (looking up from book,
                          sarcastically)
                    Could I have a little service,
                    please?

                              SODA JERK
                         (setting him up a napkin)
                    Yes, sir.

                                                     CONTINUED

75        CONTINUED

                         DOC
                  (fixing him with
                   an eagle eye)
               How long ago did you squeeze
               your orange juice?

                         SODA JERK
               It's fresh this morning.

                         DOC
               What _time_ this morning?

The soda jerk starts to smolder.  He looks over his
shoulder up at the clock, then back at his customer.

                         SODA JERK
               Exactly two hours ago.

                         DOC
               Well that's exactly an hour and
               a half too late.  Squeeze me
               some fresh ones.

                         SODA JERK
                  (ind. large pitcher
                   full of orange juice)
               I suppose you want me to pour
               this down the drain?

                         DOC
               It's Vitamin C content became
               deficient a half hour after
               squeezing.  People need Vitamin
               C.
                  (pointing to Norma)
               You take that girl there.  Hy-
               perthyroid.  Slight pituitary
               deficiency.  She'd be better off
               if she ate less eggs and drank
               more orange juice.


76        TWO-SHOT - NORMA AND DOCTOR

                         NORMA
                  (drily)
               Just leave me out of this,
               brother.  I'm doing all right.

                         DOC
               Your fingernails break too easily.

                         NORMA
                  (sarcastically)
               Fella, you marry me to a guy with
               a bankroll and I'll grow the
               nicest, longest fingernails you
               ever saw.

                                                  CONTINUED

76      CONTINUED
                                DOC
                        (studying her closely)
                    You also get a rash when you
                    swim in water containing
                    chlorine.

Norma starts to make a flip answer but stops short as
she realizes that that is exactly what does happen
to her.

                                NORMA
                        (looking into her plate)
                    What if I do?


77      MED. - AT COUNTER
                                SODA JERK
                        (still burned)
                    Look, 'Merlin' - do you really
                    want me to squeeze a fresh glass
                    or don't you?

                                DOC
                        (ignoring him and
                         moving onto the seat
                         next to Norma)
                    I'm doing special research on
                    glands and their relation to
                    vitamin consumption.  I'm a
                    doctor.

                                SODA JERK
                    Doctor Merlin - do you want a
                    California Cocktail?

                                DOC
                        (abruptly)
                    Certainly.

The soda jerk picks up a glass and, seeing that his
customer is looking at the girl, surreptitiously fills
it from the regular orange juice pitcher.

                                NORMA
                        (meanwhile)
                    If this is a line, it's at least
                    a new one.

                                DOC
                    Oh no.  I have my credentials
                    here some place ----

                                                CONTINUED

77      CONTINUED

                           DOC (cont'd.)
                    (as soda jerk sets up
                     his orange juice, he
                     turns on him fiercely)
            ---and don't think I didn't see
            you do that!  I won't drink stale
            orange juice, see?  I will pour
            it down the drain.
                    (he pours the glass of
                     juice into the sink)
            Now let me talk to the manager.


                       SODA JERK
                    (containing himself
                     with difficulty)
            Mr. Jenkins!


78      MED. - MANAGER - BEHIND DRUG COUNTER

                           MR. JENKINS
            Yes?

He comes forward.


79      MED. SHOT - GROUP - AT FOUNTAIN

Doc and the soda jerk are exchanging glares as Mr.
Jenkins enters.
                       JENKINS
            What seems to be the trouble?

                         DOC
            I have just poured a glass of
            orange juice down the sink.

                       JENKINS
            But, my good man -- why?

                         DOC
                    (turning to Norma)
            Go ahead -- you tell him.

                        NORMA
                    (taken aback)
            Tell him what?

                         DOC
            About your nails -- and those
            spells you have when you're
            terrifically thirsty and want
            to drink gallons of ice-tea...

                        NORMA
                    (looking at him with amazement)
            How do you know about that?
                                              CONTINUED

79      CONTINUED

                              DOC
                      (ignoring her - turns
                      back to Jenkins)
              See.  Symptoms of vitamin C
              deficiency.  And why?  Because the
              poor girl comes into a drugstore
              innocently expecting her daily
              vitamin content, only to be cheated
              by mass production methods.

Jenkins turns, frowning, toward the soda jerk, demanding
a full explanation.

                          SODA JERK
                      (explaining hurriedly)
              He doesn't want orange juice - he
              wants alphabet soup.  I squeezed a
              fresh batch at seven this morning.

                              DOC
                      (picking him up on it)
              And it is now--
                      (he points dramatically at
                      the clock, looks off to
                      verify exactly, then
                      does a startled takum)
              Is that the correct time?  Wow!

He grabs a heavy suitcase which has been beside his chair
and without another word dashes for the door. CAMERA PANS
with him.  Coming towards the group is Hoskins. Doc bumps
into him, nearly knocking him down.

                              DOC
                      (continuing on, but
                      turning his head back)
              Pardon me!

With that he barges right into a display of carefully piled
cold cream cans, bringing them down with a terrific clatter.
He continues out the door.

80      MED. GROUP SHOT - AT FOUNTAIN

                          SODA JERK
                      (looking after Doc
                      and shaking his head)
              A fugitive from a butterfly net

                            NORMA
                      (thoughtfully)
              No - he's a smart kid.  My finger
              nails are brittle.

Hoskins enters SCENE, dusting himself off.

80          CONTINUED

                              HOSKINS
                            (to Norma)
            Pardon me, Miss -- my other passenger
            hasn't shown up and the rest are getting
            impatient.  We'd better go.

                              NORMA
            All right.

81          MED. SHOT - GROUP AROUND TOURING CAR

            Daisy is now out on the sidewalk talking to Ferdie.
            Dr. Jackson dashes breathlessly into scene.

                              DOC
                            (to Ferdie)
            Are you the driver of this car?

                              CHUCK
                            (quickly)
            If he is, I'm walking.

                              DAISY
                            (pointing)
            Here he comes now.

            Hoskins enters scene with Norma.

                              DOC
                            (crossing to them)
            I'm Doctor Jackson.  I didn't
            know what time it was.

                              HOSKINS
                            (sarcastic)
            I can see that ----

                              DOC
            Huh?

                              HOSKINS
                            (taking his bag)
            Skip it...We almost left without you.

            He takes the Doc's bag and starts to put it up in the
            front seat.

                              DOC
            Yes, I -- I --
                            (catching sight of Norma)
            I've met you before...

                              NORMA
                            (sarcastically)
            Could it have been in Monte Carlo?

                                                  CONTINUED

                              DOC
                     (frowning thoughtfully)
               No ---
                     (trying to place her)
               Was it ---
                     (trailing off)
               No.

Hoskins reaches out to take the Doctor's small valise.

                            HOSKINS
               I'll put that up front, too, Doctor.

                              DOC
                     (hanging on to it)
               Oh, no. I have all my chemicals and
               special extracts in here. I'll hold it
               on my lap.

                            HOSKINS
               All right, sir.
                     (to the group generally)
               In that case, let's get going.

Hoskins opens the rear door and stands aside to let Norma
enter.  Doc Jackson, however, in his absent-minded way,
climbs right in and plunks down in the rear seat.  Smith
raises his eyebrows, slightly annoyed, as he 'hands' Norma
in.  That leaves room for only one more in the rear seat.
Making a quick decision, Smith elbows Daisy gently aside
and climbs beside Norma himself.  Daisy looks after him,
hands on her hips.

                             DAISY
                     (to Chuck - Ind.
                      Smith's action)
               The age of Chiselry.
                     (as Chuck shows signs of
                      getting in next; sternly)
               Stand back.
                     (to Ferdie)
               Come on, Cutie.

Ferdie lowers his eyes modestly and does face fall into the
car.  Daisy gets in next, followed by Chuck.  They sit on the
specially constructed 'jump' seats.  Chuck slams the door.

   82      CLOSE - FRONT OF CAR

Hoskins climbs behind the wheel and starts the motor.

                            HOSKINS
                     (to people in back)
               Well - we're off.

He puts the car in gear.  As it starts his face assumes
a sly, evil expression.
                                             DISSOLVE TO:

   83      LONG SHOT - COUNTRYSIDE
           A nice scenic view.  Farm country.  The car winds thru it.
                                             LAP DISSOLVE TO:

84          INT. REAR OF CAR - MED. SHOT - PASSENGERS

Doc is engrossed in a medical tome about 800 pages long.
He is halfway through.  Chuck is puffing smugly on a
cigar.

                    CHUCK
          Oh, yes, as soon as we get this
          tavern on its feet, we'll probably
          open a chain of tourist camps.
          Are you a traveling man, Mr. Smith?

                    SMITH
                (from behind his
                  cigarette)
          Now and then.

                    FERDIE
          How's the farmer's daughter?

Ferdie starts to giggle, looking at Smith. Smith gives
him a dead pan.

CAMERA MOVES in to FRAME occupants of rear seat.

                    NORMA
                (enthusiastically)
          I love to travel.  Wouldn't it be
          wonderful to be able to get up and
          go whenever you're tired of being
          where you are?

                    SMITH
                (remembering those
                  high gray walls)
          Sometimes it's practically impossible.

                    NORMA
          But what's life for, if not to travel --
          see new places -- meet new people?
                (to Doc - in an attempt
                  to draw him into
                  conversation)
          What do you think, Doctor?

Doc puts his finger carefully at the very spot where he
is reading, then closes book gently and stares at Norma.

                    DOC
                (blankly)
          About what?

                                        CONTINUED

84      CONTINUED

                          NORMA
                About 'life' ...

                          DOC
                     (academically)
                It is the most fundamental charac-
                teristic of animals and plants.

He returns to his reading.

                          NORMA
                     (trying again)
                Aren't you afraid you'll ruin your
                eyes, reading in a moving car?

                          DOC
                     (riffling from
                      page 400 to 800)
                I only have this much more to go.

                          NORMA
                     (giving up)
                Oh --
                     (to Smith, under
                      her breath)
                It takes all kinds...

                          SMITH
                     (noncomittally)
                Yeah.

85      MED. SHOT - FERDIE, DAISY & CHUCK - ON JUMP SEAT

Ferdie is looking dreamily out the window.  Daisy is
studying him with interest.

                          DAISY
                     (hesitantly)
                Mr. Jones -- are you -- married?

Ferdie shakes his head shyly.

                          DAISY
                Neither am I.
                     (quickly)
                But I haven't anything against it.

                          FERDIE
                Chuck thinks I should get married.

                          CHUCK
                Be the best thing in the world for you.

                                        CONTINUED:

85          CONTINUED

                          FERDIE
            I dunno, I was in love once.

                          DAISY
            What happened?

                          FERDIE
            I went one night to sing beneath
            her window.  I sang and I sang.
            Finally she threw me a flower.

                          DAISY
            In a mad moment of love?

                          FERDIE
            No -- in a pot.

Smith gives a dead pan.

                                        DISSOLVE TO:

86     MED. SHOT - EXT. SEDAN - NIGHT - (RAIN)

       Raindrops shine in the beams of the headlights. Thru the
       cleared semi-circle of the windshield wiper the face of
       Hoskins peers intently at the road ahead.

87     MED. SHOT - INT. SEDAN

       Ferdie has fallen asleep.  His head rests comfortably on
       Daisy's shoulder, and the actress is quite content to leave
       it there.  Ferdie's mouth drops open and he emits a low,
       rumbling snore.  Chuck turns from looking out the window
       and, reaching past Daisy, lifts his partner's unslung jaw.
       The snore is bitten off in the middle.

       CAMERA MOVES IN TO FRAME back seat.  Norma's eyes are also
       growing heavy.  Slowly they close, and she drops off to
       sleep.  Smith watches this with growing interest.  The
       doctor, meanwhile, looks vacantly out into the rain.
       Norma's head gradually lowers until it almost touches
       Smith's shoulder.  Suddenly she catches herself.
       Unconsciously she tilts her head in the other direction so
       that it rests instead on the doctor's shoulder.  The doctor
       comes out of his reverie and looks curiously at his
       companion.  His expression becomes more human for a moment,
       but then catching Smith's eyes on him, he once more looks
       out the window.

                                        DISSOLVE TO:

88     ROADSIDE GAS STATION & GROCERY STORE - EXT. - NIGHT - (RAIN)

       The lone gas pump in front of the store is sheltered from
       the falling drops by a wooden portico. The light inside

                                        CONTINUED:

88      CONTINUED

        the store glows warmly in the night.  The sedan pulls into
        SCENE and stops by the pump.  At the honk of Hoskin's horn,
        a young boy runs eagerly from the store.

89      MED. SHOT - SEDAN

                              BOY
                         (entering scene)
                    Fill 'er up?

                              HOSKINS
                    How far is it to the Forester's Club,
                    Sonny?

                              BOY
                         (frowning)
                    The what?

                              CHUCK
                         (sticking his head
                          out the window)
                    The Forester's Club.  It's on the
                    main highway around here someplace.

                              BOY
                    Never heard tell.
                         (indicating store)
                    Mebbe my old man knows.

                              CHUCK
                         (opening door
                          to Hoskins)
                    Mind waiting while we find out?

                              HOSKINS
                    No - go right ahead.  I need gas
                    anyway.

                              CHUCK
                    Come on, Ferdie.

        He heads for the store.  Ferdie Follows.

90      MED. SHOT - INT. STORE

        As Chuck, followed by Ferdie, opens the door there is
        the musical tinkle of an old-fashioned bell. The store
        is typical country style, carrying a variety of merchandise
        that runs from meat to hardware.  An old man sits by a hot
        coal stove with his chair tilted back and his feet propped
        up on the wood box. He chews tobacco and spits with unerr-
        ing accuracy onto the stove.

                                                  CONTINUED:

90      CONTINUED

>                    CHUCK
>                (to storekeeper)
>          Howdy, neighbor.

>                    STOREKEEPER
>          Howdy.

He spits at the stove and the tobacco juice hisses as it
goes up in steam.

>                    CHUCK
>          You, uh....
>                (attempting the
>                 vernacular)
>          ... ever hear tell of the Forester's
>          Club?

>                    STOREKEEPER
>          Shucks, boys, that place has been
>          closed for years.

>                    CHUCK
>          Well, we're the new owners.  We're
>          going to open it up again.

>                    STOREKEEPER
>          What fer?  Likker's legal around
>          here these days.

>                    FERDIE
>          We got a new idea.  We're gonna put
>          in a gas station and tourist cabins
>          and everything.

>                    STOREKEEPER
>          If you do, you're crazier than you
>          look.

>                    FERDIE
>                (getting tough)
>          Now wait a minute, grandpa.

>                    CHUCK
>                (restraining him)
>          Take it easy.
>                (to the old man)
>          What's the matter with that idea?

>                    STOREKEEPER
>          Can't have a tourist camp with no
>          tourists.

>                    CHUCK
>          That's our worry.  You just tell
>          us how to get there.
>                                              CONTINUED:

90          CONTINUED:2

The storekeeper shrugs.

> STOREKEEPER
> Waal - you keep agoin' for a half
> mile more.  Then where the new main
> highway turns to the right, you keep
> on the old one.

> CHUCK
> The old one!

> STOREKEEPER
> Sure - the new grade goes t'other
> side of the canyon -- nobody ever
> uses the old road no more.

91          TWO SHOT - CHUCK & FERDIE

> CHUCK
> (miserably)
> Ferdie - we've made a horrible
> mistake.

> FERDIE
> Don't look at me.  I didn't wanna
> come in the first place.  You talked
> me into this, Chuck.  Now, how about
> talkin' us back into our old jobs?

> CHUCK
> We can't go back.  We've burned our
> bridges behind us.

> FERDIE
> That's sabotage!

> CHUCK
> Quiet.  The least we can do is take
> a look at this place.  Maybe we can
> sell it for lumber.

> STOREKEEPER
> If you're stoppin' over you'll be
> needin' vittels, won't yuh?

> CHUCK
> Yes.  No matter what it is, we'll
> stay there a couple of days until
> we decide what to do.

> FERDIE
> (looking off)
> Hey, Chuck -- !

92    MED. SHOT - DISPLAY OF SPAGHETTI & NOODLES - GROUP IN B.G.

Ferdie comes toward the display and picks up a package
of spaghetti.

                         FERDIE
                      (continuing)
              Let's get some spaghetti and I'll
              make yo-yo.

                         CHUCK

              What's yo-yo?

                         FERDIE

              One string of spaghetti and a meat
              ball.

                         CHUCK

              We won't have time to make spaghetti.

He starts to turn away.

                         FERDIE
                      (detaining him)
              It don't take me long to make it.
              I just take water, add spaghetti,
              then put in some garlic and onions,
              onions and garlic, garlic and onions --
                      (etc., etc.)

                         CHUCK
              Wait a minute.  When do you eat it?

                         FERDIE
              EAT IT?  You can't even get near it.

                         STOREKEEPER
                      (coming up to them)
              Do you fellows want some meat?

                         CHUCK
              Well, what kind of fowl have you
              got?

                         STOREKEEPER

              Duck.

                         FERDIE
              Why should I duck?  Did somebody
              throw something?

                         STOREKEEPER
              No, no.  I got a duck in the ice box.

                         FERDIE
              Go ahead, we'll wait till you come
              back.
                                        CONTINUED:

92    CONTINUED

                        CHUCK
          Ferdie, he means there's a duck in the
          ice box.  Don't you know what a duck is?

                        FERDIE
          Sure.  A duck is a chicken with snow
          shoes on.
                        CHUCK
                      (disgusted)
          All right, all right.  We'll forget about
          the duck.  What do you want to eat?

                        FERDIE
                      (eagerly)
          What about a steak?

Chuck crosses casually to the meat counter and casts a
side-long glance at ...

93    INSERT - STEAK - IN COUNTER

Stuck in the middle is a price tag, $1.25 per lb.

94    TWO SHOT - CHUCK & FERDIE

Chuck clears his throat and addresses Ferdie in purpose-
ful shocked tones.
                        CHUCK
                      (shocked)
          Steak! Do you know where a steak comes from?

                        FERDIE
          Sure - a guy gets a rope and goes
          looking for a bunch of cows..

                        CHUCK
          Not 'bunch' - 'herd'...

                        FERDIE
          Heard what?

                        CHUCK
          Heard of cows.

                        FERDIE
          Certainly I heard of cows.  Do you
          think I'm a dummy?

                        CHUCK
                      (continuing)
          Very well.  And do you realize that that
          herd of cows gives milk?  Do you realize
          that if there weren't any cows, there
          wouldn't be any milk?  And if there
          weren't any milk, little babies all
          over the world would starve to death.
          But YOU don't care.  Just so that you
          can get steak, you'd let them kill
          all the cows and let the little babies
          of the world starve.
                                        CONTINUED:

94      CONTINUED - 2

                    FERDIE
                (in righteous
                 indignation)
Do you mean to say that every time
I walk into a restaurant and order
a steak, they kill a cow just for
me?  Do you mean to say that if I
walk into a place and order steak,
the waiter says, "ONE COW COMING
UP FOR FERDIE!"

                    CHUCK
All right, let's forget about steaks
and cows.  I'm not in the mood.

                    FERDIE
What mood?

                    CHUCK
A cow mood.

                    FERDIE
Who cares if it mooed?  Maybe it's
calling its children for supper.
Maybe those little children are
hungry...
                (as a new thought
                 strikes him)
Say, Chuck, what do those little
cows eat, anyway?

                    CHUCK
They eat their fodder.

                    FERDIE
                (wide-eyed)
Eat their "fodder?"  What are they,
Cannibals?

                    CHUCK
Certainly not.

                    FERDIE
Well, what does the cows' "fodder"
eat?

                    CHUCK
He eats his fodder.

                    FERDIE
                (amazed)
What do you know?...And what does
the cows' "mudder" eat?

                    CHUCK
She eats her fodder.

95      MED. GROUP SHOT

                              FERDIE
                    It's getting worse all the time.
                              (turning to
                              storekeeper)
                    Maybe you can explain this to me.
                    NOW!  When a little cow is born,
                    where is its papa?

                              STOREKEEPER
                    In the pasture.

                              FERDIE
                    All right.  Now -- does the little
                    cow eat its papa?

                              CHUCK
                    Of course not.  The little cow eats
                    its fodder.

                              FERDIE
                              (turning on
                              him angrily)
                    Well, ain't its papa and its "fodder"
                    the same thing?

                              CHUCK
                    How could it be?  A little cow gets
                    a new fodder every day.

                              FERDIE
                    A new "fodder" every day?
                              (throwing up his
                              hands in awe)
                    What romance!

                                             DISSOLVE TO:

96      MED. - CAR - EXT. OLD ROAD

        The touring cars sways and jounces over deep ruts, and
        skids thru pools of muddy water.

97      FULL SHOT - INT. SEDAN

        On Ferdie's lap is a box of groceries.

                              CHUCK
                              (after a particu-
                              larly heavy bump)
                    We're sorry to take you folks out
                    of the way like this.

                              SMITH
                              (still smoking)
                    Relax, chum.  How was I -- I mean,
                    how were we to know they'd put
                    through a new turnpike?

98        CLOSE - SIGN - LIT BY APPROACHING HEADLIGHTS

          It reads "FORESTERS' CLUB."  An arrow drawn on the bottom
          of the sign once pointed to the left, but the chain holding
          up one side has broken so the arrow now points significantly
          downward.


99        CLOSE - FERDIE

          He follows the arrow's direction, fully expecting to see
          the house submerged in a mud puddle.


100       MED. LONG - ROADSIDE

          The sedan turns off the road at the sign and heads up the
          semi-circular driveway before the Club.  The headlights
          illuminate a weather-beaten, heavily shuttered old Inn,
          utterly desolate.  The ravages of five years are only
          enhanced by the wildness of the night.


101       INT. SEDAN - FULL

          All the passengers stare curiously ahead at the Inn.

                              FERDIE
                    Boy, what a mess!

                              DAISY
                         (in a hushed
                          voice)
                    It looks just like the setting for
                    "The Death of the Howling Corpse."

                              DOC
                         (academically)
                    Miss Brewster -- a corpse is already
                    dead and it doesn't howl.

                              DAISY
                    This one wasn't -- and it did.

          On SOUND TRACK a wolf or some other denizen of the forest
          howls mournfully.  Chuck and Ferdie pale noticeably.

                              FERDIE
                         (nervously)
                    Chuck -- there's one thing I gotta
                    get straight once and for all....

                              CHUCK
                    What's that, Ferdie?

                              FERDIE
                    Is there or isn't there ghosts?

                                             CONTINUED

101    CONTINUED

                         SMITH
          Ghosts?  Of course there are ghosts.

                         DOC
          Ridiculous.  Pure aboriginal
          superstition.

                         NORMA
          I agree with the Doc.

                         DAISY
          Well, I've heard some very strange
          stories.

                         FERDIE
          What is this -- a Gallup Poll?
          I only asked Chuck.

                         CHUCK
          Stop worrying - a ghost can't hurt you.

                         FERDIE
          No - but he can make me hurt myself!

102    EXT. ROADHOUSE - MED. SHOT

       The sedan comes to a stop by the front door.  Hoskins
       gets out and pokes his head into the tonneau.

                         HOSKINS
          I want to tell you folks something.
          I don't like the looks of the road --
          especially in this weather.
                    (indicating Chuck
                    and Ferdie)
          Now, if it's all right with these
          gentlemen, I suggest we stay here
          for the night and get an early start
          in the morning.

                         CHUCK
                    (with alacrity)
          Be fine with us.

                         FERDIE
          Sure, we don't mind.

                         NORMA
                    (to Doc)
          What do you think, Doctor?

                         DOC
          It's probably the smartest thing.
          The road may be washed out further
          up.
                                        CONTINUED

102     CONTINUED

                              HOSKINS
                    Good.  Now you just leave everything
                    to me.  Get in out of the rain while
                    I get your bags.

                               SMITH
                         (as they get out)
                    Can I take that flashlight?

                              HOSKINS
                          (handing it
                           to him)
                    Sure.

The little group hurry up the stairs to the front door.
Ferdie carries the box of groceries - the Doc, his bag.


103     EXT. FRONT DOOR - GROUP

Smith holds the light while Chuck forces the key in the
rusty lock.  With a protesting groan the door swings
inward.  With Smith in the lead, the little group enters
the old tavern.


104     INT. TAVERN - FRONT DOOR

CAMERA RETREATS AHEAD of group as they enter.  They go
cautiously past the foyer and checkroom into the dining
room.


105     REVERSE ANGLE - DINING ROOM

The flashlight picks out tables and chairs piled in
corners, a large rustic-looking fireplace, hunt trophies
on the walls a moose head over the mantel. In the center
of the room is
a small dance floor.  Dust and cobwebs lie heavily everywhere.  ON SOUND TRACK the wind howls mournfully and a
loose shutter in the upper part of the house claps back
and forth.

                               CHUCK
                         (looking around)
                    At least the roof is still on.

There is a terrific flash of lightning.

                              FERDIE
                    I'm scared of lightning.  Let's
                    hide in the cellar.

                                                       CONTINUED

105     CONTINUED

                              CHUCK
               Lightning can hit you in the cellar
               too.

                              FERDIE
               Yeah - but it'll have to look for
               me.

Suddenly an automobile motor roars; a car grinds in
first gear, straining for a getaway.  The group look at
each other, startled, then with common accord rush for
the
front door.


106     EXT. FRONT DOOR - MED. SHOT

        as they rush out and look off.


107     REVERSE ANGLE - SEDAN - LONG SHOT

        It is disappearing into the night, swaying crazily from
        side to side.

108     MED. SHOT - GROUP

                              DOC
               Where's he going?

                              NORMA
               He's running off with our baggage!

                              FERDIE
               The dirty crook - my tooth brush
               is in there.

                              DAISY
               And my new nightgown and my pair of
               mules.

                              FERDIE
               Pair of mules?

                              DAISY
               Uh-huh.  I had a pair of mules
               wrapped up in my nightie.

                              FERDIE
               For goodness sake, were you afraid
               they'd catch cold?

                                        CONTINUED

108    CONTINUED

                    SMITH
          I should have known better than to
          leave that little sniper alone.
          That's the oldest chisle in the world.

                    NORMA
          What?

                    SMITH
          The wildcat bus racket:  collect the
          fares and the luggage, and then get
          rid of the passengers.  I bet nobody
          bothered to look at his license
          number...
                    (as the others
                     look blank)
          Well, neither did I.  So we're stuck.

                    CHUCK
          At least we have a place to stay.

                    FERDIE
          And food.

                    DAISY
                    (with a glance at
                     Ferdie)
          -- I'm not in a hurry to get any place.

                    FERDIE
          You ain't getting' any place.

                    DOC
          Well, let's go inside before we drown.

          They return to the tavern dining room.


109    INT. DINING ROOM

          as group enter.

                    DOC
          Perhaps I should go into town and
          contact the police.

                    SMITH
                    (quickly)
          It's too tough a night, Doc.
          There'll be plenty of time to call
          the cops in the morning -- plenty
          of time.

110    MED. GROUP

                              DOC
          In that case, let's get this place
          warm.  I'll build a fire.
                    (to Chuck)
          You see what you can find in the
          way of cooking utensils and dishes.

                              DAISY
          Yeah -- I'm starved.

                              CHUCK
          Okay.  Let us have your flashlight,
          Smitty.

                              SMITH
                    (stalling)
          Maybe I'll find a coal pile in the
          cellar and be able to send up some
          real heat.  I'd better keep the
          flashlight.

                              FERDIE
          Okay.  We'll hunt with matches.
                    (looking around)
          Where's the kitchen?

                              SMITH
                    (Pointing off
                     with certainty)
          This way --
                    (catching himself)
          --probably.

     Smith, Daisy, Chuck and Ferdie exit into the kitchen
     as Doc and Norma start to build the fire.


111    INT. KITCHEN

     It is rather small for a tavern, indicating that food
     was never a major incentive for patronage... Smith finds
     the door to the cellar with suspicious ease.

                              SMITH
                    (as he opens door)
          Well - so long.

     He starts down the cellar steps, closing the door behind
     him.

112     MED. - CHUCK, FERDIE AND DAISY - INT. KITCHEN

They are left in darkness.

                    DAISY
          Oh boy.  Romance.

She looks disappointed as Chuck strikes a match.


113     INT. CELLAR - MED. CLOSE - SMITH ON STEPS

As soon as he lands in the cellar he seems to lose all
interest in lighting the furnace.  Instead he goes to a
pile of barrels and boxes and feverishly starts to
search for something.  He casts occasional glances up
the cellar steps to be sure he is undisturbed.


114     INT. KITCHEN - MED. - CHUCK, FERDIE AND DAISY

Working by matchlight, they are opening drawers and cup-
boards, taking out pots, pans, dishes, etc.


115     CLOSE - DAISY

She opens a drawer, then looks pleased at its contents.
She takes out a number of candles.

                    DAISY
               (as she lights one)
          Look what I found!

Chuck and Ferdie enter scene.  They take candles and
light them from Daisy's.

                    FERDIE
               (as he does so)
          Gee - ain't civilization wonderful?


116     INT. DINING ROOM - MED. - DOC AND NORMA

near fireplace.  Doc has a snapping, leaping blaze
going.

                    NORMA
          That's a marvelous fire, Doc.

                    DOC
          I used to be a boy scout coun-
          selor.
               (he smiles at her)

                                        CONTINUED

116    CONTINUED

                         NORMA
              Do that again.

                         DOC
              What?

                         NORMA
              Smile.

                         DOC
                       (smiling)
              Why?

                         NORMA
                       (with critical
                        approval)
              Not bad...

                         DOC
                       (seriously)
              Oh - they're very good.
                       (showing her his
                        back teeth too)
              See?  Not a cavity.  I've always
              been careful to assimilate plenty
              of calcium.

     Norma just shakes her head.


117    INT. KITCHEN - CLOSE - DAISY

     She is taking tarnished silverware from a drawer.
     Suddenly on SOUND TRACK there is a hoarse, choking gasp,
     sounding exactly like a man being throttled.  Daisy jumps,
     grabs a knife and turns around.  Then she relaxes as
     CAMERA PANS TO:


118    CLOSE - FERDIE AT SINK

     He has turned on the dry water faucets and is examining
     them disappointingly.  It is the faucet that is giving off
     the 'no water' sound effects.

                                        CONTINUED

118     CONTINUED

                          FERDIE
                        (ind. faucet)
                Nothing.

                          CHUCK
                See if there's a rain barrel
                outside.

Ferdie picks up a bucket, starts out the rear kitchen
door.

                          FERDIE
                Gee whiz, I gotta go out there in
                the dark all by myself, with nobody
                to talk to.

                          CHUCK
                Why don't you talk to yourself.

                          FERDIE
                I get too many stupid answers.

Ferdie opens the rear kitchen door.  It leads onto a
back porch


119     MED. - BACK PORCH

Close to the door is a pump.  Ferdie spots this and
crosses to it.  He starts to work the handle, wincing
as it gives a protesting screech born of long disuse.
Chuck and Daisy come dashing out of the kitchen, brand-
ishing knives, just as water gushes from the pump's
mouth.

                          CHUCK
                        (anxiously)
                Ferdie!

                        (then - as he sees
                         Ferdie working
                         the pump)
                Oh...
                        (annoyed at his premature
                         fright - to Daisy)
                Come on.

They return to the kitchen.  Ferdie keeps pumping.  He
peers up into the mouth of the pump, to see if he can
see any water.  Then he gives a few more vigorous pumps,
waits a moment for the water to flow.  When nothing
happens he bends down to examine the pump's mouth.
Suddenly the water gushes out, smacking him in the face.

                                        WIPE TO:

120     INT. CELLAR - CLOSE - SMITH

With the flashlight propped on an old box, he is
searching the contents of a barrel. His head jerks
toward the cellar stairs, as the door to the kitchen
opens.

                    CHUCK'S VOICE
          How are you doing, Smitty?

                    SMITH
          I'll be up shortly.

                    CHUCK'S VOICE
          Need any help? We've almost
          got supper ready.

                    SMITH
          No. You stay up there. I'll
          join you.

                    CHUCK'S VOICE
          Okay.

The cellar door slams and Smith continues his search.


121     MED. - FURNACE

Fixing his beam of light on the door to the grate, Smith
opens it. Before he can move or cry out, a pair of
brutal, hairy hands reach out from inside the furnace
and clutch at his throat. Smith's eyes pop out and his
face contorts with horror. Then he drops his flashlight
and in the dim-ness that remains we can see him being
dragged into the furnace.


122     FULL SHOT - INT. DINING ROOM

By the fireplace Daisy is busying herself cooking
dinner. A large, iron kettle hangs over the fire, filled
with soup. The Doc is studiously opening cans of beans
while the boys dump the contents into another large
kettle. The scene looks like they were making camp
outdoors, miles from civilization.


123     MED. - SHOT - NORMA - EDGE OF DANCE FLOOR

She has just finished setting the table. It looks very
inviting. Two large candles, stuck in bottles, cast an
intimate night club glow. She steps back now and
admires her handiwork. Satisfied, she crosses to the
boys, CAMERA PANNING WITH HER.

                              CONTINUED

123    CONTINUED

NORMA
(playing games-
to Chuck)
Oh, proprietor..we'd like a
table for six, please.

Chuck looks at her curiously for a moment, then,
catching on, jumps quickly to his feet, whips his
handkerchief from his breast pocket and drapes it over
his arm like a napkin.

NORMA
(continuing)
And you'd better put us by the
dance floor because we're big
spenders.

CHUCK
(clicking his heels
and bowing)
Certainly, Madame.
(snapping fingers at
Ferdie)
Ferdie!  The best table in the
house for these people.

FERDIE
(giving it the business)
One best table coming up.

With grand gesture he bows and then leads Norma to the
table.  He holds her chair ceremoniously for her as she
sits.

124    MED. SHOT - TABLE

NORMA
And what time does the floor show
go on?

Chuck looks at his watch, then at the dance floor.

125    DANCE FLOOR - CHUCK'S ANGLE

The floor has sunk a bit in the middle.  A leak in the
roof has filled this depression so that it now forms a
large puddle.  Drops continue to plunk in the water from
the cracked ceiling.

126    MED. SHOT - TABLE

CHUCK
(clearing his throat)
We're, er-- presenting an aquacade
this week.  They're filling the tank now.

FERDIE
(curiously)
What's an aquacade?                          CONTINUED

                              DOC
                        (entering with the
                         bread dish - brightly)
              An H2Olio...
                              NORMA
                        (with a surprised smile)
              Why Doc!
                              DOC
                        (blinking)
              Wasn't bad, was it?
                              NORMA
                        (affectionately)
              Of course, it was bad.  That's
              what was good about it.
                              DAISY
                        (staggering up to the table
                         with the kettle of soup)
              Soup's on.
                        (she plunks it down on the table)
              Better call Mr. Smith.
                              FERDIE
                        (yelling)
              Smitty!

127     INT. CELLAR - MED. CLOSE SHOT - FLASHLIGHT ON GROUND

        The flashlight still burns on the cellar floor, mute
        evidence that neither Smith or his unseen assailant have
        returned.
                              FERDIE'S VOICE
                        (faintly)
              Come and get it...

128     MED. SHOT - GROUP AT TABLE

        They listen for Smith's answer.
                              NORMA
              I wonder what could be keeping Mr.
              Smith.
                              FERDIE
              Maybe he went to Washington.
                              DAISY
              Let's eat.

        Ferdie seats himself hurriedly and reaches across the
        table for the salt and pepper.
                              CHUCK
                        (smacking his hand)
              It isn't polite to reach -- if you
              want something, ask for it.  You
              have a tongue, haven't you?

                              FERDIE
              Sure - but I can reach farther with my hands.

        He grabs a soup spoon and starts to zup his soup avidly.
        Suddenly a strange expression comes over his face.
        Ferdie puts down his spoon and looks at the soup
        distastefully.

129    TWO SHOT - CHUCK AND DOC

They start to eat their soup, then stop as they become
aware of its peculiar taste.

130    MED. SHOT - GROUP

                    DAISY
                (shoving aside
                 her plate)
        I'm the cook so I can say it --
        the soup stinks.

                    FERDIE
                (taking a sip from
                 his glass of water -
                 wincing)
        It's the water from the pump.

                    DOC
                (lifting his glass
                 curiously)
        Let's see...
                (smacking his lips
                 professionally)
        Hmmm...very unusual.

                    FERDIE
        You said it -- from now on when
        I wanta drink, I'm gonna boil it -
        sterilize it - strain it --

                    DOC
        And then...

                    FERDIE
        I'll drink milk.

                    NORMA
                (shrugging)
        Well, anyway, the beans will
        be done in a moment...
                (looking at dance floor)
        Too bad the orchestra isn't on
        the stand.  We could dance between
        courses.

131    MED. SHOT - DAISY

She is frowning at something o.s.

                    DAISY
        Wait a minute.

She gets to her feet and crosses the dance floor, CAMERA
PANNING WITH HER.  In the shadows against the wall is an
old-fashioned mechanical phonograph, covered with a
white cloth.

132     MED. SHOT - DAISY AND PHONOGRAPH

Daisy removes the cloth.

                    DAISY
                (examining phonograph)
        Just as I thought.
                (opening the record
                 compartment)
        And it's loaded, too.
                (she removes an
                 armful of records)

                    NORMA
                (coming INTO SCENE,
                 delightedly)
        How perfect.
                (taking a record from
                 Daisy -- looking at
                 its title)
        This one.

Norma puts the record on the turntable.  It's a popular
tune of the late '20's.  The music SOUNDS cracked and
wheezy but nevertheless danceable.

                    DAISY
                (to Ferdie as she
                 recrosses the floor)
        Hey, Cutie.

                    FERDIE
                (annoyed)
        The name is Ferdie.

                    DAISY
                (lifting him from
                 his chair)
        Don't quibble -- just dance.


133     MED. SHOT - DAISY AND FERDIE

We now have a comedy dance routine.


134     MED. SHOT - DOC AND NORMA - AT TABLE

They watch the antics of Daisy and Ferdie with
amusement.

                    NORMA
        Would you like to dance?

                    DOC
        Very much.
                (as Norma gets to
                 her feet)
        Some day I'll have to learn how.

Norma sits down again, disgustedly.

:B

135     DAISY AND FERDIE

They are doing a tricky bit of dancing when the needle
gets stuck.  They are forced to repeat the same step
until the phonograph continues.  Finally the old
machine runs down.  Ferdie and Daisy change their
rhythm accordingly until they come to a slow-motion
stop.


136     TWO-SHOT - DOC AND NORMA

                    DOC
                 (worriedly)
            Maybe I better go down and see
            what's keeping Smith...

He gets to his feet.
                    NORMA
            Want a candle?


                    DOC
            No.  I have some alcohol here
            in my kit.
                 (indicating string of
                  lanterns above fireplace)
            I'll fill one of those lanterns.


137     CLOSE SHOT - DOC

He crosses to the fireplace and, stepping on the rough-
hewn stones, unhooks a latern.  As he steps down --


138     INSERT - SMALL STONE IN CHIMNEY

The Doc's hand brushes past it and it recedes an inch
or two with a sharp click.


139     MED. FULL SHOT - FIREPLACE AND WALL

There is a low rumble and a section of the wall beside
the fireplace slides to one side, the long unused
mechanism groaning and squeaking.


140     MED. SHOT - GROUP

They react appropriately.

                    FERDIE
                 (pointing)
            Hey --- look!

                    CHUCK
            Well, I'll be...
                 (turning to his partner)
            Ferdie -- go see what's in there.

CONTINUED

140    CONTINUED

                              FERDIE
                    Not me.  I ain't curious.

Doc is pouring alcohol into the lantern.

                              DAISY
                         (in hushed whisper)
                    It looks just like the secret panel
                    in the "Mummy's Claw".

                              DOC
                    Wait till I light this and we'll
                    all go in.

The Doc lights his lantern.  He leads the others to the
open panel.  The CAMERA TRUCKS WITH THEM TO INT. BARROOM.
In the light from the lantern we can make out the cobwebs
enveloping the bottles behind the long bar, the dust
clouding the mirror.

                              FERDIE
                         (looking about in relief)
                    It's a barroom.

                              NORMA
                    What a funny place to put it.

                              CHUCK
                    Sure -- that's how they fooled the
                    cops during Prohibition.  Pretty
                    clever, eh?

                              DAISY
                    You think there's anything in
                    those bottles?

                              CHUCK
                    If there is, it's bootleg hooch.
                    Remember how that stuff used to
                    start your pivot tooth spinning?
                         (he shudders)

                              FERDIE
                    I drank six bottles like that
                    and didn't even stagger.

                              DOC
                    You didn't stagger?

                              FERDIE
                    I couldn't even move.


141    CLOSE SHOT - DAISY
                              DAISY
                         (such a lie!)
                    Well, I was too young.  I --

                                        CONTINUED

141     CONTINUED

        She breaks off suddenly as she spies something on the
        floor at her feet.  She points with a trembling finger
        - he mouth wide open to scream.  Yet try as she might,
        no sound comes from her fear-frozen pipes.


142     CLOSE SHOT - SMITH'S CARNATION

        Lying on the floor.


143     MED. SHOT - GROUP

        The Doc quickly picks up the flower.

                        DOC
                  (examining it)
             It's fresh.

                        NORMA
             Smith's carnation.

                        DAISY
             But how did it get in here?

                        CHUCK
             Something must have happened to him.

                        DOC
                  (looking around)
             Maybe there's another entrance
             leading to the cellar.

        They look around quickly.

                        FERDIE
             We came in the only way there is.

                        CHUCK
             Let's go downstairs and look.
             Come on.

        He heads for the dining room.


144     MED. SHOT - INT. DINING ROOM

        The group follow Chuck as he heads for the kitchen and
        the cellar stairs.  The Doc slows up and turns to the
        girls.

                        DOC
             You girls better stay up here.
             I think you'll be safer.

        Daisy and Norma cross to the fire, Ferdie going with
        them.
                                              CONTINUED

144     CONTINUED
                           CHUCK
               Come on, Ferdie - you're no girl.

                           FERDIE
                          (alibiing)
               When I was a kid I used to play
               with dolls.

                           CHUCK
                          (grabbing his arm)
               Come on.

                                              WIPE TO:

145     FULL SHOT - INT. CELLAR

        The lighted flashlight still lies on the floor.  On
        SOUND TRACK we hear the voice of the Doc.

                           DOC
               Oh Smith....SMITH!

        The Doc comes down the cellar stairs carrying the
        lantern. With him is Chuck.  Ferdie trails behind.
        Both boys carry candles.

                           CHUCK
               Hey - there's his flashlight.

        He runs over and picks it up, playing the light about
        the room.

                           CHUCK
                          (calling)
               Mr. Smith?

146     CLOSE SHOT - FERDIE

        He peers wide-eyed into the darkness.

                           FERDIE
                          (in shaking whisper)
               Oh - Smitty....

                           DOC
               What do you suppose happened to him?

        CAMERA PANS Ferdie to where he stops before the furnace,
        holding his candle warily in front of him.  The candle
        flame highlights a pair of evil eyes that peer from be-
        hind the furnace door.  Suddenly there is a puff of
        breath and Ferdie's candle goes out.

                           FERDIE
                          (frozen in his tracks)
               Who-ooooooo.

                                              CONTINUED

146     CONTINUED

        Out of the grate a claw-like hand reaches for the back
        of Ferdie's neck.

                            FERDIE
                Chuck...CCCChuck!

        Ferdie runs out of SCENE toward Chuck not realizing
        how close he was to disaster.  The hand retreats inside
        the grate.

147     TWO SHOT - CHUCK AND FERDIE

                            CHUCK
                        (looking at Ferdie
                        disgustedly)
                What's the trouble?

                            FERDIE
                        (all a-tremble)
                S-somebody just b-blew out my candle.

                            CHUCK
                Don't be silly.  It was probably
                the wind.

                            FERDIE
                        (swallowing)
                Since when does the wind eat garlic?

        Chuck gives him a look and then starts to relight
        Ferdie's candle.

                            CHUCK
                That's ridiculous.  You're letting
                your imagination run away with you.
                Just say to yourself 'I must be brave,
                I must be strong, I must be courageous!'

                            FERDIE
                Okay!

        As they continue their search.

                            FERDIE
                        (mumbling)
                I must be brave, I must be strong,
                I must...
                        (he sees a pair of
                        evil eyes behind the
                        furnace door)
                I MUST BE NUTS!

        He makes a wild dash to find an exit, follow by Chuck.

148        INT. DINING ROOM - MED. SHOT - NORMA AND DAISY

before fireplace.

                              NORMA
                        (looking toward
                         stairway)
                    Perhaps he's upstairs all this
                    time.

                              DAISY
                        (without much
                         enthusiasm)
                    You think so?

                              NORMA
                    Let's look.  I'd like to see if
                    there's a place to sleep up there,
                    anyway.

She crosses to the table and picks up a candle.

                              DAISY
                    Well -- all right.

CAMERA RETREATS AHEAD OF THEM as they go toward the
stairs.

                              DAISY
                        (continuing)
                    But I hope this isn't like that
                    scene in "The Case of the Scream-
                    ing Parrott" where the two girls
                    got into the haunted house.


149        MED. SHOT - STAIRCASE

as Norma and Daisy start to ascend.

                              NORMA
                        (curiously)
                    Say -- about that screaming job
                    of yours -- how is it you didn't
                    even peep when you saw the flower
                    on the floor?

                              DAISY
                    I don't know.  I guess I got really
                    scared.  When I get really scared,
                    I --

She breaks off short.  Her eyes pop as she sees
something o.s.  She tries to scream, but again no sound
is forth-coming.  Norma looks at her with interest,
thinking that Daisy is merely illustraing her point.

150     REVERSE ANGLE - NICHE IN WALL ON STAIRWAY LANDING
        OVER GIRLS' SHOULDRS

        from the shadows, a pair of eyes peer luminously.


151     REVERSE CLOSE TWO SHOT - DAISY AND NORMA

                            NORMA
                    (as she talks, she
                    looks away from
                    Daisy, up the
                    staircase)
                That's funny.  You mean you can't --
                    (then she sees
                    the eyes and
                    screams sharply)

        The two girls break and run.


152     INT. CELLAR - MED. SHOT - STAIRS TO KITCHEN


        Doc comes running into SCENE, followed by Chuck and
        Ferdie.

                            DOC
                    (as he starts
                    up the stairs)
                That was Norma!


153     INT. KITCHEN - MED. SHOT - DOOR TO CELLAR

        Norma and Daisy run into SCENE just as Doc and the boys
        come bounding up the stairs.

                            DOC
                    (to Norma)
                What happened?

                            CHUCK
                Did you find Smith?

                            NORMA
                    (breathlessly)
                Someone was looking at us.  We
                were going up the stairs and --

                            DAISY
                    (breaking in)
                It's a fiend.  With fangs!

        By way of illustration, she flares her fingers from her
        jaw bone.  Ferdie is ready to go back into the cellar,
        but Chuck tries to get ahead of him.

                                            CONTINUED

153      CONTINUED

                              FERDIE
                            (screaming)
                  Lemme go, lemme go!  If you wanta
                  ride hop on - but DON'T NEVER hang on.

                              DOC
                         (with determination)
                  Come on.

He leads the way.

154      INT. DINING ROOM

CAMERA PANS Doc, Chuck and Ferdie to the staircase.

                              DOC
                         (as they cross -
                            calling)
                  Who's up there? ...Come on down,
                  whoever you are.

                              OWL
                         (hooting from
                            the darkness)
                  Whoo!  Whoo!

                              FERDIE
                  You -- you coward.

155      MED. SHOT - STAIRCASE

Doc levels his flashlight at the SOUND.  The beam hits
an owl.  The bird ruffles its feathers protestingly
and flies off to the upper recesses of the tavern.

156      MED. SHOT - GROUP

Doc turns to the girls, who have lagged behind.

                              DOC
                         (slightly annoyed)
                  It was only an owl.

                              DAISY
                         (quickly - before
                          her story can be
                          questioned)
                  With fangs.

                              DOC
                  Hmmm...What were you doing up here,
                  anyway?

                              NORMA

                  Looking for Smith -- and a possible
                  place to sleep.

                                                    CONTINUED

156     CONTINUED

                          FERDIE
                    (a slight quaver
                     in his voice)
              Sleep -- that's what I could use,
              Chuck.  A nice warm bed to hide under.

                          CHUCK
              Well, Smith isn't in the cellar.  We
              might as well take a look upstairs.

As they start up the stairs, Ferdie lags behind.

                          CHUCK
              Come on, Ferdie.

                          FERDIE
              I think I better stay down here -
              and be the look-out.

                          CHUCK
              What are you going to look out for?

                          FERDIE
              MYSELF!

                          CHUCK
              Get going --

He gives Ferdie a shove and they continue up to the
first floor landing.


157     LONG SHOT - UPPER FLOOR OF TAVERN

CAMERA is shooting down the hall to the staircase at the
far end, as the group comes up.  The hall is narrow.  On
each side are the doorways, arranged so close together
that the place looks somewhat like the corridor on board
a ship.

158     MED. SHOT - GROUP

They approach the first door.  Chuck puts his hand on
the knob.

                          DOC
              Careful now! ...

Not knowing exactly what to expect, they flatten themselves against the wall, while Chuck holds the door open
and steps quickly out of the way.  Absolutely nothing
happens.  Gingerly Doc peers inside, then waves for the
others to follow him.

159    INT. BEDROOM

the

as the group enters.  Ferdie has lantern.  The light from

lantern and the candles, plus the retrieved flashlight,
reveals a well-equipped bedroom.  As throughout the rest
of the house, this room has been carefully covered with
dust cloths.  The men remove these, revealing a bed,
equipped with a mattress and pillows, a dresser and arm
chair and table.  It's really quite an adequate room.

                    CHUCK
          Not bad...

                    FERDIE
          Yeah - but where are the other
          folks gonna sleep?

                    CHUCK
          The girls will sleep in here.

Norma opens the drawers in the bureau, pulls out a
couple of blankets and some sheets.

                    NORMA
          Look ... Blankets -- all the
          comforts of home.

                    DAISY
               (a leading question)
          Norma - we're sleeping together,
          aren't we?

                    NORMA
          By all means.

                    DOC
          I'll take the room across the hall
          if it's livable.

                    CHUCK
               (to Ferdie)
          Let's see what we can find - put
          that lantern on the high-boy.

                    FERDIE
          Sure.
               (does a take)
          The what?

                    CHUCK
          HIGH-BOY!

                    FERDIE
          Hi' Chuck!

                    CHUCK
          Put that lantern down - and come on.

     They exit.                              CONTINUED

159    CONTINUED

                              DOC
                         (pausing at the
                          door, his hand
                          on the knob -
                          to Norma)
                    Of course nothing is going to happen,
                    but just in case something does -
                    you yell.

                              NORMA
                    We will.

160    INT. HALL

Chuck and Ferdie are waiting for the Doc.  He comes
out now, and, opening the door opposite the girls' room,
flashes his light inside.

                              DOC
                    This will do me.

                              CHUCK
                    We'll be right next door.  Come
                    on, Ferdie.

Doc closes his door.  CAMERA MOVES with Chuck and Ferdie
to the next door.  Ferdie opens it confidently and is
met with a wild flurry of rain and wind. For the roof
has fallen in in this particular section, leaving this
room open to the elements.  The boys slam the door
quickly before they get drowned.

                              CHUCK
                    Can't sleep in there.

                              FERDIE
                    At least it's got running water.

CAMERA PAN THEM to room across the hall.  They open the
door carefully, find the room dry, and enter.

161    INT. MOOSE MATSON'S BEDROOM

The walls are solidly draped in heavy velvet. A luxurious
four-poster bed carries a faded monogram - "MM".  The
whole room has a purple passion conception.  Chuck and
Ferdie enter and look around interestedly.

                              CHUCK
                    Say -- this is something!

                                        CONTINUED

161     CONTINUED

Ferdie sees the initials on the bed and crosses to it.

>                    FERDIE
>                  (brightening)
>          Look -- "MM."  I'll bet this was
>          the room Moose Matson used when he
>          stayed here.

>                    CHUCK
>          Well -- I hope you're happy now.

>                    FERDIE
>          Oh sure.  I'm going to like this...

Beside the bed is a heavily embroidered bell cord.
Ferdie takes hold of it.

>                    FERDIE
>                  (continuing)
>          See?  I can ring for my breakfast
>          and everything.

He pulls it and it isn't a bell cord at all, but a draw
string for some drapes directly behind the boys, which
now part to reveal a door.

162     MED. SHOT - CHUCK AND FERDIE - BEFORE DOOR

Ferdie sobers immediately.

>                    FERDIE
>          Oh -- oh.  Let's go.

>                    CHUCK
>          Why?

>                    FERDIE
>                  (pointing)
>          The door.  The door.

>                    CHUCK
>          Certainly it's a door.  Why don't
>          you open it -- see what's inside.

>                    FERDIE
>          Not me.  What do you think I am?

>                    CHUCK
>          I think you're scared.

                                        CONTINUED

162    CONTINUED

                        FERDIE
          Of course I'm scared!

                        CHUCK
          What of -- opening a perfectly
          ordinary door?

                        FERDIE
          Chuck, if you think it's a per-
          fectly ordinary door, you open
          it.  I've seen what happens in
          those movies -- I get around.

                        CHUCK
          What happens in what movies?

                        FERDIE
          Those mystery pictures!  Somebody
          finds a "perfectly ordinary" door,
          just like that, behind a curtain;
          they open it, and zowie -- out falls
          a body, right on its kisser.

                        CHUCK
          So you think there's a body
          behind this door?

                        FERDIE
          I ain't sayin' there is and I ain't
          sayin' there isn't.  I'm only
          sayin', "Let's get out of here."

                        CHUCK
                        (sternly)
          Very well.  Since you're evidently
          determined to be a child about
          this, I'll open the door.

          He approaches the closet door, Ferdie inches toward the
          hall.


163    LOW ANGLE - CLOSET DOOR

          Chuck jerks the door open.  The sole occupant of the
          closet is a rather dusty looking hanger.


164    MED. SHOT - CHUCK AND FERDIE

          Ferdie looks sheepish.

                                        CONTINUED

164     CONTINUED

                        CHUCK
              As I suspected -- a perfectly
              ordinary closet.

                        FERDIE
                    (hanging his head)
              I'm ashamed of myself.

                        CHUCK
              You should be!

And he punctuates his anger by slamming the door.


165     MED. SHOT - CHUCK AND FERDIE - SECTION OF DRAPES IN B.G.
        LOW ANGLE

        Chuck is on one side of the screen, Ferdie on the other.
        The slam of the door billows the drapes and shakes loose
        a body which has been propped behind them, but which now
        keels over onto the floor -- into CAMERA -- in classic
        style. The body belongs to Mr. Smith and is properly
        bound and gagged.


166     LOW ANGLE - FERDIE

        He looks down at the body and proceeds to faint himself,
        also falling into camera.


167     MED. GROUP SHOT

        Chuck picks Ferdie up in his arms and staggers with him
        from the room. As he goes out the door, he cracks
        Ferdie's head against the door jamb.

                        CHUCK
                    (yelling as he goes)
              Oh, Doc! Doc! Help!


168     INT. UPPER HALL

        Doors burst open down the hall, as Doc, Norma and Daisy
        rush out. Chuck carrying Ferdie, runs out of Moose's
room
        and starts toward them.


169     MED. GROUP SHOT

        as they converge

                                        CONTINUED:

169    CONTINUED

                        NORMA
        What is it?

                        CHUCK
        It's murder!

                        DAISY
                    (indicating Ferdie)
        Cutie?  Oh.....!

She faints.  Chuck drops Ferdie and catches Daisy just
in time.  The Doc starts to kneel down to examine
Ferdie.

                        CHUCK
            No -- no.  He's all right.
                    (indicating
                    Moose's room)
            It's in there.

                        DOC
        Smith?

                        CHUCK
        Yeah.

Doc and Norma start down the hall, CAMERA RETREATING
ahead of them.  At the door to Moose's room, they stop.

                        DOC
            Perhaps I'd better go in alone.

                        NORMA
        I'm not afraid.

                        DOC
        Let me feel your pulse.

He measures her pulse rate briefly.

                        DOC
        Normal.....You'd make a good nurse.

                        NORMA
        Why, thanks, Doctor.

                        DOC
                    (brusquely)
            In fact, you might as well start
            being one right now.  Go back and
            take care of Miss Brewster.
                    (he points sternly
                    down the hall)

                                    CONTINUED

169        CONTINUED - 2

                              NORMA
                            (meekly)
                        Yes, Doctor.

She flashes him a brief, appreciative smile.  Doc enters
Moose's room.


170        INT. MOOSE'S ROOM - MED. SHOT--- CORPSE

Doc enters scene and kneels beside the corpse.  He rolls
it over and is immediately attracted by some marks on
the neck.


171        INT. UPPER FLOOR HALL - NORMA, DAISY, CHUCK AND FERDIE

Norma is rubbing Daisy's neck vigorously.  Chuck is
slapping Ferdie's face.  Daisy comes to and sees this.

                              DAISY
                        (angrily to Chuck)
                Stop slapping him, you big bully!

                              FERDIE
                        (opening his eyes
                         abruptly, to Daisy)
                You stay out of this.

He holds his face to Chuck, seemingly because he likes to
be slapped.  Chuck regards him disgustedly.

                              CHUCK
                        Get up.

Ferdie starts to get to his feet.


172        MED. GROUP SHOT

Behind them, Doc comes out of Moose's room.  They go
towards him.
                              NORMA
                            (tensely)
                        What happened?

                              DOC
                            (gravely)
                        He was strangled.

As Norma and Daisy gasp, on SOUND TRACK there is heavy
POUNDING on the downstairs front door.  All turn and look
in the general direction of the stairs.

173        EXT. FRONT DOOR - CLOSE SHOT - HAIRY HAND

        as it pounds on the panel.  It looks like the same hand
        which so efficiently strangled Smith.

174     LONG SHOT - INT. DINING ROOM - SHOOTING TOWARD STAIRCASE

on SOUND TRACK the pounding on the door continues
insis-tently.  The group come running down the stairs
and CAMERA
PANS THEM to front door.


175     MED. SHOT - GROUP - AT FRONT DOOR

                         DOC
                    (calling out)
               Who is it?

                         FIRST DETECTIVE'S VOICE
               The police - open this door.

Doc quickly opens the door and two husky plainclothes
detectives (or so they seem) enter.

                         DOC
               Are we ever glad to see you!

                         SECOND DETECTIVE
                    (flashing his heavy spot-
                    light around from one
                    place to the other)
               Oh yeah?  What goes on around here?
               Trespassers, huh?

                         FERDIE
               Oh, no -- we own this place.

                         CHUCK
               We inherited it from Moose Matson.

                         FIRST DETECTIVE
               Are you relatives of his?

                         CHUCK
               No.  But we were very close to him
               at the time of his death.

                         DOC
                    (impatiently)
               Officer, we can discuss those social
               details later.  At the moment there's
               the body of a murdered man upstairs.

                         SECOND DETECTIVE
                    (he of the hairy hands)
               How do you know it's murder?

                         DOC
               A trauma of the lower trachea causing
               embolism of the bronchi can only be
               caused by strangulation.

                         FERDIE
               Not only that - he's dead.          CONTINUED

175     CONTINUED

                              FIRST DETECTIVE
                    A doctor, huh?  Okay, Doc, where
                    is this body?

                                   DOC
                    Upstairs.

        All start toward the staircase.

                                                    WIPE TO:


176     INT. MOOSE'S BEDROOM - MED SHOT - DOOR

        The group enter, led by Doc.  He stops at the doorway
        abruptly and looks puzzled.

177     REVERSE ANGLE - OVER DOC'S SHOULDER

        The body of Smith is gone.

178     MED. GROUP SHOT

        as they sift into the room.

                                   DOC
                              (looking around)
                    Gone!

                                 FERDIE
                              (with sudden idea)
                    I know!

        CAMERA PANS HIM to the closet door. He opens it a
        little, then slams it hard and holds out his hands to
        the neighboring drapes, fully expecting to catch Smith's
        body when it falls out.  He looks disappointed when
        nothing happens.

179     MED. GROUP SHOT

                                 CHUCK
                    He was right there on the floor.

                                   DOC
                    He's disappeared.

180     CLOSE SHOT - FIRST DETECTIVE

        He nods sagely and speaks in a voice that carries
        Mysterioso overtones.

                              FIRST DETECTIVE
                    He always disappears.

181      MED. SHOT - GROUP - GATHERED AROUND DETECTIVE

                          NORMA
                       (frowning)
          Who?

                          FIRST DETECTIVE
          A dapper looking guy, with a
          flower in his buttonhole, smooth
          olive skin...

                          CHUCK
                       (interrupting)
          That's Smith.  What about him?

                          FIRST DETECTIVE
          He's been dead for fifteen years.

                          DAISY
          What?

                          FIRST DETECTIVE
                       (continuing)
          He was killed in one of Moose
          Matson's gang fights -- strangled
          to death in the cellar.  Ever since
          then he keeps coming back, luring
          people to this place and acting the
          death out all over again.

                          NORMA
          Ridiculous!  I rode beside the
          man for hours.

                          FIRST DETECTIVE
          That's what they all say.
                       (in a monotonous
                        sing-song voice)
          But he keeps getting murdered --
          and he keeps coming back.--

                          FERDIE
                       (in the same
                        sing-song voice)
          And if he keeps coming back, I'll
          Keep going away.

                          DOC
                       (to detectives)
          I'm surprised at you -- officers
          of the law, prattling an Old Wives'
          Tale.  Is that all you intend to do?

                                          CONTINUED

181     CONTINUED

                              SECOND DETECTIVE
                    Oh, no -- we'll investigate.


                              FIRST DETECTIVE
                         (droning)
                    We always investigate.

                              DOC
                    Well, he was down in the cellar
                    just before he disappeared.  I'll
                    show you.


He turns toward the door, but the First Detective puts
a restraining hand on his arm.

                              FIRST DETECTIVE
                    We know our way around.
                         (to group
                          in general)
                    But if you folks take our advice,
                    you'll get out of here right now.
                    Sometimes he likes company on his
                    return trip...

                              FERDIE
                    This is one time he's going to be
                    lonely!

The two detectives exit.



182     MED. SHOT - GROUP

        as they look after the detectives.

                              DOC
                    Fine detectives.  They acted
                    as though they were trying to
                    scare us out of the house.

                              DAISY
                         (in a hoarse
                          whisper)
                    Dead fifteen years -- we never
                    did a play like that.

                              NORMA
                    Forget it.

                                        CONTINUED

182      CONTINUED

                          DAISY
            I can't.  Let's not go to bed.
            Let's sit up all night and play
            games or something.

                          FERDIE
            Yeah -- let's play "Ghosts."
                     (as he realizes
                      what he has said)
            No!

                          DOC
            If we stay up, we'll just let
            this thing get on our nerves.
            The best thing is to go back
            to bed

                          CHUCK
            The Doc's right.  The police are
            going to handle everything from
            here on.

                          DAISY
                     (to Doc)
            Are you going to bed?

                          DOC
            Yes - as soon as I have my glass
            of warm milk.  A glass of warm
            milk before retiring is an excel-
            lent sleep inducer.
                     (to Norma)
            Can I bring you some?

                          NORMA
                     (with hidden
                      amusement)
            No, thanks.

                          DOC
                     (to group
                      in general)
            Well -- pleasant dreams.

            He gives them just enough of a blank stare so that the
            audience suspects that perhaps he is not all he seems
            to be himself.  Then he exits.  Ferdie looks around.

                          FERDIE
            Chuck - we don't want to sleep
            in this room, do we?

                          CHUCK
            You're not afraid, are you?  That's
            silly.

                                                   CONTINUED

182     CONTINUED - 2

                         FERDIE
              If it's silly, all right -- we'll
              sleep here.  But if you see a pair
              of pants flying through the air,
              don't stop them -- I'll be in 'em.

                         CHUCK
                     (getting a little
                      frightened)
              Maybe we'd better find something better.

They start to exit.

183     INT. BAR ROOM

The detectives enter and hurry behind the bar.  One of
them grabs hold of a whiskey bottle that is on one of
the shelves by the mirror.

184     INSERT - BOTTLE

It is really a lever, and, as the detective's hand pulls
it, it sets in motion some hidden mechanism.

185     HIGH SET-UP - REAR OF BAR

The CAMERA is SHOOTING over the shoulder of the
detective who pulls the lever.  The flooring behind the
bar lowers into the cellar beneath, in the same manor
that a first floor fire escape might lower.  The
duckboards turn as the section sinks, forming stairs.

186     INT. CELLAR

The two men come down the stairs.  One crosses to a
barred window and signals with his powerful flashlight,
turning it on and off.  The other drags over a box and
takes out a deck of cards.

                         FIRST DETECTIVE
                     (looking up
                      at ceiling)
              I hope them guys have pleasant
              dreams...

                                          DISSOLVE TO:

187     INT. NEW BEDROOM DOOR - MED. SHOT - CHUCK AND FERDIE

They enter, look around.

                         CHUCK
              This will do us.
                                          CONTINUED

187     CONTINUED

CAMERA RETREATS AHEAD of them, then PANS, as Chuck
crosses to another door.  When he opens it, we can see,
beyond, a bathroom, with another door in the far wall.

                        CHUCK
              Well.  A private bath.

He crosses to the other door and opens it.

188     INT. ANOTHER BEDROOM

This room is the identical mirror to the first bedroom -
the same furniture, but with the arrangement reversed.
Chuck stands in the door to the bathroom.

                        CHUCK
                  (over his shoulder
                   to Ferdie)
              Say, this is fine.  We can have
              separate rooms.

Ferdie enters SCENE and looks at the second bedroom over
Chuck's shoulder.

                        FERDIE
              You mean I'm going to sleep in here
              all alone?

                        CHUCK
              I'll be right next door.  Now go to
              bed.
                  (he turns to go)

                        FERDIE
              Chuck!

                        CHUCK
                  (turning back)
              Yes?

                        FERDIE
              Aren't you gonna come in and hear
              me say my prayers?

                        CHUCK
              You call me when you've washed
              your hands and face.

Chuck exits, leaving Ferdie alone.

189     MED. SHOT - FERDIE

He sets his candle on a small table.  He takes off his
tie and puts it on the dresser.  Beside the door to the
bathroom is a hat rack.  Ferdie now removes his coat and
hangs it on one of the hooks on the hat rack. He enters
the bathroom closing the door behind him.

190     INSERT - HAT RACK

Under the weight of Ferdie's coat, the hook depresses
slowly downwards, thereby setting off a secret
mechanism.

191     INT. BEDROOM - FULL SHOT

In shadowy foreground at one side of the screen is the
hat rack.  Beyond this, the bedroom is undergoing a
complete metamorphosis.  The chandelier lowers from the
ceiling to make a roulette wheel.  The bed disappears
into the wall, pivoting into view a crap table.  The
bureau turns into a bird cage outfit.  From a secret
panel in the wall springs a faro wheel.  (In the old
days, in case of a sudden raid by the cops, the place
could be turned into the innocent bedroom it was
originally.)

192     INT. BATHROOM

Ferdie takes a water pitcher from a shelf and crosses to
the bathroom window.  Outside, a steady stream of water
spills from a rain spout.  Ferdie opens the window and
quickly fills the pitcher from the spout.  Closing the
window, he crosses to the basin, which he now fills with
rain water.

193     CLOSE SHOT - FERDIE

He washes his face, humming contentedly to himself. He
dries himself with his handkerchief, turns jauntily to
the bedroom.

194     INT. BEDROOM - MED. SHOT - DOOR

as Ferdie enters.  He does a double take, ducks back
into the bathroom.

195     INT. BATHROOM - MED. SHOT - FERDIE

Going quickly to the wash basin, he douses more water
in his face, rubs his eyes hard, and returns for another
look.

196     INT. BEDROOM - FULL SHOT

Ferdie enters, looks around in complete bewilderment.
He even forces himself to the roulette table, which he
touches to make sure that it's real.

                          FERDIE
                        (convinced)
                    Ch-Ch-Chuck....!

He breaks and runs for the bathroom door.  As he passes
the hatrack, he grabs his coat and takes it along with
him, slamming the bathroom door behind him.

197     INSERT - HATRACK HOOK

Relieved of the weight of the coat, the hook returns to
its natural position.

198     REVERSE ANGLE - INT. BEDROOM

with the shadowy hook in f.g.  The room promptly starts
to return to its original condition.

199     INT. CHUCK'S BEDROOM

Ferdie rushes in.

                        FERDIE
                Chuck -- Chuck!  Am I awake
                or am I dreaming?

                        CHUCK
                You're awake, of course.

                        FERDIE
                Yeah, but couldn't I be dreaming
                that you're saying that I'm awake?

                        CHUCK
                What's the matter with you?

                        FERDIE
                        (excitedly)
                My room -- it's turned into a
                gambling joint -- roulette table,
                dice board, everything....

Still chattering excitedly, he drags the skeptical Chuck
toward the bathroom door.

200     INT. FERDIE'S BEDROOM

The furniture is just returning to its normal place.
Ferdie drags Chuck into the room.

201     TWO SHOT - CHUCK AND FERDIE

Ferdie blinks, bewildered.  Chuck regards him sourly.

                        FERDIE
                        (with righteous
                         indignation)
                There was a roulette table -
                right there.  If I'm dreaming, I
                dreamt it.  But if I'm awake, I
                saw it.

                                        CONTINUED

201     CONTINUED

                              CHUCK
                    Ferdie, your imagination is running
                    away with you again.

                              FERDIE
                    I couldn't imagine a thing like
                    that, Chuck.  I'm not that clever.

                              CHUCK
                         (with heavy sarcasm)
                    All right, all right, then -- the room
                    is full of roulette tables.  I like to
                    sleep on roulette tables.
                         (touching the mattress)
                    Nice, soft roulette tables.

                              FERDIE
                    That was the dice board.

                              CHUCK
                    Go to bed, Ferdie.  Take my room.
                    I'll sleep in here.

                              FERDIE
                    All right.

        Still bewildered, he goes into Chuck's room.  Chuck
        starts to undress for bed.

202     INT. CHUCK'S ROOM

        Ferdie enters and hangs his coat on the hatrack hook
        In this room.  Then he snaps his fingers as if he
        remembered something, and returns to his own room.

203     INSERT - HATRACK LEVER

        The coat pulls this lever down as well.

204     INT. FERDIE'S ROOM

        Chuck is preparing for bed.  Ferdie enters and crosses
        to the dresser, where he picks up his tie.

                              FERDIE
                    I forgot my tie.

        Chuck is still looking at him with annoyance, so he
        hurries out shamefacedly.

205     INT. CHUCK'S BEDROOM

        Gambling equipment,identical with the kind seen
        previously, is just settling into place.  Ferdie enters.

206     MED. CLOSE SHOT - FERDIE

        He does a 'doe', grabs his coat from the hatrack, and ducks
        out, slamming the door behind him.  Automatically the lever
        returns to its position and the gambling equipment starts to
        disappear.

207        INT. FERDIE'S BEDROOM

Chuck is making up his bed, when Ferdie comes running
into the room.

                    FERDIE
                 (babbling)
          Come on - in your room now --
          It's happened again!

                    CHUCK
          What has happened in my room?

                    FERDIE
          The same thing -- dice, chuckaluck,
          roulette!

                    CHUCK
          Ferdie, stop working yourself into
          one of your frenzies.

                    FERDIE
          What frenzies -- I ain't gonna be
          frenzies with nobody.

Still babbling, Ferdie grabs Chuck and drags him by main
force out of the room.

208        INT. CHUCK'S BEDROOM

By the time the boys enter, the room has returned to
normal.  Ferdie looks, starts to open his mouth to
speak, then gives it up as a bad job and shrugs
hopelessly.

                    CHUCK
          Now stop this foolishness and
          get into bed.
                    (as Ferdie gets
                     into bed)
          Now lay your little headie on the
          pillow - now I'll tuck you in.
                    (fixes cover)
          NOW - you're all ready for beddie-bye.

                    FERDIE
                 (plaintively)
          CHUCK - you didn't kiss me goodnight.

Chuck gives Ferdie a severe glare and exits into his own
room, slamming the door behind him.

209        CLOSE SHOT - FERDIE - IN BED

He is trying to figure the whole thing out.

210      INT. FERDIE'S BEDROOM

When Chuck enters, he sees Ferdie's coat lying on the
floor where the latter dropped it. He picks it up
and returns with it to the other room.

211      INT. CHUCK'S BEDROOM

Chuck enters brusquely. He slaps Ferdie's coat onto
the hat rack and exits, slamming the door. The hat
rack hook depresses.

212      INT. CHUCK'S BEDROOM - FULL SHOT

The room begins to change.

213      CLOSE SHOT - FERDIE - IN BED

He is horrified as the bed begins to raise into the
wall. He jumps out, just in time to keep from being
trapped, ducks around the roulette table that is almost
to the floor and dashes from the room, hollering
hysterically for Chuck. But as he passes the hat rack,
he grabs his coat before exiting.

214      INT. FERDIE'S BEDROOM

Chuck sits on the edge of the bed, just removing his
shoes, when Ferdie rushes in, grabs his partner, and
drags him forcibly into the other bedroom.

215      INT. BATHROOM

as the two men rush from one room to the other.

216      INT. CHUCK'S BEDROOM

with everything back to normal. When Ferdie sees that
he has once again been foiled, his face starts to pucker
up. Tears well in his eyes.

> FERDIE
> No -- no. It can't happen again --
> it can't. What have I ever done to
> deserve this?
>
> CHUCK
> (consolingly)
> Now, Ferdie...

Ferdie lays his head on Chuck's chest.

CONTINUED

216     CONTINUED

                              FERDIE
                            (sobbing)
                    I've tried to do a good deed every
                    day.  I've given old ladies my seat
                    on the streetcar -- I've brushed up,
                    brushed down on my teeth -- I've washed
                    behind my ears --

                              CHUCK
                    Sure -- sure.

                              FERDIE
                    I guess it must be so after all,
                    Chuck, no matter how hard I try.

                              CHUCK
                    What's that?

                              FERDIE
                    I'M A BAD BOY.

                              CHUCK
                    No you're not.

                              FERDIE
                            (inconsolable)
                    Oh, yes I am!  I'm the kind of boy my
                    mother don't want me to associate with.

                              CHUCK
                    Now -- now.  You'll feel better about
                    this after you've had some sleep.  Come
                    on -- we'll find you another room.

He leads the way to the hall door.


217     INT. GIRLS' BEDROOM

        Daisy is in bed.  Norma sits on the edge of the bed with
        her coat still over her slip.

                              NORMA
                            (half to herself)
                    Maybe a glass of warm milk would
                    hit the spot after all.

                              DAISY
                            (her face muffled
                             in the covers)
                    I'm sleepy now.

                                                    CONTINUED

217     CONTINUED

                         NORMA
              I'll see if the Doctor has some
              to spare.

        She exits, carrying a candle.


218     INT. DINING ROOM - MED. SHOT - DOC - AT FIREPLACE

        He is tending his pan of warm milk, which sets over
        The coals.  His eyes fall on the bucket of water and
        he frowns as he remembers its peculiar taste. Taking a
        glass from the table, he tries another sip. He grimaces,
        then tries to analyze the taste on his tongue.
        Intrigued, he carries both water bucket and personal
        medical kit to the table.  He turns his alcohol lamp up
        high, takes out chemical vials and test tubes and sets
        to work analyzing the chemical properties of the water.

        Norma enters SCENE and watches him a moment as he shakes
        a test tube in one hand, changes blue litmus paper to
        red with the other and starts to make staccato notes on
        the back of an envelope.

                         NORMA
              Now don't tell me you make your
              own milk!

                         DOC
                    (not even looking up)
              Huh?

                         NORMA
                    (coming closer)
              What are you doing?

                         DOC
                    (after a long moment
                     during which a vague
                     sound seeps through to
                     his consciousness)
              Huh?

                         NORMA
                    (sarcastically)
              I suppose if I was to tell you the
              house is on fire, you'd say "huh."

                         DOC
                    (pointing with an
                     authoritative snap
                     of his fingers)
              Hand me that blue bottle.

                                              CONTINUED

218        CONTINUED

His eyes, however, never leave his work.  Norma hastens
to do his bidding.  The Doc shakes a couple of grains
from the blue bottle into his experiment.  Then,
suddenly, he sets the bottle down, straightens up and
looks about wildly.

                         DOC
                  (alarmed - as her
                   previous remark
                   sinks in)
          What's on fire?

                         NORMA
                  (calming him)
          Nothing, nothing.
                  (as he relaxes)
          You're the concentratinest man I
          ever met.

                         DOC
                  (returning to his
                   test tubes)
          I'm analyzing this water.

                         NORMA
                  (with a little shake
                   of the head)
          Doctor, Doctor, what makes you tick?
          Here we're surrounded by murder and
          mystery, and you go your same calm,
          unconscious way.

                         DOC
                  (as he works)
          What else is there to do?

                         NORMA
          You might at least worry.

Doc looks away from his work and peers at her.

                         DOC
          Are you nervous?

                         NORMA
                  (pursing her lips)
          Mmm -- I don't know.

                         DOC
          You don't strike me as the nervous
          type.

                         NORMA
          Don't I?

                                            CONTINUED

218     CONTINUED - 2

They are close to each other now.  Their eyes meet for
a long moment.

                         DOC
               I'll be you have perfect 20-20
               Vision, too.

Annoyed at this scientific approach, Norma turns away
and crosses to the fireplace.

                         NORMA
                    (with heavy sarcasm)
               Thanks.

Doc senses that he has hurt her feelings, but doesn't
quite understand why.

                         DOC
                    (following her)
               Well -- haven't you?


219     CLOSE TWO SHOT - NORMA AND DOC - AT FIREPLACE

                         NORMA
                    (pouting at the fire)
               Is it important?
                    (turning to him, as
                    he starts to stutter
                    an explanation)
               Actually, would you prefer a girl
               with healthy eyes to a girl with
               pretty eyes who is still blind as
               a bat?

                         DOC
                    (in a voice that in-
                    dicates he never
                    thought of it that
                    way before)
               No.  I guess not.

                         NORMA
               Of course you wouldn't.
                    (removing his heavy
                    horn-rimmed glasses)
               Look at you.  Without these port-
               holes you probably can't see a thing.
               But it's a vast improvement...
                    (studying his face,
                    which is really quite
                    handsome - in softer tone)
               It really is.

                                        CONTINUED

219    CONTINUED

When their eyes meet this time, the Doc is looking
anything but scientific.

                    DOC
              (a little shyly still)
         Thanks.  I noticed you had beautiful
         eyes the first time I saw you.  I
         just didn't get around to mentioning
         it then.

                    NORMA
         Mention it now.

                    DOC
              (reaching for words)
         Well, they're soft, and limpid, and,
         and like two pools of water...
              (suddenly remembering)
         Water!  I almost forgot!


220    MED. SHOT - NORMA AND DOC

Doc makes a dive for his neglected experiment, but
stumbles over a log and falls flat on his face.  Picking
himself up, he returns to Norma.

                    DOC
         My glasses!

He grabs them from her, crams them over his eyes, and
rushes back to his work.  Norma follows him, thoroughly
annoyed.

                    NORMA
         I suppose your silly experiment
         couldn't wait a while.

                    DOC
              (from the depths of
              his scientific de-
              tachment)
         Huh?

                    NORMA
         Oh "huh" yourself...


She grabs her candle and heads upstairs.  CAMERA HOLDS
on Doc, as he manipulates another phase of his
experiment.

                                   CONTINUED

220     CONTINUED

                              DOC
                    (setting down a test tube)
          There...
                    (removing his glasses as
                    he turns toward where
                    Norma was)
          Yes -- in fact you're the most beautiful
          girl I ever saw....

He realizes she isn't there. He looks around for her,
then puts on his glasses and scans the room.

                              DOC
                    (in blank bewilderment)
          Huh?

                                        DISSOLVE TO:

221     INT. GIRLS' BEDROOM

Daisy is practically asleep, as Norma storms into the
room. She slams the door and plunks down on the edge of
the bed.

                              NORMA
                    (grumbling to herself)
          Rude, inconsiderate...

                              DAISY
                    (half asleep)
          Huh?

                              NORMA
                    (turning on her)
          Don't you start that!

                              DAISY
                    (bewildered)
          I didn't say anything.

                              NORMA
                    (setting down candle
                    and preparing for bed)
          I'll certainly be glad to get going
          tomorrow.

                              DAISY
                    (unhappily)
          It'll mean saying goodbye to Cutie.
                    (to Norma)
          You'll at least have the Doctor.

                              NORMA
                    (as she climbs into bed -
                    scornfully)
          The Doctor -- he doesn't know I'm
          alive...And I'm not sure he is.

She blows out the candle.

222        INT. CELLAR - MED. SHOT - DETECTIVES - BEFORE FURNACE

One of them has fixed his heavy flashlight so that it
hangs from the ceiling, casting a small circle onto the
up-ended box. The first detective is playing solitaire
using this box as a table.  The second detective has
tilted another box against a beam and reclines lazily on
it. The heads of both men are turned away from the
furnace door, which is in b.g.

                    SECOND DETECTIVE
                     (sleepily)
               Heard anything yet?

                    FIRST DETECTIVE
          Nope.

CAMERA TRUCKS IN to furnace door.  Slowly and silently
it opens.  A shadowy figure creeps out.


223        REVERSE ANGLE - OVER SHOULDER OF NEWCOMER

CAMERA TRUCKS WITH HIM as he approaches the unsuspecting
detectives.

                    NEWCOMER
                    (stretching forth his
                     hand and pointing to
                     the table)
               Put the black ten on the red Jack,
               why don'tcha.

224        MED. GROUP SHOT

The two detectives look up casually at the newcomer, who
has been followed by three other men.  Meet these four
seedy looking individuals: ROSIE, SNAKE-EYES, GLUM and HIGH
COLLAR--all former members of Moose's gang.  Incidentally,
also meet IRON DOME and THE STRANGLER, who have hitherto
posed as First and Second Detectives, respectively. The
newcomers shake water from their hats and turn down their
coat collars.  Iron Dome makes the suggested change in
cards.

                    SNAKE EYES
               Never mind that.
                    (nodding toward the
                     upper part of the house)
               Did you scare them out?

                    THE STRANGLER
               Nah-- but you should have heard Iron
               Dome.  He was terrific.

                                        CONTINUED

224     CONTINUED

                          ROSY
              What are we waitin'for?
                    (he reaches for his gun)

                          IRON DOME
                    (restraining him)
              I'm givin' the orders.

                          SNAKE-EYES
              But we gotta work fast.  Lefty and
              some of the boys just broke jail...

                          HIGH COLLAR
              They wouldn't dare come around here.

                          THE STRANGLER
                    (menacingly)
              If they do, they'll get what I gave
              Smitty-- the double-crossin' rat.

                          IRON DOME
              Forget that.  Our job is to find Moose's
              dough before they can start trouble.

                          GLUM
                    (nodding upstairs)
              How, if they didn't believe that ghost
              yarn?

                          IRON DOME
                    (thoughtfully)
              So far we've only told them about
              ghosts... I'll tell you what we'll
              do now...

                                        DISSOLVE TO:

225     INT. UPSTAIRS HALL

        The four gangsters tiptoe down the hall.

226     INT. FERDIE'S BEDROOM

        The little man is almost asleep when there is a loud
        KNOCK on the hall door.

                          FERDIE
                    (sleepily)
              Come in....

        Again there is a KNOCK.  Ferdie climbs out of bed,
        crosses to the door.  Behind him a panel opens in the
        wall, and Glum and High Collar step out.  They follow
        the unsuspecting Ferdie across the room.  The little man
        opens the door and nobody is there.

227    MED. SHOT - EXT. BEDROOM DOOR - HALL

Ferdie looks puzzledly up and down the empty corridor.
Suddenly the door slams closed behind him, bumping him
into the hall.  He turns and tries to open the door
again, but it refuses to budge.  He pushes hard.
Finally, he puts his shoulder to the door and gives a
real heave.  The door opens several inches, then is
obviously pushed closed by some superior force on the
other side.

                          FERDIE
                         (gulping)
              Locked!

He hurries down the hall.

228    FULL SHOT - INT. FERDIE'S BEDROOM

Glum and High Collar have had their shoulders to the
door.  The two men join Snake-Eyes now, searching rapidly
but thoroughly for Moose's hidden bank roll.  They start
to turn the place topsy-turvy.

229    CLOSE SHOT - SNAKE-EYES

He has just finished slitting Ferdie's mattress with a
wicked looking knife.  He now pulls out the stuffing,
scattering it all over the floor, and reaches in to see
if the money could be hidden inside.

230    CLOSE SHOT - GLUM

He pulls out the drawer of a small table and dumps the
contents on the floor.  Then, to make sure there are no
secret compartments, he kicks a hole through the top
and tears off the legs.

231    CLOSE SHOT - HIGH COLLAR

He rips up the carpet in a cloud of dust and looks
beneath it.

232    MED. SHOT - INT. HALL

Chuck is listening to Ferdie skeptically, as the little
man hurries him toward their bedroom door.

                          FERDIE
              It's locked tight, I tell you.

                          CHUCK
              You're sure this isn't one of your
              brain-storms?

They stop before the closed door.

                                              CONTINUED

232        CONTINUED

                              FERDIE
                         (sure of himself
                          this time)
                    Go ahead -- open it.

                              CHUCK
                         (turning the knob)
                    You mean like this?

The door opens with ease.

                              FERDIE
                         (nodding)
                    Yeah.

                         (then realizing
                          what has happened)
                    Hey!

He dashes into the room.

233        MED. FULL SHOT - BEDROOM

The room looks as though it were struck by a cyclone.
Ferdie is dumbfounded.  Chuck looks at his partner
with growing disgust.

                              CHUCK
                    Ferdie -- I'm ashamed of you -
                    absolutely ashamed.

With that he turns on his heels and exits, leaving
Ferdie to stand in the midst of the mess looking around,
bewildered.  Tears in his eyes, he carefully folds his
clothes and throws them away.

234        INT. HALL

Chuck crosses the corridor and enters another bedroom.
As he closes the door behind him, we see the shadowy
figure of the three gangsters creep toward the girls'
room.

235        MED. SHOT - EXT. DOOR OF GIRLS' ROOM

Snake-Eyes tip-toes to the door and quietly opens it.

236        MED. SHOT - NORMA AND DAISY - IN BED

In b.g. we can see the slowly opening door.

                              DAISY
                         (turning to Norma
                          restlessly)
                    Norma-- are you asleep?

                              NORMA
                    Nope.

                                        CONTINUED

236        CONTINUED

                              DAISY
                    Neither am I.

       The door in b.g. closes again.

237        TWO SHOT - SNAKE-EYES AND GLUM - INT. HALL

                           SNAKE-EYES
                           (whispering)
                    How we gonna get them out of the
                    room?

                              GLUM
                    You remember what Iron Dome said...

       Snake-Eyes nods, then points to a table covered with
       A white dustcloth.  Glum gets the idea and starts to
       remove the cloth.

238        INT. GIRL'S BEDROOM - MED. SHOT

                              DAISY
                           (sitting up in bed)
                    Didn't that warm milk make you
                    sleepy?

                              NORMA
                    I didn't have any.

                              DAISY
                    Maybe we should.

                              NORMA
                    You have some if you want to -
                    not me.

       Daisy gets out of bed and starts to slip into her coat.

                              DAISY
                           (a bit nervous)
                    Er, the Doctor's still down there,
                    isn't he?

                              NORMA
                           (half to herself)
                    His body is.

                              DAISY
                           (gasping)
                    What -- !

                              NORMA
                           (going on)
                    His mind is miles away.

                                        CONTINUED:

238     CONTINUED

                            DAISY
                          (relieved)
              Oh...
                          (as she opens door)
              I'll be right back.

239     INT. HALL - MED. SHOT

        Daisy closes the door to the bedroom and starts for the
        stairs.  Unnoticed in the shadows behind her is the
        white cloth-covered figure of Glum.  The 'Ghost' now
        follows Daisy toward the head of the stairs.

240     TRUCKING SHOT - DAISY & GHOST

        As Daisy walks toward the stairs, she becomes conscious
        of a squeaking sound that keeps time to the rhythm of
        her own footsteps.

241     CLOSE SHOT - GLUM'S FEET

        His big, heavy shoes which stick out from beneath the
        sheet SQUEAK like rusty hinges.

242     CLOSEUP - DAISY

        Her eyes drift from side to side, warily, but she
        refuses to turn her head.

243     MED. SHOT - HEAD OF STAIRS

        Daisy, with the ghost almost breathing down her neck
        now, starts downstairs.  Each step that Daisy takes is
        not only echoed by the squeak, but by the clump of
        Glum's heavy feet.  Worried now, Daisy looks down at her
        feet, wiggles her toes to see whether her shoes are
        squeaking, then carefully takes the next two steps on
        tiptoe.  However, the clump-squeak continues.  Frowning,
        Daisy takes two more steps, starts to take another -
        then, with her foot still in the air, stops suddenly.
        Glum, right behind her, takes the third step by himself.
        Daisy hurries down to the landing, as rapidly as she
        can go and again stops.  Glum follows as best he can,
        but this time he is all out of step and all out of
        rhythm.

244     MED. SHOT - LANDING

        Daisy's suspicions are pretty well confirmed, but she
        de-cides to make one more test.  She breaks into a
        little time step, leaving the final two beats
        unfinished.  Glum does it for her, with two solid
        clumps.  Slowly, Daisy turns around and looks.

245     CLOSEUP - "GHOST"

        from Daisy's ANGLE.

246     CLOSEUP - DAISY

        When she sees the "Ghost", she throws back her head and
        lets out that scream that has been dying in her throat
        all evening.  It is all the screams of the "Crimes of
        Passion" program rolled into one.  As it goes on, it
        even builds in intensity like a siren.  The shriek con-
        tinues over the following shots, all of which are fast
        3-6 foot cuts.

247     CLOSE SHOT - "GHOST"

        He takes to his heels, dashing upstairs.

248     INT. GIRLS' BEDROOM - CLOSE SHOT - NORMA

        She sits up into CAMERA, wide-eyed,

249     CLOSE SHOT - CHUCK - IN BED

250     INT. CELLAR - CLOSE SHOT - ROSY

        He looks up over his shoulder toward the sound,
        horrified, then holds his ears.

251     CLOSE SHOT - OWL - IN ATTIC

        Frightened, it flies out into the rain through a broken
        window.

252     CLOSE SHOT - DOC

        Completely unconscious of the sound, he carefully pours
        the contents of one test tube into another.

253     INT. FERDIE'S ROOM - CLOSE SHOT - FERDIE

        He is sitting up in bed, quivering.  CAMERA RETREATS to
        MED. SHOT - BED - as Glum, still wearing his sheet,
        dashes in from the hall and dives in under the covers.
        Costello takes this, then leaps out the other side and
        runs wildly to the door.

254     MED. SHOT - LANDING

Daisy is slowly running out of breath.  Her scream con-
cludes with a gasp.


255     CLOSE SHOT - DOC

                         DOC
                    (looking up from
                     his chemicals)
                What was that?


256     MED. SHOT - LANDING

                         CHUCK
                    (dashing into
                     scene, followed
                     by Norma)
                What happened?

        A ghost!
                         DAISY

                         NORMA
        A ghost?

                         DAISY
                    (illustrating)
        With fangs.

                         DOC
                    (coming into scene
                     - skeptically)
        Again?

                         FERDIE'S VOICE
                    (from stairway)
                He's in my room -- he's in my bed!
                    (entering shot)
                He pulled the covers over his head.

All rush toward his bedroom.

                                        WIPE TO:

257     INT. FERDIE'S ROOM

The group enters and looks warily toward the bed.  The
Doc crosses to it and throws back the blankets,
revealing the white cloth left by Glum.

                         DOC
        Hmmmmm....
                    (holding up the cloth)
                Here's your ghost.

                                        CONTINUED

257     CONTINUED

                              FERDIE
                    (touching it gingerly)
              There was more to him than that.

Doc lifts the sheet and puts it on a chair, disclosing
coat.

                              FERDIE
              Here, Doc, you forgot to put his
              coat on him.

                              NORMA
                    (looking suspiciously
                      at Ferdie)
              This couldn't by any chance be a
              joke, could it?

                              CHUCK
                    (sternly)
              Yes, Ferdie -- what's the big idea?
              It seems that everything happens
              to you around here.

                              FERDIE
              Everything except what happened
              to Smitty.

                              DAISY
                    (to others)
              That's right.  Somebody's trying
              to get us out of this house.

                              DOC
              Where's those detectives anyway?
              If that scream didn't bring them...

                              DAISY
                    (swallowing)
              Maybe they're...

                              DOC
              You girls get dressed and ready
              to leave.  We'll search for the
              officers and get them to take us
              into town right now.

As the group files into the hallway, Daisy and Ferdie
stop at the doorway.  Daisy is starting to eat an apple.

                              FERDIE
              Now that we're all going away,
              I guess I'll never see you again.

                                        CONTINUED

257        CONTINUED - 2

                         DAISY
              No, I guess not.

                         FERDIE
              I just met you today - but...

                         DAISY
              What is it you want?

                         FERDIE
              You wouldn't think I was fresh
              if I...

                         DAISY
              Of course not.
                         (coyly)
              What do you want?

                         FERDIE
              I never asked a girl before --

                         DAISY
              Come on, Cutie -- tell Daisy.

                         FERDIE
              I'm ashamed.  Maybe you'll get
              mad at me.

                         DAISY
              No, I won't.
                         (puckering lips)
              What does Cutie want?

                         FERDIE
              Could I have a bite of your apple?

                                             WIPE TO:


258        INT. DINING ROOM

           The table with the doctor's phials and test tubes is
           In the f.g.  The Doc, Chuck and Ferdie approach from the
           steps.

                         DOC
              Too bad I can't finish this ex-
              periment.  I'm really onto something.

                         CHUCK
              We'd better split up.  Ferdie, you
              stay here and wait for the girls.

                         FERDIE
                         (Unhappily)
              Alone?

                                             CONTINUED

258     CONTINUED

                         CHUCK
                      (continuing)
          Doc and I will search the cellar
          and the grounds.
                      (taking a folder
                       from his pocket -
                       handing it to Ferdie)
          And while you're waiting, study this
          map.  Try and figure out the nearest
          place we can get to.

Doc exits toward kitchen.

                         FERDIE
          S-sposin' that ghost shows up again.

                         CHUCK
          That ghost was only a rumor.

                         FERDIE
          I don't care if he was the landlord.

                         CHUCK
          Stop worrying!
                      (takes two candles
                       in holders, and places
                       them on table)
          Here - sit down and study the map.
          And if you want me, call me.

                         FERDIE
          Okay -- I'll call you.

Chuck starts to exit.

                         FERDIE
          Oh, Chuck!

                         CHUCK
                      (running back
                       to table)
          What's the matter?

                         FERDIE
          Come on -- what kept you?

                         CHUCK
          What's wrong with you?  When you
          called I came back just like that.
                      (snaps his fingers)

                         FERDIE
          Yeah - well, if you can get here in
          between that -
                      (snaps fingers)
          GET HERE!
                                           CONTINUED

258     CONTINUED - 2

                        CHUCK
            Give me a chance.  As soon as
            you call, I'll be here.

He exits, closing the door.

                        FERDIE
            Now I'm all alone.
                    (softly)
            Oh, Chuck - oh, Chuck.
                    (gets louder)
            Oh, Chuck - Oh, Chuck - OH, CHUCK!

This is kept up until Chuck comes in and continues until
Ferdie sees him.

                        FERDIE
            Where've you been?  Thirty-four
            times I called "Oh, Chuck".

                        CHUCK
            You're crazy.  I was in here on the
            first one.

                        FERDIE
            From now on when I call you, don't
            wait for "Oh, Chuck".

                        CHUCK
            No!  Get in here on the "Oh".

Daisy comes downstairs into SCENE.

                        DAISY
            Are you boys ready to leave?

                        FERDIE
            I was ready to leave when he put
            the key in the door to get in.

                        CHUCK
                    (to Daisy)
            Daisy, do me a favor.  Keep him
            company while Doc and I look for
            the officers.

Chuck exits and Daisy sits down beside Ferdie.

                                        CONTINUED

258     CONTINUED - 3

                        FERDIE
                     (very shaky)
          I gotta read this map to find out
          how we get out of here.  Are you
          scared?

                        DAISY
                     (shakily)
          Nooooo.

                        FERDIE
          Me neither. I would be silly if
          I was scared of a ghost.
                     (ghostly wail)
          Boy -- am I silly?!

                        DAISY
          Cutie?

                        FERDIE
          What?

                        DAISY
          You and I are all alone, aren't we?

                        FERDIE
          I hope so.
                     (studying map)
          Let's see.  I could get out of here
          on Route number 66, or I could take
          Route number 101...

                        DAISY
          Why don't you take number 158?

                        FERDIE
          If I had number 158, I wouldn't
          be here.
                     (starts reading map)
          I could take this road...

Candle moves across the table - from CAMERA left to
CAMERA right.

                        FERDIE
                     (trying to yell)
          Oh, Chuck, -- oh Chuck - etc. ad lib.


258-A   INT. CELLAR - CLOSEUP PAIR OF HAIRY HANDS - NIGHT

        The hands are pulling two strings.

258-B     INT. DINING ROOM - DAISY AND FERDIE

                    FERDIE
                 (still trying
                  to say --)
Oh, Chuck -- etc.

                    CHUCK
                 (rushes in)
What's the matter?
                 (very excited)
What's the matter?

                    FERDIE
                 (unable to speak -
                  tries to get words out)
The candle went like this...
                 (indicates)

                    CHUCK
Oh, that's only your imagination.
                 (to Daisy)
Did you see the candle go across
the table?

                    DAISY
NO!

                    FERDIE
Where were you looking?

                    DAISY
                 (indicating)
Over there.

                    FERDIE
What are you looking over there for?
KEEP YOUR EYES ON THIS CANDLE.  That's
the son of a gun that was doing all
the movin'.

                    DAISY
Okay!  I'll watch it.

                    CHUCK
                 (to Ferdie)
Now stop this nonsense and find a
road to get us out of here.

Chuck exits through door and Ferdie starts to read the
map.  Daisy is looking intently at the candle.

                    FERDIE
                 (looking at Daisy)
That's it - keep your eye on that
candle.
                 (Ferdie ad libs
                  while reading map)
                                 CONTINUED

258-B     CONTINUED

The candle to the right of CAMERA starts going up and
down.  Ferdie sees candle and vainly tries to speak
to call Daisy's attention.  Daisy continues to keep her
eyes glued to the other candle.

                    FERDIE
                (trying very hard
                 to yell)
          Oh, Chuck --
                (then he finally
                 gets the words out)
          OH, CHUCK!!!

                    CHUCK
                (rushing in)
          Now what's wrong?

                    FERDIE
                (breathlessly)
          The candle - up and down.

                    CHUCK
          Wait a minute.  Daisy, did you see
          that candle go up and down?

                    DAISY
          NO!

                    FERDIE
                (to Daisy)
          Where were you looking?

                    DAISY
          At this candle.

                    FERDIE
          What are you looking there for?

                    DAISY
          You told me to.

                    FERDIE
          Well - don't believe me - I'm a
          liar.

                    CHUCK
          Ferdie, you're wasting my time.

He leaves again.

                    FERDIE
                (to Daisy)
          Look - keep one eye on that candle
          over there - keep one eye on this
          candle over here - and with the
          other one, WATCH ME.

                                        CONTINUED

258-B    CONTINUED - 2

> DAISY
> All right!

Daisy starts looking from one candle to the other.
Ferdie watches and starts to do the same thing.

> FERDIE
> All right, all right, that's enough,
> all right, ALL RIGHT.

Ferdie places Daisy's head so she can watch both
candles, then starts to study map.  Daisy is watching
candles as a door opens and the ghost appears behind
Ferdie.

> DAISY
> (shivering)
> It's getting drafty in here.
> (her back is
> partly to Ferdie)
> Wouldn't it be nice to have a
> pair of arms to keep you warm?

By this time the ghost has come behind Ferdie and
Placed its  arms around him.

> FERDIE
> (thinking its Daisy,
> pushes the arms away)
> Lady - this is no time for fol-de-rol.

> DAISY
> Imagine a pair of arms holding you
> tight - and squeezing you!

The ghost's arms are again around Ferdie.

> FERDIE
> (still thinking
> it's Daisy)
> Stop putting your arms around me.
> When I have to get out of here,
> I don't wanta drag no woman with me.

> DAISY
> (getting indignant)
> I didn't put my arms around you.

> FERDIE
> Well, don't do it -
> (does a take)
> You didn't put your arms around me?

> DAISY
> No!

CONTINUED

258-B     CONTINUED - 3

                          FERDIE
              Something tells me there's somebody
              else in this room besides you and me.
              By and by its only gonna be you,
              'cause I'm gettin' out of here.

The ghost comes behind Ferdie, and a pair of hairy arms
reach out and put out both candles, with a buck dance
break.  In the dark there is a terrific struggle.


259       INT. KITCHEN - MED. SHOT - DOOR TO CELLAR STAIRCASE

Doc comes up from the cellar as Chuck returns from
outside.  They start toward dining room.

                          DOC
              Any luck?

                          CHUCK
              Not even a footprint.


260       INT. DINING ROOM - (STILL DARK)

The struggle is still on.

                          FERDIE
              I got you, you old ghost you, and
              I'm gonna lift up that sheet and find
              out who you are.

Doc and Chuck come in from the kitchen with the flashlight just as Daisy is indignantly straightening her
dress.  She turns and gives Ferdie a terrific slap in
the face.

                          DOC
              I wish I could figure out why
              someone is so anxious to keep
              people away from this tavern.

                          CHUCK
              Maybe it's because of Moose's
              bank roll.

                          DOC
              What bank roll?

                          CHUCK
              Moose is supposed to have buried
              his cash.

                                        CONTINUED

                          DAISY
          Around this tavern?

                          CHUCK
          Nobody knows.  All Moose would
          ever say was that he kept the money
          in his head.

                          FERDIE
                     (pointing to moose's
                      head over fireplace)
          You mean up there?

                          CHUCK
                     (with a pained
                      expression)
          Ferdie --

                          FERDIE
                     (defensively)
          That's a moose, ain't it?

                          CHUCK
                     (sarcastically)
          No.  It's a horse with a hat rack
          on its head.

                          DOC
                     (looking toward
                      staircase)
          I'm going to see if Norma is all
          right.

He exits from SCENE.

261    THREE SHOT - CHUCK, FERDIE AND DAISY

                         CHUCK
                    (continuing -
                      to Ferdie)
           I'm afraid you're just dumb.

                         FERDIE
           Who's dumb?  Didn't you say the
           money was in a moose's head?

                         CHUCK
           No.  When I say Moose kept the
           money in his head, I'm using a
           figure of speech.  Don't you know
           what a figure of speech is?

                         FERDIE
           Certainly --
                    (giving one)
           "A lot of water has gone under
           the bridge."

                         CHUCK
           Under what bridge?

                         FERDIE
           How do I know what bridge?

                         CHUCK
           Then how do you know there's water
           under it?

                         FERDIE
           There's got to be water under it.
           The boats have to go up and down!

                         CHUCK
           Why do they have to go up and down?
           Why can't they go across?

                         FERDIE
           All right, all right -- let them go
           across.

                         CHUCK
           And what happens to the boats that
           want to go up and down?

                         FERDIE
           They can't get past the bridge!
                    (to Daisy)
           I'm a sucker to get into these
           arguments.

                         CHUCK
           Then why do you start them?

                                   CONTINUED

261      CONTINUED

> FERDIE
> Who started it?  You said I didn't
> know what a figure of speech was,
> and I was dumb enough to try to
> explain.
> (to Daisy)
> Boy, talking to him is like pour-
> ing water on a duck's back.

> CHUCK
> That's fine!  Now you want to pour
> water on a duck's back.  What did
> the duck ever do to you?

> FERDIE
> Who's pouring water on a duck's
> back?  That's another expression...
> (to Daisy)
> - like "robbing Peter to pay
> Paul."

262      CLOSEUP - DAISY

As she listens to the boys argue, her head goes back and
forth as though she were a spectator at a tennis match.

> CHUCK'S VOICE
> Now you're going around robbing
> people.

> FERDIE'S VOICE
> Who's robbing people?  I don't even
> know Peter and Paul!

> CHUCK'S VOICE
> That makes no difference.  You've
> got no right to rob them.

> FERDIE'S VOICE
> I didn't rob anybody.

262A     MED. GROUP SHOT - FERDIE

> FERDIE
> Look -- robbing Peter to pay Paul
> is like I take money from one
> pocket and put it in another.

> CHUCK
> Soooo -- you're a pickpocket!
> That's the last straw.

> FERDIE
> (to Daisy)
> That's the straw that broke the
> camel's back.

CONTINUED

262A     CONTINUED

                         CHUCK
          And now you want to break camels'
          backs.  First you pour water on a
          duck, now you pick on a poor camel.
                    (as Ferdie
                     starts to answer)
          Wait a minute... Let me get in a
          word or two --
                    (as Ferdie
                     subsides)
          Don't just stand there -- say
          something!

Ferdie burns.


263      INT. GIRLS' BEDROOM

Norma is cutting wads of paper and fitting them into her
shoes to keep them dry as Doc enters.

                         DOC
          Are you ready?

                         NORMA
                    (thru set lips)
          In a moment.
                    (sarcastically)
          I'm sorry if I've kept you waiting.

                         DOC
          Oh, that's all right...
                    (then catching
                     the tone in
                     her voice)
          Say -- you're mad at me.

                         NORMA
          No.

                         DOC
          Yes you are.

                         NORMA
          That's ridiculous.


She half-turns away from him and continues putting paper
in her shoes.  Doc crosses to her and examines her face
carefully.

                                        CONTINUED

263     CONTINUED

                         DOC
            But you have all the symptoms:
            flat tone of voice, a little ridge
            here where the jaw muscles swell -
                         (he reaches out
                          a finger to
                          touch her cheek,
                          but she pulls her
                          head away)
            The only question is why are you
            mad?

Norma stops her work and looks up at Doc.

                         NORMA
                         (in a tired
                          voice)
            Let's not go into that, Doctor.


                         DOC
            If you won't tell me, I'll have
            to work it out.

                         NORMA
            You go right ahead.

She returns to her shoes.


                         DOC
            Very well...
                         (frowning)
                          thoughtfully)
            What we need here is the empiric
            approach.

                         NORMA
                         (intrigued in
                          spite of herself)
            The what?

                         DOC
            Empiric:  knowledge founded on
            direct experience.  For example --
                         (he sits on the
                          edge of the bed
                          and leans forward,
                          thinking out loud
                          with the utmost
                          seriousness)
            You could only be angry with me for
            what I have been, for what I am,
            or for what I will be... Since you
            never saw me before and have no
            knowledge of my future, we eliminate
            "was" and "will" --

                                    CONTINUED

263    CONTINUED - 2

Norma has stopped working on her shoes and is watching
him, undecided how to take it, trying still to be angry
but beginning to be a little amused -- and certainly
interested.  Doc rises and starts  to pace the floor,
warming to his subject.

                         DOC
              Therefore you are angry at what I
              am... And what am I?... Divide me
              into two categories --
                         (passing his hand
                          across his throat)
              Physical and mental.
                         (he crosses to a
                          full-length mirror,
                          in which he examines
                          himself studiously)
              First the physical.  Tall.  But not
              too tall...
                         (examines his hands
                          and fingernails)
              Reasonably clean, neat --
                         (looking at himself
                          again in the mirror
                          and brushing back a
                          loose lock of hair)
              Hair could be combed better, but
              whenever I take off my glasses, it
              gets mussed up --
                         (brought up short
                          by a disturbing
                          thought)
              Is it something my best friend
              wouldn't tell me?

                         NORMA
              I wish that was all it was, but it
              isn't.

She puts on her other shoe and crosses to the mirror,
where she starts to comb her hair.

                         DOC
              Oh...
                         (analyzing again)
              It becomes increasingly apparent
              that the cause is mental.

                         NORMA
              You're getting hot.

                         DOC
              Mental, mental -- what are my
              mental deficiencies? - from
              your point of view, of course.

                                   CONTINUED

263        CONTINUED - 3

                              NORMA
               Of course.

                               DOC
                          (pacing again)
               We hardly spoke in the car... We
               seemed to get along quite well here
               at first, but then I got interested
               in that water and after that we --
                          (suddenly the
                           light dawns)
               I got interested in the water and
               I ignored you.
                          (with happy
                           conviction)
               You're mad at me because you like
               me!

                              NORMA
                          (too proud to admit
                           it - pretending it's
                           utterly ridiculous)
               Oh!  Now after all...

She starts to put on her coat.  Doc crosses to her and
turns her to him.


264        MED. CLOSE SHOT - DOC AND NORMA

In b.g. a panel slides silently open in the wall.  They
don't notice it.

                               DOC
               But don't you like me a bit?
               Don't you feel a mite safer with
               me around?

Out of the panel a hand comes, holding a wicked-looking
knife.  The arm raises, preparing to plunge the blade
into Norma's back.

                              NORMA
               Doctor -- whenever I have to turn
               to you for protection, I'll --

At this moment, Doc sees the knife.  He whirls Norma out
of the way, throwing her to the floor, grabs the
descending wrist just in time.  A brief scuffle ensues,
in which the Doc twists the knife away from his
assailant.  The mysterious figure, however, manages to
break loose and withdraw into the panel, sliding it
closed after him.  Doc scrapes his finger nails trying
to open the panel, but to no avail. He turns to Norma,
who is just picking herself off the floor.

                                        CONTINUED

264        CONTINUED

                                    DOC
                            (helping her up)
                    Are you all right, darling?

                                  NORMA
                    Yes, dear...
                                (as realization
                                  sinks in)
                    Dear -- you called me 'darling'.

                                    DOC
                            (his arms
                              around her)
                    Darling -- you called me 'dear'.

                                  NORMA
                    Did I?

She tilts her face up to his.

                                    DOC
                    Of course we shouldn't be
                    standing here....

She closes her eyes and purses her lips.

                                    DOC
                    We should find the police and...

Then suddenly he is kissing her.


265        CLOSE SHOT - PANEL

It slides open.


266        CLOSE SHOT - DOC AND NORMA

As they kiss, two knives bury themselves in the wall,
inches from their heads.  They remain completely
oblivious.


267        CLOSE SHOT - PANEL

Snake-Eyes, the wielder of the knives, looks out at
The clinching couple.  Remembering perhaps that love
conquers all, he gives up with a fatalistic shrug and
slides the panel closed.

                                            WIPE TO:

268    MED. SHOT - CHUCK, FERDIE AND DAISY - BEFORE FIREPLACE

They sit on the floor, looking exhausted.  The argument
still rages and their voices are tired and hoarse.

                          CHUCK
                    (croaking Ferdie's
                     peccadillos)
          ...Wetting ducks, injuring camels,
          making hay while the sun shines without
          even owning the field, trying to kill
          two birds with one stone, throwing
          tailors out of work by doing your own
          stitching -- what kind of a person are
          you, anyway?

                          FERDIE
                    (hoarsely)
          I ain't gonna talk.  I'm in the
          dog house!

                          CHUCK
          And now you're in the dog house.
          Where's the dog supposed to sleep?
          Who are you to put the dog out while
          you take his nice, warm bed?

                          FERDIE
                    (to Daisy)
          I don't know how I get into these things.

                          DAISY
                    (pointing toward
                     moose head)
          You said the money was up there.

                          FERDIE
          All right!  So the money isn't up there.

                          CHUCK
          How do you know the money isn't up
          there?  Have you looked?

                          FERDIE
                    (controlling his tem-
                     per with difficulty)
          Chuck -- would it make you happier
          if I was to climb up and prove there
          isn't any money in that moose's head?

                          CHUCK
          At least you'd know what you were
          talking about.

                          FERDIE
                    (handing his candle
                     to Daisy)
          Hold this.

                                        CONTINUED

268     CONTINUED

        CAMERA FOLLOWS Ferdie to fireplace.  He starts to climb
        up onto the mantle.

                            FERDIE
                       (grumbling  as he goes)
                  If this is the only way I can have
                  a little peace around here -- okay.


269     CLOSE SHOT - FERDIE

        He crawls onto the mantle, then stands up.  This brings
        him about to the level of the moose's head.  The light
        from the fireplace and the candle barely reaches him.

                            FERDIE
                  I can't see a thing.....

        He starts to reach into the moose's mouth, but as he
        passes the tongue, something feels loose under his hand.
        Ferdie flicks the loose section out of the moose's mouth
        and it wafts toward the floor.

                            FERDIE
                  This moose's tongue is peeling.
                       (flicking several
                         more loose papery
                         pieces out)
                  Look at that....


270     MED. CLOSE SHOT - CHUCK AND DAISY

        as INTO SCENE float the loose sections -- only by the
        light of the fire they are seen to be nice green ten-
        dollar bills. Chuck and Daisy grab one each.  They
        exchange a glance of amazement.

                            CHUCK
                       (calling up to
                         Ferdie)
                  Make sure you get all the peeled
                  stuff off that moose's tongue.
                  It's very bad for him.


271     CLOSE SHOT - FERDIE AND MOOSE'S HEAD

                            FERDIE
                  Okay.

        He proceeds to flick greenback after greenback out of
        the moose's mouth.  Then he reaches his hand further
        inside.
                                              CONTINUED

271     CONTINUED

                         FERDIE
          There's some more stuff back here.

He pulls out a wad of bills thick enough to choke a
moose and drops it down to Chuck.


272     MED. CLOSE SHOT - CHUCK AND DAISY

Chuck grabs the roll.

                         FERDIE'S VOICE
                        (continuing)
          Boy, the taxidermist that fixed
          this head sure did a poor job.

Another thick roll drops into scene and is caught by
Daisy.  She takes the Doc's satchel and starts to drop
the money into it.


273     CLOSE SHOT - FERDIE AND MOOSE'S HEAD

He cleans  out the inside of the moose's head.

                         FERDIE
                        (when he is sure
                         there is nothing
                         left)
          There...


274     MED. SHOT - FIREPLACE

as Ferdie starts to climb down.  Daisy is busily
counting money.

                         CHUCK
                        (to Ferdie)
          Are you sure the head is empty?

Ferdie crosses to Chuck and Daisy.

                         FERDIE
                        (with the
                         conviction of
                         a research
                         scientist)
          There is no money in that moose's
          head.  Now go on -- argue with me!

274   CONTINUED

                    CHUCK
              (calmly starting to
               count money himself)
        Why should we argue?

                    DAISY
              (counting aloud)
        Nine hundred and ninety, one
        thousand, one thousand and ten...

                    FERDIE
              (looking from one
               to the other -
               throwing up his arms)
        I don't get it.

275   INT. DINING ROOM - MED. LONG SHOT

as Doc and Norma hurry downstairs and cross to group.  A
dim light shows through the windows.

                    DOC
        It's almost morning.  We've got to
        find those detectives and -
              (as he sees
               the money)
        What have you got there?

                    CHUCK
        Ten dollar bills.  Thousands of
        ten dollar bills !

                    NORMA
        But where -- ?

                    DAISY
        It was hidden in the moose's head.

                    FERDIE
        That's a figure of speech.

                    ROSY'S VOICE
        Just like "reach for the ceiling"!

CAMERA PANS to Rosy in doorway to kitchen.  Behind him
are several of the boys.  All heft guns.

                    ROSY
              (coming toward group)
        I suppose we ought to thank you
        people for finding this sugar...

276        MED. GROUP SHOT - AROUND TABLE

Ferdie holds the satchel full of money.

                            ROSY
                    Come on, hand it over.

Ferdie looks to Chuck for direction.  Chuck shrugs
helplessly.

                            CHUCK
                    Better do what he says.

But Ferdie is made of sterner stuff.  His mouth tightens
in grim determination.  He does hand the satchel over
the table to Rosy, but at the same time he slides the
lamp under Rosy's gun hand.  Rosy drops his gun with a
howl. Simultaneously, Ferdie grabs the satchel back and
ducks under the table.

277        CLOSE SHOT - FERDIE

He wiggles between Rosy's legs and makes a dash for the
stairs.

278        MED. SHOT - GROUP - DAISY IN F.G.

Ferdie dashes past camera.  In b.g., the gangsters start
to chase him.

                            DAISY
                      (looking after
                        Ferdie)
                    Oh, boy!

Then she sticks out her foot and trips the first
gangster. The others pile up on top of him.

279        MED. SHOT - STAIRS

Ferdie comes dashing up the stairs.  The gangsters
follow as quick as they can pick themselves up.  At the
top of the stairs, Ferdie stumbles but recovers quickly.

280        INT. HALL - MED. LONG SHOT

Ferdie runs down the hall towards camera, then ducks
into Moose's room in f.g.  The gangsters follow,
shooting wildly.  As the gangsters enter Moose's room:

281        INT. MOOSE'S ROOM - FULL SHOT

Ferdie is nowhere to be seen.  But from behind one
section of drape there is a slight movement.  The
gangsters approach this section.

282    MED. SHOT - GANGSTERS - BEFORE DRAPES

                              SNAKE-EYES
                    Come out of there... Come out, or
                    I'll let you have it.

       No answer.  Snake-Eyes fires several times into the
       drape.  The drapes billow and out falls the body of
       Smith -- still bound and gagged.


283    INT. MOOSE'S ROOM - FULL SHOT

       As the gangsters stare pop-eyed at Smith, Ferdie ducks
       from behind another section of drape on other side of
                    room and sees Smith.

                              FERDIE
                    Hi' Smitty.
                         (does a double take)

       Ferdie dashes out the door, slamming it behind him.
       On the slam, the gangsters turn and give chase.


284    INT. HALL - MED. SHOT

       Ferdie is halfway down the hall, running away from
       CAMERA.  The gangsters dash out of Moose's room in f.g.
       and start to fire at Ferdie.  He ducks into the room
       which he had previously occupied.  The gangsters dash
       after him.


285    INT. FERDIE'S ROOM

       Ferdie is making a bee-line for the bathroom door,
       which he knows will connect with Chuck's room, and
       possible escape.  Too much in a hurry to take a detour,
       he runs right over his bed.  He gets tangled in the
       sheet, however, and does a flying gruesome into the hat
       rack.


286    CLOSE SHOT - HAT RACK

       as Ferdie hits it.  His hand knocks down the lever that
       changes the room into a gambling den.


287    INT. ROOM - FULL SHOT

       The room immediately starts to change.  Ferdie scrambles
       to his feet and is out the door just as the gangsters
       enter.  High Collar, taking Ferdie's route over the bed,
       gets trapped as the mechanism starts to fold into the
       wall.  The chandelier, lowering to become a roulette
       table, conks Snake-eyes, knocking him cold.  Glum is
       knocked down by the fare-wheel as it springs from its
       panel. Only Rosy manages to stumble through.

288         INT. HALL

           Ferdie ducks out of Chuck's room and starts back down-
           stairs.  Rosy, the one gangster not trapped, follows
           after him and fires at Ferdie just as the latter reaches
           the head of the stairs.

289         INT. DINING ROOM - MED. LONG SHOT - STAIRCASE

           Ferdie throws himself over the bannister and slides
           down to the dining room.  CAMERA PANS with him, picking
           up Iron Dome and The Strangler, our two bogus
           detectives, who are just coming in the front door.
           When Ferdie sees them, he dashes over.

                               FERDIE
                     Where have you guys been?...

290         MED. SHOT - GROUP

           Doc, Norma and Daisy enter scene.

                               FERDIE
                            (continuing
                             breathlessly)
                     The joint's full of crooks.
                            (indicating
                             satchel)
                     They're after this dough!

                               IRON DOME
                     Give it to us -- we'll hold it.

                               FERDIE
                     Sure, but duck -- they got guns.

           He starts to hide behind the Strangler, nodding towards
           the head of the staircase as he does so.

291         MED. LONG SHOT - HEAD OF STAIRCASE

           The other gangsters, having extricated themselves, come
           to the head of the stairs, prepared to open fire.  They
           react, however, when they see the group below.

                               ROSY
                     Grab him, Iron Dome -- he's got
                     the money.

292         MED. GROUP - FEATURING IRON DOME

                               IRON DOME
                            (holding up satchel)
                     You mean we've got it.

293     MED. SHOT - GANGSTERS - ON STAIRCASE

They start down the stairs, putting their guns away as
they go.

                    SNAKE-EYES
                  (to Glum)
          See?  I told you Iron Dome had
          finesse.


294     MED. GROUP - FEATURING IRON DOME

He is smirking contentedly, as he rustles through the
money in the satchel.

                    NORMA
                  (arms akimbo)
          Well --- of all the dirty, double-
          crossing tricks.

                    IRON DOME
                  (beaming)
          Thanks, lady...
                  (as the others
                    enter scene)
          Okay, boys -- tie 'em up.

                    ROSY
          Right.

He shoves a chair under Doc, catching him at the knee
joints and making him sit down abruptly.

                    ROSY
          Siddown!

                    SNAKE-EYES
                  (repeating the process
                    with Norma)
          Yeah - make yourselves to home.


295     MED. SHOT - CANVAS BUNDLE - IN CORNER OF ROOM

It has been well tied with heavy rope, which Glum is now
removing.  High Collar takes the first piece that comes
loose and crosses with it to the Doc.  He starts to tie
him to the chair.

                    DOC
          Er, not too tight -- you'll
          impede the circulation.

High Collar gives him a pained look.

296    MED. SHOT - NORMA

Glum enters scene and starts to rope her.

                         NORMA
                      (nervously)
              You're not going to leave us here,
              are you?

                         GLUM
              We'll send yuh a post card.

High Collar passing in b.g. laughs.  CAMERA FOLLOWS with
him as he carries the last long piece of rope over to
where Chuck, Ferdie and Daisy are sitting.

                      HIGH COLLAR
                   (to Iron Dome -
                      indicating rope)
              This is all there is.

                      IRON DOME
              I'll show you how we'll do it.
                   (to Chuck, Ferdie
                      and Daisy)
              Stand up, you.

He puts them shoulder to shoulder in an outward facing
triangle.  Then he indicates to the Strangler to tie
them all with the one rope.  Rosy enters scene.

                         ROSY
              I'll get the car.

                      IRON DOME
              Bring it around front.

Rosy starts off toward the bar.  Iron Dome crosses to
see whether Doc and Norma have been properly tied.

297    MED. CLOSE SHOT - CHUCK, FERDIE AND DAISY

being tied by The Strangler.  He is bending over,
wrapping the rope around their ankles.

                         CHUCK
                      (growling)
              You big ape.

The Strangler straightens up and slaps Ferdie's face.

                         FERDIE
              Hey!

The Strangler resumes his tying.

                         CHUCK
              Just you wait -- Crime Doesn't Pay.
                                        CONTINUED

297     CONTINUED

The Strangler slaps Ferdie's face again.

                    STRANGLER
                  (to Ferdie)
          Shut up.

                    FERDIE
                  (bewildered)
          I didn't say nothing.

                    STRANGLER
                  (as he bends down
                   again)
          Then don't - see?

                    CHUCK
                  (mumbling again)
          You dirty crook.

                    FERDIE
                  (to Chuck)
          Cut it out, will you?

The Strangler draws back his hand to slap Ferdie,
but good.

                    DAISY
                  (to Strangler)
          You lay off him!

                    STRANGLER
                  (wagging a finger
                   in her face)
          Listen, sister ---

But Daisy sinks her teeth into the Strangler's finger,
causing him to yelp with pain.

298     INT. CELLAR - MED. SHOT - ROSY

He swings the furnace door open and is about to step
down the passage when his face suddenly undergoes a
change of expression. His jaw drops. His eyes popped
with horror. He backs away from the furnace, then turns
to make a wild dash for the Bar steps. From the interior
of the furnace, there are several shots. Rosie stumbles
and falls at the foot of the stairs.

299     INT. DINING ROOM - CLOSE SHOT - IRON DOME

He is looking over his shoulder toward the cellar steps,
the sound of the shots still ringing in his ears.

                    IRON DOME
          That must have been Rosy.

300      MED. SHOT - GROUP

The Strangler has just finished tying Chuck, Ferdie and
Daisy.

> IRON DOME
> (to his henchmen)
> Come on.

He takes one step toward the bar, then pulls up short.
He and the others slowly raise their hands over their
heads.

301      INT. DINING ROOM - PANEL TO BAR ROOM

In the opening stands LEFTY. He still wears convict's
clothes. He is a slight man, with the deeply lined face.
One arm hangs in a makeshift sling. Lefty holds a gun
in his good hand.

> LEFTY
> You ain't goin' no place, Iron
> Dome.

He comes into the room, followed by two other escaped
convicts. One tall and gangling, the other sawed-off.
In other words, BIG FINK and LITTLE FINK.

302      MED. GROUP

> IRON DOME
> (his voice quavering)
> Hello, Lefty...

> SNAKE EYES
> We heard you'd broke jail.

> THE STRANGLER
> Yeah -- we was just talking about
> it.

> LEFTY
> (sarcastically)
> My ears are ringin'.

> IRON DOME
> (thinking fast)
> We was sayin' how nice it was we
> could count you in on the split.

> LEFTY
> (unbelievingly)
> Sure.

CONTINUED

302        CONTINUED

                    THE STRANGLER
                  (casting his eyes
                   to Heaven)
          It's the way Moose would have
          wanted it.

Lefty looks pained at their feeble attempt toward
concil-iation. Since the Finks carry a rifle apiece,
he drops his revolver into his pocket and holds out his
hand to Iron Dome for the Doc's satchel which holds
the money.

                    LEFTY
          Gimme that.

                    IRON DOME
                  (as he hands it
                   over)
          Aw, Lefty.

                    LEFTY
                  (handing the
                   satchel to
                   Big Fink)
          Count it. See how much there is.

Big Fink turns to the table. He starts to move one of
Doc's phials to make room for the satchel.

                    DOC
                  (quickly)
          Don't touch that!
                  (as the man pulls
                   his hand away)
          It's sodium tetrachloride -- you'll
          get burned.

Lefty crosses to Doc.

                    LEFTY
          You a doctor?

                    DOC
          I am.

                    LEFTY
                  (to Little Fink --
                   indicating Doc)
          Untie him.

Little Fink starts to untie the Doc.

                                        CONTINUED

302 continued -2

> LEFTY
> (meanwhile - pointing
> to Big Fink)
> You -- cover these guys while
> the Doc works on me. I'll take
> care of the dough.

But Big Fink levels his rifle at Lefty instead of the others.

> BIG FINK
> (reaching for the
> satchel)
> I'll take care of it. I didn't
> break jail to be picked up by no
> cops, Lefty.

As his hand touches the satchel, Lefty clips him on the jaw with his good mitt. Big Fing goes down, his rifle slithering away from him. Quick as a flash, Lefty draws and ducks behind the table. Little Fink, having turned from untying Doc, starts to fire at him, taking cover as he does so. Almost immediately, however, Iron Dome, taking advantage of the situation, jumps on Little Fink. The other gangsters quickly drop behind suitable cover and open fire on Lefty and Big Fink, who are alternately firing at each other and at their attackers. The satchel remains on the table.

303     CLOSE SHOT - IRON DOME

He is about to shoot when a bullet knocks his bowler hat off his head. He puts it back on, again takes aim. Again a bullet knocks it off.

304     LONG SHOT- FIGHT

305     MED. SHOT - NORMA - TIED IN CHAIR

In trying to get a better firing position, the Strangler takes refuge behind her chair, using her body as a shield.

306     CLOSE SHOT - DOC

When he sees Norma's danger, he gets fightin' mad. Struggling out of his loosened bonds and whipping off his glasses, he piles into the Strangler, paying no heed to flying bullets. He knocks the Strangler down, deftly twists Norma's chair to safety and returns to the fray.

307     CLOSE SHOT - LEFTY

He is crouched behind an angle in the fireplace. On the
mantle above him is a can of tomato juice. Lefty is
taking aim.


308     CLOSE SHOT - SNAKE-EYES

He fires at lefty.


309     CLOSE SHOT - LEFTY

The bullet hits the can of tomato juice, sending a
stream of liquid down Lefty's neck.


310     CLOSE SHOT - IRON DOME

He is still trying to get in a shot. But once again his
hat is smacked off. Irate, Iron Dome crams it down over
his ears with both hands.


311     INT. DINING ROOM

The fight goes on. In the middle of the dance floor,
Chuck and Ferdie and Daisy are still tied. Bullets
whine around them.

                        FERDIE
                    (gulping
            We gotta get out of here!

                        DAISY
            How?

                        CHUCK
                    (getting an idea)
            Hop! All together!

Like an animated potato sack, they jump together across
the dance floor, Chuck counting to keep the rhythm.
Ferdie, however, gets out of step and they topple over
with Ferdie facedown in the dance floor puddle.

                        FERDIE
                    (managing to raise
                    his head)
            Hey! This isn't Saturday night.

                                        CONTINUED

311     CONTINUED

His voice trails off in a gurgle.

                         CHUCK
                       (to Daisy)
                We'll have to roll for it.

They roll a bit and Daisy goes underneath.

                         DAISY
                Do I look like the face on the
                barroom floor?

A little more progress and Chuck is face down.

                         CHUCK
                      (snappily)
                Ferdie -- what kind of bread do
                you like best?

                         FERDIE
                   (right back at him)
                Give me a roll any time.

                         CHUCK
                All right.

So they roll Ferdie onto the bottom again.

                         FERDIE
                This is where I came in.

One final effort smashes them into a pile of stacked
chairs, which crash around them, hiding them from view.


312     MED. SHOT- DOC AND THE STRANGLER

Doc puts the Strangler out of business, then hurries to
Norma and starts to untie her. As he bends down to untie
her feet, she gives him a quick kiss.


313     MED. SHOT - CHUCK, DAISY AND FERDIE - BEHIND CHAIRS

They have removed the rope that tied them together, and
Ferdie has made it into a lariat. He flips it now,
neatly roping the satchel, pulling it off the table and
over to him.


314     INT. DINING ROOM

When the gangsters see this, they forget their common
differences and start for the dough.

315     MED. SHOT - CHUCK, FERDIE AND DAISY

Behind them is the phonograph. In looking around for
weapons, their eyes light on the records. They pick
them up and start to sling record after record at the
approach-ing gangsters.


316     MED. CLOSE SHOT - LEFTY AND LITTLE FINK

They duck back to cover in a hail of phonograph records.


317     CLOSE SHOT - GLUM

On the wall behind him is an old colonial musket and
powder horn. A record flies into SCENE, cutting the cord
that holds up the mouth of the horn. It dangles from the
small end, spilling black powder all over Glum and
causing him to go into a violent sneezing fit.


318     CLOSE SHOT - IRON DOME

He raises his gun to fire.


319     CLOSE SHOT - FERDIE

as he heaves a record at Iron Dome.


320     CLOSE SHOT - IRON DOME

The record shears off the top of his bowler, revealing a
very bald head. Iron Dome burns.


321     INT. DINING ROOM

From the outside comes the wail of an approaching SIREN.
The gangsters freeze as they hear it. Then with common
accord, they break for safety. Some go through the front
door, some toward the cellar. Norma, Doc, Chuck and
Ferdie rush for the front door. Strangler is just
struggling to his feet. As Ferdie passes him he notices
that Strangler's hands are bound with rope.

                         FERDIE
              So you're the guy that hit me.
                   (business of making
                    passes at Strangler)
              Wait till I get Chuck. I'll show
              you up- you big gorilla.

He goes to the front door.

                                          CONTINUED:

321        CONTINUED:

                          DAISY
                   (groggily appears from
                   behind a chair- there
                   is a rat-tat-tat of
                   machine guns from out
                   front)
              So, wiseguys, the cops are going
              to get you.

                          STRANGLER
              Look, lady, how about giving me
              a cigarette?

                          DAISY
                   (undecided)
              Well--- okay.
                   (hands him
                   cigarette)

                          STRANGLER
              I can't smoke unless my hands
              are untied.

                          DAISY
              Oh, no...

                          STRANGLER
              You don't have to untie both of
              them-- just untie one.

                          DAISY
              That's different.

She unties the rope from Strangler's hand. Ferdie,
Chuck, Norma and Doc come in from the front door.

                          FERDIE
                   (to Strangler-
                   very bravely)
              Now I'm gonna get yuh!

Strangler keeps his hands behind him- while Ferdie makes
a few passes. Ferdie turns to the group and as he turns
back to hit Strangler, Strangler's hand fixes his tie
and then is placed quickly behind him again. Ferdie is
now in doubt as to whether Strangler is tied or not.
He slowly circles around, while Strangler circles with
him. As he holds off to hit Strangler, he gets a
terrific punch on the chin which knocks him into Chuck's
arms. As the Strangler starts toward the group, several
State Troopers rush in, guns ready for battle.

                                        CONTINUED:

321     CONTINUED:-2

                         DOC
              How did you know?

                       CAPTAIN
                    (grinning- crossing
                     to them)
              Your luggage is down at head-
              quarters. We've been laying for
              that chiseler a long time.

                       DAISY
                    (to Ferdie)
              Oh, boy!--- my new nightgown.

                       FERDIE
                    (grandly - dipping into
                     his satchel)
              Here, Officer. Here's your reward.

The captain takes a handful of bills from Ferdie's out-
stretched hand. He frowns and holds them up to the
light.

                       CAPTAIN
                    (glowering at Ferdie)
              You're a wise guy, huh?

                       FERDIE
                    (startled)
              Who?-- Me?

                       CAPTAIN
                    (continuing)
              Trying to pass off counterfeit
              money-- I oughtta run you in
              with the Matson gang.

                  CHUCK AND FERDIE
                    (together)
              Counterfeit!

                       CAPTAIN
                    (relaxing)
              I suppose you wouldn't know about
              that, though. Yeah. Moose took a
              fling at counterfeiting once, though
              we never could pin it on him. His
              first batch turned out so bad, he never
              tried it again.

                                   CONTINUED:

321 CONTINUED:-3

CHUCK & FERDIE
(together - in heart-broken tones)
Counterfeit.....

Two state troopers return from investigating the upstairs.

CAPTAIN
(indicating bag)
Well-- I better take this along.
(to Doc)
We'll send a car for you just as soon as we take Moose's gang back to jail.

He gives them a reassuring smile and exits. Ferdie looks after him sadly.

NORMA
(to Chuck and Ferdie)
Will you boys be coming back to the police station with us?

CHUCK
(looking around)
Might as well-- there's nothing to keep us here.

DOC
Oh, but this place can make you a pile of money.

FERDIE
As a convention hall for termites?

DOC
No-- as a health resort.
(nodding toward the table)
I haven't finished analyzing that water yet, but I'm certain it has immense therapeutic value. There must be an underground mineral stream that's seeped into your well.

FERDIE
(with rising excitement)
You mean people might come here just to drink our water?

DOC
And rest. After all, you're <u>off</u> the main highway, in peaceful, lovely surroundings...

LAP DISSOLVED TO:

322     LONG SHOT - 'REST HOME' - DAY

You can hardly recognize the old place, what with its
new coat of paint and landscaping. White-clad nurses are
pushing prosperous-looking men and women around in wheel
chairs, etc.

                                        LAP DISSOLVE TO:

323     INT. MOOSE'S ROOM

It, too, has been generally refurnished, but still retains enough of its former hangings and furnishings to
be recognizable. In place of the "MM" embroidery we now
have "CM & FJ" monograms. The room manages to be both
antiseptic and luxurious at the same time.

Chuck and Ferdie, in white attendant coats, are just
push-ing an old lady in a wheel chair into the room.
They look quite prosperous.

                        CHUCK
                   (as they enter)
            Oh, yes, Mrs. Giltedge. This is
            absolutely our best room.

                        MRS. GILTEDGE
                   (looking around)
            It is nice. I'm beginning to feel
            better already-- it's so restful
            here, so peaceful....

                        FERDIE
            Say, Chuck, that'd make a swell
            slogan for us-- "Rest in peace".

Chuck slaps his face behind Mrs. Giltedge's chair. At
this moment Doc, Norma and Daisy enter.

                        CHUCK
            Ah, here we are.
                   (introducing them)
            This is Dr. Jackson, our resident
            physician and--
                   (indicating Norma)
            Mrs. Jackson, who is our special
            dietician.

                        MRS. GILTEDGE
            How do you do.

                                        CONTINUED:

323     CONTINUED:

                              FERDIE
                         (indicating Daisy
                         proudly)
                    And this is our head nurse. If you
                    want her, you just ring this and---

As he says this, he grabs the bell cord by the side of
the bed and gives it a yank. Once again a pair of drapes
draw outside, revealing the closet door.

                              FERDIE
                         (continuing)
                    Oops-- wrong rope.

                         MRS. GILTEDGE
                    And what is that?

                              FERDIE
                    Oh, that-- that's a closet-- a
                    plain, ordinary closet.

With that he crosses to it confidently and swings the
door open. Out falls the body of Smith.


324     LOW SET-UP-- SMITH'S BODY

        as it crashes onto CAMERA.


325     CLOSEUP-FERDIE

                              FERDIE
                    "Smitty"!

326     CLOSEUP- DAISY

        She lets go with a super-colossal scream.

                                        FADE OUT.



                         T H E   E N D

# Hold (Back) That Ghost

Three days after "Oh, Charlie" wrapped principal photography, *Buck Privates* opened in downtown Los Angeles at the Paramount Theater. (Formerly known as Grauman's Metropolitan Theatre, it was the largest movie theater ever built in Los Angeles. Sadly, it was razed in 1960.) Bud, Lou, and co-stars Lee Bowman, Jane Frazee, and Nat Pendleton made personal appearances.

By then *Buck Privates* had earned critical praise, and by late March was being held over in theaters across the country. The *Hollywood Reporter* observed, "*Buck Privates* is headed to out gross any picture made on the Universal lot since the present organization has been there." Screenwriter Stanley Roberts (1916–1982), who was later nominated for an Academy Award for the film adaptation of *The Caine Mutiny*, worked at Universal at this time. He recalled, "They didn't realize what they had when they released *Buck Privates*, or they wouldn't have made 'Oh, Charlie' for [only] $200,000. They were trying to wash up the deal. Then, lo and behold, *Buck Privates* became the thunderclap. To this day they have no idea what the picture grossed."

As profits poured in, Universal's brain trust grew envious as well as anxious. They had pre-sold *Buck Privates* to exhibitors at the lower B-movie rental fee of 25% and weren't raking in as much of the windfall as they might have. Studio president Nate Blumberg hastened to announce that all subsequent Abbott and Costello films would carry the higher A-movie rental rate of 35%. Exhibitors in the northwest later complained bitterly over this and other studio demands, such as settling delinquent payments before allowing

a theater to book *In The Navy*. The *Motion Picture Herald* wrote, "Universal…has created for itself a whirlwind of exhibitor ill will. Angry and indignant exhibitors have flooded their office with their protest." Theater owners decried "the disdain and unappreciation for exhibitor support and good will which was given to Universal in the past several seasons… now that this company has a couple of flash-in-the pan comedians, who temporarily are boxoffice attractions."

Studio executives also fretted that "Oh, Charlie" bore no resemblance to the proven hit. A test screening confirmed their fears. According to Maxene Andrews, "They asked everybody in the audience to fill out these cards and say what they thought of the picture. Well, everybody wrote on the cards, 'Where are the Andrews Sisters?'" The script for *In The Navy*, which was nearly ready, reassuringly mirrored *Buck Privates* and included the Andrews Sisters.

On March 26, while Universal contemplated gilding "Oh, Charlie" with music, Ted Lewis' "Happiness Revue of 1941" opened in downtown Los Angeles at the Orpheum Theatre. The *Los Angeles Times* thought that Lewis "never had a better show."

A week later, the *Hollywood Reporter* stated that Universal decided to hold back "Oh, Charlie" and instead release the new naval comedy on May 30. Even with twice the budget of "Oh, Charlie," *In The Navy* would still require efficiency to make the date. Cliff Work wanted to start production on March 15, but filming did not commence until April 8. That same day, the *Hollywood Reporter* and *Variety* reported that Universal would upgrade "Oh, Charlie" with

*Re-shooting the bus exteriors in May. Ferdie has just tossed Chuck's bag onto the roof of a passing bus. Costello stands on a mat to deaden the scuffing sound of his shoes on the sidewalk. Arthur Lubin sits in shadow behind his director's chair and below the camera. Below: the framing through the camera.*

Ted Lewis *and* the Andrews Sisters, and that Lewis would also make a musical short. (It was also stated that one sequence would be based on George Gershwin's "Rhapsody in Blue.") Both acts recorded for Decca, which had a rare relationship with Universal. From 1938 to 1948, no other studio featured so many artists from the same label. Decca's president, Jack Kapp, believed that the exposure was invaluable, and pushed to showcase his acts in movies. Ironically, Decca eventually bought controlling interest in Universal-International in 1952.

Bud and Lou would not be available for the new "Oh, Charlie" scenes until mid-May, when *In The Navy* wrapped. But there was a snag: the navy would not approve the picture. In the climax, Costello tries to impress Patty Andrews by impersonating a captain and taking command of a battleship. Even though the navy brass gave the screenplay their blessing, the broad comedy on the screen now offended them.

With the May 30 release date fast approaching, Universal was in a panic. Alex Gottlieb quickly wrote two connecting scenes that played Costello's madcap maneuvers as a dream. Lubin filmed Bud and Lou on Sunday, May 18, and the navy approved the revisions on May 21. The boys also shot a newsreel promoting defense bonds and stamps with Shemp Howard and Joe LaCava.

Meanwhile, on April 14, producer Burt Kelly resigned amicably and went to Paramount as an associate producer under Sol Siegel, whom he knew at Republic. Milton Feld assigned Glenn Tryon to finish "Oh, Charlie." Tryon (1898-1970) had been a stage actor and a vaudevillian. Hal Roach signed him in 1924 to replace Harold Lloyd, who left to form his own production company. Although Tryon's two-reelers didn't click, Universal signed him for a series of features in 1927. The most significant of these was Paul Fejos' *Lonesome* (1928), with Barbara Kent. The film was panned by critics but has achieved new appreciation for its poetic, innovative, and even surrealistic camera work. In the 1930s Tryon not only acted but also wrote films; he worked uncredited on the screenplays for *Sons of the Desert* (1933) and *Room Service* (1938). At Universal he produced *Hired Wife* (1940) with Rosalind Russell, and recently directed *Double Date* (1941). After *Hold That Ghost*, Tryon produced Bud and Lou's third service comedy, *Keep 'Em Flying*, and Olsen and Johnson's *Hellzapoppin.'* He then moved back to Roach as a producer. In 1942 Tryon married actress Jane Frazee, the boys' *Buck Privates* co-star. The marriage lasted five years and produced a son, Timothy.

Feld and Tryon put a few writers to work integrating musical numbers into "Oh, Charlie" while salvaging as much original footage as possible. Lees and Rinaldo were enlisted, of course, as were Arthur T. Horman, Edward Eliscu, and Edmund L. Hartmann. "[The studio] never told you who was coming in after you," Lees said. "They never told you what they wanted you to change, because they decided if they got a new writer and told him, he wouldn't fight them." Clearly none of the other writers added more than fifty percent to the screenplay to warrant a screen credit. According to Writers Guild guidelines, "In the case of an original screenplay, any subsequent writer or writing team must contribute fifty percent to the final screenplay [to receive a credit]."

It was easy to imagine musical acts at the picture's end, when Moose's tavern would be completely refurbished. But there were different thoughts about how to wedge music into the opening. Lees and Rinaldo suggested bringing the big musical act to Chuck and Ferdie's gas station. This idea was not far-fetched; as gasoline retailing became more competitive in the 1930s, grand opening events were an important way to draw customers. In this scenario, Ted Lewis' tour bus stops for gas. Chuck thinks it's the local band he has hired for the festivities, but Ferdie, Lewis' biggest fan, recognizes him immediately. Ted offers to pay for gas with a song. At the end of their number the band hurries off to keep another engagement. The boys check their cash register and discover that the crowd was so enthralled by the music that they haven't done any business. We dissolve to the next day, and the picture picks up with the original gas station opening. Later, after Chuck and Ferdie turn the tavern into a nightclub, they hire Lewis for an unlimited engagement.

To Lees and Rinaldo this was the most efficient solution, and it preserved their screenplay. But once it was decided to film a musical short with Lewis, the nightclub idea took root, since the same set could be used for both. In a new treatment, Lees and Rinaldo kept the original opening in the gas station. Then, after Moose is killed, we find Chuck and Ferdie in jail. Matson's attorney, Bannister, shows up to arrange bail. He asks the boys to meet him at a nightclub that evening where he will explain everything. (Apparently he is so busy that he has to conduct business in his off hours.) At the club, Bannister refuses to discuss business until the featured musical act is finished. He then tells the boys about Moose's peculiar will; probate court; the Forrester's Club; and Moose's cryptic clue about keeping his money in his head. Meanwhile, in another corner of the club, Charlie Smith and a few other gang members eye Bannister, Chuck, and Ferdie. They know the will is coming up in court the next day and are determined to see that these two dopes don't inherit Matson's estate. Smith says he'll handle everything, but the other gangsters warn him not to double-cross them. There's another musical number in the club, then the original picture resumes with an abbreviated courtroom sequence.

Arthur Horman (1905-1964) proposed eliminating the gas station sequence altogether. A Chicago native, Horman began his screenwriting career in 1934 plotting crime dramas at RKO. He wrote some Little Tough Guys and Dead End Kids programmers at Universal before working on both *Buck Privates* and *In The Navy* (1941). He went on to write *Captains of the Clouds* (1942); the Oscar-nominated *Desperate Journey* (1942); the Humphrey Bogart suspense thriller *Conflict* (filmed in 1943 but not released until 1945); *Dark Waters* (1944); and *The Suspect* (1944).

*Ted Lewis and the Andrews Sisters on the nightclub set. The girls, who had just completed larger roles in* In The Navy, *were in the news because an earlier film,* Argentine Nights, *was banned in that country after violent opening night demonstrations.*

Horman also co-wrote a Universal musical, *Bowery to Broadway* (1944), that John Grant produced. His next collaboration with Grant was *Here Come the Co-Eds* (1945) for Abbott and Costello. That year, Horman was promoted to producer and his first assignment was "Meet a Genius," which he scripted for Bud and Lou to follow *The Naughty Nineties* (1945). The film was never made. In 1949 Horman began writing for Cathedral Films, which was established by an Episcopal priest in the 1930s. Horman scripted *The Fourth R,* a short film about the founding of Campbell Hall School in North Hollywood, where religion is a part of daily education. (Recent alumni include director Paul Thomas Anderson and the Olsen twins.) In 1951 Horman wrote eleven half-hour episodes of *The Living Christ* that were shown in churches and on Sunday morning TV. He also wrote *I Beheld His Glory* (1953), and Cathedral's only theatrical release, *Day of Triumph* (1954). His last film credits, *Juvenile Jungle* and *Young and Wild* (both 1958), are a cut above the usual teen exploitation fare.

Horman's idea for "Oh Charlie" begins at a nightclub where Chuck is the maître d' and Ferdie works as a parking valet. Ferdie asks Chuck about a job inside as a waiter, and Chuck half promises to see what he can do. Ted Lewis and his band arrive in their bus, which Ferdie parks with comedic results. Moose Matson pulls up with a couple of blondes. He is approached in the lobby by Lefty, who asks to be reinstated in the gang. When Matson brushes him off, Lefty in retaliation phones the police and alerts them that Moose is back in town. Meanwhile, Chuck gives Ferdie a chance as a waiter. After a musical number by Lewis, Ferdie makes a nuisance of himself with the patrons and Lewis. He suggests all of Lewis' trademark bits, such as saying, "Is everybody happy?," as original ideas to Lewis. Chuck sends Ferdie back to parking cars, but on his way out Ferdie spills something on Moose. Enraged, Matson leaves. Ferdie retrieves Moose's car, but smashes the fender as he pulls up to the club. This makes Moose more furious. Just then, thanks to Lefty's tip, the police arrive. Moose hastily pushes Chuck and Ferdie into his car and speeds away. The police give chase. After Moose is killed, the original film picks up in probate court.

Lees and Rinaldo fleshed out a script based on this scenario, adding specific gags but returning the boys to the gas station after the nightclub fiasco. Ferdie parks Ted's bus in a space so tight that he cannot open the door; he must climb out of a window. The owner of the gas station next to the club is impressed and offers Ferdie a job parking cars. Ferdie declines, saying he meets a better class of cars at the nightclub. After Lewis performs one of his numbers, the club owner complains to Chuck that more busboys are needed. Chuck wrangles Ferdie and brings him inside, where they bump into Moose and one of his gang, Harry, by the coat check. Moose spots Charlie

Smith in the lobby and they have a brusque conversation. Harry claims he saw Smith entering the district attorney's office that morning, but Smith denies it. As Moose and Harry take their seats, Charlie realizes his predicament.

Ferdie, meanwhile, stops clearing dishes and sits down next to a stuffy dowager to watch the Andrews Sisters perform. Chuck catches him and sends him back to work. In the lobby, Charlie Smith dials the district attorney but is interrupted when Harry discreetly sticks a gun in his ribs. Smith takes advantage of the crowded lobby to get away. Harry reports back to Moose and suggests he leave now and hide at the Forrester's Club the next day. As the two gangsters depart, the Andrews Sisters begin singing a rhumba. Ted commands everyone to join a conga line. Ferdie can't resist and ends up in line right behind the trio. Chuck rushes over to yank Ferdie off the floor, but the other patrons think it's part of the dance and won't let Ferdie go. The club owner dispatches two bouncers who toss the boys out onto the street. Chuck is angry with him, but Ferdie knows where they can get new jobs: the gas station next door. The original picture picks up there. After Moose is shot, the boys land in jail, where Bannister explains about the will and the tavern and gets them released. The next day, when Chuck and Ferdie exit the courthouse, the gang shoots at them. Charlie Smith observes this from behind a piece of the building.

Another scenario, dated April 17 but uncredited, eliminated Moose's will entirely, so it almost certainly did not come from Lees and Rinaldo. It is likely by Edward Eliscu (1902-1998), a jack of all trades in the Broadway theatre. His songs include "Without a Song," "More Than You Know," "Great Day," "Carioca," "Orchids in the Moonlight," and "Flying Down to Rio." His Hollywood career began with the Wheeler and Woolsey comedy *Diplomaniacs* (1933). Later that year, he and Gus Kahn wrote the lyrics for the first Fred Astaire-Ginger Rogers musical, *Flying Down to Rio*. Between 1935 and 1951 Eliscu also co-wrote a dozen screenplays, including *The Gay Divorcee* (1934); *Paddy O'Day* (1936) and *Little Miss Nobody* (1936) for Jane Withers; *Charlie McCarthy, Detective* (1939); *Something to Shout About* (1943); and Joe Besser's service comedy, *Hey, Rookie* (1944). Eliscu was blacklisted in the 1950s but continued writing under pen names. He was president of the American Guild of Authors and Composers from 1968 to 1973, and was inducted into the Songwriters Hall of Fame

in 1985.

In this scenario, Chuck and Ferdie crash a nightclub opening and enjoy free drinks, food, pretty girls, celebrities, and the music of Ted Lewis. Two bouncers discover the boys and bring them to the club owner, Mike Sheridan. Sherdian is busy with a scared man (like Billy Gilbert) who begs him to buy back the haunted Club Forrester [sic], which Sheridan had recently sold him. The man is desperate and ready to take the first offer that comes along. Sheridan refuses to buy it back, but Chuck and Ferdie jump in and purchase the club for $4.10. They excitedly go off to recruit the entertainers in Sheridan's club. Now Charlie Smith collars Sheridan. Smith has learned that Moose Matson, the original owner of the Club Forrester, hid a fortune in cash there. Sheridan convinces Chuck and Ferdie to take Smith along as an adviser and maître d'. The next morning they meet Dr. Jackson, Norma, and Camille at the bus and drive to their property. After they stop for groceries, Hoskins abandons the group at the tavern. Charlie Smith is strangled while searching for Moose's money. During one of the scary episodes, Ferdie falls and is knocked out. He has a brief, fantastic dream incorporating the Andrews Sisters, Ted Lewis, the dishonest bus driver, and the moose head. When Ferdie comes to, he is so rattled that they put him to bed. This leads to the Changing Room routine. The villain who eliminated Smith tries to get the doctor and the girls. He is also the ghost who stalks Camille and appears in the Moving Candle scene. He is revealed as a cracked old man who worked for Matson during Prohibition and doesn't want anybody else around the place. The other gang members arrive and there is a free-for-all, working up to a climax where Ferdie is knocked out again and the same vision of the moose head reappears. Ferdie wakes up quickly and proceeds to take the money out of the moose head, thinking he's still dreaming. Other gang members take the money, but the boys recover it. The scene dissolves to the Club Forrester transformed, and a musical finish.

Another proposal, dated April 19, is almost certainly from Edmund L. Hartmann (1911-2003). Hartmann helped write the stage comedies George White's "Scandals" and "Strike Me Pink" before Fox brought him to Hollywood in 1934. "There were nine studios in those days," Hartmann recalled, "and you went from one to the other, and each time you moved you got a raise. And by the time you had been fired from all nine, there were all new bosses so you could start over again." Hartmann began at Universal in 1938. He wrote the stories for the Abbott and Costello films *Ride 'Em Cowboy* (1942) and *Keep 'Em Flying* (1941), and later produced *In Society* (1944) and *The Naughty Nineties* (1945) for the team. "I also worked on the opening and closing scenes and transitions for *Hold That Ghost* so they could use what they had shot," he said. (Indeed, his name is written at the top of page 35 in the re-take script.) Hartmann also scripted *Sherlock Holmes and the Secret Weapon* (1942), *Ali Baba and the Forty Thieves* (1944), and *The Scarlet Claw* (1944). He later produced *Ghost Catchers* (1944) and *See My Lawyer* (1945) for Olsen and Johnson, and *Hi'Ya Chum* (1944) for the Ritz Brothers. In a prolific decade at Paramount, Hartmann co-scripted several Bob Hope vehicles, including *The Paleface* (1948), *Sorrowful Jones* (1949), *Fancy Pants* (1950), *The Lemon Drop Kid* (1951), and *Casanova's Big Night* (1954), as well as *The Caddy* (1953) for Martin and Lewis. In the late 1950s he switched to television and produced "My Three Sons," "Family Affair," and "The Smith Family," starring Henry Fonda.

Hartmann's story begins at the opening of a swanky nightclub featuring Ted Lewis and the Andrews Sisters. Two waiters have an accident on the slippery floor and Chuck and Ferdie, who work in the kitchen, are promoted. The severe maître d' instructs them in the art of making the customer feel at home. Moose Matson attends the opening with his lawyer, who tries to pump him about the money hidden in the Forrester's Club. Moose laughs and says the money "is in my head." We learn that the lawyer and Charlie Smith are working together against Matson. Smith phones the police to alert them that Moose is back in town. After a musical number, Ferdie and Chuck try to make the patrons feel at home but are fired. On their way out they meet and befriend Dr. Jackson.

The next day opens at the gas station, where the boys have just been hired and Ferdie parks a car in a tight space. Moose comes in for gas and the police chase him. Moose is shot, and the will is revealed. Matson's attorney explains that the boys have inherited Moose's club. He introduces them to Charlie Smith, who will escort them there. Charlie leaves, and when Chuck and Ferdie exit the building, shots are fired at them from a moving car. Smith and other gang members are in the sedan. The next morning at the bus the boys meet Charlie and the Doctor, who they invited to accompany them to the club. On the drive they stop to buy provisions at the general store. Here they pick up Norma and Camille, who have missed a bus connection. When the bus reaches the club, the driver, who is also Charlie's confederate, takes off to report back to Bannister. The original film picks up here, but trades the gang for one villain who strangles Smith, does the ghost routines and throws the knives. At the climax of the money scene, the villain is revealed as an old bartender who worked for Moose and wants the loot. The boys subdue him, recover the money, and transform the tavern into a health resort. There's a final musical production in the remodeled club.

Many elements of this scenario wound up in the final film. By April 25, it was fleshed out in a new script. Chuck and Ferdie are relief waiters under an officious maître d', at a swanky nightclub. Ferdie suggests Lewis' own trademark bits to him as original ideas. Bannister meets with Charlie Smith in the lobby. Smith is worried about Moose seeing him there. Bannister delivers the will to Moose and mentions Smith, who Moose clearly despises. During another musical number, Alderman Birch arrives with a young woman. After Bannister informs Charlie about Moose's animosity, Charlie phones the police to tell them Moose's whereabouts. Ferdie has a run-in with the Alderman. Ted introduces Andrews Sisters, and then commands everyone to dance. When the Alderman's date runs off to dance, Ferdie goes after her. They are swept up in the crowd of dancers. Ted Lewis calls figures and the patrons, including Ferdie and the girl, comply. Gregory spots Ferdie and fumes. Chuck gets an idea. Impersonating Lewis, Chuck calls figures that free his pal from the pack. He grabs Ferdie and they dash out of the club ahead of Gregory and the bouncers. The next morning the boys are back at their jobs in the gas station, and the original picture resumes.

After his Los Angeles gig and prior to filming "Oh, Charlie," Ted Lewis took his band to San Francisco for three weeks. By May 8 he was back in Hollywood where, along with Abbott and Costello and most of the industry, Lewis attended the world premiere of *Citizen Kane* (1941).

Stanley Roberts recalled: "Alex Gottlieb had been a publicity man for Ted Lewis. I was with Alex in

*Ted Lewis in 1919, uncharacteristically without his trademark battered top hat*

Milton Feld's office when Ted Lewis came in. Ted said, 'What are you doing?' Alex said, 'Haven't you heard? I'm a producer.' And Ted Lewis laughed. Alex said, 'I am. I produced *Buck Privates*.' Ted said, 'Don't be ridiculous.' He would not believe Alex. I was there."

The jazz world snickered at Ted Lewis. "Ted Lewis made the clarinet talk. What it said was, 'Put me back in the case.'" So quipped guitarist and bandleader Eddie Condon, a leading figure in the so-called "Chicago school" of early Dixieland. Lewis' "gas pipe" clarinet style—producing honks, growls, squeaks, animal noises, and even laughter from his instrument—was outdated as early as 1926. But he was one of the first to bring jazz to a mass audience and was so popular for so long that he could not help but be influential. Even in 1940 *Variety* reviewers thought that Lewis was "still a sock attraction" when he played the Oriental Theater in Chicago, and "kills 'em, as he always does" at Loew's State in New York.

"I never considered myself a musician," Ted Lewis once said. "I always considered myself a showman."

In his heyday Lewis was Columbia Record's top act, and his discs outsold those of Al Jolson and Paul

Whiteman. He was called "King of Jazz," "Sultan of Syncopation," "Swami of the Swaying Symphonies," and "The High-Hatted Tragedian of Song." Every entertainer who played clarinet (and some who did not) couldn't resist impersonating him.

He was born Theodore Leopold Friedman on June 6, 1890, in Circleville, Ohio. (Like Lou Costello, Ted took every opportunity to publicize his hometown.) He knew he wanted to be a musician early on. "I ran away from home when I was sixteen and became a clarinet player for the hoochie-koochie dancers in a carnival," he recalled. "I was a disgrace to my family."

After high school Ted went to New York where he formed an instrumental trio, Rose, Young and Friedman. Their first big-time vaudeville appearance was in 1911 at the Palace on a bill headlined by Will Rogers. After the trio broke up, Ted teamed with a young singer and comedian named either Eddie or Jack Lewis. Their act was erroneously billed as "Lewis & Lewis," but Ted liked the new name and kept it.

He formed another trio, Duffy, Geisler and Lewis. They toured with a show on the American Burlesque wheel, a subsidiary of the Columbia circuit, in 1915-16. Ted married one of the show's chorines, Adah Becker. She eventually became his manager.

In 1916 Ted joined pianist Earl Fuller's society dance band, which played the Café Aux Caprice and Rector's Cabaret on Broadway. It was at Rector's that Lewis began sporting his trademark battered top hat, which he won from a hansom cab driver named Mississippi. He told the *Boston Globe* in 1935, "[His hat] strangely fascinated me. I had a hunch [about it]. When the show was over, a couple of friends and I used to ride home in 'Sippi's cab, and I always insisted on wearing that high hat. One night we lured Mississippi into a crap game, and when it was over I'd won the topper. Then the hunch jelled—I wore it that night during my performance at Rector's because I knew it would be recognized and get laughs. And the laughs it got at Rector's it got everywhere, until it became my trademark." Lewis kept the hat in good repair. "It was second hand when I got it," he later explained, "and this hat has been stitched, re-stitched, relined and sewed. I don't think a piece of the original hat is left." He reportedly learned some of the tricks, such as rolling it down his arm, from W. C. Fields.

Lewis' catchphrase was also born at Rector's. "I couldn't ask the customers for applause, like I'd been doing at Coney Island. I had to be more discreet. So one night I just happened to ask: 'Is everybody happy?'"

He rose to fame in Fuller's group and made his first recordings for Columbia in 1917. Lewis left the band in 1919 and took Fuller's four sidemen with him. The band appeared at three Manhattan venues, sometimes on the same night. When he played the Palace again, the *New York Dramatic Mirror* wrote: "There are few who would dare dispute his title of 'Jazz King.' His middle name is rhythm and he fingers a wicked clarinet not to mention a mean shimmy..."

Lewis introduced "When My Baby Smiles at Me," which became his theme song, in the 1920 edition of the Greenwich Village Follies. There had been a dispute over the song's title. Irving Berlin wrote a song called "When My Baby Smiles." Harry Von Tilzer, who published "When My Baby Smiles at Me," claimed that it was written and published first; he said he heard it at Rector's in September 1919. But when he discovered that the song was not protected by copyright, Von Tilzer suggested the title to pianist Bill Munro, who wrote a melody and improvised lyrics for the chorus. Von Tilzer had already paid for orchestrations and advertising when he learned that Berlin had written a song with a comparable title but no other similarities. Berlin's pianist, Harry Akst, suggested that they flip a coin for the title, but Berlin refused and placed an ad in *Variety* stating that his song was registered a month earlier. Von Tilzer's song became a hit. Although he, Munro, Lewis and Andrew G. Sterling are credited, the song was written by Bill Munro and copyrighted by him in January 1920.

Ted's band grew to ten pieces by 1924 and included George Brunis, the legendary New Orleans Rhythm King trombonist, who stayed for ten years. When Lewis played the Palace again, *Variety* wrote, "There was no questioning the hit Ted Lewis...made after considerable absence. Lewis...[is] a poseur, a strutter, a jazz hound, a showman. The latter gives him the 'edge' seventeen different ways over his contemporaries. And they know it, and doubtlessly Lewis himself knows it."

In 1928 Lewis hired other musicians who gave his music added credibility. Coronetist Muggsy Spanier and Don Murray, whom Ted called the greatest clarinetist he ever had in his band, came aboard. That year Lewis added "Me and My Shadow" to his act.

With the arrival of talkies it was only natural that Lewis, like Jolson, would be tapped for films. In 1929 Warner Bros. made the musical *Is Everybody Happy*. Lewis played a character named Tod Todd. *Variety*

called it "so weakly a copy of [Jolson's] 'Singing Fool' as to border on criminal neglect of Lewis and his following." The film is considered lost but the soundtrack is preserved on Vitaphone discs. Curiously, "Me and My Shadow" was not used in that film.

Clarinetist Don Murray died tragically in 1929 and was replaced by Frank Teschemacher, whom Benny Goodman called "perhaps the most inventive musician it has ever been my privilege to hear." When Teschemacher left the band, Jimmy Dorsey replaced him. When Dorsey left a year later, Goodman joined the band. Goodman won a talent contest ten years earlier by imitating Lewis. This new line-up, supplemented by Fats Waller's vocals, produced arguably the best recordings Lewis ever made: "Royal Garden Blues" and "Dallas Blues," cut in 1931.

In 1934 Lewis signed with the new American arm of Decca Records, a British company founded by Edward "Ted" Lewis (no relation). The label's founding roster included Bing Crosby, Guy Lombardo, Tommy and Jimmy Dorsey, Ethel Waters, and the Mills Brothers. The Andrews Sisters joined in 1937.

While his new recordings didn't do as well as his Columbia discs, Lewis' live show continued to draw crowds in nightclubs and theaters. The act grew to include dancers, singers, acrobats, and even a contortionist. "I tried to surround myself with the best possible talent," he later recalled. "This became increasingly easy, because my act was the only one left in the country which could promise a performer a full year's work, year after year."

Hollywood recognized Ted's ongoing marquee value. He was top billed as "Ted Lowry" in MGM's *Here Comes the Band* (1935). Two years later, Lewis was featured in Republic's *Manhattan Merry Go Round* (1937). The film, made at the Biograph Studios in the Bronx, featured cameos by Gene Autry and Joe DiMaggio, who is forced to sing at gunpoint. DiMaggio met his first wife, actress-dancer Dorothy Arnold, on the set.

There are conflicting reports over how much time and money was spent embellishing "Oh, Charlie." Some sources state that shooting started on either May 15 or May 19, and was completed by May 23; others claim that filming lasted nearly two weeks. The budget varies from $25,000, to $100,000, to $150,000 and included a second camera for efficiency. Lubin recalled, "I think *Hold That Ghost* was the first time I used two cameras, because Lou was always changing it. If you go back for re-takes or

*Left: The Andrews Sisters perform "Sleepy Serenade" with a dramatic lighting effect by cinematographer Joseph Valentine. The girls recorded the tune for Decca a day later, on May 21. Right: Ted and Charles "Snowball" Whittier in "Me and My Shadow." On closer inspection they are never perfectly in sync. The number began to face a backlash in 1963.*

added scenes, he'd always add a little more."

A 52-page re-take script dated May 5, along with another eight pages of later undated scenes, follows this chapter. (Scenes from these pages are referred to as "re101" for example, in this chapter.) A shooting schedule no longer exists, but from other documentation it appears that Lubin bounced from set to set and sometimes doubled back again. It is not clear if he directed the musical numbers in *Hold That Ghost* or if they were directed by Larry Ceballos, who directed Lewis' musical short. Curiously, the press book lists every song number that was filmed, although only a few are in *Hold That Ghost*.

Ceballos (1887-1978) was Hollywood's first dance director. He started out in the family's trapeze act as a child, danced in vaudeville with his sister, Florence, and choreographed several Broadway shows. Warner Bros. brought him to Los Angeles to produce the dance numbers at the Hollywood Theater. When talkies came in he began choreographing films for Warners and First National. Vitagraph released a series of shorts under the title *The Larry Ceballos Revue.* His feature credits include *On With the Show, Gold Diggers of Broadway, Show of Shows, Sally, Everything,* and *No, No Nanette.* At other studios he choreographed *Sitting Pretty, Murder at the Vanities, The Music Goes 'Round, Make a Wish* and *Pot o' Gold.* Ceballos helmed several musical shorts at Universal in 1940 and 1941, and choreographed *One Night in the Tropics* and *Spring Parade.*

Elwood Bredell was assigned to the Lewis short, while Universal's star cinematographer, Joseph Valentine (1900-1949), filmed the added sequences in "Oh,

Charlie." *American Cinematographer* wrote, unkindly, "Valentine's contributions does wonders with the by no means photogenic Andrews Sisters—even better, in fact, than he did in their previous appearance in 'In the Navy.'"

Ted Lewis began filming "Isn't She a Pretty Thing" on the nightclub set on May 19. The number, which features Jeanne Blanche, a glamorous tap and ballet dancer, appears only in the short.

Next, the Andrews Sisters shot "Sleepy Serenade," which was written by Mort Greene with music by Louis C. Singer. It was first recorded two months earlier by another Decca artist, Woody Herman. Greene, who wrote principally for RKO, switched to comedy writing in the late 1940s. He later produced Bob Cummings' first television sitcom, *My Hero.* He wrote briefly for a 29-year-old Johnny Carson, then worked on the Perry Como and Red Skelton TV shows. Lou Singer was a child prodigy who taught himself piano. After studying at Julliard, he worked on radio and as an arranger for Duke Ellington and Lou Levy (who managed the Andrews Sisters and was briefly married to Maxene). Singer's brother, Al, was one of the creators of *Name That Tune.* Lou co-wrote the music for two cartoon series his brother produced, *Big World of Little Adam* and *Gigantor.*

The next day, May 21, the Andrews Sisters recorded *Sleepy Serenade* at Decca's Hollywood studio. It charted on October 4 and reached No. 22.

"Me and My Shadow" was filmed next. There is still some controversy over the writing credits. In 1927 Billy Rose bought the title for $15 and roughed out some lyrics. He gave the idea to composer Dave

*After Ferdie is knocked down by the kitchen's swinging doors, he runs into the Andrews Sisters. This scene (Re-14) was cut, but Ferdie references meeting the girls when he catches up to Chuck and Gregory.*

Dreyer, who composed the music and rewrote the lyrics overnight. He presented the song to Rose, who changed one word and then wrote his own name at the top of the sheet music. Rose, who always considered it his favorite song, is credited with the lyrics, while Dreyer and Al Jolson are credited with the music. (Rose's authorship of the lyrics to "I Found a Million Dollar Baby [in a Five and Ten Cent Store,]" and "It's Only a Paper Moon," are also contested. Composer Harry Warren once explained that Rose "mostly stimulated the real lyricists to produce" good work, for which he then took full or partial credit.)

Jolson introduced "Me and My Shadow" in blackface in his Broadway show, "Big Boy." About a year later a diminutive white dancer and comedian named Eddie Chester improvised the "shadow" bit in Ted's show. "He deserves the credit for originating my shadow," Lewis told the *Los Angeles Times* in 1955. However, the *Los Angeles Times* reported that Jay Hurley and Glen Putnam, a pair of young vaudevillians, performed a "smart takeoff on Jolson's 'Me and My Shadow'" several months before Chester.

When Chester left the act after a few months, Lewis hired Charles "Snowball" Whittier, a teenaged dancer whom he saw in a black nightclub, the Apex Cafe, in Los Angeles. In a 1935 interview in the *Pittsburgh Courier,* an African-American newspaper, Whittier said, "Any success I enjoy throughout my lifetime I owe to [Ted Lewis]...When we trouped through the South, he made it possible for me to play every major theater in all the key cities. Whenever the band is registered in a hotel in the South and I am refused admittance, Mr. Lewis finds another place. He says anything that isn't good enough for me isn't good enough for him either. Once, one of the fellows in the band called me a n——. Mr. Lewis fired him." Whittier went on to say, "You know, many white and colored artists claim sincere friendships, but they are false. The white man usually uses the Negro as a tool. But I can truthfully say that is not true in my case, because Mr. Lewis is like a real father to me. I suppose that's why he says 'Charlie, my boy' and I call him 'Pops.'"

The *Chicago Defender*, another African-American newspaper, reported that when the band arrived in Miami in 1937, the club owner told Lewis that black and white performers could not share the same stage. Lewis ordered the band to pack up and leave immediately. The club owner pleaded with him to keep Whittier out the show, but Ted refused. The owner relented, but Whittier received death threats from the Ku Klux Klan. Lewis hired two body guards for him and the Miami shows went on without incident.

"Me and My Shadow" appears in both *Hold That Ghost* and the short, although Whittier performs an extended tap dance in the short while Lewis makes unfunny, condescending, and racist comments off camera. "Show the people those teeth I bought you," Lewis says. In the short, Whittier is dressed all in black except for a gray derby. Lewis asks the audience, "Is the *hat* visible from where you're sitting?"

Four other acts were filmed on this set, but only two made it into the short: an acrobatic ballroom dance trio, Kay, Katya, and Kay, and the Four LeAhn Sisters, a swing quartet. Byron Kay, Katya Komer, and Edwin Kay worked together from 1933 to 1942. They joined Ted's show in the fall of 1940. The act consisted of each man dancing with, lifting, flinging, or spinning Katya. They performed two numbers in the

MISCHA AUER

*Left: The boys vex maître d' Gregory (Mischa Auer). Right: a 1930 trade ad touts the young actor's range in character parts.*

short, including one with Katya made up like a rag doll (and handled like one). The LeAhn Sisters sang a swing version of "Three Blind Mice" with racist overtones. Other numbers by Gladys Tell, a swing singer, and Geraldine Ross, a singing and dancing comedienne, didn't make the cut.

Abbott and Costello started on the club's kitchen set with one of Hollywood's inimitable character actors, Mischa Auer (1905-1967). Auer signed a long-term contract with Universal in 1936 after his Oscar-nominated performance as Carlo, the freeloading gigolo, in *My Man Godfrey*. "I was usually a leering villain, killed in the first reel," Auer once recalled. "I hit the Hollywood mother lode [with *Godfrey*]. That one role made a comic out of me. I haven't been anything else since. It's paid off very well." Auer was filming *The Flame of New Orleans* when "Oh, Charlie" began production, and had just finished shooting *Cracked Nuts* (1941) before being cast as the maître d' Gregory.

Auer was born Mikhail Ounskovsky in St. Petersburg, Russia. His father, a naval officer, was killed in the Russo-Japanese War when Mischa was three. Mischa and his mother, the daughter of celebrated violinist Leopold Auer, were separated during the Bolshevik Revolution. He and other displaced children were sent to Siberia where they roamed the streets and begged for food. "We were such a problem that they finally sent us back to St. Petersburg to find

our families," he recalled. "I found my mother by chance and we went to the south of Russia. There still wasn't enough to eat."

His mother, trained by the Red Cross during the war, contracted typhus in Constantinople and died. Mischa dug her grave with his own hands. He was able to get to Italy where a family friend contacted his grandfather, who was now in New York. He brought Mischa to America, where the boy took his grandfather's surname and learned to play violin and piano.

As a teen Auer was attracted to acting. He made his Broadway debut in 1925. His first screen role was in *Something Always Happens* (1927), and he spent the next few years playing exotic foreigners. "It took me three years to make a living in Hollywood," he once said, "but it's a wonderful country. You can live on oranges and credit, and have a car to boot."

After *My Man Godfrey*, Auer specialized in eccentric foreigners. He was the ballet instructor in 1938's Best Picture, *You Can't Take It with You;* a prince-turned-fashion designer in Walter Wanger's *Vogues of 1938;* and a hen-pecked Russian cowboy in *Destry Rides Again* (1939). His other Universal films include *East Side of Heaven* with Bing Crosby; *One Hundred Men and a Girl* and *Spring Parade* with Deanna Durbin; *Hellzapoppin'* with Olsen and Johnson; and *She Wrote The Book* with Joan Davis.

Auer asked Universal for his release late in 1941 and returned to Broadway in "The Lady Comes

264

*In a cut scene, Bobby Barber lends his head to a math problem. Bobby became part of Lou's entourage several years later and a member of the stock company of* The Abbott and Costello Show.
*Below: Ted Lewis tries to help solve the plate-counting problem.*

Across." His reviews were harsh and the show closed after one night. Auer's film characterizations also began to wear thin with critics and the public. In 1943 *Photoplay* wrote, "Mischa Auer grows cornier by the Auer." He did better on live television and received raves for a 1953 *Omnibus* presentation of George Bernard Shaw's "Arms and the Man." His later stage work in a revival of "Tovarich" in Paris and "The Merry Widow" at Lincoln Center were also highly praised. Auer and his family settled in Austria in the 1950s and he worked in European-made films, including Orson Welles' *Mr. Arkadin* (1955).

Auer was married four times. He wed Norma Tillman in 1930 and had a son and a daughter with her. The couple divorced in November 1940. During retakes on "Oh, Charlie," he announced his engagement to singer Joyce Hunter. The marriage ended in 1950. That year he married Susanne Kalish, with whom he had a daughter. They divorced in 1957. His fourth wife was Elise Souls Lee (1965-1967). Auer died in 1967 after suffering two heart attacks.

With Lewis and his orchestra pantomiming in the background, Gregory orders Chuck to make a waiter out of Ferdie (Re-15). Chuck demonstrates how to slide a chair in or out for a guest and explains that after taking an order, Ferdie must show his slip to the checker. (The checker tallied up the items on the bill.) Ferdie says he isn't wearing one. The scene cuts to "Me and My Shadow," deleting a forgettable math

routine (Re-15). Chuck explains that dinner costs $3, and that three dinners are $9. Ferdie, however, claims that three times three is ten. As they argue, Ferdie draws another waiter into the dispute. The waiter says the answer is eleven. Ted Lewis steps in and says the answer is fourteen. To prove it, he counts dinner plates and somehow gets to fourteen. When Ferdie counts plates, he only gets to nine. In frustration he grabs a tenth plate and slams it down. It isn't apparent if there was more to this bit than what appears in the script. It was cut for any number of reasons, most likely because a far better math routine, "7x13=28," had appeared in *In The Navy*.

Bobby Barber, a familiar face to Abbott and Costello fans, plays the waiter. Born in New York City on Dec. 18, 1894, Barber worked in vaudeville and

265

*Top: Ferdie pulls a chair out for a diner (William Ruhl), who lands on the floor. The roll-up vest gag is repeated here, too. Center: Bannister delivers the will to Moose. The two women seated here are also seen with Ruhl. Bottom: Charlie Smith confronts Bannister in the lobby.*

on the stage before migrating to Hollywood. He broke into films in a Lloyd Hamilton short, *Nobody's Business* (1926), and turned up in over 200 films and TV shows. He also had a side career as a professional jester. The Hollywood elite (including Jack Benny) hired him to appear at parties as a waiter and annoy the guests. (This may explain why so many of his bit roles were as waiters.) Barber appeared in films with nearly every famous comedy team, as well as *Modern Times, Dodsworth, Beau Geste, Vivacious Lady, They Knew What They Wanted, My Favorite Spy, I Walk Alone,* and *Man of a Thousand Faces.*

In 1947 Charles Barton was directing *The Wistful Widow of Wagon Gap* with Bud and Lou. Barton had previously worked with Bobby and hired him for a bit part as a waiter. During production Lou's father, Sebastian Cristillo, died unexpectedly. Bobby's wife, Maxine, recalled: "Lou and Bobby weren't close until Lou's father died. Lou's father had a special chair on the set. Lou walked on the set, saw the chair, started to cry, and walked out. They told Bobby, 'Go get him.' Bobby ran after Lou and walked and talked with him. I don't know what Bobby said to him, but he got Lou to come back. After that, they were inseparable."

When he wasn't doing bits in the boys' films, TV shows, or live appearances, Bobby was their off-camera court jester. "Bobby loved doing anything that made people laugh," Maxine said. "You might say he was the scapegoat, but as long as people laughed, he didn't care." Bobby died on May 24, 1976.

Next, Lubin shot Charlie Smith's encounter with Bannister in the club's lobby (Re-21). Marc Lawrence had picked up more work after "Oh, Charlie." He was placed in *The Man Who Lost Himself* and the Richard Arlen-Andy Devine programmer *A Dangerous Game* at Universal; *Blossoms in the Dust* at MGM; and the gangster comedy *Lady Scarface* at RKO. Russell Hicks had worked on *Sergeant York* (1941) and was making *The Little Foxes* (as was Richard Carlson) when retakes were shot.

The scene between Bannister and Moose was likely also covered at this time. William Davidson recently worked in *In The Navy* as Captain Richards, and in *Sun Valley Serenade* (along with Joan Davis) as the resort's owner. Moose is seated with "two glamorous looking blondes" (Re-18). Breen warned, "These women should not be suggestive of women of loose morals." (Their morals may be fine but they do get around; they are also in the chair gag scene, which was supposed to come after Moose dismisses them.) Significantly, we hear Moose tell Bannister, whom he does not fully trust, that the money is "in my head." Other lines of their dialogue alarmed the Breen Office. They wrote, "The character of Attorney Bannister in this scene is unacceptable, for the reason that it shows him as an accessory to Matson's crimi-

*Left: In Bannister's office, Smith says he has arranged to take the boys for a ride. Right: Smith and members of the gang. Ed Pawley drives, with (left to right) Frank Penny, Nestor Paiva, and Harry Wilson in the back.*

nal activities. This characterization will also cause widespread criticism of this picture generally by members of the bar. We refer especially to the dialogue, 'Charlie Smith knows you pulled the Worthington payroll job. He wants fifty percent of the proceeds to keep quiet.' Then follows similar dialogue, and further reference to the 'payroll money.' We urge and recommend that you change these speeches so that Bannister will be discussing a legitimate business deal with Matson, perhaps something to the effect, 'Charlie Smith wants you to settle up for that property you bought,' and carry on from there with suitable changes of the other dialogue."

Rather than adopt the censors' fix, Milton Feld, in a phone call with the PCA on May 15, agreed to change Bannister from a lawyer to Moose's right-hand man. An unseen attorney ostensibly drew up Matson's will, which Bannister merely delivers. This change necessitated replacing the probate court scenes, where Bannister is clearly identified as an attorney, with a new scene in his office. Breen cautioned, "It should not suggest a lawyer's office, with law books in the background, etc., so that there can be no question in the minds of the audience that Bannister is not a lawyer." Most viewers, however, assume that he is a lawyer. In another change, Bannister introduces the boys to Charlie Smith.

Back on the nightclub set, Chuck continues to train Ferdie (Re-23). He tells him there are three pat answers when a customer complains: "Three dollars," "Tell it to the manager," and, "If you don't, someone else will." After Ferdie slides a chair out and a customer lands on the floor, he uses all three responses out of context with the livid patron. (Ferdie's victim

was originally one of these women, who threatened to call Moose.) William Ruhl (1901-1956), a prolific character actor of the 1930s, 1940s and early 1950s, is the victim. Sadly, according to one source, Ruhl's wife, actress Lu Miller, died about three weeks before these scenes were shot.

The following day, Bud, Lou, Joan Davis, Richard Carlson, and Evelyn Ankers reported to the tavern's dining room set for re-takes. They were joined by Ed Pawley, Harry Wilson, Nestor Paiva, Frank Penny, and a brand new rival for Moose's stash.

Carlson came over from Goldwyn Studios, where he was playing Teresa Wright's love interest in *The Little Foxes*. (Wright, in her film debut, was nominated for Best Supporting Actress.) Director William Wyler reportedly shot around Carlson, although that may have been unnecessary. On May 12, star Bette Davis famously walked off the film for three weeks after clashing with Wyler. Meanwhile, Mona Carlson gave birth the couple's first child, Richard Henry.

Carlson's role in the period film required longer sideburns that were not trimmed when he returned to Universal. In the sequences after Ferdie empties the moose head, Carlson's sideburns change length as new footage mixes with old. They are longer in the new finale as well. (His sideburns are hard to spot in the new exterior bus scene because he is partially obscured.) Costello's grooming and wardrobe also betray the new footage. His hair, cropped closer for *In The Navy*, is noticeably shorter in the re-takes; also, his fedora does not sit as far back on his head, and the hat's decorative feathers are more prominent.

It was long assumed that Joan Davis was unavailable for re-takes because she was filming *Sun Valley*

*Contrary to some claims, Joan was not doubled in the last tavern scenes. She and Carlson were working at other studios but returned for re-takes. Compare his sideburns here with the photo on page 78 from the original production. They are longer because he was making the period film* The Little Foxes. *The feathers on Ferdie's hat in these re-takes do not match the original footage, either.*

*Serenade* at Fox. But that picture wrapped two weeks earlier. She was making another film, *Two Latins from Manhattan*, at Columbia. Director Charles Barton worked around her on the day or two she was needed at Universal. Joan clearly re-shot the wildcat bus scenes and some tavern scenes and was not doubled, as others have surmised. Her character was written into a quick gag in the new finale (Re-116), but she does not appear. Instead, Ferdie explains her absence with the "runaway marriage" joke (re93).

After Evelyn Ankers completed "Oh, Charlie," Universal tossed her into *Hit the Road* with the Dead End Kids and Little Tough Guys. She later recalled rebuffing the unsolicited amatory advances of Huntz Hall. "I responded as my daddy taught me to—I let him have it with my knee right between his legs," she recalled. In March, Evelyn was cast in another Burt Kelly production, the Baby Sandy picture *Bachelor Daddy*, which was also scripted by Lees and Rinaldo. In April she made *Burma Convoy*. Since *Hold That Ghost* was not released until August, *Hit the Road* and *Bachelor Daddy* were Evelyn's first American releases.

When she was reunited with her "Oh, Charlie" cast mates in May, a gossip columnist reported that Evelyn was engaged to Major Byron Ashford Russell of the British Army. They supposedly met on the set of her British film *Second Thoughts* (1938) when he was a critic for the *London Star*. It was reported that they planned to wed after the war, but there are no further references to Russell; Ankers will soon begin a relationship with actor Glenn Ford.

The re-take script expands on Norma and Dr. Jackson's courtship, no doubt to bolster an element the studio believed contributed to the alchemy of *Buck Privates*: romance. Scenes Re-80 to Re-83 were proposed to replace Sc. 263, where Jackson deduces that Norma is angry with him because she likes him. In the new scenes Norma spots a "Wishbloom tree" from the bedroom window. She considers it a romantic talisman, but the Doctor recognizes it as a perennial plant native to places with hidden springs. This leads back into Sc. 264 in the original film, where a knife-wielding hand appears from behind a painting. The Wish-bloom tree is reprised on opening night at the resort. With Ferdie's labored help (Re-104 to Re-116), the tree affirms Norma's belief in its romantic power. These scenes, however, were not filmed.

The retake script adds two memorable lines when Ferdie searches the moose head: "Don't bite me," and "I'll never join your lodge!" (Re-84). This suggests that the sequence needed punching up. However, there may be another explanation. In the event that Joan Davis had limited availability, the new script has Camille excuse herself before the "figure of speech" argument (Re-79). With her gone, the boys' dialogue, as well as Ferdie's search of the moose head, would need to be completely re-shot with only he and Chuck. Ferdie's line, "Camille, does mooses have ton-

*Left: Costello adds choice dialogue to his encounter with the moose head. Right: The Mystery Man, Frank Richards, demands the loot. Note that Costello's hair and the feather in his hat do not match the original footage.*

sils?," (which was added during the original shoot), would have to be addressed to Chuck (Re-86). For this reason, dialogue is duplicated in the re-take script even though it may have been shot earlier. It is possible that "Don't bite me" and "I'll never join your lodge" were already in the original footage but repeated in the new script to cover them without Camille.

Costello embellishes the bare bones of the line "Don't bite me" when he first approaches the stuffed animal. He explains, "Now look, I'm gonna put my hand in your mouth. Don't *bite* it. This one's goin' in. This is the one I eat with." He gently pats the moose and boasts, "I got a way with animals."

The "lodge" line is a reference to the Loyal Order of Moose, a fraternal and community service organization founded in 1888. (The Elks were founded twenty years earlier.) Originally exclusively male and white, it later expanded to include women and minorities and is now known as the International Order of Moose. Depending on the source, it has anywhere from 650,000 to one million members in 1,600 to 2,400 Lodges in the U.S., Canada, Great Britain and Bermuda. According to the organization, Abbott and Costello were members of Lodge 216 in Atlantic City, although their membership may have been honorary and, perhaps, a result of this scene.

Soon after Ferdie recovers the money the resentful "Mystery Man" emerges from the shadows (Re-90). Edward Eliscu and Edmund Hartmann both wrote this character into their treatments, possibly at the suggestion of the producers. This is all new footage; notice Carlson's sideburns and Costello's hat.

The Mystery Man (or "Gunman" in the credits) is played by Frank Richards (1909-1992), recognizable to fans of TV's *The Adventures of Superman*. He menaced Lois and Jimmy in the episodes "Tin Hero," "Shot in the Dark," and "Night of Terror." (In "Night of Terror," Richards was supposed to hit Phyllis Coates to prevent her from leaving a tourist cabin. Coates missed her mark and Richards knocked her out cold. The punch was left in the episode.) A New York native, Richards made his stage debut in 1938 and worked in Hollywood from 1940. His 150 film and TV credits include *The Cowboy and the Indians* (1949), *Pat and Mike* (1952), and *A Woman Under the Influence* (1974). Richards appeared in an episode of *The Abbott and Costello Show* that echoed *Hold That Ghost* and Fox's *The Ghost Talks* (1929), which was based on the comedy-mystery play "Badges." In "Private Eye," Lou takes a correspondence course to become a detective and tries to help a young woman recover some valuable bonds from a house that is "haunted" by a disgruntled cousin; Richards is one of his henchmen. In 1954, Richards and Nestor Paiva appeared with the boys on a *Colgate Comedy Hour* where Costello impersonated the ruler of a fictional South American country. Richard's last role was as a security guard in a two-part episode of *Diff'rent Strokes* (1984). He died in Las Vegas.

The Breen Office warned, "The Mystery Man's line, 'Stick 'em up,' and the voice [Rosy] saying 'Reach for the ceiling,' may be deleted by some political censor boards." After Ferdie drags the unconscious Mystery Man away, the original gang members appear and demand the loot (Re-94). Again, new footage briefly blends with old in a shortened fight sequence, which completely eliminates the escaped convicts and the reprise of the phony detectives.

*Top left: The group quickly defeats the gang in re-takes. Top right: In the original footage, Chuck runs to answer the siren at the front door. Note the broken records on the floor, and their absence in the shot on the left.*
*Bottom left: The new ending with Dr. Jackson and Norma as newlyweds. Ferdie explains Camille's absence with the "runaway marriage" joke. Bottom right: Alderman Birch (Thurston Hall) and his young date (Janet Shaw).*

However, a vestige of the original fight remains. When Chuck runs to answer the siren at the front door, the dining room floor is littered with broken records. This shot, which pans with Chuck to the door and reveals Ferdie as the source of the siren, was in the original footage. There is also a continuity error. Chuck carries the bag of money in the original footage, but when he starts for the door in re-takes, running away from the camera, he is empty-handed.

Other re-takes on the tavern set included Dr. Jackson professing the therapeutic value of the water and Ferdie restating his ambition to hire Ted Lewis and the Andrews Sisters (Re-98). The old money-counting bit in this scene is not in the script. This gag really *is* old; it appears in a compilation of bits from the *commedia dell'arte* dated 1618 and is probably older.

Next, Lubin shot the end gag at the tavern's cash register with Chuck, Ferdie, Dr. Jackson, and Norma (re93). There was an additional routine (re94-96) that

was not filmed. After the Doctor and Norma exit, Ferdie laments that although he and Chuck are now successful, they don't have anyone to dance with. Just then a young woman walks by and accidentally drops her purse. A young man promptly returns it to her and asks her to dance. This gives Chuck an idea. He tells Ferdie to toss money on the ground, stop the next girl that comes along, and point out the lost money. She'll deny that it's hers, but Ferdie will have a chance to ask her to dance. After a couple of bad candidates, one young woman is honest and denies that it's her money. Chuck, however, has Ferdie insist that she take it. She refuses at first but then gives in, takes the cash, and walks off. When Ferdie surreptitiously retrieves his money from her purse, he and Chuck are arrested. They are put in a paddy wagon…along with Charlie Smith's body.

Lubin and the boys returned to the nightclub set for the sequence with Alderman Birch and his young date. (An alderman is a member of a city council.) The Breen Office warned, "We assume there will be nothing sexually suggestive about this 'baby-faced cutie.'"

The alderman is played by Thurston Hall (1882-1958), who had just appeared as a senator in *In The Navy*. Born in Boston, Hall's Broadway credits include two dozen shows between 1914 and 1934. His film career began in 1915, and he supported Theda Bara in her vamp dramas. He later specialized in pompous or blustering authority figures. His best-known television role was as Cosmo Topper's boss, Mr. Schuyler, in the 1950s TV series, *Topper*. Hall also appeared in two episodes of *The Abbott and Costello Show*. He played philanthropist J. Peter Stuyvesant in "The Actor's Home," (which includes "Who's On First?"), and the bank manager in "The Tax Return."

Janet Shaw (1919–2001) plays the alderman's date. Born Ellen Martha Clancy Stuart, her film career began at age fifteen as one of several young hopefuls in the short *A Trip Through a Hollywood Studio*. Grooming her for bigger roles, Jack Warner signed her to a seven-year contract and changed her name to Janet Shaw. He expanded her role as Molly Allen in *Jezebel* (1938), the film that earned Bette Davis her second Academy Award. Alfred Hitchcock saw Janet in *Night Monster* (1943) at Universal and cast her as Louise Finch, the dispirited waitress, in *Shadow of a Doubt* (1943). Shaw appeared in about sixty films during the 1930s and 1940s. Her last role was in an episode of *City Detective* in 1955. She died after a long battle with Alzheimer's disease in her native town, Beatrice, Nebraska.

Back on the club's kitchen set, Lubin shot the sequence where Gregory catches Chuck and Ferdie shooting craps with the other waiters (Re-11 and Re-12). These scenes, which introduce the boys in the film, clearly exploit the Dice routine in *Buck Privates*. As it had with *Buck Privates,* Breen cautioned, "We assume no money will be shown in this gambling game. Otherwise, this scene may be deleted by some political [local] censor boards."

Gregory criticizes the boys' appearance and orders Ferdie to straighten his vest. It rolls up like a window shade. Perhaps this inspired the film's end gag. The company returned to the tavern's cash register set for an end sequence that is not in the re-take script. Chuck, suspicious of Ferdie, counts the money in the register and finds a single dollar. He slaps Ferdie, whose vest rolls up to reveal a stash of money.

The Andrews Sisters performed "Aurora" on the

*Above: Gregory catches Chuck and Ferdie shooting dice. Below: Ferdie's vest rolls up, perhaps inspiring the end gag (bottom), shot soon afterward.*

271

*Top: The Andrews Sisters perform "Aurora" at the refurbished tavern. Center: After re-shooting the bus exteriors, the boys help themselves to the alderman's duck dinner and are thrown out of the club. Bottom: A fourth(!) reprise of the vest gag, this time with Gregory.*

tavern's pavilion set. "Aurora" was a Brazilian song written in 1940 by Mario Lago, a composer, actor, poet, and lawyer, and Roberto Roberti, who penned numerous *marchas* for Rio's annual Carnival. Pedro Berrios wrote the Spanish lyrics. The Andrews Sisters

recorded the song with English lyrics by Harold Adamson in New York in March. (Adamson wrote the English lyrics for two earlier Andrews Sisters hits, "The Woodpecker Song" and "Ferryboat Serenade," both of which were originally in Italian.) Adamson's own songs appeared in *Around the World in 80 Days*, *Gentleman Prefer Blonds*, and *An Affair to Remember*. He was nominated for Academy Awards five times. His most popular songs include "Did I Remember?," "Comin' in on a Wing and a Prayer," "I Couldn't Sleep a Wink Last Night," and the theme for *I Love Lucy*. ASCAP has a songwriter's workshop named in his honor funded from his royalties.

The Breen Office objected to the lyric, "I'll give you this and give you that" because of its sexual suggestiveness. Milton Feld assured Breen that no salaciousness was intended. (Actually, the lyric in every version is, "I'll buy you this and buy you that," including the girls' Decca recording.) The Production Code's South American expert, Addison Durland, believed another line, "Is it me or just my money," would prove offensive to Latin Americans. (The PCA was overly cautious given the recent uproar over the sisters' film *Argentine Nights*.) Feld assured the censors that the song was already a hit in South America.

The Andrews Sisters' Decca recording charted on May 31 and ultimately reached No. 10. The chorus from "Aurora" can be heard in the coda of the 1976 dance hit "Cherchez La Femme," written by Gloria Estefan and performed by the swing-influenced disco group, Dr. Buzzard's Original Savannah Band.

Ted Lewis performed "On the Sunny Side of the Street" on this set; it's not in *Hold That Ghost* but opens the two-reel short. The song is credited to Jimmy McHugh (music) and Dorothy Fields (lyrics), although some sources state that Fats Waller wrote it then sold the rights. It was introduced in the 1930 Broadway musical *Lew Leslie's International Revue*, but Ted Lewis was the first to make it a hit; his melancholy version reached No. 2.

Lubin moved to the back lot to re-shoot the wildcat bus exteriors (Re-67 to Re-76). These scenes were revised because Charlie Smith's role had changed and the grocery store sequence had been deleted. Watch closely as Hoskins (Milton Parsons) mixes up the boys when he introduces them to Norma. There is one snippet left of the original footage here. Ferdie inadvertently tosses Chuck's bag over Hoskins' sedan and on top of a passing bus. Step through the high angle shot that tracks the flight of the bag. Chuck and

*Chuck's handprint on Ferdie's cheek does not quite match between the medium close up (left) shot on a sound stage with rear screen projection, and the wider exterior (right). In the script, Ferdie squirts himself.*

Hoskins are wearing coats at the very head of the shot. When re-takes were filmed, it was sunny and the temperature reached the mid-90s.

Lubin then returned to the nightclub set to film another scene that appears in the undated pages as re44. When his young date gets up to dance, the Alderman leaves in a huff. Chuck and Ferdie help themselves to his duck dinner. (In the May 5 script, Re-37 to Re-58, Ferdie dances with the girl until Chuck retrieves him.) The verbal mix-up over the verb "duck" and the noun "duck" was salvaged from the grocery store scene. As Ferdie struggles to carve the bird, Gregory surprises them, and the fowl naturally ends up in Gregory's face. The boys bolt out of the scene as Gregory starts after them. Gregory's line, "You're both fired! Get out!" and Ferdie's line, "Back to our old job at the gas station!" were both post-dubbed; their mouths don't move.

Then it was back to the tavern's cash register set. In the script (Re-104), Gregory is revealed as the boys' maître d' in a quick sight gag. A longer bit was developed where he shows up as a relief waiter. In a duplicate of their scene at the beginning of the film, Ferdie gives Gregory a similar dressing down and orders him to fix his vest, which also rolls up.

With the addition of the opening nightclub scenes, dialogue in the gas station sequence needed revising. The boys had to reference the previous night's debacle and Ferdie had to vow to hire Ted Lewis and the Andrews Sisters when he had his own club. In the new scene, Ferdie squirts Chuck with a grease gun and Chuck slaps him. In the script, Ferdie squirts himself (re61). A close-up of the slap was filmed on a sound stage with rear-screen projection, but Chuck's

handprint on Ferdie's face does not quite match the medium exterior shot. Both men have black smears on their faces. Ferdie says, "Now we're a couple of shadows," an unfortunate reference to Ted Lewis' act. Chuck scoffs at Ferdie's dream of his own nightclub. Lou interrupts and ad-libs, "Don't look now, but your eye is dripping." Abbott barks, "Quiet!" He continues to scold Ferdie, but slightly garbles his line: "You just had us thrown out of one! And if you don't get on, uh, the job you'll have us throw us [sic] out of here!" Costello imitates Abbott's little flub with a tongue trill. Bud turns and stifles a laugh. (It is unclear how they could be fired from their own gas station.)

The boys wipe the grease off their faces (so that they will match the original opening footage), and Ferdie repeats his vow to someday hire Ted Lewis and the Andrews Sisters. He picks up the air hose and pulls a balloon out of his pocket. This action dovetails into the film's original opening footage: Chuck writes on the blackboard and the camera pans over to Ferdie, who has a few inflated balloons around him. Ferdie approaches Chuck and stuffs the air hose with a balloon attached into his back pocket. A few women dressed in long coats pass in the background; this footage was originally shot in late February.

On the night of May 21, Bud and Lou threw a party for friends at Leone's, the Hollywood branch of the New York celebrity restaurant. In 1959 the Manhattan eatery was sold, expanded, and renamed Mama Leone's.

Lubin wrapped re-takes on May 23 and Phil Cahn set about weaving them into a revised cut. Meanwhile, Universal considered changing the film's title. On June 9, *Daily Variety* reported that "Oh, Charlie"

The animated titles, created by Walter Lantz Productions, were a departure from the preceding and succeding service comedies. A portion of this footage was used in the opening titles of Olsen and Johnson's Ghost Catchers (1944).

was now called *Hold That Ghost.* (Lou's young daughters, Paddy and Carole, however, reportedly referred to it as "Holy Ghost.") There had been other "Hold That" films: *Hold That Girl* (1934); *Hold That Kiss* (1938); and *Hold That Woman* (1940). But perhaps the idea came from Joan Davis' film *Hold That Co-Ed* (1938), in which she played a talented kicker on a college football team.

The film continued through post-production, adding animated opening titles and a music score. The titles, by Walter Lantz Productions, were likely animated by Alex Lovy and either Frank Tipper or Verne Harding, one of the first woman animators. The firm began as Universal's in-house studio in 1929. Lantz (1900-1994) had tried to start his own studio while working in a series of odd jobs, including chauffeuring Carl Laemmle. Lantz explained to Don Peri in *Working with Disney: Interviews with Animators, Producers, and Artists:* "[Laemmle] asked me if I would set up a cartoon studio for them. I'd had ten years' experience producing cartoons before I came out here...I set up a whole department for them—built desks, had a camera built, and everything. We had over a hundred people working in that department."

Lantz broke away in 1935 and formed his own company. He continued, "Then later, in 1937... Universal was having financial troubles and couldn't produce cartoons. They asked me if I would produce them independently [and they] would release them." Lantz supplied cartoons until 1972, including a series inspired by a pesky woodpecker during his honeymoon in a rural cabin. Woody Woodpecker was introduced in *Knock! Knock!* (1940) and was a big hit. Later in 1941, Lantz produced a car-

toon of "Boogie Woogie Bugle Boy" (1941) featuring black caricatures that was nominated for an Academy Award. Today his company exists in name only as a subsidiary of Universal Animation Studios, which owns all rights to his characters.

The music supervisor, Hans J. Salter (1896-1994), began scoring films at Germany's UFA studios in 1928. He immigrated to the United States in 1937 and signed with Universal, where he worked for nearly thirty years arranging, composing, conducting, and serving as musical director.

"You know what they used to call me in those days?" Salter asked Preston Neal Jones in *I Talked with a Zombie: Interviews with 23 Veterans of Horror and Sci-Fi Films and Television.* "'The Master of Terror and Suspense!' [laughs] Pretty good?"

Salter scored 150 movies and was nominated for six Academy Awards, including consecutive years for *The Amazing Mrs. Holliday* (1943), *Christmas Holiday* (1944), and *This Love of Ours* (1945). His other memorable scores include *The Wolf Man* (1941), *Scarlet Street* (1945), *Bend of the River* (1952), *Creature from the Black Lagoon* (1954), and *The Incredible Shrinking Man* (1957).

Salter supervised the recording sessions for the musical numbers in *Hold That Ghost* and selected pre-recorded background cues from earlier Universal films. Many cues in *Hold That Ghost* were lifted from his score for *Black Friday* (1940). In *Film Score: The Art and Craft of Movie Music,* Salter explained to Tony Thomas, "A great deal of music was used and reused at Universal in those years. We were always fighting time, and it was a matter of necessity. I would use bits and pieces of scores from the library, including my own. Charlie Previn [Universal's musical director] used to call this process 'Salterizing.'"

Other recycled cues were composed by Previn, Ralph Freed, Charles Henderson, Milton Rosen, and Frank Skinner. Skinner (1897-1968) also wrote the main title theme, which transitions into "When My Baby Smiles at Me." Before joining Universal in 1935, Skinner orchestrated and arranged dance band music. He and Salter often collaborated on the studio's horror fare. "I can't speak too highly of Frank Skinner," Salter said. "He often did more than he needed to do, such as coming to my rescue when I couldn't finish a sequence on time." Skinner's contemporaneous scores for *House of the Seven Gables* (1940) and *Back Street* (1941) were nominated for Academy Awards. He later wrote the score for *Abbott and Costello Meet Frankenstein* (1948), which was re-cycled in later A&C horror spoofs.

The trailer for *Hold That Ghost* was finished in mid-July. Trailers, posters and other marketing materials were created by the publicity and advertising specialists of National Screen Service (NSS). NSS had a production facility on Santa Monica Boulevard in Hollywood, and a group of NSS employees were in residence at each movie studio. Beginning in 1939, Robert Faber produced, wrote and directed coming attractions and shorts for Universal for over forty years. He once explained, "One of our prime rules is never to satisfy an audience with our trailer. Our job is to tease the audience into wanting to see more—even when there may be no more to see."

The surviving trailer for *Hold That Ghost* is from the 1948 Realart re-release. It omits several scenes in the original trailer, including Richard Carlson (before Joan Davis) and Evelyn Ankers (after Mischa Auer). Then, following a clip of the gang fight, Bud and Lou addressed the audience from bed. Costello says, "Ever since we started making that picture 'Hold That Ghost,' I keep seeing spooks, ghosts, secret panels, bodies falling—oh, oh, oh—"

Abbott says, "Naturally, it's supposed to be a comedy. It's all in fun."

"It may be fun to you, Abbott," Lou says, "it may be fun to you—and if I had to do it all over again—I'd do it. It was fun to me, too."

Bud says, "All right, all right, Costello. Go to sleep. Come on." A transition wipe brings on nightclub footage with Ferdie, the alderman and his date.

Ted Lewis' two-reeler, *Is Everybody Happy*, was released on Sept. 3. It was produced by Will Cowan (1911-1994), a former song and dance man who oversaw Universal's musical shorts from 1940 to 1956. Cowan, who was born in Scotland, turned out one short a month featuring nearly every big band or musical act of the era. He also produced the Inner Sanctum mysteries *Dead Man's Eyes* and *The Frozen Ghost* (the latter with Evelyn Ankers); *Jungle Woman* (also with Ankers); *Idea Girl*; and *Cuban Pete* with Desi Arnaz. After the musical shorts had run their course, Cowan produced and directed the Grade-Z horror movie *The Thing That Couldn't Die* (1958). He went on to head the new TV commercial production units of Universal, Warner Bros., and finally Filmways of California. In 1972 he bought Filmways of California and renamed it Will Cowan Productions.

The short includes "On The Sunny Side of The Street," "Me and My Shadow," "Three Blind Mice," "Isn't She a Pretty Thing," and "Leader of the Town Brass Band." "Murder," and another Lewis favorite, "Just Around the Corner," were filmed but not used. Ted performed "Just Around the Corner" in Universal's all-star musical *Follow the Boys* (1944).

On May 26 Lewis and his orchestra cut "Just Around the Corner," "Down the Old Church Aisle," "Tiger Rag," and "Jazz Me Blues" at Decca's Hollywood studios. These were the last recordings he ever made. Promotional discs featuring the original scoring stage performances of "Me and My Shadow" and "Sunny Side of the Street" from *Hold That Ghost* were sent to radio stations, but carried the film's original title, "Oh, Charlie." A ten-inch, double-sided 78 of musical excerpts by the Andrews Sisters and Lewis was also made available for publicity.

*Variety* called Ted's two-reeler a "showmanlike presentation." *Film Daily* said, "It is hard to get tired of Ted Lewis' style and he pleases as he always did." But *Showman's Trade Review* rated it "Fair" and wrote, "[F]or those who can take Ted Lewis and the way he talks a song, it will be quite acceptable. Others may find it not so entertaining." An exhibitor in Alfred, New York, wrote to *Motion Picture Herald*, "Not bad if you like Ted Lewis." But the manager of the Rialto in Marengo, Indiana, complained, "This is about the worst two reeler I have run. Why doesn't Lewis give up? The music is poor and his moaning is awful. A customer said after hearing him, 'If he's in such misery, why don't they shoot him?'"

In 1949, Castle Films released a one-reel edition entitled *Ted Lewis And His Band* as part of the "Band Parade" series.

# "Oh, Charlie" Revisions Script

Here is the 52-page revisions script dated May 5, more than two weeks before filming began, followed by eight pages of undated scenes that were written closer to the shoot date.

The script describes where these new scenes pick up from or dovetail into scenes in the original screenplay. While ideas from several writers are incorporated, no specific credit is given. The biggest contributor, however, appears to be Edmund L. Hartmann; his name even appears at the top of page 35. Still, some other ideas and scenes were apparently developed and shot on the fly.

Surprisingly, the script has a quick final gag with Camille, Ferdie and Charlie Smith's body. Unfortunately, Joan Davis was ultimately written out of the ending because of limited availability.

"OH, CHARLIE"

FADE IN:

Over Ted Lewis' music.

RE- 1    LONG SHOT - EXT. CITY STREET (STOCK) - DUSK

Hurrying pedestrians.  The lamp posts suddenly light up.

RE- 2    LONG SHOT - EXT. CITY STREET (STOCK) - NIGHT

Against the dark sky overhead the electric signs
are turned on and begin to blink all over town.

RE- 3    MED. LONG - CITY STREET - NIGHT - STREET CORNER

A few pedestrians waiting for the traffic signal to
change.  A man notices something overhead and o.s. which
amuses him.  He nudges the girl with him.  She looks
up too.

RE- 4    CLOSE SHOT - ELECTRIC SIGN (SLIGHTLY TILTED)

An outline of Ted Lewis in high hat, attached to sign.
Because only part of the letters are lighted it reads:

```
*******************************
*                             *
*       CHEZ GLAMOUR          *
*        TED LEWIS            *
*                             *
*         I     N             *
*                             *
*       DRES     SES          *
*                             *
*******************************
```

RE- 5    MED. CLOSE - EXT. STREET CORNER - NIGHT

a larger crowd enjoying the sign, paying no attention
to the cop's whistle.

RE- 6    CLOSE SHOT - ELECTRIC SIGN

as more bulbs light up, it reads:

```
*******************************
*                             *
*        CHEZ GLAMOUR         *
*                             *
*          TED LEWIS          *
*                             *
*           AND HIS           *
*                             *
*         DRE S S    ERS      *
*                             *
*******************************
```

And then rapidly it becomes:

```
*******************************
*                             *
*        CHEZ GLAMOUR         *
*                             *
*          TED LEWIS          *
*                             *
*         AND HIS BAND        *
*                             *
*        ANDREWS SISTERS      *
*                             *
*******************************
```

                                                    DISSOLVE THRU SIGN

on a sustained clarinet note to:

RE- 7    LONG SHOT - INT. CHEZ GLAMOUR

A crowded, well-appointed night club.  At the far end
TED LEWIS and his band performing one of his trade
mark numbers, probably "When My Baby Smiles At Me".
The CAMERA MOVES IN during the number.  When it is over:

RE- 8    CLOSE SHOT - TED LEWIS

                    TED LEWIS
                 (in his well
                  known manner)
            Yes, sir, is everybody happy?
                 (starts "Isn't She a
                  Pretty Thing?")

RE- 9    MED. LONG

Lewis does "Isn't She A Pretty Thing?"

RE-10    MED. SHOT - DANCE SPECIALTY

"Isn't She A Pretty Thing?"

RE-11    MED. SHOT - NEAR ENTRANCE TO KITCHEN

GREGORY, the large, severe maitre d'hotel, seems distracted trying to seat people at a table who bustle
and crowd around him.  A bus boy comes up to him.

                    BUS BOY
          Mr. Gregory --

                    GREGORY
               (turns around)
          Yes, what is it?

                    BUS BOY
          The relief waiters are here.

                    GREGORY
          About time.  Don't stare at me --
          help that waiter.

The CAMERA PANS him over to the kitchen door.  As he
reaches the door:

                    FERDIE'S VOICE
               (o.s.)
          Come on you guys, get your money
          out - before I shoot.

Gregory reacts - reaching for a gun in his hip pocket.

                    FERDIE'S VOICE (Cont'd)
               (o.s.)
          Put the dough in a pile, and don't
          try any tricks, when I say I'll shoot,
          I MEAN I'LL SHOOT.

RE-12    INT. FOOD CHECKING ROOM- LEADING TO DANCE FLOOR

GREGORY comes stealthily in - only to discover FERDIE
rolling dice with CHUCK and a couple of waiters (or
cooks.)  The waiters scramble out of SCENE - as Gregory
grabs Ferdie and pulls him to his feet.  Both Chuck
and Ferdie are dressed as waiters.

                                        CONTINUED

RE-12   CONTINUED

                    GREGORY
        Who are you?

                    FERDIE
        We're the relief waiters.

                    CHUCK
        The employment agency sent us.


RE-13   MED. CLOSE SHOT - GREGORY, FERDIE AND CHUCK

                    GREGORY
        With all the people out of work,
        the employment agency had to send
        you two.

                    FERDIE
        It's nice of you to say that.

                    GREGORY
        Keep quiet.  With that crowd out
        there, I'll have to make the best
        of it.
                (to Chuck)
        Fix your tie - straighten your
        trousers --
                (to Ferdie)
        Pull down your vest.

Ferdie pulls down vest and his shirt front rolls up
like a window shade, clipping him on the chin.  Gregory
starts for Ferdie, who steps behind Chuck for protection.

                    GREGORY
        Look, I don't want any trouble
        with you.

                    CHUCK
        No sir.

                    GREGORY
        Just make one mistake, and I'll
        throw you out.

                    FERDIE
                (aggressively)
        You'll throw who out?


                            CONTINUED

RE-13    CONTINUED

                    GREGORY
          I'LL THROW YOU OUT.

                    FERDIE
          You're the guy that can do it,
          too.

                    GREGORY
                  (disgustedly)
          Come with me.

Ferdie opens the swinging door and starts out at exactly
the same moment as Gregory.  They get wedged in the door
together.  Ferdie backs out - holds door for Gregory.
Chuck thinks he is holding it for him, too, but Ferdie
lets it slam on him; as Ferdie looks at door to see
where Chuck is, Chuck comes thru the door slamming it into
Ferdie's face.


RE-14    GREGORY, CHUCK AND FERDIE

approaching the CAMERA single file.  The CAMERA PANS
with them as they come to a table at which the ANDREWS
SISTERS are seated.  Ferdie looks at the girls and turns
back.  Gregory and Chuck continue out of SCENE.

                    FERDIE
          Excuse me - but you look just
          like the Andrews Sisters.

                    PATTY
          We are the Andrews Sisters.

                    FERDIE
          Isn't that a coincidence - wait
          till they come out to sing - then
          you'll see how much you look like
          them.

Ferdie starts off - does take - and returns.

                    FERDIE
          Hey, you're the Andrews Sisters.

                    PATTY
          That's right.

Ferdie does his whistle and dashes out.

RE-15   MED. SHOT - GREGORY AND CHUCK IN F.G. NEAR VACANT TABLE

They are waiting for Ferdie who is just leaving the
Andrews Sisters and approaching them.

                    GREGORY
          Maybe nobody will notice you two
          back here.

                    FERDIE
               (brightly)
          Hey, I just met the Andrews Sisters.

                    GREGORY
          Pay attention to me.  A new night
          club's success depends upon the
          patron's making themselves at home.
          We want the people who come to the
          Club Glamour to feel that they're
          members of one big happy family.
          Do you understand?

                    CHUCK
          Yes, sir.

                    GREGORY
               (to Chuck)
          These are your tables -- these two.
               (then wheeling
                on Ferdie)
          And you -- remember what I said.

                    FERDIE
          Yes, sir -- everybody's one big
          family.

                    GREGORY
          Your tables are these two behind
          the post.
               (to Chuck)
          Try to make a waiter out of that guy.

Gregory glares at Ferdie and leaves the scene.

                    CHUCK
          I've got to make a waiter of you.
          So pay attention.  When a person
          comes to the table push the chair
          under them like this -
               (demonstrates)
          - Now, when they get up you take
          the chair away.

                              CONTINUED

RE-15    CONTINUED

                         FERDIE
              That's easy.


                         CHUCK
              Okay - now when you take a person's
              order, go over to the checker and
              show him your slip.


                         FERDIE
              I can't.  I'm not wearing any.


                         CHUCK
              Show him what food has been
              ordered.  For instance, dinner
              is $3.00 a plate.  If your table
              is filled that's three dinners -
              so the check will be $9.00.


                         FERDIE
              It will be ten dollars - 3 times
              3 -- is ten.


                         CHUCK
              Three times three is nine - look.

Chuck counts the three plates three times, arriving
at the figure nine.


                         FERDIE
              Three times three is ten - look.

Ferdie counts the plates as Chuck did and arrives
at the figure six.  This leads into a short ad lib as
to whether it's nine or ten.  As a waiter comes into
SCENE - Ferdie stops him.


                         FERDIE
              Hey - how much is three times three?


                         WAITER
              Eleven.

Ferdie and Chuck immediately start another argument.


                         WAITER
              I say three times three is eleven.

The waiter counts plates and ends up getting the figure
eleven.  Again the argument starts - and Ted Lewis comes
into SCENE.


                                   CONTINUED

RE-15   CONTINUED - 2

                              FERDIE
                    Hey you --

                              CHUCK
                    Ferdie, this is Ted Lewis.  He
                    works here, too.

                              FERDIE
                    Which table?

                              LEWIS
                    I lead the band - you know, direct
                    the numbers.

                              FERDIE
                    The numbers - oh yes - Mr. Lewis,
                    we got an argument.

                              CHUCK
                    Yes, Mr. Lewis, I say three times
                    three is nine.

                              FERDIE
                    And I say three times three is
                    ten - now how much is three times
                    three --

                              LEWIS
                    Three times three is fourteen.

                              FERDIE
                    That's ridiculous.

                              LEWIS
                    I'll prove it.

Ted counts plates ending up with figure fourteen.

                              FERDIE
                    I still say 3 times 3 is ten -

                              CHUCK
                    Money talks.

                              LEWIS
                    And I listen.

They make bet.

                              FERDIE
                    I'LL PROVE 3 times 3 is ten -

                                        CONTINUED

RE-15    CONTINUED - 3

As Ferdie starts to count - several waiters come into b.g.
One has tray with dishes on.

                          FERDIE
              One, two, three, four, five, six,
              seven, eight, nine -
                        (he finds he's still
                         short a dish, grabs
                         it from waiter's
                         tray and bangs it on
                         table, breaking it)
              AND ONE IS TEN.

                                              DISSOLVE


RE-16    LONG SHOT - INT. CLUB GLAMOUR

The SOUND OF APPLAUSE before the scene is fully shown,
then we see the crowded night club with the patrons
applauding.  In b.g. we see Ted Lewis and his band.


RE-17    MED. SHOT - INT. LOBBY - NEAR CHECK ROOM

Charlie Smith is just turning away from the check room
counter to join Bannister (Matson's lawyer).  They start
into the Club together.  Suddenly, Bannister sees someone
inside the club o.s.  He draws back, pulls Charlie back
with him.  Charlie follows his gaze; his expression hardens.


RE-18    REVERSE ANGLE - MED. LONG SHOT

On Moose Matson, seated at a table with two glamorous
looking blondes.  The Moose is laughing and enjoying
himself.


RE-19    MED. FULL SHOT - CHARLIE AND BANISTER

Charlie glares furiously at Bannister.

                          CHARLIE
              You knew Moose Matson was here!
              You framed this!

                                              CONTINUED

RE-19    continued

                          BANNISTER
          Simmer down! You've been seeing
          too many gangster movies. You
          don't suppose I'd want my two most
          important clients to kill each other.
                    (casually)
          I'll have a drink with him - get
          everything settled.

                          CHARLIE
                    (coldly)
          Let him know I've got him hooked -
          but good. I'll be waiting for
          you.

Bannister nods and goes into the Club. Charlie looks after
him, his eyes narrowing. Then he turns back to the check
room.


RE-20    INT.  CLUB (SHOOTING TOWARD THE ENTRANCE FROM LOBBY)

Bannister enters and peers around. Gregory approaches
him. Bannister indicates that he has located the table
he is looking for. CAMERA PANS with Bannister as he
makes his way between the tables and stops at a table
where MOOSE MATSON is sitting with two giddy blondes.
He is laughing uproariously. Banister
stands uncertainly for a moment. Moose sees him and
greet him broadly.

                          MATSON
                    (expansively -
                     still laughing)
          Oh, hello... hello... sit down.
          Meet the girls.
                    (to the two blondes)
          Girls, this is my lawyer, Mr.
          Bannister.

Bannister nods and sits down. Bannister takes a folded
document from his pocket.

                          BANNISTER
          I was lucky to run into you
          tonight. There are a couple of
          important matters-

                                        CONTINUED

RE-20    CONTINUED

                    MATSON
                (squinting)
        Don't talk shop.  It's after
        office hours --

                    BANNISTER
                (persisting)
        But here's that legal matter you
        asked me to draw up.

Matson sobers, takes the document and looks it over quickly.

                    MATSON
                (soberly)
        Will this hold up in court?

                    BANNISTER
                (nodding)
        It's ironclad --
                (very seriously)
        There's something else -- the
        Worthington affair.
                (as Moose hesitates)
        It's urgent.

He indicates the two blondes.  Matson turns to them, grimly.

                    MATSON
                (coldly)
        Get yourself a cup of coffee or
        something - beat it.

The blondes hurriedly move away.  Bannister turns back
to Matson.


RE-21    MED. SHOT - MATSON AND BANNISTER

                    MATSON
        All right.

                    BANNISTER
        Charlie Smith knows you pulled the
        Worthington payroll job.  He wants
        fifty per cent of the proceeds.

                    MATSON
        Tell that rat I can get a coffin
        for him, wholesale.

                                CONTINUED

RE-21    CONTINUED

                              BANNISTER
                He says if you don't come across,
                he's going to tell the D. A.

                              MATSON
                              (grimly)
                And my mother said stool pigeons
                don't sing.

                              BANNISTER
                It's serious, Moose.  If you've
                still got the cash, I think you
                ought to make him an offer -

                              MATSON
                I've got the cash all right -
                              (coldly)
                But you tell Charlie I can out-think him
                with one hand behind my back.  Tell
                him he's gotta find the dough before
                he can cut in on it.
                              (laughing)
                And he won't find it -- the dough
                is in my head!

                              BANNISTER
                              (pressing)
                Moose -- you can confide in me.

                              MATSON
                I don't confide in anybody.  I
                said the money was in my head.

                              BANNISTER
                I want to be sure that payroll money
                is just safe before I reject Smith's
                offer.

                              MATSON
                              (icily)
                Okay --   so you're sure --

                He takes a drink.  The subject is closed.  Bannister
                shrugs, nods, turns away.  Matson turns to watch the show.


RE-22    MED. LONG SHOT - SPECIALTY NUMBER - KAY, KATJE & KAY

                Adagio and doll dance, from Ted Lewis' act, during
                which we

                                                CUT TO

RE-23    MED. Close shot-Chuck and Ferdie - at table

Guests in b.g.

                         CHUCK
              We've got to get busy.  Can you
              remember everything I told you?

                         FERDIE
              Sure.  When a person sits down
              push the chair in - when they get
              up pull the chair away.

                         CHUCK
              Right - and remember the three
              answers.  How much is dinner - $3.00
              - That's too much - Tell it to the
              manager - I don't think I'll eat here -
              If you don't somebody else will.

                         FERDIE
              Three dollars - tell it to the manager
              and if you don't somebody else will.

                         CHUCK
              That's right - I've got to take
              care of a table - you just keep
              running over what I told you.

As Chuck goes OUT OF SCENE - CAMERA DOLLIES with Ferdie
who goes to nearest table - seated at the table facing
CAMERA are two blondes drinking coffee.

                         FERDIE
                      (repeats to
                       himself)
              If they sit down - push the chair
              in - if they get up - take the
              chair away.  Three answers - three
              dollars - tell it to the manager -
              if you don't somebody else will.

The first blonde starts to rise from the chair.  Ferdie
immediately pulls the chair away.  Meanwhile, the blonde
changes her mind and sits down again.  She does a pratt
fall.  She rises angrily and grabs Ferdie.

                         BLONDE
              What did you pull that chair for?

                         FERDIE
              Three dollars.

                                        CONTINUED

RE-23    CONTINUED

> BLONDE
> I'll report you for this.

> FERDIE
> Tell it to the manager.

> BLONDE
> I oughta have Moose Matson punch
> you in the nose.

> FERDIE
> If you don't somebody else will.
>           (suddenly, he takes
>            it)
> Did you say "Moose Matson" - that
> bad man?

The blonde nods, Ferdie whistles and scrambles away as
fast as he can go.


RE-24    MED. SHOT - INT. LOBBY NEAR CHECK ROOM

as Bannister gets his hat and coat and turns toward the
exit, he is met by Charlie Smith, who steps out of an
alcove.  Charlie eyes Bannister questioningly. Bannister
shakes his head.

> CHARLIE
>           (angrily)
> Okay - I gave the Moose his chance.
> I was gonna be fair and split with
> him.  Now I'll get him out of the way,
> and grab it all.

> BANNISTER
>           (worried)
> He's still got the cash, but I
> couldn't find out where he's hiding
> it.  He keeps saying he's got the
> money in his head!

> CHARLIE
>           (savagely)
> I'll have plenty of time to look for
> it.  The District Attorney is gonna
> be nursing the Moose for a long while.

He goes out followed by Bannister.

RE-25     MED. SHOT - INT. LOBBY - GREGORY IN F.G.

His face lights up with anticipation as ALDERMAN
BIRCH, a baldish-oldish-small time politician,
approaches him.

                    GREGORY
          Good evening, Alderman.  I'll
          get you a nice ringside table.

                    ALDERMAN
                 (ill at ease)
          No, please -- you see I -- that
          is -- I'd like a table in a
          corner somewhere.

At this moment the reason for his embarrassment enters
the SCENE -- a baby-faced cutie.

                    GIRL
          Here I am, Daddy.

                    GREGORY
                 (understanding,
                  but discreetly)
          Oh.
                 (bows to girl)
          This way, please.


RE-26     MED. LONG SHOT - KAY, KATJE AND KAY


RE-27     MED. SHOT - INT. CLUB - GREGORY, ALDERMAN AND GIRL

                    GIRL
          Can we have that table down there?
                 (indicates o.s.)

                    ALDERMAN
          It's too noisy there.  We'll take
          that quiet one in the corner.
                 (he indicates the
                  opposite direction)


RE-28     MED. CLOSE SHOT - SHOOTING TOWARD TABLE IN CORNER FROM
          THEIR ANGLE

Ferdie stands behind a vacant table vigorously applauding
the number which has just finished.  Gregory, the Alderman
and the girl enter SCENE.  Gregory looks at Ferdie, furious.

                                        CONTINUED

RE-28    CONTINUED

Ferdie pays no attention.  Gregory seats the girl.
The Alderman seats himself.  Gregory angrily taps
Ferdie.  Ferdie steps to the table as Gregory goes out
of SCENE.

                    FERDIE
          Good evening, folks - how about
          starting with a little soup.

                    ALDERMAN
          I don't like soup.

                    FERDIE
          Give me a reason.

                    ALDERMAN
          I don't have to give any reason,
          other than I don't like soup.

                    FERDIE
          Maybe she wants soup.

                    ALDERMAN
          She doesn't want any soup either.

                    FERDIE
          It's good soup.

                    ALDERMAN
          I don't care how good it is -
          we don't want any soup.

                    FERDIE
          Somebody's got to eat it.

                    ALDERMAN
          Feed it to the chef.

                    FERDIE
          He's all souped up now.

                    ALDERMAN
          Then feed it to the hogs.

                    FERDIE
          Then you want some soup.

                    GIRL
          I think I'll have some soup.

                                        CONTINUED

RE28    CONTINUED - 2

                    ALDERMAN
          You'll do nothing of the kind.

                    GIRL
                  (pouting)
          Oh, Daddy.

                    FERDIE
          Why don't you listen to your
          father.

                    ALDERMAN
          I'm not her father.

                    FERDIE
          Then why don't you let her have
          some soup?

                    ALDERMAN
          All right, bring her some soup,
          bring me some soup, BRING US BOTH
          SOME SOUP.

                    FERDIE
          Sorry, we're all out of soup.


RE29    MED. LONG SHOT - TED LEWIS SPECIALTY

        Ted Lewis does "Leader Of The Home Town Band" which
        includes "Me and My Shadow."


RE30    MED. CLOSE SHOT - FERDIE'S TABLE

        Chuck comes INTO SCENE.

                    CHUCK
          Good evening, folks.  What are
          we eating?

                    FERDIE
          I asked them that.

                    CHUCK
          I'll take the order.  How about
          an order of frankfurters?

                    FERDIE
          Yeah - frankfurters - that's baloney
          with an inferiority complex.

                                        CONTINUED

RE30   CONTINUED

> GIRL
> Daddy can't eat frankfurters.

> CHUCK
> Then how about a seafood plate?

> ALDERMAN
> Seafood?  Have you any weak fish?

> FERDIE
> Weak fish?  I don't know about their
> physical condition, but we got some
> little fish out in the kitchen.

> ALDERMAN
> Smelt?

> FERDIE
> And how.

> CHUCK
> How about a lobster?

> GIRL
> Is your lobster fresh?

> FERDIE
> Fresh?  It's positively insulting.

> CHUCK
> Keep quiet.

> ALDERMAN
> Never mind the seafood.  Bring two
> orders of roast duck with apple dress-
> ing, candied yams, corn on the cob,
> fresh string beans, hot biscuits,
> roquefort salad - and coffee.

> CHUCK
> Yes, sir.

He goes out of SCENE.

> ALDERMAN
> (to girl)
> After we finish that, what else will
> we get?

> FERDIE
> Indigestion.

RE-31    MED. CLOSE - GREGORY

He is standing at Chuck's table when Chuck approaches him.

> CHUCK
> Mr. Gregory --

> GREGORY
> (sharply)
> What is it?

> CHUCK
> Those two people -- they're
> asking for something. --

> GREGORY
> (tersely)
> Whatever it is, give it to them --
> always do what the customer says.

Chuck shrugs and leaves.


RE-32    MED. SHOT - FERDIE AT HIS TABLE

He is helping the Alderman up.

> FERDIE
> Excuse me.

> ALDERMAN
> Stop being so clumsy.

> GIRL
> He's only trying to help us
> have a good time.

> FERDIE
> That's the idea.  We want you
> to be happy.
> (imitating Ted Lewis)
> "Is everybody happy?"

From o.s. there is a roll on the drums which frightens him.


RE33    CLOSE - TED LEWIS - AT THE BANDSTAND

He introduces the Andrews Sisters.


RE-34    MED. SHOT - ANDREWS SISTERS SPECIALTY

When this is over:

RE-35    MED. SHOT - THE ANDREWS SISTERS' ENCORE

The Andrews Sisters start novelty number.  It is really a
variation of the Big Apple, in which figures are called.
Ted Lewis should call the figures.


RE-36    MED. SHOT - SHOOTING OVER HEADS OF PEOPLE - TOWARD TED LEWIS)

                    TED LEWIS
          Everybody on the floor...
          Everybody dance!


RE-37    MED. FERDIE'S TABLE

                    GIRL
          Come on, Daddy.

                    ALDERMAN
          No, thank you.

                    GIRL
                (wailing)
          I'm not having any fun.

                    TED LEWIS (o.s.)
          Everybody dance!

                    FERDIE
                (to Alderman)
          Didn't you hear what Ted Lewis
          said?  Everybody dance!

                    GIRL
          I'll find myself a partner.

                    ALDERMAN
          If you do I'll leave.

                    FERDIE
                (troubled - to Alderman)
          She's only kidding.
                (girl walks out
                 of shot)
          Wait!  I'll get her.


RE-38    MED. SHOT

The girl weaves her way through the tables.  Ferdie
goes after her and catches her hand.

RE-39    REVERSE ANGLE - MED. SHOT - FERDIE AND GIRL - EDGE OF
         DANCE FLOOR

They are swept on the floor by dancers who are just
coming from their tables.


RE-40    CLOSE SHOT - GREGORY

His eyes popping out.


RE-41    MED. SHOT - FERDIE AND THE GIRL

He forgets his position and begins to lose himself in
the dance.


RE-42    MED. SHOT - CHUCK

Coming along with a trayful of food, he approaches the
Alderman who is standing angrily in the f.g. watching
the dance floor.


RE-43    MED. SHOT - FERDIE, GIRL AND DANCERS


RE-44    MED. CLOSE - AT FERDIE'S TABLE

Chuck is about to put down the tray.  The Alderman
stands glaring o.s.

                         CHUCK
                Your food, sir.

                         ALDERMAN
                       (furiously)
                Eat it yourself.

He turns on his heel and strides out of the SCENE.
Chuck looks after him, puzzles.  He looks at the
dance floor., o.s.


RE-45    MED. LONG - DANCE FLOOR

A clearing has been made and Ferdie is now doing what is
almost an exhibition dance with his partner.  This is
applauded by the couples who then reassemble for the
dance.

RE-46    C. U. TED LEWIS

RE-47    shouting dance figures.

RE-48    MED. LONG - DANCE FLOOR

RE-49    as people obey Ted Lewis' commands.


RE-50    MED. CLOSE

The CAMERA SWIFTLY PANS Chuck toward the dance
floor. He glances o.s. and looks frightened.


RE-51    MED. SHOT - EDGE OF DANCE FLOOR - FROM CHUCK'S ANGLE

Gregory, flanked by two husky men, obviously bouncers,
and obviously waiting to get Ferdie.


RE-52    CLOSE SHOT

Chuck worried -- then getting an idea.


RE-53    ANOTHER SHOT - DANCE FLOOR

A change in the figure as ordered by Ted Lewis.


RE-54    MED. SHOT - NEAR BANDSTAND

Taking in Ted Lewis and Ferdie, who is dancing close
to the bandstand, and Chuck who is hiding beside it.


RE-55    CLOSE SHOT

Chuck, imitating Ted Lewis, gives a command ordering
the men to dance with each other.


RE-56    MED. SHOT

The whole dance floor obeys -- couples breaking up
and men starting to choose other men.


RE-57    CLOSE SHOT - TED LEWIS

He whirls around, amazed.

RE-58    MED. SHOT

Chuck grabs Ferdie and yanks him away.  The CAMERA
TRUCKS with them as they go sashaying between the
tables.

                         FERDIE
                      (delighted)
             We're in!

                         CHUCK
             Oh, now we're not -- we're out!


RE-59    MED. CLOSE

Gregory and the two bouncers go after them.


RE-60    MED. CLOSE

Ferdie and Chuck look behind them and run right
into the CAMERA.

                                        FADE OUT

FADE IN

RE-61     ESTABLISHING SHOT - FILLING STATION


RE-62     MED. SHOT - GAS STATION

Chuck at the blackboard.

                    FERDIE
                    (o.s.)
          Hey, Chuck --

                    CHUCK
          Don't bother me -- I'm busy -- and
          stop playing with that balloon.


RE-63     CLOSE SHOT - FERDIE WITH BALLOONS

                    FERDIE
                    (sighing)
          Life is very dull here.

CAMERA PANS with him as he comes toward Chuck.

                    CHUCK
                    (bitterly)
          We were lucky to get this job --
          after the way you acted at the
          night club!

                    FERDIE
                    (wistfully)
          Remember the good old days of
          Cafe Society with Ted Lewis and
          the Andrews Sisters?

                    CHUCK
          What are you talking about?  That
          was only last night.

                    FERDIE
                    (surprised)
          It was?  I sure am a sucker for the
          fast life.

                    CHUCK
          I hope you've learned your lesson.
          You get an opportunity, then what
          do you do?  You forget yourself.
          You become important -- you become
          all puffed up.

By this time Ferdie is well inflated.

GO TO SCENE 5 IN SHOOTING SCRIPT AND CONTINUE
PHOTOGRAPHED ACTION THROUGH SCENE 52.


SEQUENCE "B"

RE-64     (THIS SCENE REPLACES SCENE 53 OF SHOOTING SCRIPT COURTROOM)

CLOSE SHOT - WILL

held by Bannister at his desk in his office.  As he
speaks the CAMERA PULLS BACK to include Charlie Smith
leaning back in a chair beside the desk -- and then
Chuck and Ferdie seated opposite Bannister.

                    BANNISTER
          So you see, according to Mr.
          Matson's Will, the inheritance
          goes to whoever was with him
          at the time of his death.

                    CHUCK
               (to Ferdie -
                amazed)
          That's us.

                    FERDIE
          You mean we get his money?

                    SMITH
               (sharply)
          There is no money.

                    BANNISTER
               (smoothly)
          Moose Matson always said he kept
          his money in his head.  We never
          learned what he meant.  We found
          no cash or bonds.
               (holds up a large
                roll of paper)
          The only tangible asset bequeathed
          to you is a tavern on what used to
          be Highway 129.

Chuck and Ferdie rise to look at the paper.

                    FERDIE
          A what?

                    SMITH
          The old Forrester Hotel.  Moose used
          to operate it.

                              CONTINUED

                    CHUCK
                  (enthused)
          Ferdie!  We own a hotel!

                    FERDIE
                  (excited)
          Maybe we can get some cheap
          rates - if it's our own place!

                    SMITH
          I haven' been out there in
          several years - I don't know
          what shape it's in.

                    FERDIE
                  (insistently)
          Then it should be very cheap -
          they can't hold me up!  Not to
          stay on a hotel I never heard
          about - besides it belongs to
          us!  I'm going to talk to the
          manager!

                    SMITH
          You'll need a guide familiar
          with the territory.  As an old
          friend of Moose, I'll show you
          around any time you say.

                    FERDIE
                  (jumping at it)
          What are you doing tomorrow?

                    CHUCK
          What are you rushing the man for?

                    SMITH
          I'd like nothing better than to take
          you two for a ride.

                    FERDIE
          You mean it?

                    SMITH
          Of course.  I'm going to take care
          of you two boys.  It'll be a pleasure.
          Leave everything to me.
                  (he nods and leaves)

RE-65    MED. CLOSE SHOT - FERDIE, CHUCK AND BANNISTER

                        FERDIE
               Now that's what I call a nice
               fellow.

Bannister picks up his hat and the paper.

                        BANNISTER
               We'll go down to the courthouse
               and make this legal.

As they start for the door -

                                        WIPE TO

SCENE 68 IN SCRIPT ALREADY PHOTOGRAPHED


                    CONTINUE 68-A

RE-66    LONG SHOT - THE FLEEING CAR * (ALREADY PHOTOGRAPHED)

CLOSE SHOT - PROCESS

Charlie Smith and three men (the same men who take part
in the chase and fight in the later sequences - ALREADY
PHOTOGRAPHED.


                        SMITH
                     (furiously)
               You missed them!

                                        CONTINUED

RE-66    CONTINUED

                    1ST GANGSTER
                  (apologetically)
          The little guy ducked!

                    SMITH
                  (angrily)
          I didn't want them bothering me
          at the Forrester Club!

                    GANGSTER
          You won't be able to search that
          hotel -- not with these two dopes
          watching you!

                    SMITH
                  (bitterly)
          They won't be watching me for long!
          They think they inherited the hotel!
          All they're gonna get is a couple
          ounces of lead!

                    GANGSTER

          Maybe they'll recognize this car.
          They'll get suspicious -- and won't
          go --

                    SMITH
          I thought of that.  I arranged for
          Harry to take them.  He's a very
          innocent looking monster --

          He sits back, tight-lipped.

                                        DISSOLVE


RE-67    CLOSE SHOT - SIGN

          soiled and not too professional, hung by a piece of
          cord from a car door.  It reads:

                    HARRY HOSKINS
                    BUS SERVICE

          CAMERA PULLS BACK to reveal Chuck reading the sign,
          holding two suitcases.  Ferdie carries the box of
          groceries.  (TO MATCH BOX ALREADY PHOTOGRAPHED IN LATER
          SEQUENCE).  The car is parked near a corner.

                    CHUCK
          Yep -- this is the bus all right.

                                        CONTINUED

                         FERDIE
            I'll put this inside.
                    (he pushes the box
                     into the car)

From out of the drug store in b.g. comes Harry Hoskins,
heading for the car.

                         CHUCK
            Say, are you Harry Hoskins?

                         HOSKINS
                    (evasively)
            Who are you?

                         CHUCK
            I'm Chuck Murray -- this is Ferdie
            Jones.  We're supposed to pick up
            a ride here.

                         FERDIE
            Our pal, Charlie Smith, arranged it.

                         HOSKINS
            Oh... I'm Harry Hoskins.  Let me
            take those bags.

                         CHUCK
                    (to Ferdie)
            Why don't you help the man?

At this moment a large bus comes through the SCENE.
Ferdie throws the suitcase high into the air.  It
lands on top of the bus which carries it out of the SCENE.

                         FERDIE
            Which way are you going?

                         HOSKINS
            North.

                         FERDIE
                    (to Chuck)
            Don't you wish we were going South?

                         CHUCK
            Why?

                         FERDIE
            That's the way your bag went.

                                        CONTINUED

RE-67    CONTINUED - 2

                    HOSKINS
          We'll be leaving as soon as the
          other passengers get here.

Norma enters the SCENE.

                    NORMA
          Mr. Hoskins?  I'm Norma Lind.

He takes her bag.

                    HOSKINS
          This is Mr. Murray -- Mr. Jones --

                    NORMA
          How do you do.

                    CHUCK
          The pleasure's all mine.

                    FERDIE
          Don't I get a little of it?

                    NORMA
          Will I have time for some breakfast
          before we leave?

                    FERDIE
          Sure - take your time -- we'll wait
          for you.

                    HOSKINS
          Two of the passengers haven't arrived
          yet.

                    NORMA
          Call me when you're ready to go.
          Goodbye for now.
                    (exits from scene)

                    FERDIE
                    (gazing after her)
          Goodbye for now ---

Camille's voice is heard o.s.

                    CAMILLE (o.s.)
          Mr. Hoskins -- Mr. Hoskins!

Camille runs into the SCENE.  She collides with Ferdie.
His feet go into the air.  They both fall.

                                        CONTINUED

RE-67     CONTINUED - 3

                              FERDIE
                    What's the matter -- can't you see?

                              CAMILLE
                    I hit you, didn't I?

                                                          CUT TO

(SCENE 75 OF SHOOTING SCRIPT
 AND CONTINUE DRUG STORE EPISODE AS PHOTOGRAPHED
 TO THE END OF SCENE 79)


RE-68    MED. SHOT - NEAR CAR - CAMILLE, CHUCK AND FERDIE

         Ferdie looks dead pan at Camille as she chatters.

                              CAMILLE
                    Are you sure you never heard me,
                    on the radio?
                              (he shakes his head)
                    Camille Brewster?
                              (he shakes his head)
                    Don't you recognize this?
                              (she screams -- he leaps
                               into Chuck's arms)

         Doc dashes into the SCENE.


                              DOC
                         (to Ferdie)
                    Are you the driver of this car?

                              CHUCK
                    If he is I'm walking.

         Norma enters with Hoskins.

                              NORMA
                    Are we all here?

                              FERDIE
                    My pal, Charlie Smith ain't here and I
                    ain't leaving without him.


                                                        CONTINUED

RE-68    CONTINUED

                        CHUCK
            I can't figure out what's keeping
            him!

                        CAMILLE
                    (brightly)
            Maybe Mr. Smith went to Washington.

Ferdie makes as though to hit her -- Chuck restrains him.


RE-69    MED. SHOT - EXT. STREET - OUTDOOR PHONE BOOTH IN F.G.

Charlie Smith enters, looks down the street.


Re-70    MED. LONG SHOT - GROUP (FROM HIS ANGLE)

Norma entering car.  Camille indicates she'd rather wait
outside with Ferdie.


RE-71    CLOSE SHOT - EXT. PHONE BOOTH

Charlie enters and dials number.


RE-72    MED. SHOT - CORNER OF CHEAP ROOM

One of Charlie's mob at the phone, calls to the others:

                        1ST GANGSTER
            It's Charlie!

The others quickly come into the SCENE.

                        1ST GANGSTER
                    (into phone)
            Yeah - I'm listening.


RE-73    CLOSE SHOT - SMITH - IN TELEPHONE BOOTH

                        SMITH
            I can handle this myself -- but
            if anything should go wrong and
            you don't hear from me by six o'clock,
            come after me -- the old Forrester
            Club...Right.
                    (he hangs up)

RE-74    MED. SHOT - CAMILLE, CHUCK & FERDIE OUTSIDE THE CAR

Hoskins stands apart, looking o.s.  Norma and Doc are
inside.

                         FERDIE
                    (to Camille)
          I don't care how late it's getting
          to be.  I --

                         HOSKINS
          There's Mr. Smith.
                    (he starts out of SCENE)

                         FERDIE
                    (to Camille)
          It's my pal!
                    (calling)
          Oh, Charlie!

                         CHUCK
          Keep quiet.


RE-75    MED. LONG SHOT - STREET - CAR AND GROUP IN B.G.

Hoskins meets Smith and takes his bag.  Their actions are
formal, though it's clear their relations are not.

                         SMITH
                    (angrily)
          You little chiseler.  I told you
          not to pick up any other passengers.

                         HOSKINS
          It'll look more on the level with a
          bus full.  They're just three traveling
          dopes - they won't even remember you!

                         SMITH
          They'd better not.


RE-76    GROUP AT CAR

Smith enters the SCENE.  Hoskins puts his bag away and
gets in the driver's seat.

                         FERDIE & CHUCK
          Good morning.

                         SMITH
          Good morning, boys.  Sorry I held
          you up.

                                        CONTINUED

RE-76    CONTINUED

                          CAMILLE
                      (putting out her
                       hand)
              Good morning, Mr. Smith.
                      (he mistakes her
                       gesture to mean
                       "you first", and he
                       enters the car.
                       Camille stands, arms
                       akimbo, burning)
              The age of chiselry!

Chuck is about to enter the car when Ferdie restrains
him.

                          FERDIE
              Ain't you got any manners?

Chuck stands back.  Before Camille can get started
Ferdie steps up to the car, bumps his forehead against
the top.

                                        DISSOLVE TO:


(SC. 84 OF SHOOTING SCRIPT

NOW THE ACTION CONTINUES AS IN THE SHOOTING SCRIPT UP
TO THE MIDDLE OF SC. 132.  THE VICTROLA IS TURNED ON
AND THE MUSIC BEGINS.  BEFORE THE DANCE

                                        CUT TO:)


RE-77    CLOSE SHOT - MYSTERIOUS FIGURE IN THE SHADOWS

         opening a door just a little.  The music grows a bit
         louder from the suggestion of the lighted room in b.g.
         As the door closes again,

                                        DISSOLVE TO:


SC. 136 IN SHOOTING SCRIPT

WHICH IS PLAYED THROUGH SC. 139

                                        CUT TO:)

RE78    CLOSE SHOT - IN THE SHADOWS

As the panel opens the Mysterious Figure, surprise, flees.


(CONTINUE FROM SC. 140 OF SHOOTING SCRIPT
RIGHT THROUGH 220.   DISSOLVE FROM 220 to:

SC. 238 - AND CONTINUE AS PHOTOGRAPHED RIGHT
THROUGH SC. 260)


RE79    THREE SHOT - CHUCK, FERDIE & CAMILLE

                    CAMILLE
          You two can sit here arguing.
          I'm going to pack.
                    (she exits)

                    CHUCK
                    (continuing - to Ferdie)
          I'm afraid you're just dumb.

                    FERDIE
          Who's dumb?  Didn't you say the
          money was in a moose's head?

                    CHUCK
          No.  When I say Moose kept the
          money in his head, I'm using a
          figure of speech.  Don't you know
          what a figure of speech is?

                    FERDIE
          Certainly --
                    (giving one)
          "A lot of water has gone under
          the bridge."

                    CHUCK
          Under what bridge?

                    FERDIE
          How do I know what bridge?

                    CHUCK
          And how do you know there's water
          under it?

                    FERDIE
          There's got to be water under it.
          The boats have to go up and down!

                    CHUCK
          Why do they have to go up and down?
          Why can't they go across?
                              CONTINUED

RE79    CONTINUED

                    FERDIE
          All right, all right-- let them
          go across.

                    CHUCK
          And what happens to the boats that
          want to go up and down?

                    FERDIE
          They can't get past the bridge!
          I'm a sucker arguing with this guy.

                    CHUCK
          Then why do you start it?

                    FERDIE
          Who started it?  You said I didn't
          know what a figure of speech was,
          and I was dumb enough to try to say
          water under a bridge -- I could have
          said gone with the wind.

                    CHUCK
          What wind?

                    FERDIE
          How should I know what wind?

                    CHUCK
          Then what are you bringing it
          up for?

     Ferdie burns.


RE80    MED. CLOSE INT. GIRLS' BEDROOM

     Norma stands at the bay window looking out, lost in reverie.
     She has opened the window.  The moon light streams in.
     A breeze is stirring.  Sound of a door being shut.

                    DOC (o.s.)
          Are you ready?

     Doc comes into the shop, stands beside Norma.

                    DOC
          Why, it's stopped raining.

     CAMERA COMES UP to a CLOSER SHOT

                    NORMA
          That must have been a lovely
          garden once.
                                        CONTINUED

RE30     CONTINUED

                              DOC
                          (excitedly)
               Of course!  Of course!  That
               explains the water!

                             Norma
                          (puzzled)
               What?

                              DOC
               That tree!  It grows only near
               hidden springs --


RE31     MED. LONG - EXT. GARDEN

         Part of the ruined garden, featuring a tree (to be used
         later) all shimmering after the later rain.


RE32     CLOSE SHOT DOC AND NORMA

                             NORMA
               When I was a little girl we
               called it the Wishbloom tree.

                              DOC
               I beg your pardon?

                             NORMA
               The Wishbloom tree.  If you
               wished a certain person were in
               love with you and the blossoms of
               that tree fell on him, then your
               wish was granted.

                              DOC
               What wish?

                             NORMA
                          (patiently)
               That the person will fall in
               love with you.

                              DOC
               But what possible relation can there
               be between falling of blossoms and
               falling in love?

                             NORMA
                          (wearily)
               Let's skip it.

                              DOC
               Believing in a thing like the
               Wishbloom tree is sheer superstition.

                                        CONTINUED

                              NORMA
                         (grimly)
               Okay.  Let's talk about something
               else.
                         (changes the subject)
               What kind of doctor are you?
               Patent medicine or quack?

Doc looks at her very peculiarly.  For the first time, we
see that there is something behind his vagueness; something
more than has appeared, to his studied absent mindedness
toward Norma.

                              DOC
                         (slowly)
               I don't know, yet.  I've just finished
               my internship.  Now I'm on my way to
               Paducah Falls.

                              NORMA
                         (surprised)
               Your arrival will double the
               population --

                              DOC
                         (seriously)
               There aren't many potential patients
               there -- but I'm taking over my
               father's practice.

                              NORMA
               That's falling into a gold mine --

                              DOC
                         (smiling)
               Unfortunately, I'll be taking over
               nothing more than a lot of unpaid
               bills and some good wishes. It will
               be a long time before I can make a
               living --
                         (softly)
               --before I could even dream of trying
               to make two livings --

For a second they eye each other tenderly.  Then Norma
swallows hard; tries to be flip.

                              NORMA
               What are you kicking about?  I had
               a job in Carterville.  All I had to
               do was get there within twenty-four
               hours.  Thirty bucks a week -- dictation
               and typing. Eats and shelter - regular --.
               Heaven on earth.

                              DOC
               And now?

RE32      CONTINUED

                          NORMA
             By tomorrow – there won't be any
             job waiting.
                    (wryly)
             Goodnight, Doc. I suppose we
             can waste the moonlight okay ––
             it's all we've got plenty of.

She turns away. CAMERA HOLDS on Doc looking after her
tenderly. He adjusts his glasses, starts to go back into his
vague character. Then he makes up his mind; sets his lips
grimly. He starts toward Norma.


RE33      MED. CLOSE (This leads right into Sc. 264)

Norma is standing in front of a picture. The panel
slides silently open in the wall and the rest of the
scene is the same through 266. The knives are thrown
at their heads. They remain oblivious.


                                       WIPE TO:


RE34      TWO SHOT – FERDIE & CHUCK

                         FERDIE
             I'd like to know how I get
             in these arguments.

                         CHUCK
             You said there was money in the
             moose's head.

                         FERDIE
             All right –– there ain't no money
             in the moose's head.

                         CHUCK
             Why don't you stand up for what
             you believe in?

                         FERDIE
             When I believe in something I do
             stand up for it.

                         CHUCK
             Like what?

                         FERDIE
             Like the Star Spangled Banner––
             and that's no figure of speech!

                                   CONTINUED

RE34    CONTINUED

                    CHUCK
                (shaking his head)
            Now you're talking... Say...
            Suppose Moose Matson's money were
            really up there.

                    FERDIE
            That's the limit. Now I'm mad...
                    (climbs up on chair)
            ... and I'm going to prove what
            I say is right.

                    CHUCK
            Take it easy.

                    FERDIE
            It's awful dark up here-- I can't
            see a thing.
                    (puts his hand in
                     the moose's mouth)
            Don't you bite me.  Cut that out or
            I won't join your lodge.  This
            moose must have been eating a lot of
            paper when they shot him--
                    (he pulls some
                     out-- a few bills
                     begin to float down)
            -- or maybe it's the stuff that the
            taxi driver-- I mean the taxi dancer--
            I mean the taxidermist used--
                    (takes more money out)


RE35    CLOSE SHOT - CHUCK - IN THE LIGHT

        as the money floats down and they begin to grab it avidly.

                    CHUCK
                (excitedly)
            Keep it up, Ferdie.


RE36    TWO SHOT - FERDIE ON LADDER - CHUCK BELOW

        catching the shower of money.

                    FERDIE
            Hey-- have mooses got tonsils?

        He extracts a large wad of bills and throws it down.

                    CHUCK
            What a tonsil!

                            CONTINUED

RE36     CONTINUED

                    FERDIE
          Now that I'm through with that
          stuffing, if I had a light I could
          look for the money.  Hey, Chuck,
          hand me that candle.  I--

As he looks down he sees Chuck jamming the money into the
satchel.


RE37     CLOSE SHOT - FERDIE

as he suddenly realizes what has happened.  He makes a
flying leap for the satchel and begins whimpering.

                    CHUCK
          Take it easy, Ferdie-- put it
          in the bag.

                    FERDIE
          It's in the bag all right!


RE38     MED. SHOT - DOC, NORMA AND CAMILLE COMING DOWN STAIRS

                    DOC
               (holding a corked vial)
          You see I keep it in this little
          vial and--
               (looking o.s.)
          What are you two doing there?


RE39     MED. CLOSE SHOT - CHUCK & FERDIE

                    CHUCK
          Look!  A thousand dollar bill!

                    FERDIE
          Boy, I'd like to run through this
          in my bare feet!

The others enter the shot.

                    NORMA
          Where did you--

                    CAMILLE
          Ferdie--
               (she dives for the bag)

                    FERDIE
          Lay off!

                              CONTINUED

RE89    CONTINUED

                        CHUCK
            Take it easy, folks, there's enough
            for everybody.


RE90    MED. SHOT - SHOOTING TOWARD ENTRANCE TO BAR

        The sliding panel opens and the Mystery Man comes into
        the light for the first time, gun in hand.  He is a
        gnarled, menacing looking man.  Over this we hear Ferdie's
        voice:

                        FERDIE (o.s.)
                        (rapidly)
            I'm going to open the biggest cafe
            in the world with Ted Lewis, the
            Andrews Sisters-- music and night
            life and glamor.  You got no idea
            what I'm going to do with this money--

                        MYSTERY MAN
            Oh, yes I have-- you're going to
            hand it over.


RE91    CLOSE SHOT - GROUP

        as they stare astonished at the man.

                        MYSTERY MAN (o.s.)
            All right, stick 'em up.


RE92    MED. SHOT

        The Mystery Man eyes them all and advances slowly.

                        MYSTERY MAN
            I've got to give you credit.
            You found in one night what I've
            been hunting around here for ten
            years.

                        FERDIE
            I thought it was f-f-finders
            keepers.

                        MYSTERY MAN
                        (laughs)
            Sure... you're the finder,
            and I'm the keeper--

RE93    CLOSE SHOT FEATURING DOC

He gets an idea, glancing at the vial in his hand.
Over this comes the Mystery Man's voice:

                    MYSTERY MAN (o.s.)
                    (snarling)
          I didn't tend bar and slave for
          Moose Matson for fifteen years just
          to let someone else get the gravy--

                    DOC
                    (suddenly)
          Look out!  I'll throw this!


RE94    THE GROUP - MED. SHOT

The Mystery Man's attention is distracted.  Chuck makes
a leap for him; so does the doctor.

                    FERDIE
                    (to the girls)
          Watch the money.


They overpower the Mystery Man and roll him toward the
door to the bar.  Ferdie opens the door.  They roll the
Mystery Man inside and lock the door.  Camille rushes
over to Ferdie.

                    CAMILLE
          My hero!

                    NORMA
                    (to Doc)
          Are you all right?

                    FERDIE
                    (crossing to table)
          That's who was after us.  Now we
          got nothing to worry about.

                    DOC
                    (panting)
          But you still haven't told us where
          you got the money...

                    CHUCK
          It was hidden in the moose's head.

                    FERDIE
          That's a figure of speech.

                    VOICE (FROM ORIGINAL SOUND TRACK)
          Just like "reach for the ceiling."

(FROM THIS POINT ON THE ACTION CONTINUES
THROUGH THE SCENE WHERE FERDIE'S HEAD GOES
THROUGH THE WALL.)


RE95    MED. SHOT - SHOOTING UPSTAIRS

The gang rushes down to the dining room.

                                        WIPE TO:

(GANG TYING UP PEOPLE SCENE AS PHOTOGRAPHED
THROUGH 298 and 299)


RE96    INT. CELLAR - MED. SHOT - NEAR FURNACE DOOR

Harry tottering.  He has just been shot.  He shoots
twice into the furnace.  We see the outlines of the
Mystery Man's body as he topples and falls.


RE97    Iron Dome is about to go to the cellar.  Doc trips
him up.  The gun goes off.


(LONG SHOT - OF FIGHT AS PHOTOGRAPHED AND SHOT
INCLUDING 321 WHICH IS FERDIE PRETENDING TO BE
SIREN.  After line "And single-handed, too!"

                                        WIPE TO:

RE98    FOOT OF STEPS - CHUCK, FERDIE, CAMILLE, NORMA & DOC

Ferdie sits despondent.
                            FERDIE
                But I'm sad I tell you -- I'm sad.

                            CHUCK
                What are you sad about?  Those guys
                got what they deserved -- and we got
                all this dough.

                            FERDIE
                Money ain't everything.  What's going
                to happen to this place?  I thought it
                was going to be nice and lively with
                music and dancing -- but it's too
                quiet -- nobody will come here.

                            DOC
                You're wrong -- a lot of people will.

                            FERDIE
                You mean as a last resort?

                                        CONTINUED

                              DOC
          No-- as a health resort.  I
          haven't finished analyzing that
          water yet but I'm certain it has
          immense therapeutic value.

                              FERDIE
          You mean people might come here just
          to drink our theres -- our water?

                              CHUCK
          Sure -- and to relax.

                              FERDIE
          It ain't our racket.

                              CHUCK
          Sure it is -- a modern hotel --
          important people -- a big dance
          pavilion --

                              FERDIE
                    (getting the idea)
          With Ted Lewis?

                              CHUCK
          Sure.

                              FERDIE
          And the Andrews Sisters?

                              CHUCK
          Of course.  And Doc will take
          charge of the health departments.

                              FERDIE
          And I'll take charge of the
          business!

Chuck reaches over, lifts up the satchel of money and
hands it to Norma.

                              CHUCK
          Put this in a safe place
          will you?

                                        QUICK FADE.

OH, CHARLIE - REVISIONS

FADE IN on a succession of QUICK WIPES
accompanied by lively music, the tempo and excitement increasing with each wipe.

re99    MED. SHOT - EXT. FORRESTER CLUB

Carpenters, painters and plasterers are seen
busily repairing the exterior of the club while a
gardener works in the f.g.

re100   MED. CLOSE SHOT - EXT. FORRESTER CLUB

A carpenter hammering.  Chuck and Ferdie stand beside
him.  Chuck holds out his hand to Ferdie.  Ferdie
takes some nails out of his mouth, hands them to Chuck,
who in turn hands them over to the carpenter.  Suddenly
Ferdie swallows a nail and begins to cough.  Chuck
slaps him on the back.

                                            WIPE TO:

re101   CLOSE SHOT - PAINTER ON LADDER WITH A FEW BUCKETS
        OF PAINT

Below him stand Ferdie and Chuck arguing.  Ferdie
instructs the painter, who makes a light stroke on
the wall.  Chuck countermands this, insisting he
use the dark paint. The painter obeys.  This battle
of the light and dark paint is repeated a few times
until the painter in desperation begins to paint the
two different colors wildly, one with each hand.

                                            WIPE TO:

re102   MED. SHOT - SHINY DANCE FLOOR - PART OF AN OUTDOOR
        PAVILION

In b.g. a partly finished bandstand.  In f.g. a man
sprinkles something on the floor and then dances
around on it alone.  He bows to Chuck and Ferdie to
try it.  Chuck and Ferdie bow to each other, begin
to waltz around...and suddenly they slip and fall.

                                            WIPE TO:

OH CHARLIE - REVISIONS

rel03    LONG SHOT - EXT. MOOSEHEAD SPRINGS - NIGHT

This is an outdoor dining and dancing pavilion with the
hotel buildings in b.g.  Ted Lewis and his orchestra are
playing a cheerful tune.  People are dancing.  The
atmosphere is bright and summery.

rel04    MED. SHOT - AT ENTRANCE GATE - NIGHT

Chuck and Ferdie in person - and in flannels - greeting
new arrivals.

> CHUCK
> Welcome, folks.

> FERDIE
> Drink our waters -- they taste
> terrible -- but they make you
> feel fine.
> > (his face lights up
> > as he spots the
> > Alderman -- this time
> > with his wife)
> Hi ya, Alderman?

> ALDERMAN
> How do you do?  I didn't have
> time to phone for reservations --

> FERDIE
> I know what you like -- we'll
> put you behind a tree some place.
> > (turns and calls
> > sharply to someone o.s.)
> Take care of the Alderman -- and
> be quick about it.

The CAMERA SWINGS AROUND to include Gregory.  He
bows the Alderman and his wife out of the shot as
the Doctor comes toward them carrying his bag.

> DOC
> Did you send for me?

> CHUCK
> There's a girl waiting for you?

> DOC
> Patient?

CONTINUED

rel04    CONTINUED

                         FERDIE
          I'll say she is -- she's been
          waiting for six months.

                         CHUCK
                    (indicating o.s.)
          She's right over there under
          that tree.

                         DOC
          I can't treat her there.  Send
          her to my office.

                         FERDIE
          I'm the boss and I say you treat
          her under that tree.

Doc shrugs and starts out of scene.  Ferdie starts
to follow him.

                         CHUCK
                    (angrily whispering)
          Where you going?

                         FERDIE
          Leave it to me -- I'll fix
          everything.

                         CHUCK
          I'll bet you do.

Ferdie runs away.


rel05    MED. LONG - NEAR THE WISHBLOOM TREE

         A few couples are strolling.  Norma sits on a grassy
         mound looking wistful.  The Doc approaches from b.g.
         unseen by her, and after him tiptoes Ferdie.


rel06    MED. CLOSE - NORMA AT TREE

         She gets up and sighs.


rel07    MED. SHOT

         Norma looking around.  Doc approaches from the b.g.
         Ferdie steps near the tree and peeks.

                         DOC
          I beg your pardon -- are you
          the young lady who --
                                        CONTINUED

rel07    CONTINUED

                          NORMA
                     (looks around)
          Doc!

                           DOC
          Well, this is pleasant.
          How do you do, Miss Lind?

                          NORMA
                     (discouraged)
          Well enough.  Don't you remember
          the last time we met?

                           DOC
          Which experiment was I making?

                          NORMA
          I believe it was something to do
          with the heart.

                           DOC
          Yours or mine?

                          NORMA
          Both.

                           DOC
          I don't recall a thing.

                          NORMA
          We talked about the moonlight
          and a certain tree -- The
          Wishbloom Tree --


THE CAMERA BEGINS TILTING UP towards the tree.


                          NORMA (o.s.)
          -- and I told you about the legend
          of the blossoms falling --


                                        CONTINUED

rel07     CONTINUED - 2

We see Ferdie perilously perched in the tree trying to
coax a few blossoms to fall down.

                          FERDIE
                        (whispering)
                Go on -- fall -- fall!


rel08     MED. CLOSE - DOC AND NORMA

                          DOC
                    (trying to remember)
                I remember.  I was on my way to
                Paducah Falls-- I believe you
                were going to Carterville --
                Something about a job --

                          NORMA
                       (plaintively)
                I'm talking about that awful night!
                We were right here!

rel09     CLOSE SHOT - FERDIE - IN THE TREE

                          FERDIE
                     (in attitude of
                      supplication)
                Fall, you dope -- fall!


rel10     MED. CLOSE - DOC AND NORMA

                          DOC
                What happened?

                          NORMA
                    (desperately -
                     almost
                     angrily)
                Don't you remember?  What did
                you do?

rel11    MED. CLOSE - FLASH - FERDIE IN TREE

He tries to reach the blossoms -- loses his balance and
yells.  The blossom falls - he is left swinging on the limb.


rel12    CLOSE SHOT - NORMA AND DOC

The blossoms fall on Doc's head.  Norma, frightened by
Ferdie's yell, leaps into Doc's arms.  He puts them around
her and their eyes meet.

                          DOC
                       (smiling)
             Of course - this is what I did!
                    (kisses her again)

Over the scene comes Ferdie's voice yelling:

                       FERDIE (o.s.)
                Help!  Help!

They pay no attention to him, but walk away from the tree
and out of the shot, her head on his shoulder.


rel13    MED. SHOT - FERDIE

falls out of tree


rel14    MED. CLOSE - SHOOTING TOWARD TREE

Ferdie, under tree, howling as the blossoms tumble on his head.


rel15    MED. CHUCK AND CAMILLE - AT THE ENTRANCE

He is just shaking hands with her when they hear Ferdie
yell.  They turn and dash out of scene toward the tree.


rel16    MED. SHOT - FERDIE IN F.G. UNDER TREE

Some blossoms still dropping down on him.  He staggers
to his feet.  Chuck runs into the scene.  Ferdie, overcome,
embraces Chuck.  Chuck pushes him out of the way just
as Camille rushes into the scene.  Ferdie embraces Camille.

                       CAMILLE
                At last!

As they embrace, the body of Charlie Smith falls out of
the tree onto their laps.  They react.

                       FERDIE
                    (screaming)
                Oh Charlie!  Charlie!

                                        CONTINUED

rell6    From o.s. a fanfare and roll of the drums.


rell7    LONG SHOT — TED LEWIS & HIS ORCHESTRA

         beginning a number.  During this CUT TO:


rell8    MED. SHOT

         An Abbott and Costello routine.


rell9    LONG SHOT

         The "Aurora" number, sung by the Andrews Sisters.
         This works into a production number using all the
         people, including Chuck and Ferdie, winding up with
         the peanut throwing bit.


rel20    A TAG

         relating back to the routine just before this
         number.

                                          FADE OUT.

Chuck is about to put down the tray.  The Alderman stands
glaring o.s. as Ferdie helps Chuck with food.

                    CHUCK
          Your food sir.

                    ALDERMAN
          Eat it yourself.

                    FERDIE
          Thanks -- you're a swell guy.

They hurriedly seat themselves at the table as  the
Alderman angrily walks OUT OF SCENE.

                    FERDIE
                 (looking at duck
                  on big platter)
          What kind of meat is that?

                    CHUCK
          Duck.

Ferdie dives under table, sticking head up.

                    FERDIE
          What's the matter did somebody
          throw something?

                    CHUCK
          That's a duck on the table.

                    FERDIE
                 (pointing
                  to duck)
          Oh, this!  I wonder how old it is?

                    CHUCK
          How can you tell a duck's age?

                    FERDIE
                 (getting ready
                  to carve)
          By the teeth.

                    CHUCK
          A duck hasn't any teeth.

                    FERDIE
          No - but I have.  What part of
          the duck do you want?

                    CHUCK
          I'll take the two legs --

                                        CONTINUED

FERDIE
Okay - I'll take the wings.

CHUCK
No you won't, I want the two wings
too.

FERDIE
(in disgust)
All right -- I'll take the breast
and the neck.

CHUCK
How do you like that - you give me
the legs and the wings -- I want
the breast and the neck too.

FERDIE
All right -- all right -- go ahead
take the wings, the legs, the breast
and the neck --

CHUCK
What about you?

FERDIE
I'll sit on the fence and get mine
as it goes by.

CHUCK
Go ahead - carve it.

Ferdie goes to stick fork in duck and it bends double.
He picks up carving knife and in his struggle to cut a
leg - the duck flies into the air - hitting Gregory in
the face as he comes into SCENE.  The boys make a dash
out of scene - followed by Gregory.

RE-61    ESTABLISHING SHOT - FILLING STATION - MED. SHOT

        Chuck busy outside station - Ferdie's voice comes
        over SCENE singing "WHEN MY BABY SMILES AT ME"
        CAMERA PANS OVER - FERDIE IS DOING AN IMITATION
        OF TED LEWIS - using a grease gun as a clarinet-
        as he moves gun he accidentally pushes plunger
        getting a kisser full of grease.

                        CHUCK
                Now look what you did.  Forget
                Ted Lewis and get busy.

        (balance of scene according to script)




RE-93        INSERT GAG AFTER CHUCK'S LAST SPEECH

                        CHUCK
                We moved all your stuff into
                the Bridal Suite - Compliments
                of the Management --

        Norma and DOC look at each other in amazement, they
        go into a clinch - and as the boys start to move away.


                        DOC
                By the way Ferdie - what happened
                to Camille?

                        FERDIE
                We had a runaway marriage.

                        NORMA
                A runaway marriage?

                        FERDIE
                Yeah - she got the license and I
                ran away.

MED. SHOT - FERDIE & CHUCK - TABLES IN B.G.

As MUSIC comes over SCENE, the boys are apparently watching the dancers.

> FERDIE
> Gee, Chuck, we got money, we own
> this place, but we haven't even
> got a girl to dance with.

> CHUCK
> Well we can't just strike up an
> acquaintance with a girl -- we
> need some sort of an introduction.

A nice looking girl passes and accidentally drops her
purse; as the boys start for it, a young chap steps in
and picks it up.

> MAN
> Pardon me, miss, you dropped your
> purse.

> GIRL
> So I did! Thank you.

> MAN
> Suppose you thank me on the dance
> floor.

> GIRL
> I'd love to.

They go OUT OF SCENE toward dance floor.

> CHUCK
> That's an idea Ferdie, the next
> girl comes along - you drop your
> money - then you say "Pardon me,
> miss, but you dropped your money,"
> naturally she will say it isn't
> hers -- you strike up a conversation
> and you invite her to dance.

> FERDIE
> That's a swell idea -
>        (does take)
> - but it's no good.  She might take
> the money.

> CHUCK
> Nonsense - she won't take it.  Now
> get your money ready, and we'll wait
> till a girl comes by.

Ferdie puts hand in pocket, a girl passes by and Ferdie
throws a quarter - the girl goes OUT OF SCENE.

CONTINUED

                            CHUCK
                      (grabbing Ferdie)
              What's the idea of throwing a quarter?


                            FERDIE
              That's all she was worth.


                            CHUCK
              Look, Ferdie, you've got to throw
              big money.


                            FERDIE
              Why don't you throw your own money?


                            CHUCK
              That's a fine thing to say.  I gave
              you the idea, didn't I?


                            FERDIE
              Sure.


                            CHUCK
              Well, you can't expect me to give
              my own idea - and use my own money
              to try it out.  That would be selfish.


                            FERDIE
              Maybe I should give you back your idea
              and you throw your money.


                            CHUCK
              Stop worrying - she won't take it.
              Now the next time drop a bankroll.


Ferdie puts hand in pocket as girl passes - he throws the
money toward her feet, she makes one dive for it but
Ferdie gets there first - the girl goes OUT OF SCENE.


                            FERDIE
              She won't take it huh?  Brother, she
              grabbed at that like a wife grabs for
              a husband's pay envelope.


                            CHUCK
              You didn't even give her a chance to
              strike up a conversation.


                            FERDIE
              She didn't want any conversation --
              Did you see those lunch hooks go
              after that dough?


                            CHUCK
              I told you she wouldn't take it.
              We'll try it just once more.  Get
              the money ready.


                                        CONTINUED

                              FERDIE
                    Maybe it would be better if I
                    nailed it to the floor.

                              CHUCK
                    I told you - she won't take it.

Another girl passes by - Ferdie throws the money at
his feet.  He warily kicks money with his foot toward
girl, as Chuck urges him on - as the money gets near
the girl's feet.

                              FERDIE
                    Miss, as you was passing by, you
                    dropped your money.

                              GIRL
                    That isn't my money.

Ferdie and Chuck give each other a look, as if the idea
was working out okay.

                              FERDIE
                    But I saw the money fall, as you
                    went by.

                              GIRL
                    I'm sorry - I couldn't take money
                    that doesn't belong to me.

                              CHUCK
                         (calling Ferdie aside)
                    Insist - it's her money.  INSIST
                    she takes it.

                              FERDIE
                    I INSIST YOU TAKE.

As Ferdie turns to Chuck, the girl stoops and picks up
the money.

                              GIRL
                    Well, if you insist - okay.

She goes OUT OF SCENE with money - Ferdie gives a very
satisfied look to Chuck, turns and sees girl is gone,
does a double take - and almost collapses in Chuck's
arms.

RE-95 A

    During the AURORA NUMBER we CUT TO Chuck and Ferdie
    going from table to table looking for the girl.  As
    we get to the close of the number - they find her
    seated with back to them, and her pocketbook laying
    on the table.  Urged by Chuck in pantomime, Ferdie
    reaches in her purse and takes out his bank roll.


RE-96   MED. SHOT - CHUCK AND FERDIE

                        FERDIE
                  (stuffing bankroll
                   in his pocket)
              I got my money back anyway.

    GIRL and COP comes into scene.

                        GIRL
              Those are the men that took my
              money officer.

                        CHUCK
              Now just a minute miss --

                        FERDIE
              It was MY money.  I ain't got
              your money.

                        COP
              I'll just search you and make sure.

    He puts hand in Ferdie's pocket and pulls out bankroll.

                        COP
                  (to Girl)
              Could you identify your money?

                        GIRL
              Certainly -- it was green and had
              numbers on it.

                        COP
              That's right.
                  (hands girl money)

                        FERDIE
              Certainly it had numbers on --
              they all got numbers ---

                        COP
              And I got a couple of numbers to
              put on you guys - come on.

    The cops grab Chuck and Ferdie by the collar, and
    takes them struggling OUT OF SCENE.

RE-96-A- LONG SHOT - PATROL WAGON - leaving front of
MOOSEHEAD SPRINGS.


RE-96-B- INTERIOR PATROL WAGON - CLOSE SHOT - FERDIE & CHUCK

They are sitting disconsolately looking at each
other.

                    CHUCK
          Well, at least the three of
          us are together.

                    FERDIE
          You mean the two of us.

                    CHUCK
          I mean the three of us - LOOK.

The CAMERA PANS - and there is CHARLIE SMITH
SITTING STIFFLY AT THE END OF THE PATROL WAGON.

                    FERDIE
          OH CHARLIE! See Chuck, he
          don't scare me anymore.

As he makes this speech he gets up bravely, then
does a face fall right into CAMERA.

                                        FADE

# "The Screamingest Riot the Boys Have Turned In"

One week before it opened in theaters, *Hold That Ghost* debuted on *Hollywood Premiere,* one of several radio shows that presented streamlined adaptations of current movies. These programs, featuring the original stars, amounted to half-hour commercials. Louella Parsons, queen of the gossip columnists, hosted the series, which aired on CBS. The radio version is closer to Lees and Rinaldo's original concept. Bud and Lou returned to the program by popular demand in September for an adaptation of *Ride 'Em Cowboy,* and did *Buck Privates* on Lux Radio Theater in October.

Despite efforts to bring the film *Hold That Ghost* in line with *Buck Privates* (and *In the Navy* for that matter), the picture remained an anomaly. The story revolves around Bud and Lou, while in the previous films the boys share the screen with romantic subplots and musical numbers. Unfortunately that trend continued for the next four films, until *Who Done It* (1942), which eschewed musical acts and kept Abbott and Costello on screen virtually the entire time.

The film was previewed on July 25 at the Alexander Theater and released nationally on August 6. The *Hollywood Reporter* observed, "Abbott and Costello get more of a story in 'Hold That Ghost' than they have had heretofore. Fred Rinaldo and Robert Lees have tailored a perfect fit for the stars and John Grant's gag material is his best film contribution yet."

*Variety* agreed: "Script provided by Lees, Rinaldo and Grant takes full advantage of Abbott and Costello's special talents, providing the pair with socko material that eliminates recourse to their familiar routines of previous pictures. As result, picture is a slam-bang and knockabout comedy, silly and ridiculous, but a laugh-creator and audience-pleaser."

*Showman's Trade Review* noted, "With a better story, costlier production and a bang-up supporting cast, [Abbott and Costello] romp through their assignments like a couple of veterans."

Others, however, didn't think there was much of a story. *Motion Picture Daily* wrote, "'Hold That Ghost' is, with a few modernizations and no trimmings, the classic skit of the medicine-show era, known variously as 'Over the River, Charlie,' 'Oh, Charlie,' etc., which had ghosts shuttling in and out of a haunted house or hotel to the consternation of the comedians and, of course, the onlookers. 'Hold That Ghost' has more ghosts, all phony, and more shuttlings, all timed to a nicety, than your grand pappy ever dreamed of."

The story was undermined by edits that made room for the music. *Boxoffice* described the plot as "meager." *Independent Exhibitors Film Bulletin* said, "The story is slight—much of it is never explained, but this matters little, for what counted with the preview audience were the routines of the amazing new comics. And how they deliver!" The *New York Herald Tribune* was typical: "The picture is quite a hodgepodge, but it doesn't seem to matter." *The New Yorker* said, "[Abbott and Costello] are top-notch burlesque comedians, and there's no higher praise than that. They are severely handicapped, though, by the necessity of maintaining an interest in a purely nominal plot."

The film's paltry budget, and the haste in refurbishing it, was apparent to others. The *Hollywood Reporter* thought it "...lacks the polished production which Alex Gottlieb gave 'Buck Privates' and 'In the Navy.'"

*Trade ad for* Hold That Ghost. *(The 16,000 theaters represented nearly every theater in the United States in 1941—wishful thinking.)*

*Independent Exhibitors Film Bulletin* complained, "It is all as tawdry and hackneyed as can be, the production is even cheap and careless—but the public will laugh like hell at the antics of Abbott and Costello."

Of course Lou received the lion's share of the accolades. *Exhibitors Film Bulletin* proclaimed, "Costello is the funniest guy to hit the screen in years and 'Ghost' proves it." *Film Daily* thought, "Lou Costello has never been funnier. At times his comedy is so fast that lines of dialogue are ignored and the audience roars at the pantomime he uses with his lines." The *New York Herald Tribune* echoed, "When dialogue and situations fail to keep the comedy at fever pitch, Costello's masterful pantomime usually assumes the burden of entertaining." The *Washington Post* noted, "'Hold That Ghost' gallops along like a cyclonic nightmare. This is to be blamed principally upon the infinite capacity for fear and fumbling manifested by the cherubic Lou Costello, who can get himself into more jams to the square minute than all the rest of the company put together…" The *Hollywood Reporter* noted, "Costello hits the top of his comic form and has two long scenes by himself that had the crowd in near hysterics." The *New York Sun* cracked: "The fat boy has a fat part, all built to order for him."

Bud Abbott, as usual, was commended for his work as a straight man. The *Washington Post* asserted, "Bud Abbott, as always, is the perfect 'straight man' who often makes his partner seem a greater funster than he is." Bud was also praised for his acting. The

*Hollywood Reporter* remarked, "Bud Abbott feeds less lines to his roly-poly partner in this and does more acting. He's good, underplaying for a sock appearance." *Independent Exhibitors Film Bulletin* concurred: "Abbott is less of a stooge in this picture, playing what amounts to a straight part."

Still, the boys' teamwork shined. The *Brooklyn Daily Eagle* observed: "You can probably guess most of the slapstick tricks. But you've got to see them again, brightened with the Abbott and Costello polish, to realize how funny they are. Depend upon these two to make even old saws keen again. That's what makes them the movies' cleverest comics." The *Los Angeles Examiner* proclaimed, "Lou Costello is a great comedian. Not since Chaplin has any comic conveyed more wistful bewilderment performing his outlandish clowning. Bud Abbott is a terrific straight man—and without him Costello could not be half as funny. As a team, they are a riot."

The *Philadelphia Inquirer* agreed: "Costello's pathetic, human comedy has genuine appeal, with Abbott's straight man stuff to complement it." The *Baltimore Evening Sun* said, "[Abbott and Costello] seem to be having a high old time as they tear about threatening to wreck the scenery, and, fortunately, their enthusiasm is contagious." *Film Daily* predicted, "Following the formula of the former A&C hits, with the sure-fire locale of a haunted tavern, and a rapid succession of those old-new burlesque routines, 'Hold That Ghost' is a cinch to please all those theater

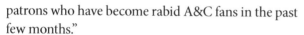

*Above: Animated lobby display from the Orpheum Theater in Philadelphia. Green lights blinked on and off in the eyes of the ghost above the house; the ghost on the left waved its arms and nodded its head. Right: The Senator Theater had four white-robed, ghost-masked men drive around Pittsburgh in an antique automobile.*

patrons who have become rabid A&C fans in the past few months."

The opening stanza in the nightclub, however, was not appreciated. The *Los Angeles Times* complained, "You have to endure preliminaries that are chock full of routine gags…Abbott and Costello have their first adventure as waiters, under the supervision of Mischa Auer, and that sequence is just fair, for it drags." The *Washington Post* called it "…a creeping start that betrays nothing of the hysteria that is to follow…"

Joan Davis was deservedly singled out. The *Los Angeles Times* enthused: "…Joan Davis [reveals] herself as the best rough-and-tumble comedienne on the screen. She and Costello have a dance and a water splashing episode that is corny as sin, yet brings down the house." The *New York Herald Tribune* agreed, "…Costello finds a smart, comic partner in Joan Davis. They…do a slapstick waltz and a show-stopping rumba…"

The *Hollywood Reporter* gushed, "Joan Davis is immense with the best role she's had in years and wraps it up for a smash…The dance by Joan Davis and Costello is a hilarious highlight." The *Dallas Morning News* wrote, "…Joan Davis turns loose her eccentric dancing. A turn with Costello ending with a water bucket where a bustle once was worn is a riot." *Variety* declared: "Miss Davis also clicks in major fashion with her comedic surprise throughout the proceedings, and is an excellent laugh teammate for Costello." *Independent Exhibitors Film Bulletin*

thought, "Joan Davis has a juicy spot and the comedienne makes the most of it."

Richard Carlson and Evelyn Ankers, however, received cursory attention. The *New York Herald Tribune*: "Richard Carlson and Evelyn Ankers play very subdued romantic roles well, Carlson as an absent-minded chemist with glasses and Miss Ankers as a pretty girl." *Independent Exhibitors Film Bulletin*: "Richard Carlson and Evelyn Ankers handle the slight romantic thread in satisfactory fashion." *Philadelphia Inquirer*: "There are others in the cast besides Bud and Lou, not that it matters much. Joan Davis does an eccentric dance with Lou, and lets out a scream or two. Evelyn Ankers provides the pulchritude, and Richard Carlson opposite. But you won't worry about any plot—Costello will see to that."

The harshest criticism was leveled at the musical numbers. The *Baltimore Evening Sun* complained about "…some night-club hanky-panky thrown in for what the producers erroneously thought was good measure. This latter consists of barbershop chords and whinnies from the awkward Andrews Sisters and Ted Lewis, the band leader, waving his battered silk hat and wanting to know whether everyone is happy, and repeating his similarly battered old theme song, 'When My Baby Smiles at Me.'"

The *Philadelphia Inquirer* grumbled: "…Universal dusted off Ted Lewis and the Andrews Sisters, inserting them in nightclub sequences fore and aft to add a bit of 'name' value. For our money…they only pad

*Before* Hold That Ghost *opened, the manager of the Loew's in Evansville, Indiana, sent six ushers around town wearing these ghost costumes. They also walked up and down the theater aisles when trailers were shown.*

out the picture…" The *Los Angeles Times* was more severe: "Ted Lewis moans through some numbers, including the old 'Me and My Shadow,' which loses its flavor in the current tune treatment…Lewis doesn't add much." *Variety* summed up, "…finale with the entertainers on again is nothing more than an anti-climax."

The *New York Times* was more objective: "Preceding and succeeding the haunted-house routine, Universal has draped 'Hold That Ghost' with night-club production numbers in which Ted Lewis and the Andrews sisters run through 'Me and My Shadow,' 'When My Baby Smiles at Me,' 'Sleepy Serenade' and 'Aurora.' But while these interludes are entertaining of themselves, they tend to slow up the film's pace and before the final fade-out one is all too conscious that 'Hold That Ghost' runs eighty-six minutes."

Many critics thought *Hold That Ghost* was better than the boys' previous films. *Motion Picture Daily* raved, "'Hold That Ghost' is, in the vernacular, hotter than a firecracker. It is, to use some more vernacular, by far the corniest comedy the Abbott and Costello duo has committed, but don't get me wrong—for "corniest" is, in this case, a synonym for best…On the evidence provided by a capacity audience which witnessed the preview at the Alexander Theater in Glendale, this is the screamingest riot the boys have turned in—and I mean screams, not just guffaws, blurts and haw-haws, but screams! Indeed, shrieks! Not even 'Buck Privates,' nor 'In the Navy,' had them yelling so loudly, long or often."

*Variety:* "Although the story utilizes mechanical devices and foolproof situations…it depends on its own dialog and situations to get across the laughs without inclusion of the Abbott-Costello routines that have already become familiar and threadbare in the comics' previous film appearances…[S]ituations are neatly set up to make Costello and Joan Davis the major victims of the surprise happenings. As a result, episodes fall on top of each other with crazy and ridiculous happenings that are still good for hefty laughs despite audience familiarity and forewarning of what's coming."

*Independent Exhibitors Film Bulletin:* "'Hold That Ghost'…was exactly what the doctor ordered to make the sure-fire capers of Abbott and Costello click again after the let-down they suffered in 'In the Navy.' *Newsweek:* "'Hold That Ghost' is very low comedy with a high percentage of rumbling, unabashed belly laughs. To students of the muscle-and-meringue school of comedy, and/or admirers of the comedy team, the new film will prove as funny as 'Buck Privates.'"

The *Atlanta Constitution* proclaimed, "'Hold That Ghost' tops Abbott and Costello's 'Buck Privates' and 'In the Navy.' It is a picture for laughs." The *New York Daily News* agreed: "Seems to me it's funnier than [*Buck Privates* and *In The Navy*]. Better lines and bits of business plus something laughable in the way of a plot." The *Los Angeles Times* called it "their most wild-eyed and perhaps uproarious comedy, once it really gets going." *Dallas Morning News:* "The third Abbott and Costello picture (in order of release) is the merriest as far as we are concerned." *Harrison's Reports* predicted, "This latest Abbott and Costello comedy should provoke laughter of even greater intensity than that provoked by…'Buck Privates' and 'In The Navy' [because] not only are the stars known far better now…but the picture has a greater number of

*Universal plastered the Hold That Ghost 24-sheet poster on the billboards outside the studio. (Courtesy of Robert Rinaldo.)*

laugh-provoking situations."

But some critics tempered their enthusiasm. The *New York Herald Tribune* wrote, "Even these zanies aren't always able to keep 'Hold That Ghost' from becoming a bit tiresome, but these lapses are generally welcome as breathing spells before the next stomach earthquake. In contrast to the usual languor of a summer morning audience, the one at the Capitol's first show yesterday howled with glee. They had no reservations in their appreciation of 'Hold That Ghost,' nor did we. Abbott and Costello continue their amazing success."

The *New York Post* confessed, "…this department (and we're still an A and C fan—especially C) must report that the Capitol's current opus didn't have us in the aisles—as did both 'Buck Privates' and 'In the Navy'—not to forget their charming contribution to 'One Night in the Tropics.'"

The *New York Daily Mirror* said, "Though 'Hold That Ghost' doesn't reach the high mark set by 'Buck Privates' and the even more amusing 'In the Navy,' it packs sufficient fun to satisfy comedy seekers and should not be missed by Abbott and Costello fans."

The *New York Times* observed, "Yes, the boys are immensely funny as they romp through a ramshackle house abounding in secret passageways, sliding panels, clutching hands, eerie sound effects and all sorts of trick contraptions. An ideal background, to be sure, but the boys linger in it a little too long. For while their bag of tricks is considerable, it is by no means inexhaustible. But in spite of a tendency to drain every situation, there is many a hearty laugh to be had out of 'Hold That Ghost.'"

The *Dallas Morning News:* "We think Abbott and Costello milk their sequences, meaning that they protract a scene until the cream of the jest turns sour. If each were trimmed a bit, the audiences would be craving more, which is the best way to leave an audience."

The *New York Morning Telegraph* opined, "To an impartial observer, however (of which there are admittedly only a few in the world), it does seem that the boys are running short of material. 'Buck Privates' was a howl, principally because Abbott and Costello went through their routines with that split-second timing, that rapid precision that has brought them to where they are today. 'In the Navy' had a little less routine and a little more slapstick, which the Three Stooges could have done equally as well, and now 'Hold That Ghost' only occasionally has the boys firing the questions and answer business at each other, which much more of the siding door business thrown in than they really need…'Hold That Ghost' is good rowdy, risible slapstick. But it should have been better Abbott and Costello."

Two reviewers were far more critical. The film set an opening day record at the Senator Theater in Pittsburgh and was held over. Yet the critic for the *Pittsburgh Post-Gazette* fixated on the film's checkered production history—the low budget, extraneous musical numbers, added scenes, etc.—and it tainted his opinion. He moaned, "…'Hold That Ghost' is a pretty tired whodunit in which Abbott and Costello…work under the theory that if a thing is funny for 20 seconds it will be 10 times as funny if it consumes 200 seconds…they play the old spook stuff to death and at least half the footage is consumed by Mr. Costello's double-takes, the longest on record and better-

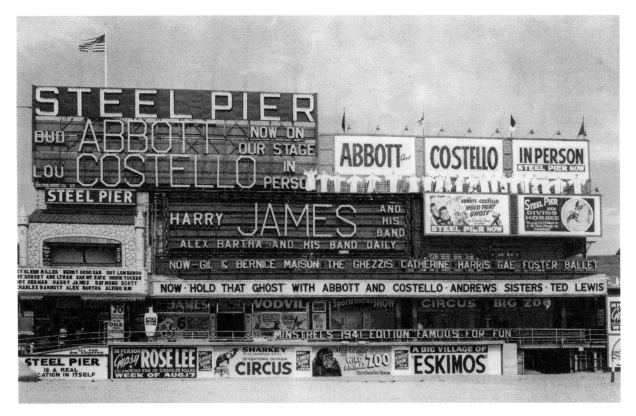

*The boys and* Hold That Ghost *headline the Steel Pier. The team had been there in a minstrel show only four years earlier.*

ing Mr. Edward Everett Horton's previous mark by at least several hundred feet of celluloid…To be sure, 'Hold That Ghost' will no doubt make a million bucks, chiefly on the strength of 'Buck Privates' and 'In the Navy,' neither of which, by the way, it even remotely approximates in entertainment…Consider this a minority report, though. The audience at the Senator [Theater] early yesterday afternoon split their sides at 'Hold That Ghost.' Most of them were kids."

The critic for the *Cleveland Press* was also sour: "This picture is probably the corniest offering put out by the Universal Studios in a long time. The oldest gags in the business, including the trusty rusty haunted house, are dragged out to make Bud Abbott and Lou Costello look good. If acting consists of running into doors, slapping each other and looking around as if waiting for a director to bark out commands, then Abbott and Costello have really got something. Personally speaking, they seem to have as much acting ability as a mummy."

But audiences loved it. The *Motion Picture Herald* marveled, "Yes, Ladies and Gentlemen, they've done it again. In fact by count and with witnesses, the Messrs. Abbott and Costello got more, louder and longer laughs in 'Hold That Ghost' at its Hollywood preview than they did in 'Buck Privates' or

'In the Navy.' Veritably, it is to be doubted if any two comedians ever got so many laughs in one picture any time, anywhere…Previewed at the Alexander Theater, Glendale, to a mixed audience, paying and professional, who set a new high in Glendale annals for volume, consistency and duration of laughter."

The *Hollywood Reporter:* "This review started taking shape about nine days ago, when your critic attended a show at the Pantages and happened to catch the trailer on 'Hold That Ghost.' The audience went into spasms at the few teaser scenes presented them. Those spasms were nothing compared to the roar that greeted the main title of 'Universal presents Abbott and Costello in–' at the Glendale preview Friday night, and the cleverly animated title, 'Hold That Ghost.' As with the audience that saw the trailer, just the mere idea of the comics in a haunted house mystery comedy was enough to insure their complete enjoyment. And the picture didn't let them down. If this seems more a review of the audience reaction than of a picture, it's because everyone knows by now that Abbott and Costello are funny in almost anything, that their shows are currently outgrossing anything else on film and story doesn't mean a thing as long as boys give out with their routines… [T]he laughs come so fast and furious that a great many lines are entirely drowned out. At one point, about half the audience was saying 'Sh' to the other half. It will be wise if Universal digs out some edited footage and puts it back in the picture to allow for proper lapses and timing for the laughter." (Editor Phil Cahn had already done just that.)

The *Boston Globe* noted: "From one stock situation to another, this pair of former burlesque comedians take themselves through an orgy of laugh-provoking scenes. The audience that witnessed the first showing yesterday nearly rolled in the aisles… and believe this reporter, it's a night of hilarity."

The *Washington Post* observed, "Abbott and Costello are their own yardstick. The antic lunacies they bring to the screen cannot be judged by standards applicable to the insanities of any other team of comedians enlivening the cinema with the aberrations of the crazy house. By slightly modifying and considerably refining the hoariest of burlesque's slap-stickeries and the most palpable of ancient 'gags' they have become, of a sudden, the one brace of low comics who infallibly can roll an audience up and down the aisles in convulsions of hysterical mirth. They prove it again in 'Hold That Ghost,' the new attraction at RKO Keith's Theater.

The *Baltimore Sun:* "'Hold That Ghost' is the same old hokum that's been dished out in the movies since the Keystone cops were throwing custard pies. But it keeps the audience roaring, and there are probably more laughs per pennyweight for the audience in this film than in a dozen comedies cast in a more subtle mode." *Billboard* remarked, "About 90 per cent of this spooky comedy is a rehash of the team's old vaude and burly gags and, judging by the response, audiences still consider them screamingly funny. Riding on the crest of the wave, Abbott and Costello can get away with almost anything and still panic the customers." The *Dallas Morning News:* "[T]he screams of the Palace patrons Friday indicated a ravenous appetite for this kind of fun."

The *New York Times:* "The arrival of 'Hold That Ghost' yesterday at the Capitol makes it three straight hits in a row for Abbott and Costello, judging by the gales of laughter which greeted their every turn…"

The *Philadelphia Inquirer:* The audience at the Stanley [Theater] yesterday laughed so much that many of the gag lines were missed, but there was always another gag quickly following." (*Variety* reported that a woman complained to the manager of the Rivoli Theater in Toledo that she and her fam-

American Cinematographer *and* The Hollywood Reporter *and both singled out this scene when Ferdie timidly calls Charlie Smith in the cellar. This scene is not in the script and was expanded on set.*

ily couldn't hear many lines of dialogue because of audience laughter. The manager gave the family of seven free tickets for another night.)

The *New York Post* wrote: "Yesterday's premiere was launched with a street line 'way around the block, and by this time, there's probably standing room only. The boys have caught on; here's hoping they don't outwear their welcome by too frequent release of their wares."

The craftsmen behind the camera were also acknowledged. *Independent Exhibitors Film Bulletin* wrote, "Arthur Lubin, who delivered the previous A and C hits, has done a magnificent job of direction. It's not often that gags are so well planted and that business is made to account for so much humor."

*The Hollywood Reporter* observed, "It was a surprise…to hear the applause which greeted the title: 'Directed by Arthur Lubin.' That was not studio inspired, for no studio claque could make that much noise. It was a sincere tribute from an audience, which recognized Lubin's name…and was prepared to see another hit from him. And Lubin's third straight hit is what they got…It's a whale of a job that Arthur Lubin has done on the direction, with a number of outstanding examples of set business, particularly the timing of the scene where Costello gets in a closet with a dead body and walks out instead of running, and a scene where we see only his shadow at the head of the stairs…." (Both scenes were added on the set.)

*Variety* thought, "Arthur Lubin…carries this one along at a fast pace, highlighting every possible situation available for laugh purposes."

*Left: Italian poster for* The Illusive Ghost, *with original artwork highlighting the comic dance. Right: French poster for* Ghosts on the Loose, *utilizing Universal's artwork. Note that Shemp Howard rates a credit.*

*American Cinematographer* praised Elwood Bredell's camera work: "Bredell's handling of the production should advance his prestige many a notch upward. The greater part of the action takes place in a haunted house, with the inevitable effect-lightings such a locale would inspire. Bredell handles these very artistically, yet so skillfully that no comedy action is lost because of his pictorial shadowing—a more than praiseworthy achievement. To this writer, as apparently to many of the preview audience, a standout scene was that in which Costello, timorously seeking the missing Charlie Smith in the basement of the abandoned inn, fearing to come down in to the basement, stands at the head of the stairs and quavers 'Oh, Charlie.' This scene is played entirely in an effect-lighted long shot—with the star shown only by his feet and a long shadow. This concept, together with Bredell's lighting, makes the scene infinitely more effective and amusing than any more literal treatment could. Bredell deals excellently with the players, presenting the two feminine principals—Evelyn Ankers and Joan Davis—to special advantage."

When *Hold That Ghost* was released in August, Bud and Lou had just finished *Ride 'Em, Cowboy.*

They flew to Reading, Penn., for a personal appearance, then did eight days at the Steel Pier in Atlantic City. They also appeared the Capitol Theater in Manhattan, and Keith's in Boston. *Variety* wrote, "With their 'Hold That Ghost' in its third week at the Keith Memorial, after a very recent five-week run of 'In the Navy,' Abbott-Costello in person are jamming 'em in at the Boston. Ex-burley comics jump right into a line of chatter that the mob is waiting for, Costello fools around with the orchestra a bit, then they encore with that terrific routine ["Who's On First?"]."

A few days after *Hold That Ghost* was released, Bud and Lou signed a revised contract with Universal. The studio took up a two-year option on the team (rather than the usual one year) "to give them a feeling of security in their new homes." The new contract called for three pictures a year, plus one annual outside job at MGM. In addition, the boys were handed a bonus of $29,000 on each of two completed films, *Buck Privates* and *Hold That Ghost.*

In September *Hold That Ghost* was playing at the Alexander Theater in Glendale when Laurel and Hardy's service comedy, *Great Guns* (1941), was previewed. It was Stan and Ollie's first feature after leav-

*Above: Post-war German poster for "das beliebte komik-erpaar" (the popular comedy pair) in* Caution Ghost!

ing Hal Roach. The *Motion Picture Herald* reported that "the audience which, having just viewed 'Hold That Ghost', laughed itself into near hysterics at this."

In a year-end poll of exhibitors, *Showman's Trade Review* compiled the twenty-five "Leaders of 1941."

There were three Abbott and Costello films on the list: *Buck Privates* (No. 2, behind *Men of Boys Town* and ahead of *Caught in the Draft*); *In the Navy* (No. 7); and *Hold That Ghost* (No. 11, after *The Philadelphia Story*). They were the only Universal films on the list. *Variety* reported, "The quartet of pictures turned out by Universal starring newcomers to films Abbott and Costello rate special mention…They will bring in a total of around $6,000,000 in the domestic market. For a starring team, this is miraculous. Universal, in its entire history, has not had any such coin-attracting combination for the box office."

On the strength of those films, Abbott and Costello placed third on the list of Top Ten Box Office stars of 1941. (*Variety* rated them No 2.) In 1942, the team would rank Number 1.

In November 1941 *Hold That Ghost* became the second Abbott and Costello film to open in London. (*In The Navy* preceded it that summer.) The *Times* wrote, "Bud Abbott [sic] is an American comedian who has a most resourceful talent for gibbering with fright. His incarceration in a haunted house gives this talent fullest possible scope. The film is good slapstick entertainment."

The picture played in Cairo a year later, and reached Australia in the spring of 1943. *Variety* reported, "Abbott and Costello still remain top faves with Aussies. Latest pic to hit here, 'Hold That Ghost,' is breaking records for Greater Union Theaters."

Universal's other comedy team, Ole Olsen and Chic Johnson, made their own haunted house comedy, *Ghost Catchers*, in 1944. In a plot taken from D.

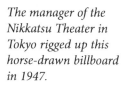

*The manager of the Nikkatsu Theater in Tokyo rigged up this horse-drawn billboard in 1947.*

W. Griffith's *One Exciting Night*, the duo discover that gangsters have been trying to scare a family out of their home in order to steal some valuable pre-Prohibition liquor hidden in the cellar. The film not only used part of the animated opening from *Hold That Ghost* but also includes a riff on the Moving Candle routine. As they undress for bed, Olsen says, "Remember Abbott and Costello in *Hold That Ghost?* The whole thing turned out to be gangsters."

"That was a very unbelievable picture," Johnson replies.

"Yeah," Olsen says, "especially when that candle started moving back and forth in front of Costello."

A candle slides along a table.

Olsen: "Like that."

They casually watch the candle slide back and forth numerous times with increasing speed, then Olsen and Johnson rapidly spin around several times, appear in pajamas, and go to bed.

World War II disrupted the flow of American movies to the European continent. These audiences got their first taste of Abbott and Costello in 1946 with *Hold That Ghost, Hit the Ice,* and *Pardon My Sarong.* Bud and Lou became so popular that they were given the distinction of local nicknames. In France the boys were called "Les Deux Nigauds" ("The Two Nitwits"), while in Italy they were affectionately known as Gianni e Pinotto ("Johnny and Little Pig").

That year, Bud and Lou made a supernatural comedy, *The Time of Their Lives.* Costello plays a spirit from the Revolutionary War, and Abbott plays a dual role across the decades. Although it is now a favorite of critics and fans, it was unappreciated in its day, and the boys fell from the ranks of Top Ten box office stars. Their new producer, Robert Arthur, decided to reboot the team's film career by revisiting their earlier hits. Abbott and Costello made *Buck Privates Come Home* (1947), a sequel to their first starring film, and a horror comedy that raised the fright quotient exponentially, *Abbott and Costello Meet Frankenstein* (1948). To underscore it's kinship with *Hold That Ghost,* John Grant reprised the Moving Candle bit in a unique way: sliding across the lid of Dracula's coffin as it slowly opened from inside. According to Bud's nephew, Norman Abbott, Costello resisted this twist on the routine until Grant demonstrated how it worked.

When *Abbott and Costello Meet Frankenstein* became a huge hit, Realart and Eagle-Lion reissued *Hold That Ghost* that fall. A theater manager in Holliday, Texas, reported to *Box Office*: "This is an oldie that topped all A&C pictures except 'Abbott and Costello Meet Frankenstein.' Business was fine both nights. My only complaint was from headaches caused by the shrieks and screams of the kid patrons." An exhibitor in Anthon, Iowa, wrote, "Excellent all the way around…Again I say the all-around quality of these older pictures is hard to find today." An exhibitor in Washburn, North Dakota, reported: "There comes a time when the elements will be stronger than the urge to see Abbott and Costello. Eight inches of loose snow on the ground and…business was still 85%."

*Hold That Ghost* made the rounds of revival houses and Saturday matinees through 1959, when it was released to television. In New York, it debuted on WOR's "Million Dollar Movie" on December 27. According to *Motion Picture Daily*, "Million Dollar Movie," which played the same film sixteen times a week, outdrew network programming. Viewers voted *La Strada* (1954), *Hold That Ghost,* and *Naked City* (1948) the three outstanding hits of the year.

The picture remained in syndication with twenty-seven other Abbott and Costello Universal features for nearly three decades. In 1977 the Museum of Modern Art in New York mounted a 65th anniversary salute to the studio. *Hold That Ghost* closed the six-month festival on January 29, 1978.

*Hold That Ghost* was released on videocassette in February 1983 and laser disc (paired with *Time of Their Lives*) in February 1996. Its first DVD release was in 2004.

It continues to turn up in revival houses, including the scene of its original triumph, the Alexander Theater in Glendale in 2010.

Dan Akroyd told the *New York Times* in 2008 that *Ghostbusters* (1984), was inspired by classic scare comedies like Bob Hope's *Ghost Breakers, Hold That Ghost,* and the Bowery Boys' *Ghost Catchers* (1951), and by having grown up in a haunted farmhouse in Canada.

*Hold That Ghost* had an impact on actor Ryan Gosling, who saw it when he was eight years old. "I saw *Hold That Ghost* and I had a completely weird, visceral experience watching it," he recalled. "I was scared and I was laughing and I felt so vulnerable and tender. I just didn't know what was going to happen, because it was like ballet: so elegant and masterful and beautifully shot." Clearly his affection for the film runs deep. He called *Hold That Ghost* "kind of a masterpiece," and has repeated the "Post Office" gag and Lou's sputtering scare take in his own films.

# Post-"Ghost"

Ten days after he finished re-takes, Arthur Lubin started another film with Bud and Lou, *Ride 'Em, Cowboy.* Like "Oh, Charlie," it was also held back several months so Universal could quickly push through a third service comedy, *Keep 'Em Flying.* After that—his fifth Abbott and Costello picture in just ten months—Lubin called it quits. "As we progressed from picture to picture," Lubin told the *Hollywood Reporter* in 1990, "as their popularity continued to grow, pressures came in on them. Frankly, they became difficult to direct. They were late getting to the set. Many times they didn't know their lines. Obviously, it's not easy to go from nowhere to becoming among the top ten boxoffice, where they remained for many years. Anyway, Abbott and Costello, who were basically great, decent guys, started acting up."

Lubin, in another interview, explained, "The studio felt that maybe they needed a new director to give them some incentive. But it was five fabulous pictures with those boys. They were very good for me. They gave me a reputation. I learned everything about timing from them."

Lubin was rewarded with the opportunity to direct one of the studio's prestige dramas of 1942, *Eagle Squadron,* for producer Walter Wanger. "It was a big chance for me to break away from slapstick," he said. "I don't regret leaving the boys. I wanted to leave them at a high point in my life with them and a high point in their career. I was never asked to direct them again, and I wanted to keep the memory of them the way I originally knew them. It was a sad parting for me. I loved those guys very much. But I don't think any of their later pictures ever equaled the five that I directed."

Lubin, who spent thirty years at Universal, was also entrusted with the studio's lavish remake of *Phantom of the Opera* (1943), starring Claude Rains. But high-camp opuses followed, including *White Savage, Ali Baba and Forty Thieves,* and *The Spider Woman Strikes Back* (which Lubin detested).

Lubin directed *Night in Paradise* (1946), starring Turhan Bey as Aesop, for Wanger. Bey, whom Lubin discovered, complained that the director was giving co-star Merle Oberon too many close-ups, and not enough to him. "He didn't have me fired," Lubin said, "but the studio didn't pick up my contract."

In 1949 Lubin became enchanted with David Stern's novel "Francis," about a talking mule, and wanted to turn it into a film. In order to persuade Universal's skeptical front office, Lubin offered to cut his salary and accept a percentage of future profits. "They loved the story," he recalled, "but there were technical problems getting a mule to move his mouth in sync with the dialogue. At the same time, they had a deal with Donald O'Connor—they had to find a script for him by a certain date or else they had to pay him anyway."

O'Connor was cast in the film, and by trial and error a well-guarded technique was developed to make the animal appear to talk (likely a nylon string). When *Francis the Talking Mule* became a hit, Lubin shared the windfall. He directed six of the seven sequels, and Francis, like Abbott and Costello before him, joined every branch of the service.

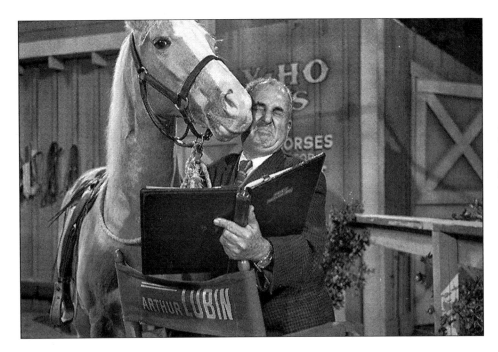

*Arthur Lubin with Mr. Ed. He produced and directed the series which ran from 1961 to 1966.*

In 1954 Lubin directed Clint Eastwood's screen test and arranged for the inexperienced actor to receive a studio contract. In *Clint: The Life and Legend*, author Patrick McGilligan quoted Lubin: "He was quite amateurish. He didn't know which way to turn or which way to go or do anything. I said, 'Don't give up, Clint. I'll suggest that you go to the dramatic school on the back lot." Lubin put Eastwood under personal contract and gave him bit parts in four films through 1957, including *Francis in the Navy* (1955) and *Lady Godiva of Coventry* (1955). That was nearly half of Eastwood's movie output then. Lubin also used him in a 1959 episode of TV's *Maverick*, "Duel at Sundown." Soon after, Eastwood was cast in the series *Rawhide* (1959-66) and his career took off. "As time went on," Lubin remarked, "he forgot Arthur Lubin." Then, after Eastwood won an Oscar for directing *Unforgiven* (1992), he called Lubin and the two chatted for the first time in decades.

In 1961 Lubin adapted Francis for TV as *Mr. Ed*. He produced and directed the series, which ran for five years. Mae West and Clint Eastwood made guest appearances as themselves. Bud Abbott was reportedly asked to do a guest spot but never did.

Lubin often lamented that he'd be remembered for talking mules and horses, but his sixty-odd credits include *Rhubarb* (1951, about a cat that inherits a baseball team), *Thief of Baghdad* (1953), *The First Traveling Saleslady* (1956), *The Incredible Mr. Limpet* (1966), and *Hold On!* (1966) with Herman's Hermits.

In December 1994, Lubin suffered a stroke and entered a nursing home. When his condition deteriorated he was moved to Glendale Adventist Medical Center, where he died on May 11, 1995. A respiratory therapist at the facility was later convicted in a series of mercy killings, and Lubin's true cause of death will always be uncertain. Arthur Lubin was 96.

Milton Feld continued to oversee the Abbott and Costello films until December 1945, when he resigned ahead of Universal's merger with International Pictures. Feld announced that he would enter independent production, and his first venture was scheduled to be the film version of Mike Todd's 1944 Broadway musical "Bloomer Girl." The project, which Feld tried mount at Universal-International, fell through.

Bud and Lou, meanwhile, signed a new contract with the studio permitting them one outside picture per year. *Boxoffice* reported that the team formed Abbott and Costello Productions with Feld as a partner. Their first venture would be *The Noose Hangs High*, with Charles Barton directing. In August 1947, however, Feld unexpectedly fell into a coma and died three weeks later on September 7. He was 53. He left a wife, Shirley, and a son, James, who was adopted as "Oh, Charlie" finished production. Feld was buried in his native Kansas City. Barton produced and directed *The Noose Hangs High*, with Shirley Feld and Lolly Cristillo, Lou's mother, credited as associate producers.

Producer Burt Kelly left Universal a month before retakes on "Oh, Charlie" and went to Paramount, where he produced *Pacific Blackout* (1941), *Priorities on Parade, Street of Chance,* and *Lady Bodyguard* (all 1942). In mid-1943 he moved to Columbia, where Sam Bichoff, his old partner from Tiffany and KBS, was in charge of production. In 1944 the studio resurrected the *Blondie* series by popular demand. Kelly produced the next nine *Blondie* films. When the series ended in 1950, Kelly resigned but remained active in the producer's guild. He died of heart failure on March 5, 1983 at the Motion Picture Home and Hospital in Woodland Hills, Calif. He was 84 and had resided there for several years after a stroke. His widow, Adrienne Doré, died in 1992.

Richard Carlson's role as the earnest and analytical Dr. Jackson foreshadowed his work in several sci-fi classics of the 1950s. But during the early 1940s, Carlson played first or second male lead opposite several notable leading ladies. After *The Little Foxes* (1941), he was seduced by Hedy Lamarr as Tondelayo in *White Cargo* (1942), and was a young playwright in one of Judy Garland's biggest hits, *Presenting Lily Mars* (1943). (Van Heflin, who was in Carlson's play "Western Waters," played a Broadway producer.) After making *The Man From Down Under* (1943) with Charles Laughton, Carlson enlisted in the Navy and worked on training films at the primary East Coast submarine base in Groton, Conn. In August 1943 his second son, Christopher, was born; he passed away in 2002.

After his discharge, acting jobs were few and far between. He told a columnist that during the lull he took up the art of upholstering "to keep from going nuts." He also became a freelance writer. Carlson's first film after the war, and his last youth role, was in Edward Dmytryk's *So Well Remembered* (1947). He played Martha Scott's son, who is disfigured in World War I. Carlson reportedly was considered for *Mexican Hayride* (1948) with Bud and Lou. In Budd Boetticher's film noir *Behind Locked Doors* (1948), Carlson played a private detective who goes undercover in a lunatic asylum to find a missing judge. He and Boetticher became good friends. Then he joined the Chicago stage production of "Mr. Roberts" in the title role. (Henry Fonda was starring in the Broadway production.) Carlson did the play for 35 weeks.

Back in Hollywood he turned down a leading role in another film to take a smaller part in the epic *King Solomon's Mines* (1950). "I figured it is better to have even a mediocre role in a hit than a good role in a picture that wouldn't make any money," he said. The film, starring Stewart Granger and Deborah Kerr, was shot on location in the Belgian Congo, Kenya, Tanganyika, and Ruanda-Urundi. Carlson later told reporter Bob Thomas, "There are discomforts on any film location. Multiply this by one hundred and you get a picture of what we went through. Naturally there was a lot of grumbling. But also I think we realized we were getting something really great on film. That helped compensate for the discomfort." He added, "I defy anyone to sleep soundly when their camp is surrounded by growling lions."

Carlson wrote about his experiences for *Collier's* magazine and the articles were reprinted in *Reader's Digest*. He was suddenly in demand as Hollywood's resident expert on Africa. With Fred L. Packard, son in law of J. Arthur Rank, Carlson planned a 26-episode TV series about Africa, and Columbia hired him to write a jungle movie. He intended to return with his good friend, William Holden. (A few years later, Holden established a wildlife foundation in Kenya that is still active today.)

Carlson's post-war career had more outlets, including live theater, films, and live television. He appeared in the underrated noir *The Sound of Fury* (1950); the play "Arsenic and Old Lace" at the La Jolla Playhouse; and in a live TV adaptation of Joseph Conrad's "Heart of Darkness," a novel set in Africa. (Francis Ford Coppola refashioned the story for *Apocalypse Now* [1979].)

Carlson relished live television, calling it "summer stock with 20 million people watching." He appeared in thirty live productions in the 1950s, including "Now, Voyager" and "The Philadelphia Story," on shows like *Lux Video Theater, Studio One in Hollywood* and *Schlitz Playhouse*. Beyond working live, Carlson also appreciated television's broader influence. In an interview in the *Los Angeles Times* he remarked: "I think that television is a great new stimulus, and that it is already spurring the picture industry to develop a higher grade product...At the same time my youngsters have taught me that TV is accomplishing something quite remarkable. It is stirring their imagination, especially through the science fiction it presents." That last remark was prophetic.

Meanwhile, he continued in films, usually as the second lead. He was Jane Wyman's love interest in *The Blue Veil*; Fred MacMurray's best friend in the screwball comedy *A Millionaire for Christy* (1951); and a

*With Communist hunter Herbert Philbrick, the inspiration for the TV series* I Led Three Lives.
*Right: On the set of* The Creature from the Black Lagoon *(1954) with Julia Adams and Ben Chapman.*

movie director in *Valentino* (1951). He played the detective hero of *Whispering Smith Investigates* (1952), and was the husband abandoned by Barbara Stanwyck in *All I Desire* (1953). Carlson reunited with director Budd Boetticher for *Seminole* (1953), where he played against type as a severe and racist army major.

Carlson had planned two television ventures, a travel show, "Around the World in a Week," and "Richard's Almanac," a series set in his own home with his family, but neither sold.

In August 1952, Carlson, producer Ivan Tors, and screenwriter Curt Siodmak formed A-Men Productions to make a series of low-budget science-fiction films. Tors hoped that the movies, which followed agents from the fictitious "Office of Scientific Investigation," would lead to a television series. Their first entry, *The Magnetic Monster* (1953), was built around special effects footage from the German film *Gold* (1934). *Variety* wrote, "Carlson's performance is charged with an earnestness and sincerity that the rest of the players fail to match."

At Universal, staff director Jack Arnold (1916-1992) was preparing the studio's first 3-D venture, *It Came From Outer Space* (1953). He cast Carlson in the lead role of an astronomer. Carlson's conviction in the

genre was a key asset. *Variety* gave the film a mixed review, but called Carlson "excellent."

His next assignment was *The Maze* (1953), a 3-D horror film directed by William Cameron Menzies. Carlson played an American who returns to his ancestral Scottish home to confront a bizarre family secret. Among the cast: Hillary Brooke, who had worked for Menzies in *Invaders from Mars* (1953).

Carlson then signed to star in the television series *I Led Three Lives,* based on a memoir by Herbert Philbrick, an advertising executive who infiltrated the Communist Party for the FBI. Like *Dragnet*, the stories were taken from real cases and featured Jack Webb-style voice-overs by Carlson. The half hour show was produced and syndicated by Ziv Television, which had twenty-five series on the air in the 1950s, including *The Cisco Kid, Highway Patrol* and *Sea Hunt.* Carlson's deal included ten percent of the gross and the chance to write and direct some episodes. "When [*I Led Three Lives*] came along," Carlson told the *New York Times*, "it had all the elements I was looking for—truth, timeliness, even a chance to be of public service. The only trouble was, I didn't want to tie myself down to one job—I've got these other things I like to do, too." Carlson was permitted to appear in films and on live televi-

*Carlson reprises Costello's necktie gag with an alcoholic drink in a 1963 episode of* Burke's Law. *The cast and crew burst into applause after this scene. Coincidentally, the show's star, Gene Barry, was represented by Bud and Lou's agent, Eddie Sherman.* Daily Variety *reported that Bud was sought for the 1964 episode "Who Killed Vaudeville?" but did not appear.*

sion between seasons.

When *I Led Three Lives* debuted in the fall of 1953, it was carried on 94 stations (*I Love Lucy* was on 79). Carlson was making *Creature from the Black Lagoon* (1954) at the time. His co-stars were Julia Adams, Richard Denning (Evelyn Ankers' husband), and Nestor Paiva, who played the faux ghost in *Hold That Ghost*. The lead actors never left Universal City; the underwater footage was shot in Florida using stunt doubles including Ricou Browning, who did the Creature's swimming scenes. Ben Chapman played the Creature on dry land in Hollywood, and "met" Abbott and Costello in a *Colgate Comedy Hour* sketch two weeks before the film was released. Universal made two *Creature* sequels, but Carlson was not in either.

His next film, *Riders to the Stars,* was made with his partners, Tors and Siodmak. Carlson waived his acting fee to direct and receive a percentage of the profits. The movie, about a mission to capture a meteor, is told with a documentary-like realism but falls short of other space travel films of the era.

Meanwhile, *I Led Three Lives* had expanded to 157 stations by May 1954. It was nominated for Emmy awards in 1954 and 1955, and both years won *Billboard*'s poll for Best Non-Network Series and Best Non-Network Adventure Series. Additionally, Carlson won Best Actor in a Non-Network Adventure Series in 1954 and 1955. Plans were announced for an *I Led Three Lives* theatrical film. In an article for the *New York Herald Tribune* in 1955, Carlson wrote, "…[T]he most important thing this role has given me was a new-found awareness of the grave events happening all around me. Subversion was a real and frightening thing, something I had shrugged away, perhaps like the average citizen. I also felt that my role in the series was a real contributing factor to waking people up as

to the dangers around them. This, believe me, is not just in the sense of flag-waving patriotism. It's being aware of yourself as a citizen and your responsibilities to your community."

Between seasons of his TV series Carlson directed the Rory Calhoun western *Four Guns to the Border* (1954) at Universal. He later directed Calhoun in *The Saga of Hemp Brown* (1957).

In 1955, Mona Carlson appeared in an episode of *I Love Lucy* set at a celebrity fashion show with Sheila MacRae and the wives of William Holden, Dean Martin, and Van Heflin.

Director Frank Capra enlisted Carlson in 1957 for a series of television science specials for Bell Labs. Using on camera talent, animation, and marionettes, the programs explained scientific concepts from solar energy to the body's circulatory system. Carlson was in *Strange Case of the Cosmic Rays* and *Hemo the Magnificent* (both 1957). He appeared in and directed *The Unchained Goddess* (1958), an episode about weather that anticipated climate change caused by human activities. After the installment drew disappointing ratings and poor reviews, Capra and Carlson left the series. It was taken over by Warner Bros. and then Walt Disney, until 1964.

While Carlson was working on the Bell specials, CBS prepared *Perry Mason* for television. Carlson, Fred MacMurray, Efrem Zimbalist Jr., and William Hopper were each considered for the title role before Raymond Burr. (Hopper was cast as Paul Drake.)

The following year Carlson starred in another Ziv television series, *Mackenzie's Raiders*. The show was based on the 1955 book *The Mackenzie Raid* by Colonel Russell "Red" Reeder. Colonel Ranald Mackenzie had secret orders from President Grant to defend the border between Texas and Mexico. Cavalry raids into

Mexico risked international incident, but Mackenzie pursued bandits, gun runners, and renegade Apache knowing that if he were caught he would be disavowed by his own government. Carlson wrote and directed a few of the 39 episodes. He also enjoyed the same deal he had with *I Led Three Lives:* profit participation and few restrictions on outside assignments.

In a 1959 *New York Times* profile with the headline, "Carlson, Actor, is Thinking Man," he said, "Examine the men who have been successful in television. They're almost always people whose careers have gone down or, like myself, whose careers are not likely to get any bigger. I was the guy who did not get the girl. I was not going any higher." His deals with Ziv were lucrative, and by 1959 *I Led Three Lives* had reportedly grossed $8 million. "I have little patience with people who think that the money in television is tainted," he said. "I love money. The more of it, the better. I want prosperity for my family, and television gives it to me."

After starring in Bert I. Gordon's film *Tormented* (1960), where he was taunted by a vengeful ghost, Carlson used his triple-threat talents acting, writing and directing in series television. He appeared on *Voyage to the Bottom of the Sea, Wagon Train, Perry Mason,* and *It Takes a Thief,* among others. In a particularly memorable inside joke in an episode of *Burke's Law,* "Who Killed Sweet Betsy?," Carlson duplicated Costello's necktie gag from *Hold That Ghost,* but with an alcoholic drink. Carlson penned scripts for shows including *O'Hara, U.S. Treasury; Owen Marshall, Counselor at Law;* and *Mannix.* He drew on his experiences in Africa to write a few episodes of *Daktari,* which was produced by his former partner, Ivan Tors. Carlson directed episodes of *The Detectives, The Loretta Young Show, Men Into Space,* and *Thriller.*

His last film roles were in George Pal's murder mystery *The Power* (1968); *Valley of the Gwangi* (1969, featuring the stop motion effects of Ray Harryhausen); and Elvis Presley's *Change of Habit* (1969), in which Carlson was cast as a Catholic bishop. In the 1970s he turned up in episodes of *Cannon, Owen Marshall,* and *Mobile One.* Carlson also did commercial voice overs for Pillsbury, GTE, Goodyear, and Max Factor.

Carlson retired in the San Fernando Valley. He succumbed to a cerebral hemorrhage on November 24, 1977 at age 65. His wife, Mona, died in 1990. Two sons survived them. "Mom and Dad were great parents," their son, Richard, said. "He never brought his work home with him. I can't recall which movie set I was on, but I remember one of the crew came up to me out of the blue and said, 'You know, your dad is one of the best-liked people in the business.'

Evelyn Ankers had a few months off after shooting re-takes for *Hold That Ghost.* By now she was romantically involved with actor Glenn Ford, and the gossip columns reported that they planned to wed late in 1941 or early in 1942.

Beginning in September, Evelyn made four films in quick succession. The first was *North to the Klondike* with Lon Chaney Jr. and Broderick Crawford. Chaney and Ankers got off to a bad start, however. Universal gave the dressing room bungalow Chaney shared with Crawford to Ankers and Anne Gwynne because the two men habitually drank, brawled, and trashed the place. Chaney held a grudge against Ankers.

Her next two films, also with Chaney, were more memorable: *The Wolf Man* and *The Ghost of Frankenstein.* Screenwriter Curt Siodmak created *The Wolf Man* and established the werewolf lore. (Universal's other monsters were based on books and plays.) Chaney was the only actor to play the role in four other films, including *Abbott and Costello Meet Frankenstein* (1948). During production, Chaney, in full Wolf Man make-up, relished sneaking up behind Ankers, tapping her on the shoulder and, when she turned around, snarling and grabbing her. "He had to hold me," Evelyn recalled, "or I would have ended up in the rafters!" In another incident, she *did* end up in the rafters. A bear got loose during the film's carnival sequence and chased Ankers up a ladder, where a studio electrician helped her escape onto a platform. Another time, Evelyn was overcome by the fumes of fog machines and passed out on the soundstage forest floor.

Three weeks after wrapping *The Wolf Man,* production began on *The Ghost of Frankenstein.* Co-star Ralph Bellamy, in James Bawden's book, *Conversations with Classic Film Stars,* grumbled: "Ugh. It sort of picked up the story from *Son of Frankenstein* (1939). Chaney was the monster this time and he really resented that. Cedric Hardwicke was Ludwig Frankenstein, Lionel Atwill was the doctor, Bela Lugosi was Ygor, and Evelyn Ankers, a wonderfully sensitive British lady, was Elsa Frankenstein. The damned dumb director was Erle C. Kenton, complete with whip and an air of pomposity. On one scene he was giving Evelyn directions: 'Elsa, your father was killed by the monster, your husband dragged off by Ygor. Now what

*Evelyn with Lon Chaney Jr. in* North to the Klondike *(1941), the first of their six films together. Their second was* The Wolf Man *(1941). Their professional relationship was not as harmonious as these photos would indicate.*

I want from you is one clear emotion—that you're fed up with it all.' At which moment Sir Cedric lay on the floor howling with laughter and he couldn't stop for some time. And forever afterwards at Hollywood parties I'd see him and he'd shout, "Fed up with it all?" (Kenton's next assignments were two of Abbott and Costello's better comedies, *Pardon My Sarong* and *Who Done It?*, both 1942.)

Ankers' relationship with Glenn Ford cooled, and her press agent arranged for her to meet another client, Paramount contract player Richard Denning. The publicist brought Evelyn and her mother to the final rounds of Denning's bowling league tournament. Denning ignored her and continued to bowl, leaving Ankers to wonder why she agreed to go. When he finally finished, Denning asked Evelyn if she'd like to bowl. Although she never had, she said yes. She kicked off her high heels and tossed a strike while her tight black silk dress ripped up the side. The couple hit it off immediately. In *Glenn Ford: A Life*, Ford's son, Peter, wrote: "Evelyn was ready to settle down, but Dad was not. On one occasion when my father was out of town on location, Evelyn met and began dating actor Richard Denning…One night Denning insisted on putting Evelyn in his car and driving over to Dad's house. He instructed Evelyn to go inside and talk to my father about his intentions. Denning gave her fifteen minutes, and if she didn't come out within the appointed time, he said he would drive away and accept the fact that she loved Dad best. Evelyn went into the house, she

and Dad talked, and she came out in a timely fashion and drove away with her future husband."

Evelyn and her vocal cords were spared horror films for the rest of 1942, but she was required to pose for cheesecake photos. Her next film assignment was Walter Wanger's World War II drama, *Eagle Squadron*, which reunited her with director Arthur Lubin. After that she was loaned to MGM for the inane *Pierre of the Plains*, featuring John Carroll as a singing French-Canadian trapper.

Back at Universal, Evelyn was cast opposite Ralph Bellamy in the espionage thriller *The Great Impersonation*, the third screen version of E. Phillips Oppenheim's most famous novel. (Oppenheim, a British writer, invented the contemporary spy novel.) Ankers recalled the film for Doug McClelland in *Film Fan Monthly*: "I was called on to the set and Mr. Bellamy was already there. He was one of my idols but I'd never met him. [Note: they were both in *The Wolf Man* and *The Ghost of Frankenstein*.] The director, John Rawlins, who I had also never met, said, 'Hi, are you ready to shoot?' I replied, 'You must be Mr. Rawlins.' I was anxious to rehearse, as I had to lean over and kiss Bellamy in a vampy, Mata Hari style. Suddenly I heard, 'Okay, action!' There was deathly silence as Ralph and I sat looking at each other with our mouths open…we hadn't even been informed where the director wanted to start and finish the scene. Mr. Rawlins finally yelled 'Cut!' and asked us what the problem was. I managed to stutter, 'First, I would like to meet my leading man,

Left: Evelyn shows her horror resumé to Mad Ghoul (1943) co-star David Bruce. Right: On the set of the Sherlock Holmes entry The Pearl of Death (1944) with Nigel Bruce and her husband Richard Denning, serving stateside in the Navy.

as I have never kissed a man without being introduced to him. Second, it would help us both if we knew where you wanted to start and end the scene…'"

Rawlins cast Ankers in his next film, *Sherlock Holmes and the Voice of Terror* (1942). It was the first film with Holmes and Watson in the present day. When the picture was released in September 1942, Ankers and Denning eloped to Las Vegas. He was in the middle of making *Quiet, Please, Murder* (1942). A few weeks later, Denning enlisted in the Navy, eventually serving as a yeoman on submarines. Evelyn now worked to support her mother and a husband. "Her mother didn't want her to get married," Denning confided to Tom Weaver, "because, to put it bluntly, she thought this might be the end of her meal ticket." (Evelyn's mother died in 1954 after a long illness.)

At the end of the year Evelyn made two horror films back to back: *Captive Wild Woman* and *Son of Dracula*. In *Captive Wild Woman*, an endocrinologist (John Carradine) creates an ape woman (Acquanetta) who falls in love with Ankers' fiancé, a circus trainer (Milburn Stone). *Son of Dracula*, with Lon Chaney Jr. in the title role, was the first Universal Dracula film set in the United States and the first where a vampire is actually seen transforming into a bat. Ankers, second

billed behind Louise Allbritton and playing her sister, doesn't even meet the count. Perhaps Chaney and Ankers were kept apart for a reason. At a studio function, Ankers, Denning, and Chaney were seated together when Chaney made a crack about Denning wearing a Navy dress uniform while serving stateside. As the insults mounted, Chaney tossed food on Denning's uniform and Denning shoved ice cream in Chaney's face. They nearly came to blows—halted by, of all things, a genuine scream from Evelyn.

Ankers included her next film, *All By Myself*, among her favorites, and named Felix Feist her favorite director. In this romantic comedy, she is jilted by Neil Hamilton (later Commissioner Gordon on *Batman*) and gets Patric Knowles to pose as her fiancé to make him jealous. Of course, Ankers and Knowles eventually fall in love.

Evelyn was then cast in supporting roles in two high-profile Deanna Durbin musicals. In *Hers to Hold*, the third film in the "Three Smart Girls" trilogy, Ankers and debutant Durbin were coworkers at an aircraft plant. In *His Butler's Sister*, Evelyn played a Manhattan socialite who loses Broadway composer Franchot Tone to Deanna.

In between these roles, Ankers dashed off *The Mad*

*Ghoul.* She played a singer whose fiancé (David Bruce) is turned into an obedient zombie by his chemistry professor (George Zucco), who lusts after her. The studio promised Evelyn the chance to sing but she wound up lip-synching to a Lillian Cornell recording. Still, she called working on the film "a pleasure," and named her co-stars "gentlemen, quite a unique characteristic in Hollywood in those days." Evelyn reportedly had her tonsils removed after this film; two years of screaming at Universal had irritated them.

David Bruce also played Evelyn's jilted fiancé in her next film, the musical *You're a Lucky Fellow Mr. Smith.* (The song and title came from *Buck Privates.*) To fulfill the conditions of a large inheritance, Ankers hastily marries a soldier (Allan Jones) but eventually realizes that she really loves him.

Evelyn was selected "Queen of National Swim-for-Health Week" in 1943, which required her to pose poolside in a bathing suit for a phalanx of photographers. That fall, MGM wanted to borrow her for the role of the frowzy maid in *Gaslight* with Ingrid Bergman and Charles Boyer. Universal refused, and put Evelyn in Walter Wanger's *Ladies Courageous,* a film about female pilots who ferry Army transport planes. Angela Lansbury played the maid in *Gaslight* and was nominated for an Oscar.

Another pair of horror jobs inevitably followed: *Weird Woman* and *The Invisible Man's Revenge.* Arguably the best of the studio's six Inner Sanctum mysteries, *Weird Woman* was adapted from Fritz Leiber Jr.'s novel, "Conjure Wife," which was later remade as *Burn Witch Burn* (1962). Lon Chaney Jr. plays a college professor who marries a voodoo priestess (Ann Gwynne) and has to contend with a jealous ex-girlfriend (Ankers) determined to destroy the marriage. In *It Came from Horrorwood,* Anne Gwynne told Tom Weaver, "Evelyn and I were such very good friends. She was the matron of honor at my wedding [in 1945] and I stood up for her when she got her citizenship papers [in 1946]. There was a scene in *Weird Woman* where she was flaring her nostrils at me. It all seemed so funny, because in real life we were so close. We broke down and laughed away. It took quite a while before we could compose ourselves."

In *The Invisible Man's Revenge,* scientist John Carradine successfully tests a formula for invisibility on escaped fugitive Jon Hall, who then terrorizes Ankers' parents (Gale Sondergaard and Lester Matthews), whom he believes cheated him out of a fortune years earlier. This was followed by what Evelyn later called

*Evelyn is suspected of bumping off rival strippers in* Queen of Burlesque *(1946).*

her favorite role as the jealous fiancée of playwright Patric Knowles in *Pardon My Rhythm,* a lightweight musical directed by Felix Feist and featuring Gloria Jean and Mel Torme.

Her next film, *Jungle Woman,* a sequel to *Captive Wild Woman,* is arguably Universal's all-time worst horror movie, but it permitted Evelyn to play against type as the villain. Her following assignment, in *Pearl of Death,* considered among the best in the Sherlock Holmes series, continued the trend, with Evelyn as a mistress of disguise.

Evelyn was pregnant when she played a Gay Nineties burlesque queen in *Bowery to Broadway* (produced by John Grant during Costello's illness). *Variety* also reported that Ankers, Turhan Bey, Jon Hall, and Frances Langford made a special short film specifically for television, but Universal later denied it.

In June 1944, Hedda Hopper wrote that Ankers and Grace MacDonald (who had been in *It Ain't Hay* with Abbott and Costello) were both fed up with their roles at Universal and would part ways with the studio. After one final Inner Sanctum with Chaney, *The Frozen Ghost,* Evelyn quit to await the birth of her daughter, Diana, in October. Ankers had appeared in Universal's Frankenstein, Dracula, Wolf Man and Invisible Man

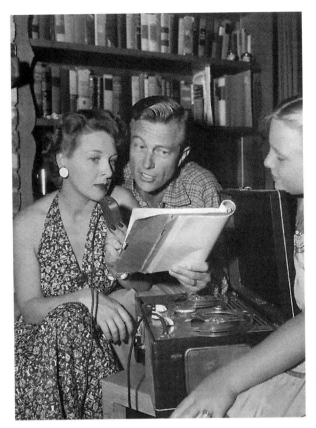

*Recording a rehearsal with husband Richard Denning while daughter Diana looks on.*

old house we'd bought, repaired and resold. But, as the months went by, our cash reserve went down the drain…" The couple bought a trailer and lived at the beach in the summer and in Palm Springs in winter. Between jobs Denning worked as a lobster fisherman. "Yet we were never happier," he reflected.

Evelyn appeared in a poor atomic spy drama, *Flight to Nowhere,* with Alan Curtis, and *Spoilers of the North,* a crime drama centered on Alaskan salmon fishing. She had little to do in *Last of the Redmen,* an adaptation of James Fenimore Cooper's "The Last of the Mohicans," but was strong as musical comedy star and murderess in *The Lone Wolf in London.*

In 1948 Denning was cast as Lucille Ball's banker husband in the radio series "My Favorite Husband." (He replaced Lee Bowman, who did the pilot but couldn't commit to the series.) The program ran for three years until March 1951. Meanwhile, Evelyn continued in low-budget films. She played an aviatrix in *Tarzan's Magic Fountain,* and was a gang member in the melodrama *Parole* (both 1949). At this time she also did her first television projects. She appeared in "Adventure of the Speckled Band," with Alan Napier as Sherlock Holmes, and in the first episode of *Public Prosecutor* with her pal, Anne Gwynne. (The latter TV series sat on shelf for three years.)

Evelyn's final feature was *The Texan Meets Calamity Jane* (1950). *Variety* thought she came off okay as Calamity, but called the picture "generally bad in all respects, even for a low-budgeter." That year Denning and Ankers filmed a TV pilot, "Ding Howe and the Flying Tigers." Denning played Chinese born Ding Howe, a former Flying Tigers pilot who returns to China to help General Ching defend his people from the terror raids of the Flame Dragons, renegade pilots led by the evil bandit Hu Fang (Richard Loo). Evelyn played a reporter who covered the squadron's exploits. No sponsor or network picked up the show.

Meanwhile, CBS wanted Lucille Ball and Denning to do a television version of "My Favorite Husband." Ball famously refused to do the show without real-life husband Desi Arnaz. The network reluctantly agreed, and the concept was reworked as *I Love Lucy.* CBS then cast Denning and Barbara Britton as married amateur sleuths in the TV series *Mr. and Mrs. North.* Evelyn made a guest appearance in the first season episode "The Nobles." *Mr. and Mrs. North* lasted two seasons and influenced such later series as *McMillan & Wife* and *Hart to Hart.*

In 1953 Ankers appeared with Cecil Kellaway in

franchises and was named "Queen of the Horrors."

If Evelyn bemoaned her Universal years, she may have grudgingly come to appreciate them after working as a freelancer at Republic, PRC, and Columbia. Later that year, after Denning's discharge from the Navy, the couple made their only film together, *Black Beauty.* Critics thought this third version of Anne Sewell's juvenile classic was fine for kids but torture for the adults who accompanied them.

In 1946 Ankers got a taste of Abbott and Costello's world when she starred in *Queen of Burlesque* as a suspect in a series of backstage murders. Real-life burlesque queen Rose La Rose was Evelyn's technical advisor and appears in the film. Bud and Lou's crony Murray Leonard played the show's top banana. Appropriately enough, the previous year Ankers and four other actresses, including Nina Foch and Ann Miller, played a game of strip poker in Beverly Hills to publicize a clothing drive for the liberated countries in Europe.

Although Ankers and Denning were both working, it was sporadic and for small salaries. "Money was very hard to get," Denning recalled for *Radio-TV Mirror* in 1954. "We had *some* savings and a small profit on an

"Sam and the Whale" on TV's *Cavalcade of America*, and with Preston Foster in a *GE Theater* murder mystery, "The Hunted." In 1955 she was on *Screen Director's Playhouse* in "The Silent Partner," a comedy about a once great but forgotten film comedian, played by once great but forgotten film comedian Buster Keaton.

After *Mr. and Mrs. North* ran its course, Denning worked in several sci-fi films including *Unknown Island, The Creature from the Black Lagoon, Target Earth!, Creature with the Atom Brain,* Roger Corman's *The Day the World Ended* and *The Black Scorpion.* He also played the rejected suitors of Maureen O'Hara in *The Magnificent Matador* (1955), Deborah Kerr in *An Affair To Remember* (1957), and Lana Turner in *The Lady Takes A Flyer* (1958).

In 1956 Evelyn returned to London for the first time since 1939 to join Denning, who was filming *Million Dollar Manhunt* and promoting *The Day the World Ended.* Denning did two more short-lived TV series, *The Flying Doctor* (1959-1960), which was filmed in England and Australia, and *Michael Shayne* (1960-1961), an hour-long private-eye drama set in Miami.

Evelyn's last TV appearance was in a 1958 episode of *Cheyenne*, starring Clint Walker. Her final film was a short she made with Denning for the Lutheran Church called *No Greater Love* (1960).

Denning told Greg Mank, "Evie never really liked acting. Period. She didn't like the work; she didn't like to have to get up at five in the morning and all that. So it was a real strain on her. Evie was a wonderful, wonderful gal, but she had a very strong personality, and a very definite temperament—she could only take so much." Even so, Ankers never betrayed her feelings in her work. Her performances are always sincere and believable even in the most far-fetched and thankless situations.

Denning signed for the sitcom *Karen,* one of a trio of unrelated comedy series set in the same apartment building, "90 Bristol Court." "It was something that I always wanted to do, a comedy," he said. Only *Karen,* with teen Debbie Watson in the title role and Denning as her father, lasted the 1964-65 season. (*Karen* was produced by Joe Connelly and Bob Mosher, who produced *The Munsters.* Watson played Marilyn in the 1966 theatrical film *Munster Go Home.*)

In 1968 the Dennings retired to Hawaii, which he described as "about as close to paradise as we could find on earth." One day he read in a newspaper column that the producers of *Hawaii Five-O* were looking for

him to play the governor on the series. "I said I would consider it if I didn't have to go back to the mainland or sign a contract in case I didn't want to do a show," Denning told *The Honolulu Star-Bulletin* in 1996. "I wasn't interested in working anymore, but they agreed to everything." He was in seventy-three episodes.

After a long illness, Evelyn died of cancer on August 29, 1985, in her home in Haiku on Maui. She was 67. "We felt closer, I think, in those last few months than we did even on our honeymoon," Denning told Greg Mank. Horror film historian Carlos Clarens wrote that Evelyn "succeeded Fay Wray as the most persecuted heroine in films." She was the archetypal horror victim: an intelligent, often reserved woman who was reduced to primal screaming by something menacing and usually male. Jamie Lee Curtis was later called "The Boomer Evelyn Ankers." More recently, Brazil's R. F. Lucchetti, who has published over 1,500 pulp novels using pseudonyms like Vincent Lugosi, Brian Stockler and Isadora Highsmith, singled out Evelyn's films as especially inspiring.

After a long battle with emphysema, Richard Denning died of cardiac arrest in Escondido, Calif., on October 11, 1998. He was 85. Survivors included his daughter with Evelyn Ankers, Diana Dwyer, two granddaughters, and his second wife, Patricia Leffingwell.

Just before Universal released *Hold That Ghost,* Paramount issued *Shepherd of the Hills,* a film Marc Lawrence had made nearly a year earlier. Lawrence was given a rare chance to show his range as a gentle, mute hillbilly. "[Director] Henry Hathaway was an asshole," Lawrence told Anthony Slide. "He didn't want me in *Shepherd of the Hills.* He said, 'How can a Jew play a hillbilly?' Then he said, 'I'm one-fourth Jewish; it's nothing against Jews.'"

While the film received lukewarm reviews, Lawrence was singled out by *Variety*: "Marc Lawrence, as the mute simpleton, gives one of the most outstanding support performances seen for months. It's a radical departure for Lawrence, who has previously been typed by producers in gangster pictures." Lawrence named it his favorite film. "It's my favorite because I didn't say a word," he said. Lawrence played John Wayne's brother. "I liked him," Lawrence told *Film Comment.* "He was a very straightforward guy. He was a little insecure at that time about his acting. He worked with coaches. He asked me to work with him

*With the boys again in* Hit the Ice *(1943), and strangled again, this time by Gary Cooper, in* Cloak and Dagger *(1946).*

on acting…A guy called Paul Fix took that job."

A few weeks after shooting retakes on "Oh, Charlie," Lawrence worked for Hathaway again, this time as an Arab in *Sundown,* starring Gene Tierney. Lawrence was soon back in familiar roles, however. He appeared in *This Gun For Hire* (1942), one of the first important film noirs and a star-making turn for both Alan Ladd and Veronica Lake. At Republic he was reunited with Joan Davis in *Yokel Boy* (1942). Lawrence was cast as a member of Bugsy Mallone's mob and Joan played Bugsy's sister. (Davis was a last minute replacement for Betty Keane, who replaced Judy Canova, who originated the role on Broadway.)

Lawrence's next part, while not a gangster, was still unsympathetic: one of the leaders of the lynch mob in *The Ox-Bow Incident* (1943). It took director William Wellman, screenwriter Lamar Trotti, and star Henry Fonda two years to bring the dark, disturbing novel, which was seen as a parable to the events in Europe, to the screen.

Soon after, Lawrence was working with Abbott and Costello again in *Hit The Ice* (1943), playing one of Sheldon Leonard's henchmen. "I did three pictures with [Abbott and Costello]," he told *Film Comment.* "Costello was a clever little guy, but pushy. He was the star and wanted everybody to know it. Bud Abbott was a very sweet guy, very lonely. Didn't have all those Italian hangers-on like Costello. Bud invited me to his house. I didn't know him really. I thought there would be other people, but it was just my wife and myself and Abbott and his wife. Nice guy. A lonely man."

Following *Hit The Ice,* Lawrence married screenwriter Fanya Foss, whom he met at a screening of *Citizen Kane.*

In 1946 Lawrence played an Italian Gestapo agent in Fritz Lang's espionage thriller *Cloak and Dagger.* He and star Gary Cooper engaged in a grisly on screen fight. Lawrence told *Film Comment,* "Lang had it worked out for these intense close-ups—the hands, the face, fingers in the eyes, the nose—as these two guys tried to kill each other…And Fritz Lang would go, 'Harder! With the fingers, harder!' Six fucking days of this…Fritz Lang loved this kind of scene—technical, visual. He wasn't interested in the people."

In *Key Largo* (1948) Lawrence was Edward G. Robinson's fellow mobster, Ziggy, who shows up to buy a shipment of counterfeit money. His character's name was later referenced in *The Honeymooners* episode "Funny Money," which also featured counterfeit cash.

Lawrence played Cobby, the bookmaker turned stool pigeon, in John Huston's crime drama, *The Asphalt Jungle* (1950). That year he also had a cameo in *Abbott and Costello in the Foreign Legion* (1950) as a mobster who loans the boys $5,000 to import an Arab wrestler to the U.S.

Lawrence was working in Bob Hope's *My Favorite Spy* when two men from Washington showed up to ask about his alleged communist connections. Actor Ward Bond may have informed on him. "I got a subpoena," Lawrence recalled in 1994. "That was tantamount to a guilty verdict." He was called to testify before the House Un-American Activities Committee (HUAC) in Washington, D.C.

HUAC was established in 1938 by Congressmen Martin Dies, Jr. (D-Texas) and Samuel Dickstein (D-New York) to investigate both left wing and right wing political groups. It never probed the Ku Klux Klan, however, because Dies and other Southern committee members were Klan sympathizers. Instead, HUAC concentrated on the American Communist Party and its influence on labor unions and the Federal Theater Project. Membership in the Communist Party was never illegal, but the party and its allies had played an important role in the labor movement since 1919, and industrialists routinely blamed labor strikes on communist instigation, not on low wages or working conditions.

HUAC scrutinized Hollywood as early as 1938 after several stars including Clark Gable, James Cagney, and ten-year-old Shirley Temple sent ingenuous anniversary congratulations to a Communist-owned French newspaper, *Ce Soir*. Secretary of the Interior Harold Ickes jeered the HUAC probe: "They have found dangerous radicals [in Hollywood] led by little Shirley Temple." Dies nonetheless proclaimed that communism was pervasive in Hollywood and kept prying.

Dies should have looked closer to home. Based on research in the KGB archives, it was revealed in 1999 that HUAC co-founder Samuel Dickstein maintained a covert relationship with the NKVD, the predecessor of the KGB, from 1937 to 1940. He not only supplied illegal visas for Soviet operatives but offered to spy for the NKVD in return for cash.

In 1940 a former communist party member in Los Angeles met privately with Dies and identified forty-two people in the industry as communists. Many names were leaked to the press, including those of Humphrey Bogart, Katharine Hepburn, Melvyn Douglas, and Fredric March. Although they were ultimately cleared, Dies reasserted his belief that "numerous actors and screen people" were communists or sympathizers.

The rise of labor unions and organized strikes in Hollywood prompted more probes for communists and "subversives" in the guilds. When Disney cartoonists, the lowest paid animators in town, went on strike in 1941, Walt Disney ran an ad in *Variety* blaming communist agitators. HUAC, Los Angeles County, the California General Assembly, and other political groups investigated several Hollywood labor unions but turned up nothing. A banner headline in *Variety* proclaimed, "Can't Make Red Slur Stick." The hunt for communists temporarily cooled during World War II when the United States and the Soviet Union were allied against the Axis.

In October 1943, UCLA co-sponsored a three-day Writer's Congress that brought 1,300 people in the entertainment industry together to discuss "the social obligations of the mass media during and after wartime." It concluded with the adoption of several resolutions and called on President Roosevelt to create a cabinet-level department of arts and letters. A few months later, a group including Walt Disney, Gary Cooper, and director Sam Wood organized the Motion Picture Alliance for the Preservation of American Ideals (MPA) in response to the Writer's Congress, which the MPA saw as communist-inspired.

Within weeks, HUAC began investigating studio employees. Hollywood's seventeen unions denounced the MPA as anti-labor, racist and reactionary, and in response created the Council of Hollywood Guilds and Unions. In 1945 the MPA issued a pamphlet advising movie producers: "Don't smear the free-enterprise system…Don't smear industrialists…Don't smear wealth…Don't smear the profit motive…Don't deify the 'common man.'"

Anti-communist sentiment escalated after the war, fueled by Soviet repression in Eastern and Central Europe and a conservative, Republican-dominated Congress. Martin Dies was no longer a part of HUAC, but his colleague, John E. Rankin (D-Mississippi), declared that "one of the most dangerous plots ever instigated for the overthrow of this Government has its headquarters in Hollywood…the greatest hotbed of subversive activities in the United States."

In July 1946 the publisher of *The Hollywood Reporter*, William R. Wilkerson, obliged Rankin with a column entitled "A Vote For Joe Stalin." Among others, he named Dalton Trumbo, Maurice Rapf (Fred Rinaldo's roommate at Dartmouth), Howard Koch, and Ring Lardner Jr., as Communist sympathizers. Subsequent columns named more people and charged that some moviemakers were producing films with pro-communist propaganda. (In 2012, Wilkerson's son explained that his father was motivated by revenge for his own thwarted ambition to own a studio.)

Wilkerson's columns stirred HUAC to subpoena forty-three Hollywood figures for hearings in October 1947. They were nearly equally divided between "friendly witnesses" and those known or alleged to have been members of the American Communist Party. The friendly witnesses included Jack Warner, Louis B. Mayer, Gary Cooper, Robert Taylor, Walt Disney, and Ginger Rogers' mother, Lela, who was a newspaper reporter, scriptwriter, and movie producer and a supposed expert on detecting Communist themes in films.

The unfriendly witnesses, later known as the

*Marc Lawrence testifies before HUAC on April 24, 1951.*

*Radio and Television,* naming 151 actors, writers, musicians, broadcast journalists, and others in the entertainment industry. (Some of them were already blacklisted.) CBS, the Screen Actors Guild, and the Directors Guild demanded loyalty oaths.

In 1951 HUAC launched a second round of hearings targeting Hollywood. Over one hundred men and women were subpoenaed; fifty-eight were cooperative witnesses. *Variety* reported, "There is some belief that if a man purges himself and answers frankly, he will probably escape suspension and discharge from his studio." These witnesses acknowledged their idealistic Communist pasts and informed on an additional two hundred people. In *The Inquisition in Hollywood,* authors Larry Ceplair and Steven Englund wrote, "In short, it finally came down, not mainly to disillusionment, nor to prison even—neither of which necessitated informing—but to the blacklist...four dozen witnesses so feared losing their careers and their income that they cooperated."

The other fifty-two witnesses who refused to answer changed tactics and invoked the Fifth Amendment's protection against self-incrimination. That way, a witness could avoid naming names without being indicted for contempt of Congress, but was still certain to be fired and blacklisted. In either case, dozens of careers were ruined and a number of artists were compelled to relocate to Mexico or Europe.

Screenwriter Robert Lees testified on April 11. Marc Lawrence testified on April 24. Lawrence tried to make light of it and told the committee that he joined because fellow actor Lionel Stander told him it was a good place to "get to know dames." In 1999, Lawrence told Anthony Slide, "That was my way of trying to escape. I didn't know if I was going to talk or not up to the very minute. But the pressure is so strong, absolutely overpowering."

The Committee was unrelenting. "I kept drinking to give me courage," he told Slide, "but it never gave me courage. It deadened all my senses...I would have said, 'Fuck you. I played the gangsters, [but] you're the gangsters now. Get off my back. If you want to burn me, put a fire under me and burn me.' I should have said that and walked out."

Lawrence told the committee that he quit the party in 1939 after attending twelve meetings. "I just wanted to investigate and find out, not participate," he testified. "I'm a curious kind of a schmoe, the kind of guy who likes to listen to speeches and hear ideas defended. I didn't defend the ideas. I just listened and found it a

Hollywood Ten, had each joined the Communist Party during the Depression, when capitalism failed spectacularly. Some were no longer party members, but all refused to answer questions about their membership and cited the guarantees of the First Amendment. They, and most legal experts, were confident that the Supreme Court would vindicate them. However, they were all cited for contempt of Congress. The next day, the president of the Motion Picture Association of America, Eric Johnston, established the Hollywood blacklist, proclaiming that the Ten would be fired and not re-employed until they were cleared of contempt charges and swore that they were not Communists. Any hope that the Supreme Court would side with the Hollywood Ten vanished in the summer of 1949 when two liberal justices died and their conservative successors refused to review the convictions. The Ten began serving one-year prison sentences in 1950. Even so, the 1947 HUAC hearings failed to find any evidence that moviemakers were secretly disseminating Communist propaganda.

Two years later the Soviet Union exploded its first atomic bomb and Communist forces took control of China. The two largest nations were now Communist and the Russians had the bomb. American politicians and organizations continued to rant about spies and the dangers of communism and communist sympathizers. American Business Consultants, Inc., an organization led by three former FBI agents, published *Red Channels: The Report of Communist Influence in*

very destructive thing and refused to participate."

Following a nervous breakdown, Lawrence reluctantly gave up a few names, including Sterling Hayden, Anne Revere, Larry Parks, Jeff Corey, and Lionel Stander. Stander sued him for slander two days later and asked $500,000 in damages, but never pursued the suit. "He wanted to protect himself," Lawrence explained. "I like Lionel, despite all this."

When actor Jeff Corey was called before HUAC, he was asked if he knew Lawrence. Corey said, "I know him as an actor who played an informer, with great verisimilitude, in a picture called *Asphalt Jungle*." Thereafter, Corey pleaded the Fifth throughout his questioning. He was blacklisted despite his World War II service record. He recalled in "SAG Remembers The Blacklist" in *National Screen Actor* (1998), "I was in the Navy and received a citation, signed by Navy Secretary Forrestal, for outstanding achievement in combat photography for putting myself at risk while shooting a photo sequence of a kamikaze attack on the *U.S.S. Yorktown*." At the urging of friends, Corey soon became one of Hollywood's most respected acting coaches. His students included Carol Burnett, James Dean, Jack Nicholson, Robert Blake, Anthony Perkins, Jane Fonda, Leonard Nimoy, and Sheree North. He eventually returned to acting after twelve years. He never forgave Marc Lawrence and would not appear at the same event if he were present.

Lawrence, meanwhile, suffered from guilt and depression for years afterward. He told Anthony Slide, "The point is, in making it a secret society, they made it treacherous. Where there's smoke, there's fire; and where there's silence there's guilt. If it were an open society, they wouldn't have to ask you who was a member of the Communist Party. They could look it up... None of these guys had the courage to say, 'I am a Communist.' They had been told to keep quiet. I can see it plainly now."

Lawrence was among 320 people blacklisted by the industry. He relocated his family to Paris, then Italy. "Italy was a savior to me," he told Slide. "As Hemingway said, it's like having died and gone to heaven. I couldn't believe the adulation they gave me...You see, the moment an American actor came to town in Italy, there would be big headlines in the paper. I was much happier in Europe than I was in America." He acted in a dozen films and even directed a few.

In 1958 he returned to the stage and received acclaim for his portrayal of longshoreman Eddie Carbone in the London production of Arthur Miller's "A

*Lawrence played a gangster in the Bond films* Diamonds Are Forever *(1971), and* The Man With the Golden Gun *(above, 1974).*

View From the Bridge." Lawrence returned to California with the play in 1959 and picked up work in episodic television. After a guest shot on *M Squad*, Lee Marvin suggested Lawrence work as a director. When he wasn't acting on shows like *Playhouse 90, Peter Gunn, The Rifleman*, and *The Untouchables*, he was directing episodes of *M Squad, Lawman, Bronco, The Roaring Twenties, 77 Sunset Strip*, and *Maverick*.

In 1963 he was back on the big screen playing a deported Mafia don in *Johnny Cool*. The next year he directed, co-produced and co-wrote the low-budget film *Nightmare in the Sun* (1965), starring John Derek and his wife Ursula Andress.

In the mid-1960s Lawrence bumped into John Wayne in Italy. An ardent anti-communist, Wayne even played a HUAC investigator in *Big Jim McLain* (1952). "He was a wealthy guy, and most guys with money hated communists," Lawrence told *Film Comment*. "They felt they were privileged people and they wanted to keep it that way. John Wayne wasn't a dyed-in-the-wool hater like some of them...I saw him in Rome, a big grin on his face. He says, 'Come on, you commie prick, let's have lunch.'"

In the 1970s Lawrence appeared on *Bonanza, Mannix, McCloud, Here's Lucy, Baretta, CHiPs, Wonder*

*Lees and Rinaldo wrote the original story for this 1943
Claudette Colbert-Fred MacMurray hit.*

*Woman, The Dukes of Hazard,* and *The A-Team.* His
movie work included *Diamonds are Forever* (1971),
*The Man With the Golden Gun* (1974), *Marathon Man*
(1976) with Laurence Olivier and Dustin Hoffman,
and *Foul Play* (1978) with Chevy Chase. He also wrote,
produced, directed and appeared in the 1972 thriller
*Daddy's Deadly Darling* with his daughter, Toni Lawrence, who later wed Billy Bob Thornton.

In 1991 he appeared in *Newsies* (1991) for Disney.
That year he published his autobiography, *Long Time
No See: Confessions of a Hollywood Gangster.* The title,
he said, came from a quip made by mobster Lucky
Luciano in 1957 when the actor asked him a favor.
"The line also is a metaphor for a blindness—an inabil-
ity to see oneself without the protective shell we use to
avoid seeing ourselves," he said. "I began writing years
earlier. It started out as a very bitter book. Then I
showed it to Ray Bradbury. He told me to lighten it up.
My son still says I was too hard on myself."

He continued working into his eighties and nine-
ties. Lawrence attended the Abbott and Costello Fan
Club convention in 1992. He appeared in the films
*Ruby* (1992), about the Dallas nightclub owner who
shot and killed Lee Harvey Oswald, and Quentin
Tarantino's *From Dusk Till Dawn* (1996), as well as the
TV series *Star Trek: The Next Generation, ER,* and *Star*

*Trek: Deep Space Nine.* He finally played a real Mafioso,
Carlo Gambino, the most powerful don in America,
in the Emmy award-winning *Gotti* (1996). His last
movie was *Looney Tunes: Back in Action* (2003) as one
of many sinister Acme vice presidents.

Marc Lawrence died on November 26, 2005 in
Palm Springs, Calif., of heart failure. He was 95. Fanya
Foss died in 1995. He was survived by his second wife,
Alicia, whom he married in 2003, and by two children
from his first marriage and a stepdaughter.

Leonard Maltin observed that Lawrence "was perhaps the only character actor of the 1930's and 1940's
still being cast in similar gangsterish roles in the 1980's
and 1990's."

"If being recognized for a particular type of role
brings fame to an actor," Lawrence said, "hey, you're
among the lucky ones."

Despite his prolific career, Marc Lawrence was not
included in the previous year's necrology at the 2006
Academy Awards.

Robert Lees and Fred Rinaldo were very busy in the
spring of 1941. After they delivered their screenplay
for "Oh, Charlie," producer Burt Kelly assigned them
his next two pictures: the horror comedy *The Black
Cat,* and the Baby Sandy opus *Bachelor Daddy.* Then
Alex Gottlieb put them on the next Abbott and
Costello film, *Ride 'Em, Cowboy.* "We never really got
along with Alex Gottlieb," Lees said. "I think the problem was, Gottlieb had a writer's head, not a producer's
head." Gottlieb liked some of the situations in their
script and other contributions from Edmund L. Hartmann and Harold Shumate. True Boardman and John
Grant wrote the screenplay, and Lees and Rinaldo
returned to "Oh, Charlie" to work on the re-take script.

In June the screenwriting team was on the Film
Committee of the Fourth American Writers Congress
in New York. Others on the committee included Ring
Lardner Jr., Paul Jarrico, Lester Cole, and Frank Tuttle.
The Film Committee prepared two papers for the
Writers Congress: "The Use of Motion Pictures as
Propaganda," and a general paper examining the cul-
tural role of the writer in relation to motion pictures.

With the success of *Buck Privates* and *In The Navy,*
several writers were assigned to develop a third service
comedy for Abbott and Costello. Lees and Rinaldo
focused their treatment on paratroops and visited a
nearby training area for research. Their story, however,
was not selected for *Keep 'Em Flying* (1941), but did

evolve into a later script, "Ready, Willing and 4-F," for Paramount.

After producer Burt Kelly moved to Paramount, Lees and Rinaldo picked up an assignment there from Sol Siegel, who knew Kelly from Republic. Their treatment, "Two Bad Angels," didn't move forward, but Paramount bought an idea of theirs that was inspired by *Life* magazine photojournalist Margaret Bourke-White. It was about a female photographer who, while photographing "sandhogs" constructing a tunnel, becomes attracted to one of the men. The studio adapted it for Fred MacMurray and Claudette Colbert as *No Time for Love.* After several delays the film was directed by Mitchell Leisen and released in 1943.

Back at Universal, Lees and Rinaldo were called in to plot *Juke Box Jenny,* a picture originally intended for the Andrews Sisters. The manufacturers and distributors of coin-operated record players deplored the term "juke box"; they preferred "music machines." The word "juke" as used by African-Americans in coastal South Carolina and Georgia means disorderly, rowdy, or wicked. A "juke joint" could refer to a roadside cafe or bar, but also a brothel. But "Juke box" came into popular use beginning in 1940 and was embraced by Hollywood; in 1941, Paramount registered the title "Jukebox Johnny," Universal registered "Jukebox Jenny" and "Juke Box Hits of 1941," and Fox registered "Juke Box War." The Andrews Sisters, however, didn't want to displease the record industry and dropped out of the picture. It's not known at what point Lees and Rinaldo became involved with this thankless project. The *New York Times* wrote: "...[T]his salute to the mechanical music-box trade is nothing more than a series of musical shorts strung out to feature-length running-time by means of a feeble yarn about a music snob who unknowingly becomes queen of the jitter bugs through some fancy manipulation of her classical recordings. If you can take sixty minutes of almost continuous swing by the orchestras of Charles Barnet and Wingy Manone, the Milt Herth Trio and the King's Men, then 'Juke Box Jenny' is your dish."

Based on the success of *Hold That Ghost,* Lees and Rinaldo developed a new horror comedy for Abbott and Costello early in 1942 titled "By Candlelight" (later retitled "You Hypnotize Me"). In the story, Bud and Lou run afoul of the sinister Dr. Ayoff (Basil Rathbone), a phony psychic who uses an incredible machine to tap into the preserved brains of his former clients. Ayoff learns all the intimate details of the lives and, more importantly, their finances. This script was intended for production in 1945 but shelved. Lees and Rinaldo salvaged some of the situations and atmosphere for their later masterpiece, *Abbott and Costello Meet Frankenstein* (1948).

Alex Gottlieb put the pair on another Abbott and Costello project, a remake of *Oh, Doctor!* (1925). The original was based on a novel by Harry Leon Wilson, whose novels "Merton of the Movies" and "Ruggles of Red Gap" were also made into films. *Oh, Doctor!* follows Rufus Billop, a hypochondriac who stands to inherit $750,000 in three years but is sure he'll be dead before then. A group of businessmen offer Rufus $100,000 now if he signs his future fortune over to them. Since he believes that he has only weeks to live, Rufus agrees. To be certain that Rufus stays alive, however, the loan sharks hire a pretty nurse to take care of him. When Rufus learns that she prefers strong, courageous men, he tries to impress her with a series of dangerous stunts to the distress of his creditors.

In time, however, a different story emerged about a gangster (Sheldon Leonard) who feigns illness to establish an alibi while he and his henchmen (Marc Lawrence and Joe Sawyer) rob a bank. Abbott and Costello are wrongfully accused of the crime and try to clear themselves by tracking the hoods to Sun Valley. Lees and Rinaldo, supplemented as always by John Grant, wrote the screenplay based on a story by True Boardman. The result was *Hit the Ice* (1943), another of Bud and Lou's best efforts.

In the fall of 1942 Lees and Rinaldo wrote a script titled "Party Line." Given their association with the Communist Party, it was an interesting pun. More likely it was about neighbors sharing a telephone party line, which were cheaper than private lines and were often the only thing available during wartime. As late as 1950, 75% of phones in the U.S. were still on party lines. Users were encouraged to limit calls to five minutes, and eavesdropping was always a concern. Nothing came of their script, however.

Early in 1943, when Abbott and Costello were sidelined by Lou's illness, Alex Gottlieb prepared a second picture for Olsen and Johnson. The veteran comedy team had great success with live shows, culminating in their freewheeling 1938 Broadway production "Hellzapoppin." (They also co-produced Abbott and Costello's Broadway show, "Streets of Paris.") Universal filmed *Hellzapoppin'* in 1941, and much of the humor satirized the process of trying to adapt the show to film. The movie was a critical flop but made money, so Universal brought Olsen and

*Lees and Rinaldo had the distinction of writing screenplays for both of Universal's comedy teams in 1943.*

Johnson back for another picture, *Crazy House.*

Gottlieb, who had produced and co-written the screenplay for *Hellzapoppin',* engaged Lees and Rinaldo, and they treated *Crazy House* as a sequel in the same satiric, absurdist vein. Lees recalled, "We really let ourselves go wild on that one. It turned out that the studio really had a sense of humor about being made fun of." It opens with Olsen and Johnson staging their own welcome back parade on Hollywood Boulevard. Inside Universal, however, word of their imminent approach sends the entire lot into a panic. Performers and crew scatter and hide. The studio gate is barricaded and the guards are heavily armed, but Ole and Chick launch themselves onto the lot by canon. They land in the offices of an executive producer and announce themselves over the intercom: "Universal's most sensational comedy team outside!" The producer cheerily replies, "Oh, Abbott and Costello. Send them right in." Although the comics have a two-picture deal, the studio refuses to make the second film because most of the staff has threatened to quit if they return. Undaunted, Olsen and Johnson hire the assistant director from their last film, find talent and financial backing, and make an independent film that they trick Universal into buying.

Gottlieb was set to produce *Crazy House* and write the screenplay based on Lees and Rinaldo's treatment. However, a week before production began, Gottlieb left Universal for a job at Warner Bros. "I finally realized I was going to be marked as just making Abbott and Costello pictures," Gottlieb explained in 1979. "I wanted to get away from Abbott and Costello because when they go down, I'd go down with them."

*Crazy House* was ultimately produced by Erle C. Kenton and directed by Eddie Cline. Most critics panned the picture, but *Variety* hailed it: "Olsen & Johnson's screwball antics…make for solid entertainment results." Robert Lees said, "The finished product was a disappointment once again because the producer insisted on putting every musical and dance act in show business into the picture. But we did have a gag that everyone has taken since: 'Miracle Productions. If It's Worth Seeing, It's a Miracle.'"

Around this time, Lees, Rinaldo, and Lester Cohen also wrote a film for Frank Capra's Army filmmaking unit called *Substitution and Conversion.* It showed how industry had converted to production for war. The three screenwriters also narrated the picture.

In the second half of 1943, Lees and Rinaldo had three films in release: *Hit the Ice, Crazy House,* and *No Time for Love.* Around this time they joined Frank Tuttle, Waldo Salt, Irving Pichel, Jules Dassin, Fred Zinneman, and others to teach pro bono classes in directing, screenwriting, radio writing, and comedy to budding directors and writers.

By then Lees and Rinaldo had also signed a three-year contract with Paramount. One of their first assignments was a Dorothy Lamour film, *Rainbow Island,* to be directed by Frank Tuttle. Lamour, however, was reluctant to do another sarong picture. It's

*Robert Lees and Fred Rinaldo wrote the screenplays for three hits in a row:* Buck Privates Come Home, The Wistful Widow of Wagon Gap *(1947), and* Abbott and Costello Meet Frankenstein *(1948).*

not clear when the team was put on the project, but they are not credited on the final film. Lamour did end up in a sarong, however, along with bit players Yvonne DeCarlo, Elena Verdugo, Audrey Young, and Noel Neill. Marc Lawrence played Lamour's jealous fiancé, Alcoa.

Lees and Rinaldo developed two war-themed comedies at Paramount. The first, "Ready, Willing and 4-F," came out of their unsold treatment for an Abbott and Costello air corps comedy. "It was about the straight man of a comedy team who gets drafted into the paratroops but the comic has a bad ear so he's 4-F," Lees recalled. "The straight man smuggles his partner into the army so they can perform in camp shows. We wrote it for Buddy DeSylva, the head of Paramount, who thought it was the funniest screenplay he ever read. We were suddenly the fair-haired boys of Paramount." Bob Hope, Eddie Bracken, Danny Kaye, and Billy DeWolfe were all mentioned at various times for the film. "The studio was so desperate," Lees said, "they even considered bringing in Cantinflas from Mexico! Anyway, [our script] wound up on a shelf."

The duo's other wartime comedy, "Girls Town," cast Bob Hope as the only male worker at a defense plant with 5,000 women. *Variety* reported that it would go into production in June 1944. It didn't. In three years at Paramount Lees and Rinaldo pitched stories or worked on screenplays without earning a single screen credit. The Lees and Rinaldo Papers preserved at the Margaret Herrick Library in Los Angeles contain treatments, outlines and some complete scripts for fifty unrealized productions over their joint and solo

careers. Some of the scripts include "Murder Farm," "Bedside Manner," "All American Girl," and "The Odyssey of Ulysses Brown."

Late in 1945 they worked on two short subjects at their alma mater, MGM. *Now We've Got to Pay For It* promoted Victory Bonds to finance the post-war programs necessary to transition America to peacetime. Edward Arnold was the on-camera narrator, and Harold Russell, the amputee who later appeared in *The Best Years of Our Lives* (1946), is shown in a clip. Lees and Rinaldo also worked on a documentary about moviemaking for the Academy of Motion Picture Arts and Sciences (AMPAS). It was produced by Dore Schary, the head of production at MGM, and screened at the Academy Awards and distributed to schools.

The duo was back freelancing at Universal the following year. A new producer, Robert Arthur, was preparing his first Abbott and Costello assignment, *Buck Privates Come Home.* Arthur (1909-1986) had been a screenwriter at MGM in the 1930s when Lees and Rinaldo were juniors there. During World War II he helped write and produce hundreds of briefing films for the Army Air Force. Except for a three-year hiatus when he worked at Warners and Columbia, Arthur worked at Universal for over twenty years. He produced six Abbott and Costello films, the Francis the Talking Mule series, five Rock Hudson pictures, and helped launched the careers of Blake Edwards and Stanley Shapiro. In 1965 the studio honored him with a lifetime contract.

*Buck Privates Come Home* was not just a sequel, but a pivotal reboot of Bud and Lou's careers. Their most recent films, *Little Giant* and *The Time of Their Lives* (both 1946), departed from the usual formula and were box office disappointments. Even before Arthur's arrival, a handful of writers took a crack at a follow-up to *Buck Privates,* including Arthur T. Horman, who wrote the original. Costello, however, insisted on hiring higher caliber talent. Richard Macauley, who had scripted comedies for Joe E. Brown and dramas for Cagney, Bogart, and Edward G. Robinson, was hired in April 1946. (Macauley later testified as a friendly witness before HUAC, where he asserted that the Screenwriters Guild was Communist-controlled. He named twenty-nine people in the industry as having links to the Communist Party.)

Macauley, whose salary was $2,000 a week, turned in a treatment that contained many of the elements in the finished film. Arthur then hired a less expensive writer, Bradford Ropes, to hone the story before he gave Lees and Rinaldo the screenwriting chores. "We liked working for Robert Arthur better than Alex Gottlieb," Lees recalled. "I thought Arthur was a fine producer who didn't try to write your picture the way Alex did." The story had more dimension and emotion than *Buck Privates*. Returning from Europe after the war, Abbott and Costello smuggle a six-year-old French orphan girl into the country. The film follows their efforts to find housing and jobs, adopt her, and avoid their old nemesis, Patrolman Collins (Nat Pendleton). It was one of Bud and Lou's best pictures.

The team's next film, *The Wistful Widow of Wagon Gap*, was originally intended for Jimmy Stewart. It was based on a screenplay by D. D. Beauchamp and William Bowers from a short story by Beauchamp. Costello is wrongfully accused of shooting a brawling townsman. He is spared from lynching by an obscure Montana law that holds the survivor of a gunfight responsible for the dependents and debts of the victim. Lou becomes liable for the dead man's boisterous widow and unruly children. Since no one will dare shoot Costello for fear of inheriting his dreadful responsibilities, the citizen's committee realizes that Lou will make an invincible sheriff who can clean up the town once and for all. Robert Arthur put Lees and Rinaldo on the screenplay and the film was another critical and popular success.

While Lees and Rinaldo were working on *Wistful Widow*, Robert Arthur came up with an idea for the next Abbott and Costello picture. "At that time," Arthur recalled, "Ed Muhl and I used to sit around and wonder, 'What do we do next?'" Muhl worked at Universal for 45 years. He started in the accounting department in 1927 and by 1947 was vice president and general manager of studio operations. "Ed was the fellow who realized what Abbott and Costello meant to the studio," Arthur explained. (Muhl may have seen Bud and Lou as a great asset, but in a brief interview shortly before he died he told me he didn't find Costello funny.) Arthur continued, "One night I thought, 'Who could they meet? Suppose they met Frankenstein.' I came back a few days later and told Ed the idea: A guy has the Frankenstein Monster, and the Monster's getting too smart. They need a pliable brain to put in the Monster's head, so they pick Costello's. Ed gave me the go ahead. He said, 'But why does it have to be some legitimate character that has the Monster? Why can't it be Dracula?' And instead of having some leading man warn Bud and Lou, we added the Wolf Man—just kicking it around in Ed Muhl's office at night."

There were at least two false starts by other writers before Arthur's idea crystalized. With a clearer concept, he put Lees and Rinaldo on the project, which was initially titled "The Brain of Frankenstein." Lees loved the idea. He recalled, "One of my major theories is that comedy is rooted in fear. So when you get Abbott and Costello meeting not only Frankenstein but Dracula and the Wolf Man, you can't miss. The minute the studio told Fred and I the basic idea, we said, 'This is the greatest idea for a comedy that ever was.' But that's all they gave us. We came up with the rest. Some of the best lines in the picture, like 'I'll bite'—'No, I will,' or when Chaney tells Costello the full moon turns him into a wolf and Costello says, 'You and twenty million other guys'—that was all Fred's stuff. He was so good with verbal jokes. I would say I did about two-thirds of the story and Fred did two-thirds of the dialogue."

Remarkably, Lou hated the script. Arthur recalled, "In fact he came charging in the office once day and said, 'My daughter could write a better script than this.'" Lees explained, "You have to remember that Abbott and Costello were stand-up comics from burlesque. So they were nervous about new material, and *Abbott and Costello Meet Frankenstein* was all new. I think the 'Moving Candle' was the only stock routine in it. I credit Bob Arthur for that, because he knew when he had a good story and a good script and he did what he could to protect it. That's the first Abbott and Costello picture Fred and I could look at and say, 'That's the script.'"

Of course, the picture was an instant classic and

Abbott and Costello's most popular film. It inspired meetings with Universal's other monsters. "For the end gag we had the Invisible Man," Lees recalled, "and Bob Arthur said, 'That's your next picture.'"

Not yet. After *Abbott and Costello Meet Frankenstein,* Lees and Rinaldo wrote a screenplay called "Three For The Money," where Costello plays triplets. The original story was written by Selma Diamond and Onnie Whizen, who worked on the Jimmy Durante-Gary Moore radio program; Diamond was on the writing staff and Whizen was the script girl. (Diamond was later part of the legendary writing staff of Sid Caesar's TV show and an inspiration for the Sally Rogers character on *The Dick Van Dyke Show.*) "Three For The Money" was scheduled to be Bud and Lou's next film, but was bumped by *Mexican Hayride* (1948).

Lees and Rinaldo finished their script for *Abbott and Costello Meet the Invisible Man* in January 1949, but production was delayed for almost a year when Lou suffered a relapse of rheumatic fever. The film was released in March 1951 and was another hit for the comedy and writing teams.

While other writers plotted Bud and Lou's next films—*Africa Screams, Mexican Hayride, Abbott and Costello Meet the Killer,* and *Abbott and Costello in the Foreign Legion*—Lees and Rinaldo pitched other projects. They wrote "Air-Crash," an original story about how the Civil Aeronautics Authority (CAA) investigated plane crashes. In 1947 there were six domestic air disasters with a total of 234 fatalities. As Lees and Rinaldo were polishing their story, a DC-6 en route to LaGuardia Airport crashed in Pennsylvania, killing all 43 passengers and crew. Universal hired another writer, Michael Blankfort, to write the screenplay, but the project was ultimately shelved.

In 1949 RKO bought Lees and Rinaldo's script "Make Way for the Bride" for Dorothy Lamour. She became pregnant with her second son, however, and the project was canceled.

At Columbia, the team wrote a draft of *The Fuller Brush Girl* for Lucille Ball, but director Frank Tashlin ended up writing his own screenplay. Lees and Rinaldo then wrote a script for Desi Arnaz called *Holiday in Havana* (from a story by Morton Grant). Arnaz's role as a Cuban bandleader anticipated his later role on *I Love Lucy.* The film was directed by Jean Yarbrough, who accepted a job directing the Abbott and Costello television series just before Lucy and Desi asked him to direct theirs.

Lees and Rinaldo also wrote a short film, *Speak*

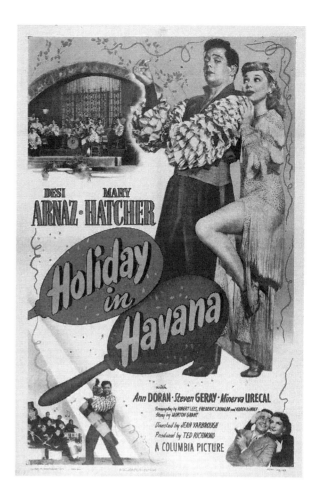

*Your Peace* (1950), warning against nuclear proliferation. It was produced by the the National Council of Arts, Sciences and Professions, an organization critics considered Communist influenced or controlled. "The day they started shooting," Bob Rinaldo said, "the Korean War broke out." Meanwhile, Lees and Rinaldo started their last screenplay for Abbott and Costello, *Comin' Round the Mountain* (1951). They also scripted "Casey Jones" for Donald O'Connor and Jimmy Durante, a follow-up to *The Milkman* (1950), but O'Connor started the *Francis the Talking Mule* series instead.

The screenwriters were working at Republic on *Oklahoma Annie* for Judy Canova when they were subpoenaed to appear before HUAC. The studio fired them and Jack Townley wrote the script. Meanwhile, *Abbott and Costello Meet Invisible Man* was about to be released. Lees was quoted in *Tender Comrades,* "Fred was advised to avoid a subpoena by leaving town. He hid out in his brother's mountain cabin. I visited him there to say good-bye before leaving on the train to join a group of other subpoenaed witnesses."

Lees traveled to Washington with writers Paul Jarrico, Richard Collins, Waldo Salt, and actors Larry

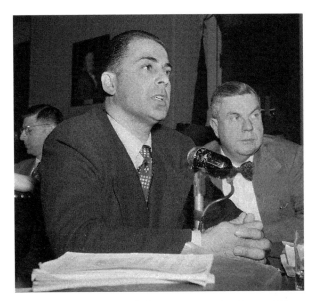

*Robert Lees testifies before HUAC on April 11, 1951.*
Abbott and Costello Meet the Invisible Man, *which he wrote with Fred Rinaldo, was in theaters.*

Parks, Howard DaSilva, Sterling Hayden and Gale Sondergaard. On April 10, Hayden testified that he had been a member of the Communist party in 1946 but quit in disillusionment. He told the committee that he knew the full name of only one other member of his "cell," Robert Lees. Hayden was remorseful, but he was welcomed back in Hollywood and returned to work on the film *Journey into Light* (1951).

Lees testified the next day for ninety minutes. The committee displayed his Communist Party registration cards for 1943, 1944 and 1945, and asked him to confirm or deny Hayden's testimony. Lees was then asked about his background, career, how he obtained screenwriting assignments, who his agents were, and with whom he worked. In his best efforts not to name Fred Rinaldo, Lees inadvertently turned the interrogation into an Abbott and Costello routine:

> *Tavenner:* Did you have an associate writer or partner?
> *Lees:* I think that's a matter of public record, the associate that I have worked with. I have been a member of a team for a great number of years.
> *Tavenner:* Well, who's on the team?
> *Lees:* I think you could find that out very simply by consulting the public records. It's on the screen and so forth and so on.
> *Wood:* Well, do you know? You know who it is, don't you?
> *Lees:* Well, I just simply say that this is something that the committee is asking me about which, as I

said, is a matter of public record, and I think that the committee could find out very simply by consulting those records. It probably knows by consulting those records already. I'm curious as to—
> *Wood:* You're asked to name them.
> *Lees:* What's that?
> *Wood:* You're asked who they were. Do you know?
> *Lees:* I say that this is a matter of public record. I know who I collaborated with.
> *Wood:* Well, would you mind telling the committee? I don't know.
> *Lees:* Is there any particular reason in regard to this question?
> *Tavenner:* A very definite reason.
> *Lees:* Could you clarify that?
> *Tavenner:* No. I'm asking you to answer the question.

Lees declined to answer on the grounds of the Fifth Amendment, but another committee member pursued the question.

> *Lees:* I do decline to answer it because I believe that's the same question I declined to answer before, Mr. Doyle.
> *Doyle:* Well, very frankly, I figured it was an honest-to-God way, my question, to ask you a frank, open question. I'm not trying to trap you. But when you voluntarily allow your name to be associated in the public record on a film or script and tell us that it is a public record, why then you hesitate to tell us the names of those people or where the record is, I don't savvy.
> *Lees:* Mr. Doyle, I think you just answered the question yourself. You said where the names can be found.
> *Doyle:* Well, where can they be found?
> *Lees:* You just said so.
> *Doyle:* Where?
> *Lees:* It's in the record at the moment, I believe, if you want to reexamine the question you just asked.
> *Doyle:* What record?
> *Lees:* I think you answered the question.
> *Doyle:* I don't know any record. I haven't seen any record where your associates are listed.
> *Lees:* Well, Mr. Doyle, I do feel that I have answered the question as clearly as I can, and I have stood on my privilege, and that's the best I can do.

Lees refused to answer whether he had been a member of the Communist Party, or contributed to organizations and publications deemed "subversive," or was acquainted with certain people. He continued to plead the Fifth.

*Velde:* There have been quite a number of cooperative witnesses who admitted to this committee that they have been members of the Communist Party and have answered the questions to the best of their ability. Have any of those in your knowledge been prosecuted for any type of crime whatsoever?

*Lees:* I don't know actually what's happened in prosecution, but I do know that there has been a great deal of reaction generally to people who have come before this committee and have cooperated with it. I know that there has been all kind of problems. I know that people who are simply subpoenaed by this committee have found themselves blacklisted or no longer able to work. I figure there's all kinds of jeopardy involved in this committee, either whether you're friendly or not.

Doyle asked Lees if he understood the purpose of the committee:

*Lees:* I know what has been listed organization wise. I know the number of people who have been blacklisted. I know the number of people who no longer can work. I know the number of careers that have been completely destroyed. I know a great number of things that have happened.

*Kearney:* Is that due to the company they kept?

*Lees:* All I know is that these people are respected citizens, and I have been living a very respectable and very, very upright life. I have been born in a great State and lived in that State, as Mr. Doyle has just pointed out. And I feel that 17 years of work in the motion picture industry of which I have devoted my time and my effort has been destroyed by this committee.

*Doyle:* Now, I would assure you that as a member of the committee there is no purpose or intent to destroy the career of any person nor harm any person. But as long as it appears you rely upon your counsel because you haven't had the time or taken the time to read the law and the jurisdiction of this committee, let me just quote the purpose of it, if I may, to you and see if you are in accord with this sort of purpose. Under Public Law 601 the Committee on Un-American Activities as a whole or by subcommittee is authorized "to make from time to time investigations of the extent, character, and objects of un-American propaganda activities in the United States." Do you or do you not feel that that is a worthy purpose?

*Lees:* Mr. Doyle, I have my opinion on what constitutes disloyal activities, and I base my opinion on the first amendment, and I consider disloyal activities that abridge anyone's right to speak or to join organizations of his free will, any rights of religion or beliefs, and I know some organizations that do persecute people because of their religion or their beliefs. I know of organizations that have persecuted people because of their race…I believe that these organizations infringe on the rights of the American people in the first amendment, and I feel that any infringements on the rights of the first amendment must be defended and the organizations that do these things must be attacked. On this basis I clearly see the right of this committee to attack those organizations and to ferret those organizations out, as I understand the first amendment and the right of the people under the first amendment…

*Doyle:* Mr. Lees, this is my final statement or question. One reason I have asked you these questions involving more or less the philosophy of certain thinking is that I wanted to try to convince you if I could as a much younger man that this committee is not interested in persecuting anybody, not you, not even the Communist Party. We are interested in fulfilling our responsibilities to the American people, which charges us with ferreting out and discovering and bringing before the law, as you stated, every person and every organization that is interested, has an objective in upsetting by force if necessary the American form of government. And I hope you will go back to Hollywood and to my native State with a firm knowledge of the fact that this committee is not apparently functioning the way you thought it was functioning when you came here as a witness. In other words, we are not interested in persecuting.

*Lees:* Mr. Doyle, I would like to go back to California and believe that, but I am going back to California and I know other witnesses and other people who have been before this committee maybe can't go back to California because there's no point in going back there because they can no longer work in the motion-picture industry, and they might try to find a job somewhere else. I don't know how you term this, as persecution or what, but I feel that this certainly comes under the heading of some kind of pressure that can be termed "blacklist," if you will, and that I don't feel that a blacklist denying people employment for whatever political beliefs they might hold is American.

Producer Robert Arthur, who was secretary of the MPA, also identified Lees as a communist. "He said he

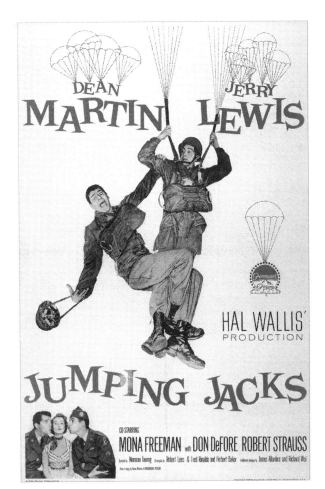

*Although blacklisted, Lees and Rinaldo received credit for the* Jumping Jacks *(1952) screenplay.*

had to watch that we didn't put anything subversive into the Abbott and Costello pictures," Lees recalled. "What subversive line could Abbott say? Was 'Who's on first?' supposed to be Stalin? I don't know!"

Lees and Rinaldo's careers were not quite over, however. Dean Martin and Jerry Lewis had made two hit service comedies, *At War With the Army* (1950) and *Sailor Beware* (1952), and Paramount, like Universal with Abbott and Costello a decade earlier, scrambled to put the comedy team into a third. Lees recalled, "They pulled the *Jumping Jacks* script off the shelf to do it with Martin and Lewis. Then they thought, 'My God, we can't do this—it's written by a couple of blacklisted writers! We can't give them any credit.' So they got Herbie Baker, who was a friend of ours. He told me this story. They said to him, 'Rewrite this script so we can get these guys' names off it.' Herbie told them he couldn't rewrite it and keep it the same picture." (*Los Angeles Times* columnist Ed Schallert reported that John Grant, who had worked on *Sailor Beware*, was working on it, too.)

Paramount put the picture into production in December 1951. When *Jumping Jacks* was released six months later, Brig. Gen. Frank Dern, deputy chief of the Army's information office, praised it and predicted it would "contribute to troop morale within the Army." Despite the Army's approval, the *Hollywood Reporter* condemned the picture because the screenwriters— Lees, Rinaldo, Brian Marlow and Richard Weil—were all implicated as Communists during the HUAC hearings. Producer Hal Wallis' attorney pointed out that, with the exception of Weil, the writers worked on the screenplay in 1943 and did not "benefit financially" from the sale of the script. Lees recalled, "Even though we were on the blacklist the Writer's Guild said they had to keep our names on it. So Paramount took out full-page ads in the trades saying that because of the screenwriter's guild they had to leave the names of the original writers on it. By then I was working as a maître d' at the Hotel Westerner in Tucson, and *Jumping Jacks* was playing first run, and an old Abbott and Costello film was still floating around—both of them with our names in plain view. I think that was a lot funnier than the pictures."

"It was pretty awful," remembered his son, Richard. "We couldn't say a word about what our father did [in Hollywood] under any circumstances. We were always looking over our shoulder. The guy knocking on the door could be the mailman or the FBI with another subpoena." But the humble job added much to Lees' experience. "He once told me," Richard said, "that on some level he probably would have had a more miserable life if he hadn't been blacklisted. That once out of the cocoon of being a famous Hollywood writer and being forced into the real world seasoned him in ways that wouldn't have been possible otherwise."

Bob Rinaldo recalled, "My uncle, Kyle Palmer (1891-1962), was the editor of the *Los Angeles Times.* He was the most influential power broker in the state and engineered Richard Nixon's career. Kyle told my father that he would 'fix it' for him so my father could go back to work. My father turned him down because my father was a man of tremendous principles."

In 1953, twenty-three actors and writers, including Lees and Rinaldo, sued the HUAC members, Hollywood studios, studio heads, and organizations for lost wages due to the blacklist. Each person sought $2.25 million, for a total of $51,700,000. While their appeal reached the Supreme Court in 1957, it was tossed out because members of Congress have immunity when performing their duties. Three years later, twelve writers and actors, including Fred Rinaldo, Ned Young (who had won an Oscar for *The Defiant Ones*), Lester Cole, and Gale Sondergaard, initiated a lawsuit against the Hollywood studios for creating and maintaining a blacklist. The suit was settled out of court in 1965 for $80,000.

Lees said he became disenchanted with communism around 1956 after details emerged about the atrocities committed under Stalin. He returned to Los Angeles and opened a dress shop with his wife. "There was a schism between Lees and Rinaldo when Bob Lees returned from Arizona," Bob Rinaldo said. "The blacklist was a searing experience. Everything disappeared for them overnight. Their relationship was never the same."

Fred took a job as a salesman for a wholesale paper company until his retirement in 1984. "He hated his job," Bob Rinaldo said. "It was torture for him, but he had to work to support his family. But he never stopped writing." Fred wrote two cult cheapies, *Robot Monster* and *Cat Women of the Moon* (both 1953). In the mid-Fifties, Hannah Weinstein (1911-1984), an American journalist, publicist and left-wing political activist who moved to Britain during the anti-Communist hearings, became a television producer. She created and executive produced *The Adventures of Robin Hood* (1955–59) and hired blacklisted writers Waldo Salt, Ring Lardner Jr., Ian McLellan Hunter, and others, using pseudonyms. Bob Rinaldo said, "She was sympathetic, but she also got topflight writers at a bargain because they were very hungry." The success of *Robin Hood* led Weinstein to create four more television series: *The Buccaneers* (1956–57) starring Robert Shaw; *The Adventures of Sir Lancelot* (1956-57); *Sword of Freedom* (1958-60); and *The Four Just Men* (1959). Fred Rinaldo wrote for *Robin Hood* and *The Adventures of Sir Lancelot*. "Dad never lost interest in writing," Bob Rinaldo said. "He wrote a play about Abraham Lincoln and a screenplay about William Shakespeare, two of his favorites."

Bob Lees also continued to write using his uncle's name, J. E. Selby, as an alias. "I lost my collaborator," Lees said, "I had to write all on my own for the first time." Lees scripted multiple episodes of *Lassie, Rawhide, Flipper,* and *Daktari,* as well as single episodes of *Alfred Hitchcock Presents, Gilligan's Island, The Green Hornet,* and *Land of the Giants.* His last credit was a 1983 episode of *The New Scooby and Scrappy-Doo Show.*

Lees and Rinaldo continued to speak out politically. In 1967 they joined 8,000 other California Democrats and signed an open letter to President Lyndon Johnson against the escalation of the Vietnam war.

Lees' wife, Jean Abel, died of cancer in 1982. Fred Rinaldo died on June 22, 1992 in Los Angeles of complications following an operation for a broken hip. He was 78. His wife, Marie, passed away in 2008.

In 1997 the American Film Institute famously refused to honor director Elia Kazan with a Lifetime Achievement Award. (The AFI celebrated Roger Corman instead.) Kazan testified before HUAC in 1952, named eight friends, and continued his career. An opinion piece by Martin E. Marty in the *Los Angeles Times*, "Elia Kazan: Can 'Naming Names' Be the One Unforgivable Sin?" prompted a response from Lees:

> Kazan did more than hand over to the committee the names of eight members of his Group Theatre to be blacklisted. He became infamous because of full-page ads he took in the *N.Y. Times* and *Variety* to make sure that his self-abasing confessions would be seen by everybody in show business. The following day Kazan signed a contract with 20th Century-Fox. Kazan's opportunity in the film industry to add to his lifetime achievements, such as "On the Waterfront," came at the expense of friends he named.
>
> Unlike film star Sterling Hayden, who named me before the committee, Kazan has remained silent. In his autobiography, "Wanderer," Hayden wrote to his psychiatrist: "If it hadn't been for you, I wouldn't have turned stoolie for Hoover. I don't think you have the foggiest notion of the contempt I have had for myself since I did that." All of which makes forgiveness in Hayden's case easy to come by.
>
> Marty should understand that there is a great deal of difference between immorality committed for monetary gain—Judas Iscariot's 30 pieces of silver—and that of the whistle-blower who loses his job.
>
> —ROBERT LEES

The debate wasn't over. In 1999 Kazan was awarded a lifetime achievement Academy Award, prompting a series of protests from some blacklisted writers and their families and supporters. Lees joined the protesters and carried a sign that read, "Don't Whitewash the Blacklist!" Later that year, prompted by Kazan's controversial award, the UCLA Screenwriters Showcase dedicated their graduation ceremony to twenty-three blacklisted writers, including Dalton Trumbo, Waldo Salt, Paul Jarrico, Robert Lees, and Fred

Rinaldo.

Lees enjoyed seeing renewed appreciation for his work with Fred Rinaldo. He was interviewed in several books about the blacklist, comedy writing, and Abbott and Costello. He appeared at many blacklist retrospectives, including some with Fred's son, Bob. "He never had a down moment," Rinaldo observed. "His disposition in life contributed to his longevity."

Early on the morning of June 13, 2004, Lees' long life ended suddenly and horrifically. A 27-year old drifter, high on methamphetamines and Ecstasy, entered Lee's home and decapitated him. He then carried the severed head into the home of Lee's neighbor and stabbed him to death, too. Lees' girlfriend of two decades, Helen Colton, lived across the street. She discovered his mutilated body hours later when she went to pick him up for an evening event at the Academy of Motion Picture Arts and Sciences. "I couldn't believe it," she said. "It was like a movie, not real life."

The killer was arrested the next day, about two miles away near Paramount Studios. He pled guilty in 2008 to two counts of first-degree murder along with eight other charges including torture, mayhem, and burglary. He was sentenced to two life terms without the possibility of parole and ordered to pay $9,000 in restitution and court fees.

"Dad had a premonition from his youth that he would die violently," his son, Richard, told the *Los Angeles Times*. He had left his father's house only a couple of hours before the killer entered, according to police. "I think when you have a sensitive child like Dad and put him in a universe of murder and wars and the rest of it, you internalize the worst of it and start to think why am I any better than that guy who got shot at Guadalcanal, the Battle of the Bulge or in Korea, Vietnam or Iraq? He was a dear fellow, a sweet man, who was like everybody else trying to make it through this business we call living."

Helen Colton recalled a plaque that Robert Lees had kept from his childhood bedroom. The inscription read: "The world is my home, all men are my brothers." Holding back tears, Colton told a reporter, "And he lived that out. He really did," "I've thought about what Bob would have made of his death," she said. "I think he would have said to that man, 'You're not worth losing my head over.' That's the kind of man he was."

After filming his musical numbers for *Hold That Ghost*

and the short *Is Everybody Happy?*, Ted Lewis toured the Midwest and east. Appearing in a hit Abbott and Costello picture certainly gave him an added boost. That fall, a poll conducted by a newspaper columnist compiled the five greatest showmen of modern times: Enrico Caruso, Will Rogers, Charlie Chaplin, John Barrymore—and Ted Lewis. A year earlier, in a similar *Billboard* poll, Lewis placed in the top twenty.

His former label, Columbia, released "Is Everybody Happy?" (Columbia C-9), a collection of reissues including "Blues My Naughty Sweetie Gives to Me," "Goodnight," "Somebody Stole My Gal," "Tiger Rag," "Have You Ever Been Lonely," "The World is Waiting for the Sunrise," "Some of These Days" (with Sophie Tucker) and "On the Sunny Side of the Street." Lewis was recording with Decca at the time, and had released "Jazz Me Blues, "Down the Old Church Aisle," and "Just Around the Corner."

The following year, Columbia made another faux biopic, *Is Everybody Happy?* It has been erroneously reported that Larry Parks played Lewis, but Ted played himself. (Parks, who had a supporting role, later played Al Jolson in *The Jolson Story*.) *Variety* called the film, which was directed by Charles Barton and laden with eighteen musical numbers, "pure corn." Another Lewis biopic was rumored in 1956 but nothing came of it.

*Billboard*'s reviews of Lewis' act in the 1940s acknowledged his crowd-pleasing showmanship, but complained that he "still retains the habit of grabbing most of the spotlight for himself, very often denying his supporting acts an encore where one is warranted and at times stretching one of his own pieces of business to the milking point..." Lewis often asked for applause or acknowledgement from his audience and sometimes continued to perform in blackface in a number called "Bring Back Those Minstrel Days."

After the war he performed in Las Vegas annually, and attracted capacity crowds there and elsewhere into 1950s. None of his reviews throughout the 1950s were negative; terms like "crowd-pleasing" and "sure-fire" reappear every time. Remarkably, he retained his audience without the benefit of records, and his TV appearances were rare. Performers as diverse as Joey Bishop and Leslie Uggams were still offering Lewis imitations in their acts in the 1950s.

Ted addressed his critics in an interview in the *Los Angeles Times*: "Corn? Sure it's corn. And let me tell you, son, it's corn people live on. Y'understand? Why, way back in 1926 the magazine *Downbeat* gave me an award for playing the corniest clarinet in the business.

And boy, was I proud!"

In 1956 Elroy Pease became the fourth performer to play Lewis' shadow. At a hotel in the Deep South, however, an outraged white politician threw a bread tray on the stage and disrupted the act. According to the *Chicago Defender*, "All Ted did was lambast the offender verbally; all the other guests did was rush the red-faced politician from the room and set up a barrage of applause that made Lewis very happy." It was still taboo for black performers to share the stage with white ones.

Lewis was the subject of Ralph Edwards' *This Is Your Life* on March 4, 1959 (the day after Lou Costello died). In the 1960s he refreshed the act by reuniting with some of his old collaborators, including Sophie Tucker, at the Riviera in Vegas. *Variety* praised the two veterans and called the act "one of the rare treats in the cafe orbit. Both of these stars add to the stature of the other. It's a happy combination." They combined for "Me and My Shadow," with Lewis shadowed by Pease and Tucker shadowed by Paul White in drag. Lewis also reconnected with his original shadow, Eddie Chester, and trombonist George Brunis.

In 1963, however, when John Bubbles, of Buck and Bubbles, became Lewis' new shadow, *Variety* called the bit "a sad anachronism" in the defining year of the civil rights movement. Still, Lewis did the bit with his fifth shadow, Harold Stumpy Cromer, on *The Hollywood Palace* in 1964.

In the mid-1960s Lewis, Tucker and George Jessel teamed up for a cabaret show. *Variety* wrote: "These headliners may have been in the entertainment business years without end; but, what is important, they know their business." They played New York's Latin Quarter to capacity crowds. But in 1966, when the show returned to New York, Tucker became ill and died soon after. Lewis tried unsuccessfully to revive the act with comedienne Totie Fields.

In 1967 he did a cringe-worthy, semi-rock n' roll version of "Me and My Shadow" with host Donald O'Connor on *The Hollywood Palace*. But rock music sent Lewis into what he considered an early retirement. "They think Ted Lewis is too corny," he said in 1970. "They probably think the parade has passed me by. If they threw me a couple of bones I'd grab them in a minute." He said, "When it gets in your blood, as it has in mine ever since I was a little kid, you just can't get away from it. It's my life." He said of some of the current entertainers, "They make a hit record and overnight go out and get $10,000 a week and still don't

*With Sophie Tucker in the early 1960s. Lewis and his band backed Tucker on her classic million-selling recording of "Some of These Days" in 1926.*

know how to walk on a stage. In my day, we did six to ten shows a day and you had to be a real showman."

Lewis didn't have much to look forward to. Even in the sanctuary of the Friar's Club, comedian Alan King relished beating him at gin rummy and taunting him with "Is Ev'rybody Happy?" because Lewis apparently was a sore loser. The highlight of 1970 for Lewis was his 80th birthday, which he celebrated in his adoring Circleville.

Ted Lewis died in his sleep on August 25, 1971. He was 81. Following a funeral service in Manhattan his body was brought to Circleville where thousands walked past his coffin. He was buried there at Forest Cemetery, where a family grave marker has his hat and cane incised upon it. Ted's beloved wife Adah, who died in 1981, rests beside him.

The Ted Lewis Museum, located across the street from where he was born, was dedicated on June 5, 1977 and was recently refurbished. A theater within the museum provides an opportunity for visitors to see Ted in performance by means of early TV and movie clips—including *Hold That Ghost*.

# *Credits and Pressbook*

Directed by . . . . . . . . Arthur Lubin
Associate Producer . . . . . .Burt Kelly
Associate Producer . . . .Glenn Tryon
Screenplay by . . . . . . . Robert Lees
Fred Rinaldo
John Grant
Original Story by . . . . . Robert Lees
Fred Rinaldo
Music by . . . . . . . . . . Hans J. Salter
(uncredited)
Cinematography by. . Elwood Bredell
Joseph Valentine
Film Editing by . . . . . . . Philip Cahn
Art Direction by . . . . . Jack Otterson
Set Decoration by . . . .
Russell A. Gausman
Costume Design by . . . . . Vera West
Assistant Director . . Gilbert J. Valle
Dialogue Director . . Joan Hathaway
Second Unit Director . . . .
John Rawlins (uncredited)
Associate Art Director . . . .
Harold H. MacArthur
Sound Supervisor. . Bernard B. Brown
Technician . . . . . . . . . . William Fox
Stunt Double for Lou Costello . . . .
Pat Costello (uncredited)
Musical Numbers Staged by . . .
Nick Castle
Musical Director . . . . . . . H.J. Salter
Stock Music Composers . . . .
Ralph Freed (uncredited)
Charles Henderson (uncredited)
Charles Previn (uncredited)

Milton Rosen (uncredited)
Hans J. Salter (uncredited)
Frank Skinner (uncredited)
Main Title Theme. . . . .
Frank Skinner (uncredited)

Bud Abbott . . . . . . . . . Chuck Murray
Lou Costello . . . . . Ferdinand Jones
Richard Carlson . . . . . Doctor Jackson
Joan Davis . . . . . . . Camille Brewster
Mischa Auer . . . . . . . . . . . . . Gregory
Evelyn Ankers . . . . . . . . Norma Lind
Marc Lawrence . . . . . . Charlie Smith
Shemp Howard . . . . . . . . . . Soda jerk
Russell Hicks . . . . . . . . . . . Bannister
William Davidson . . . . Moose Matson
Ted Lewis and His Orchestra
The Andrews Sisters
Milton Parsons . . . . . . Harry Hoskins
Frank Penny . . . . . . . . . Snake-Eyes
Edgar Dearing . . . . . . . . . . Irondome
Don Terry . . . . . . . . . . . . . Strangler
Edward Pawley . . . . . . . . High Collar
Nestor Paiva . . . . . . . . . . . . . . Glum
Spencer Charters . . . . . . Storekeeper
Paul Fix . . . . . . . . . . . . . . . . . Lefty
Howard Hickman. . . . . . . . . . . Judge
Madge Crane . . . . . . . Mrs. Giltedge
Harry Hayden . . . . . . . . . . . . Jenkins
William Forrest . . . . . . State Trooper
Charles B. Smith . . . . . . . . . . . . Kid
Paul Newlan . . . . . . . . . . . . Big Fink
Joe La Cava . . . . . . . . . . . Little Fink
Harry Wilson . . . . . Harry (uncredited)

Chuck Hamilton . . . . . .
Police Car Driver (uncredited)
Hans Herbert . . Mobster (uncredited)
Frank Richards . . . . . . . .
Gunman (uncredited)
Stanley Smith . . . . . . . . Clerk of court
(uncredited)
Thurston Hall . . . . . . Alderman Birch
Bobby Barber . . . Waiter (uncredited)
Brooks Benedict . . . . . .
Maître d' (uncredited)
Jeanne Blanche . . . . . .
Pretty Girl (uncredited)
Ralph Brooks . . . . . . . .
nightclub Patron (uncredited)
Jack Deery . . . . . Waiter (uncredited)
Joe Gilbert . . . . . . . . . .
nightclub Patron (uncredited)
Dick Gordon . . . . . . . . .
Club Patron (uncredited)
Kay Katya and Kay . . . . . . Dancers
Barry Norton . . . . . . . . .
Club Patron (uncredited)
Ronald R. Rondell . . . . . .
Headwaiter (uncredited)
William Ruhl . . . . . . . . . .
Nightclub Patron Who Falls
(uncredited)
Jeffrey Sayre . . . . . . . . . .
Chorus Boy (uncredited)
Janet Shaw . . . . . . Alderman's Girl
Larry Steers . . . . . . . . . . .
nightclub Patron (uncredited)
Amzie Strickland. . . . . . .
nightclub Patron (uncredited)

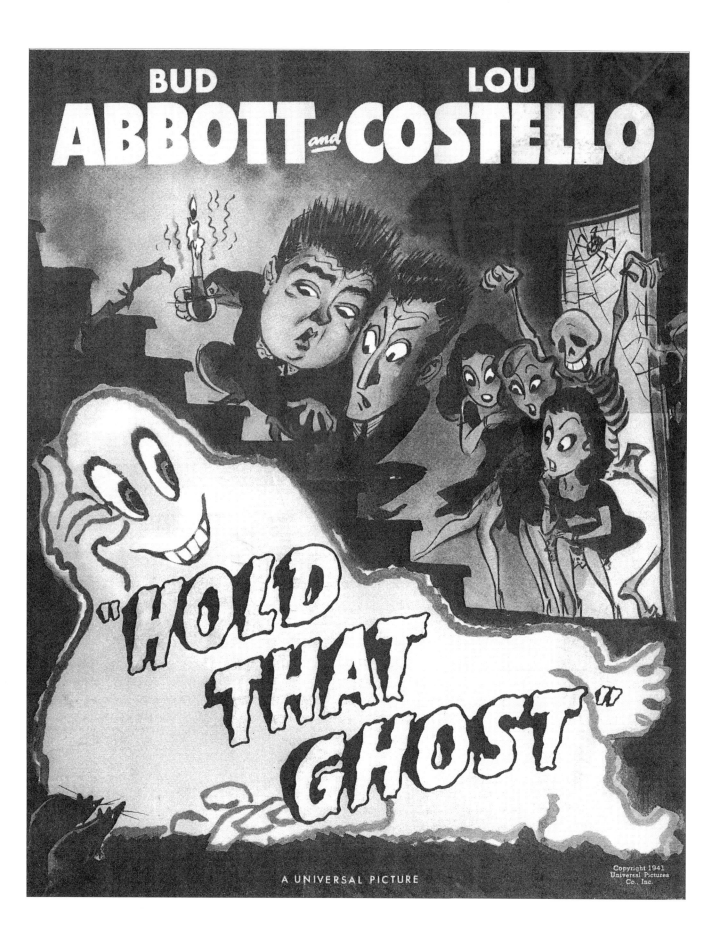

# Goblins Pursue Abbott and Costello

## Comedians Have Augmented Cast in 'Hold That Ghost'

### (Advance)

Bud Abbott and Lou Costello, laugh hits of two Universal box-office sensations, "Buck Privates" and Abbott and Costello and Dick Powell in the Navy, are coming back to the screen in another Universal comedy, "Hold That Ghost," which promises to outdo their previous successes from the standpoint of mad hilarity. The new offering has been booked into the .................... Theatre starting ....................

Evelyn Ankers and Lou Costello in "Hold That Ghost."
(Mat 12)

## Lou Costello Is Ex-Pugilist

### (Advance)

If you've ever wondered how a prize-fighter feels when he's on the receiving end of a solid sock, Lou Costello can enlighten you.

The roly-poly member of Universal's stellar comedy team of Abbott and Costello, when he was eighteen, fancied himself as something of a pugilist. He had figured in several bouts before his father discovered him in the ring and abruptly halted his boxing career.

During the filming of "Hold That Ghost," Universal's new mystery comedy, which co-stars the duo and which comes to the .................... Theatre next ...................., Lou was recalling his glove-tossing experiences. It was in Columbus, Ohio, where, broke, he was forced to accept a fight in order to eat.

"My opponent caught me on the right ear in the first round," Lou said. "I took such a terrific beating that it cost me all I earned to pay off the doctors."

In "Hold That Ghost," Costello and his partner, Bud Abbott, are surrounded by an imposing cast which includes Richard Carlson, Joan Davis, Mischa Auer, Evelyn Ankers and Shemp Howard.

Featured prominently in the spectacular musical sequences are the Andrews Sisters and Ted Lewis and his orchestra.

Arthur Lubin directed the eerie comedy. Burt Kelly and Glenn Tryon were the associate producers.

---

Playing in support of the stellar comics are such outstanding marquee "names" as Richard Carlson, Joan Davis, Mischa Auer, Evelyn Ankers, Shemp Howard, the Andrews Sisters and Ted Lewis and his orchestra. "Hold That Ghost," most of which is backgrounded within a long-abandoned and supposedly haunted roadhouse, was directed by Arthur Lubin, who piloted Abbott and Costello in both "Buck Privates" and the Navy feature.

### Story Called Rip-Roaring

Carrying a rip-roaring story as a means of holding together their zany dialog and gags, and given a far more elaborate mounting than any of their earlier films, "Hold That Ghost" promises to elevate Abbott and Costello to new heights of cinematic popularity.

Opening in a night club, where Lewis and his band and the Andrews Sisters supply the entertainment, the vehicle moves speedily to a gas station, where Abbott and Costello accidentally become entangled with a gangster, inheriting the deserted inn when he is slain by police. With ghosts serving as their stooges, Abbott and Costello are said to make the sky the limit for their laugh-provoking antics.

Carlson and Miss Ankers provide the romantic interest in "Hold That Ghost."

Ted Lewis and the Andrews Sisters appearing with Abbott and Costello in Universal's "Hold That Ghost."
(Mat 11)

## English Actress Born in Chile

### (Current)

Evelyn Ankers, who plays the romantic lead in Universal's new Abbott and Costello starrer, "Hold That Ghost," current attraction at the .................... Theatre, probably is the only Hollywood actress who ever rode a llama.

Born in Valparaiso, Chile, of British parents, Miss Ankers spent the first ten years of her life in South America. Her first—and last—llama jaunt took place in Peru when she was only nine years old.

"The beast didn't take kindly to toting me on its back," she said, "and tossed me off onto a pile of rocks."

Bud Abbott (L) and Lou Costello starring in Universal's hilarious comedy production, "Hold That Ghost."
(Mat 21)

---

## CREDITS

*Universal Pictures presents*
**BUD ABBOTT & LOU COSTELLO**
*in*
**"HOLD THAT GHOST"**
*with*
Richard Carlson, Joan Davis, Mischa Auer, Evelyn Ankers, Shemp Howard and
**THE ANDREWS SISTERS**
*and*
**TED LEWIS & BAND**

| | |
|---|---|
| *Screen Play* | Robert Lees |
| | Fred Rinaldo |
| | John Grant |
| *Original Story* | Robert Lees |
| | Fred Rinaldo |
| *Cameramen* | Elwood Bredell |
| | Joseph Valentine |
| *Art Director* | Jack Otterson |
| *Costumes* | Vera West |
| *Sound Supervisor* | |
| | Bernard B. Brown |
| *Musical Director* | H. J. Salter |
| *Director* | Arthur Lubin |
| *Associate Producers* | Burt Kelly |
| | Glenn Tryon |

## MUSIC

*Sung by*
**THE ANDREWS SISTERS**

**"SLEEPY SERENADE"**
*Written by* Mort Greene
Lou Singer
*(Published by Leeds)*

**"AURORA"**
*Written by* Mario Lago
Roberto Roberti
*English Lyrics by* Harold Adamson
*(Published by Robbins)*

*Sung by*
**TED LEWIS**

**"ISN'T SHE A PRETTY THING?"**
*Written by* Ernest Longstaffe
*(Published by Chappel)*

**"MURDER"**
*Written by* Ernest Longstaffe
*(Published by Chappel)*

**"LEADER OF THE TOWN BRASS BAND"**
*Written by* Ernest Longstaffe
*(Published by Chappel)*

**"ME AND MY SHADOW"**
*Written by* Al Jolson
Dave Dryer
Billy Rose
*(Published by Irving Berlin)*

**"JUST AROUND THE CORNER"**
*Written by* Harry VonTilzer
Dolph Singer
*(Published by Broadway Music)*

**"ON THE SUNNY SIDE OF THE STREET"**
*Written by* Jimmy McHugh
Dorothy Fields
*(Published by Shapiro-Bernstein)*

**"WHEN MY BABY SMILES AT ME"**
*Written by* Andrew B. Sterling
Ted Lewis
Bill Munro
*(Published by Harry VonTilzer)*

---

## THE CAST

| | |
|---|---|
| *Chuck Murray* | Bud Abbott |
| *Ferdinand Jones* | Lou Costello |
| *Doctor Jackson* | Richard Carlson |
| *Camille Brewster* | Joan Davis |
| *Gregory* | Mischa Auer |
| *Norma Lind* | Evelyn Ankers |
| *Charlie Smith* | Marc Lawrence |
| *Soda Jerk* | Shemp Howard |
| *Bannister* | Russell Hicks |
| *Moose Matson* | William Davidson |

**TED LEWIS & HIS ORCHESTRA**
**THE ANDREWS SISTERS**

## SYNOPSIS

### (Not for Publication)

Chuck Murray (Bud Abbott) and Ferdinand Jones (Lou Costello), co-operators of a gas station, get themselves jobs as relief waiters at a new night club where Ted Lewis and his orchestra and the Andrews Sisters are heading the floor show.

Accidently, Chuck and Ferdie become entangled with a gangster. When he is "rubbed out," they inherit, through his strange will, an abandoned tavern, supposedly the cache for his swag.

Chuck and Ferdie engage passage in a wildcat car which also carries Dr. Jackson (Richard Carlson), Norma Lind (Evelyn Ankers), Camille Brewster (Joan Davis) and Charlie Smith (Marc Lawrence). Arriving at the tavern in a storm, Chuck and Ferdie invite the others inside. The driver runs away with their baggage, leaving them marooned.

Smith, exploring the basement for hidden loot, is murdered. Then, through some weird hokus pokus, his body is found in the gangster's luxurious bedroom.

While Ferdie's party searches the place, many spooky manifestations become apparent. Lights go out, and there are moans and unearthly knocks. Meanwhile, former followers of the gangster-owner invade the tavern and hide in the cellar, revealing their presence when Ferdie uncovers a huge pile of greenbacks in a moose head.

Rival gangsters appear. There is a terrific fight, but Ferdie and his crowd, headed by Dr. Jackson, finally subdue the crooks just as the police arrive.

The money is counterfeit, but Chuck and Ferdie cash in on their inheritance by converting the tavern into a health resort with Jackson as chief physician and Norma, now his wife, as head nurse. Camille, who is romantically pursuing Ferdie, remains to assist in its operation.

◆ ◆ ◆

## Jazz Maestro

### (Current)

Ted Lewis, who is featured with Abbott and Costello in Universal's new laugh sensation, "Hold That Ghost," now at the .................... Theatre, is the dean of America's contemporary "name" band leaders. Lewis made his professional debut in Cincinnati, Ohio, at the age of 17 and has been the head of his own organization for 30 years. Six of his musicians have been with him for nearly two decades.

Page Three

# 'Hold That Ghost' is All-Out Comedy

## Total Laughs Promised in Abbott, Costello Fun Film

*(Review)*

Bud Abbott and Lou Costello have done it again! Following up their sensational successes in Universal's "Buck Privates" and Abbott and Costello and Dick Powell in the Navy, these two stellar comedians crash the screen with even more hilarious performances in the same company's "Hold That Ghost," which opened yesterday at the ..................... Theatre.

Equipped with even a more diverting story thread than the earlier Abbott and Costello vehicles, and carrying a more imposing supporting cast and an elaborately impressive mounting, "Hold That Ghost" is probably destined to surpass even the enormous grosses piled up by Universal's Army and Navy laugh-jerkers.

### Big Player Roster

Featured in the big player roster, in addition to Abbott and Costello, are such important marquee "names" as Richard Carlson, Joan Davis, Mischa Auer, Evelyn Ankers, Shemp Howard, the Andrews Sisters and Ted Lewis and his orchestra.

That Abbott and Costello are destined to hold for some time to come the high cinematic positions they have so suddenly gained, is clearly demonstrated by their riproaring contributions to this newest Universal hit. They definitely are solid entertainers with a broad appeal for the masses.

This time Bud and Lou, operators of a gas station, accidentally become entangled with a gangster and just as accidentally become his heirs. Their chief inheritance is a long-abandoned and supposedly haunted tavern, headquarters for rum-runners and gamblers during the prohibition era.

"Hold That Ghost" opens in a new night club, where Ted Lewis and his orchestra and the Andrews Sisters are supplying the entertainment, and where Abbott and Costello, weary of the dreariness of their business, get jobs as relief waiters. Lewis and the Andrews Sisters sing several song numbers in the nitery scenes and in the garden party sequence that brings the feature's final fade.

Abbott and Costello are in top form throughout "Hold That Ghost's" unfoldment, leading their audiences from laugh to laugh in an unbroken chain. Carlson is excellent as the young doctor, sharing romantic honors with the beautiful and equally-talented Evelyn Ankers.

### Comics Run Race

Joan Davis, Mischa Auer and Shemp Howard run a neck-and-neck race for secondary comedy honors. Lewis and his crew are entertaining from start to finish, while the Andrews Sisters show to better advantage than ever before.

Arthur Lubin, who directed "Buck Privates" and Abbott and Costello and Dick Powell in the Navy, has guided his puppets with fast and telling pacing.

Burt Kelly and Glen Tryon are credited as associate producers and the cameramen were Elwood Bredell and Joseph Valentine.

"Hold That Ghost" is recommended as tops in contemporary entertainment.

Bud Abbott (L), Lou Costello, Evelyn Ankers, Joan Davis and Richard Carlson in one of the spooky sequences of Universal's comedy riot, "Hold That Ghost." Ted Lewis and his orchestra and the Andrews Sisters are featured prominently in the eerie funfilm.

(Mat 22)

## Richard Carlson Haunted By Reputation of 'Genius'

*(Advance)*

Richard Carlson, who heads the supporting cast in Universal's newest Abbott and Costello starrer, "Hold That Ghost," which opens .................... at the ..................... Theatre, is happy in Hollywood—and for a most unusual reason. He has finally lost the tag of "genius" which haunted him throughout his school and university days.

When Carlson was a freshman in high school he wrote a play which was presented in Minneapolis. Newspaper critics immediately hailed him as a "young genius."

At the University of Minnesota he made such a scholastic record that he again was heralded as a "genius," and when he followed this up by writing several successful plays, the label became more securely fastened to him than ever.

Even after graduation, when he launched a theatrical project in Minneapolis, where he produced and acted in shows, he still was called a "genius." The thing became sickening to the would-be thespian.

Finally, Carlson came to the film capital, won a contract and now is a fast-rising leading man. But so far no one has stamped him as a "genius."

"Geniuses are a dime a dozen in Hollywood," he said. "In fact, you almost have to be one of them in order to make good. However, I'll make my screen climb the hard way, for I've had enough of the 'genius' business to last me a lifetime."

With Abbott and Costello and Carlson in "Hold That Ghost" are such outstanding performers as Joan Davis, Mischa Auer, Evelyn Ankers, Shemp Howard, the Andrews Sisters and Ted Lewis and his orchestra.

Arthur Lubin directed the eerie funfilm from a screenplay by Robert Lees, Fred Rinaldo and John Grant. Lees and Rinaldo are credited for the original story.

Burt Kelly and Glenn Tryon were the associate producers.

## Build Strange Setting for Spooky Comedy

*(Advance)*

One of the spookiest sets ever devised for a motion picture is said to provide the background for much of the action in Universal's new mystery comedy, "Hold That Ghost," which stars Bud Abbott and Lou Costello, and which opens ................. at the ................. Theatre.

### Sets Are Described

To all intents and purposes, the layout is an elaborately-furnished bedroom in a long-abandoned roadhouse to which the two comedians fall heir. But by the simple application of pressure to the wall of a clothes closet, the place suddenly comes to life, with the bed, dresser and other furnishings disappearing from sight. In their stead appear roulette and crap tables and other gambling devices.

The tavern at one time supposedly had been a gambling spot and hangout for gangsters.

Costello, roly-poly member of the laugh-making duo, attempts to bed himself down in the room with hilarious results.

### Cast Is Imposing

Playing in support of Abbott and Costello in the offering, which Arthur Lubin directed, are such important players as Richard Carlson, Joan Davis, Mischa Auer, Evelyn Ankers, Shemp Howard, the Andrews Sisters and Ted Lewis and his orchestra.

Special photographic effects in the eerie comedy were accomplished by Elwood Bredell and Joseph Valentine, noted Hollywood cameramen.

Burt Kelly and Glenn Tryon were the associate producers.

Lou Costello (L) with Mischa Auer and Bud Abbott in one of the side-splitting sequences of "Hold That Ghost." The Andrews Sisters and Ted Lewis and his orchestra are featured in the spectacular Universal comedy production.

(Mat 23)

## Home Towns, Birth Dates of Players

| | | |
|---|---|---|
| Bud Abbott | Atlantic City, N. J. | Oct. 2 |
| Lou Costello | Paterson, N. J. | Mar. 6 |
| Richard Carlson | Albert Lea, Minn. | April 29 |
| Joan Davis | St. Paul, Minn. | June 29 |
| Mischa Auer | St. Petersburg, Russia | Nov. 17 |
| Evelyn Ankers | Valparaiso, Chile | Aug. 17 |
| Shemp Howard | New York City | Jan. 16 |
| Marc Lawrence | New York City | Feb. 17 |
| Patty Andrews | Minneapolis, Minn. | Feb. 16 |
| Maxene Andrews | Minneapolis, Minn. | Jan. 3 |
| LaVerne Andrews | Minneapolis, Minn. | July 6 |
| Ted Lewis | Circleville, Ohio | Dec. 3 |

Page Four

# Spooks, Screams in Hilarious Film

The Andrews Sisters (L to R) Patty, Maxene and LaVerne, with Bud Abbott and Lou Costello in Universal's hilarious comedy production, "Hold That Ghost."

(Mat 24)

## Acrobatic Dance Brought Film Luck to Joan Davis

#### (Current)

Ability to absorb punishment isn't absolutely essential for success in Hollywood, but Joan Davis would be the last to deny it.

## Spider Webs in Motion Picture Are Imitations

#### (Advance)

Enough webs to accommodate all the spiders in California—and there are plenty of them—were spun by studio special effects technicians to provide the proper spooky atmosphere for Universal's new Bud Abbott-Lou Costello starring comedy, "Hold That Ghost." Much of the action in the picture, which opens .......... at the .......... Theatre, takes place in an abandoned and supposedly haunted roadhouse that once served as an underworld gang's headquarters.

It is no longer a secret that cobwebs, even more convincing for screen purposes than the real things, can be readily made in any spot desired. Their principal ingredient is rubber cement.

Abbott and Costello have been given a big supporting cast in "Hold That Ghost." In featured roles will be seen such outstanding performers as Richard Carlson, Joan Davis, Mischa Auer, Evelyn Ankers, Shemp Howard, the Andrews Sisters and Ted Lewis and his orchestra.

Arthur Lubin directed "Hold That Ghost" from the screenplay by Robert Lees, Fred Rinaldo and John Grant. The original story was authored by Lees and Rinaldo.

Burt Kelly and Glenn Tryon were the associate producers.

Filling one of the featured roles in Universal's hilarious new Abbott and Costello starrer, "Hold That Ghost," now screening at the .......... Theatre, Miss Davis literally fell into pictures.

A "falling" comedienne in vaudeville, Miss Davis and her partner and husband, Si Wills, headed for the film capital half a decade ago when variety house bookings became scarce. But she couldn't get inside a studio, despite the fact that she had starred on Broadway.

#### Meets Mack Sennett

So she persuaded a friend who knew Mack Sennett to invite the veteran producer to her home. Miss Davis did her famous ballet dance in the midst of which she does a comedy fall. Sennett was convulsed and immediately signed her for a two-reeler.

The short paved the way for a contract at 20th Century-Fox, from which she was borrowed by Universal for "Hold That Ghost."

"But if it wasn't for my ability to take falls and make them seem funny," she said, "I'd probably still be sitting at home waiting for some studio to give me my first call."

#### Big Supporting Cast

Playing in support of Abbott and Costello, in addition to Miss Davis, are Richard Carlson, Mischa Auer, Evelyn Ankers, Shemp Howard, the Andrews Sisters and Ted Lewis and his orchestra.

Arthur Lubin directed "Hold That Ghost" from the screenplay by Robert Lees, Fred Rinaldo and John Grant. The original story was authored by Lees and Rinaldo.

Burt Kelly and Glenn Tryon were the associate producers.

## 'Hold That Ghost,' Smash Hit for Abbott and Costello

#### (Current)

Bud Abbott and Lou Costello, who are co-starred in Universal's smash comedy, "Hold That Ghost," now at the .......... Theatre, are two of the most ardent comic strip fans in Hollywood. Both frankly admit their addiction to the black-and-white newspaper drawings and the colored Sunday supplements.

In fact, if pressed, they will tell you that they feel they owe much of their sensational success to the fact that they have been close students of the newspaper strips since boyhood.

#### Make Discovery

"Some twelve years ago," said Costello, "we discovered that millions of people, like ourselves, are regular followers of the comic strips. It surprised us, for up to that time we had kept our addiction under cover as being rather juvenile.

"We made a survey of the most popular strips, searching out those in which two men figure—strips on the order of Mutt and Jeff.

"Right then an idea was born. Why couldn't we be animated comic strips? Abbott could be the straight man—the wise guy who knows all the answers—while I could be the butt of most of the jokes, turning the tables on my partner just often enough to keep the customers interested and amused."

#### Act Is Modeled

It was on this basic principle that Abbott and Costello modeled their first vaudeville act, gradually devel-

oping the technique as time went on. Finally, while appearing in a Broadway vaudeville theatre, a radio scout "caught" their act and put them on the air.

They've been soaring ever since.

#### Low Comedy Defended

"Sure, we know it's low comedy that we do," Abbott confessed, "but that's apparently just what the public wants, judging from the millions who follow the newspaper strips every day.

"We figure that 100,000,000 Americans can't be wrong, and so long as we can keep up the wise-guy-and-sap combination, we ought to get along."

Abbott and Costello scored their first screen success in Universal's box-office record-breaker, "Buck Privates," and followed it up in the same company's Abbott and Costello and Dick Powell in the Navy.

#### Outstanding Players

Featured in the big cast playing in their support in "Hold That Ghost" are such outstanding players as Richard Carlson, Evelyn Ankers, Mischa Auer, Joan Davis, Shemp Howard, the Andrews Sisters and Ted Lewis and his orchestra.

## Evelyn Ankers Prominent in Cast of Comedy

#### (Current)

Evelyn Ankers, beautiful blonde English actress, who has the romantic lead in Universal's new Abbott and Costello starrer, "Hold That Ghost," is being groomed for stardom by that studio, where she was recently signed to a long-term contract.

Miss Ankers is featured in the supporting cast of "Hold That Ghost," current attraction at the .......... Theatre, with such outstanding performers as Richard Carlson, Joan Davis, Mischa Auer, Shemp Howard, the Andrews Sisters and Ted Lewis and his orchestra.

Although her parents are English, Miss Ankers was born in Valparaiso, Chile, where her father was a civil engineer and where she spent the first ten years of her life. She was educated in England, where she began her histrionic career.

After playing in British films and on the London stage, she came to the United States, making her American footlight debut in "Ladies in Retirement," after which she came to Hollywood, where Universal added her to its player roster.

Miss Ankers speaks Spanish as fluently as English.

Bud Abbott (L) and Lou Costello in "Hold That Ghost."

(Mat 13)

## Role in Comedy Wins Laughs For Mischa Auer

#### (Current)

Mischa Auer, portraying a Czarlike head waiter, turns in one of the finest performances of his entire screen career in support of Abbott and Costello in Universal's hilarious new comedy, "Hold That Ghost," now at the .......... Theatre.

"Hold That Ghost" opens with Auer as the maître in a swank night club, where he hires Abbott and Costello as relief waiters, only to discharge them the same evening because of their mad antics. The final scenes, however, show the two stellar comedians turning the tables on Auer, when they hire him as a mere waiter at their rest home and put him through all the tortures he had earlier inflicted upon them.

Other important "names" in the big cast, in addition to Abbott and Costello and Auer, include Richard Carlson, Joan Davis, Evelyn Ankers, Shemp Howard, the Andrews Sisters and Ted Lewis and his orchestra.

♦ ♦ ♦

## Star Performs Own Film Stunts

#### (Current)

Once a stunt man, always a stunt man, according to Lou Costello, roly-poly comedian.

Although he is now a full-fledged star and entitled to use a "double" when called upon to risk life and limb before the cameras, the heavyweight half of the team of Abbott and Costello, who top the big cast in Universal's riotous laugh hit, "Hold That Ghost," current at the .......... Theatre, insists upon doing his own stunts.

By all the rules of the game Pat Costello, Lou's stand-in, should also serve as his "double" and take the bumps for him, but his famous brother won't permit it.

"I'm afraid he'll hurt himself," Lou explains.

Lou first crashed Hollywood's gates as a stunt man.

Bud Abbott (L), Joan Davis and Lou Costello in one of the spooky sequences of Universal's sensational comedy "Hold That Ghost." The Andrews Sisters and Ted Lewis and his orchestra are featured prominently in the gay film.

(Mat 14)

Page Five

# Comedy Reaches All-Time Laugh High

## Lou Costello Satisfied to Be Low Comic

*(Current)*

Comedians may roughly be divided into two classes—those toting a secret yen to put aside their comic trappings and play Hamlet, and those whose drolleries have a hidden significance perceptible only to the intelligentsia.

Lou Costello, who with his partner, Bud Abbott, is starred in Universal's hilarious new comedy, "Hold That Ghost," now being screened at the .................. Theatre, is unique in that he fits into neither class.

"I'm just a low comedian," says Costello, "who gets a lot of fun out of doing screwy stunts."

The fact that the public is willing to pay large prices for which tomfoolery, is merely incidental so far as Costello is concerned.

Featured in "Hold That Ghost" are Richard Carlson, Joan Davis, Mischa Auer, Evelyn Ankers, Shemp Howard, the Andrews Sisters and Ted Lewis and his orchestra.

The Andrews Sisters, Patty (top), Maxene and LaVerne with Bud Abbott (L) and Lou Costello in "Hold That Ghost."

(Mat 15)

## Ted Lewis, Band Featured With Abbott and Costello

*(Current)*

Ted Lewis, Circleville, O., boy who made good in the show business, is celebrating the 35th anniversary of his start with a featured spot in Universal's hilarious new Abbott and Costello starrer, "Hold That Ghost," which is currently holding the screen at the .................. Theatre. Lewis was only 17 when he ran away from home and landed a job in a Cincinnati amusement park band.

## Quake Fails to Daunt Comedians

*(Current)*

When jolts and shocks are a part of your daily routine, a little thing like an earthquake can be passed off with a shrug.

At least that's what Bud Abbott and Lou Costello, starring in Universal's newest laugh success, "Hold That Ghost," current at the .................. Theatre, have demonstrated.

The setting for their new ribtickler is a haunted tavern and ghosts pop out of dark corners, mysterious rappings are heard within the walls and hair-raising screams are part of the regular routine.

Consequently the famous comics didn't realize it when, in the midst of a scene, a tremor shook the stage on which they were working. They didn't know about it until Director Arthur Lubin mentioned it later.

"Earthquake!" they exclaimed. "We thought it was just another gag for the picture!"

Ted Lewis and his orchestra, the Andrews Sisters, Richard Carlson, Joan Davis, Mischa Auer and a host of other Hollywood favorites are seen with Abbott and Costello in "Hold That Ghost."

Lewis and his entire troupe, including orchestra and song-and-dance acts, are featured in the elaborate night club and garden party sequences in "Hold That Ghost."

**Names Are Imposing**

Other imposing marquee "names" included in the big cast playing in support of the comedy heroes of Universal's box-office sensations, "Buck Privates" and Abbott and Costello and Dick Powell in the Navy, include Richard Carlson, Joan Davis, Mischa Auer, Evelyn Ankers, Shemp Howard and the Andrews Sisters.

Lewis, who has trouped the Western hemisphere with a band longer than any other contemporary baton wielder, is also rated as the wealthiest. It was in 1917 that he was designated as the "King of Jazz," the first person to bear the title.

Asked if he ever thought of retiring, Lewis answered in the affirmative. Then he shook his head and added: "I think about it, but that's all."

**Wants to Settle Down**

Although Lewis would like to settle down in Circleville, where he is the town's top realty owner, he insists he must think of the members of his organization.

"Why, some of them have been with me 20 years," he went on. "I've got to keep going to protect their jobs for them."

Arthur Lubin directed "Hold That Ghost."

## Famous Andrews Sisters Sing in 'Hold That Ghost'

*(Advance)*

The Andrews Sisters, who are featured with Abbott and Costello in Universal's laugh riot, "Hold That Ghost," which opens .................. at the .................. Theatre, have suddenly blossomed forth as Hollywood's newest Cinderellas. The three comediennes—Patty, Maxene and LaVerne—spanned the rags-to-riches gap in the brief space of four years.

Born in Minneapolis, where their father was a restaurant owner, the sisters had demonstrated their ability as entertainers before reaching their teens. During their school days they were in demand for appearances at private parties, school and church functions, the while marking time until their educations would be completed and they could go on tour.

**Success Delayed**

But success with the paying customers didn't come as easily as it had before home town audiences.

After months of playing small vaudeville circuits and cheap night clubs, the trio arrived in New York jobless and down to their last two dollars. Only a few years later, however, their earnings from motion pictures, personal appearances, radio and phonograph recordings touched the $200,000 mark, and under contracts already signed, they may soon garner better than $250,000 a year.

The thing that carried the Andrews Sisters to the top was their ability, discovered overnight, to warble "hot tunes." They are now credited with having made the nation boogie-woogie music-minded.

**Continue to Climb**

Starting their screen careers in Universal's "Argentine Nights," the sisters have continued to climb as cinematic attractions, becoming a smash hit in the same studio's "Buck Privates." They have since appeared in Abbott and Costello and Dick Powell in the Navy and now in "Hold That Ghost."

## Tin Bucket is Important Prop For Comedienne

*(Current)*

Joan Davis, the comedienne, in her five years in pictures has been measured for every type of costume from a ballet costume to a nightgown. But the topper of her whole screen career came when she was measured for a pail.

It was done for a scene in Universal's hilarious new Abbott and Costello starrer, "Hold That Ghost," current attraction at the .................. Theatre, in which Miss Davis winds up sitting in a bucket.

It was quite essential that Miss Davis should fit the container when she did her comedy fall without either losing too much skin, or, on the other hand, without rattling around like a bean in a gourd. So the studio tinsmith applied the tape measure to her anatomy. A special pail was tailored to size and Miss Davis escaped without a bruise.

Other featured players in "Hold That Ghost" include Richard Carlson, Mischa Auer, Evelyn Ankers, Shemp Howard, the Andrews Sisters and Ted Lewis and his orchestra.

Lou Costello (top), Bud Abbott, Richard Carlson and Evelyn Ankers in "Hold That Ghost."

(Mat 16)

## Story of Star's Film Career Has Amusing Climax

*(Advance)*

All Cinderellas don't wear skirts! Take, for instance, short, rotund Lou Costello, who with his partner, Bud Abbott, is co-starred in Universal's hilarious new comedy "Hold That Ghost," which opens .................. at the .................. Theatre.

**Voiced Defiance**

Several years ago, when Lou was a youth of nineteen, he voiced tearful defiance to a Hollywood assistant director who had just turned down his plea for an extra role in "The Trail of '98." The job meant everything to the young atmosphere player and stunt man, because without it he would be unable to eat.

"Some day you'll be working for me," Costello half sobbed. The assistant director merely shrugged.

Costello returned East and became a burlesque comedian, finally teamed with Abbott and together they became nationally famous a few years ago as radio comics. They were next heard from on Broadway. Then they came West to star at Universal studios.

**Face Is Familiar**

Checking in at Universal for the first day of "shooting" on "Hold That Ghost," Costello thought the face of the assistant director was familiar. Then he heard his name —Willard Sheldon. Immediately there flashed through the comedian's mind a picture of that offstage scene of a decade and a half earlier.

"You're the only one who ever threatened me and made good on it," Sheldon told Costello.

Playing in support of Abbott and Costello in "Hold That Ghost" are such important "names" as Richard Carlson, Joan Davis, Mischa Auer, Evelyn Ankers, Shemp Howard, the Andrews Sisters and Ted Lewis and his orchestra.

Ted Lewis (L), Lou Costello and Bud Abbott in Universal's spectacular comedy production, "Hold That Ghost."

(Mat 25)

# Accessories

## ★ RADIO SPOTS

**25 Words** The BIG news today is that Abbott and Costello are back in town . . . back from "Buck Privates" and "In The Navy" . . . back in their new hit "Hold That Ghost" at the Rivoli Theatre now.

**50 Words** Bud Abbott and Lou Costello have taken the nation by storm. First in "Buck Privates." Then "In The Navy." Now they are back in town in the funniest of all their fun-shows . . . "Hold That Ghost." It's a spooker-duper of hilarity, now showing at the Rivoli Theatre.

## ★ DISPLAY LINES

It's a ghost-to-ghost hook-up as these funatics of merriment give you even greater laughs than in "Buck Privates" or "In The Navy."

★ *Those funny men-iacs are here again! Merrier . . . madder . . . mirthier than "Buck Privates" and "In The Navy."*

★ A haunting they will go . . . scaring your blues away. Less private and more bucking than "Buck Privates" . . . sailing more riotously than "In The Navy" . . . an eerie-cheerie rampage of fun.

★ *You knew you were seeing things in "Buck Privates." And hearing things in "In The Navy." But you've seen nothing, heard nothing, till you get a load of "Hold That Ghost."*

★ Hold your sides! Hold onto your seat! "Hold That Ghost" can't hold any more laughs!

★ *The All-American laugh team is tackling new worlds. Shaking the spooks with laughter.*

★ W-h-o-o-o-o-o-o---PEE!!! Who's afraid of the big bad ghost? Those "Buck Privates" are spooker-dupers now! Those "In The Navy" gobs are in with the phantoms . . . and you're in for greater fun than ever!

## ★ FULL COLOR GIANT STANDEE

Standing six feet high, a flashy, full color, eye-stopping standee is available on this picture. The heads of Abbott and Costello predominate this piece. It's die cut and easel-backed, comes packed in sturdy cartons. Plant it well in advance, it's a great sales piece.

**$3.00 Each**
**UNIVERSAL BRANCHES**

★ **Set of eight 11 x 14's**

★ **WINDOW CARDS**

*Midget*

*Regular*

★ Order direct from your nearest UNIVERSAL BRANCH!

★

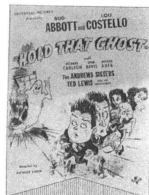

★ **22 x 28**

★ **14 x 36**     ★ **BANNER $1.50**

★ **HERALD** 7 x 10 INCH THREE COLOR **$3.50** PER 1000
AT  ALL  UNIVERSAL  BRANCHES

# THE MUSIC!

Top tunes from the nation's outstanding song writers! A scintillating score that has the power to get those extra windows, special displays and plugs in every music store, on the air and in every night spot in town! Two new hit-paraders sung by the sensational Andrews Sisters . . . and other favorites by that favorite music-maker, Ted Lewis! Put them to work FOR YOU!

★ "Sleepy Serenade"　　　　　★ "Aurora"

★ "When My Baby Smiles at Me"

★ "Me and My Shadow"

Hit Paraders—Old Favorites

Music to Match the Merriment!

Music to Hypo Your Campaign!

★ **SHEET MUSIC**　"Sleepy Serenade" and "Aurora" have both been published with special covers featuring the Andrews Sisters and Ted Lewis, and giving full picture credit! The balance of the numbers are scheduled for special picture-crediting reissue in time for your play-dates. Every music store counter, window and song plugger is a potential tie-up. Arrange for special displays of the song covers, providing blow-ups and accessory material for the lay-outs! Wherever piano players are used as "come-ons," get them to do some extra plugging.

★ **RECORDINGS**　The two pace-setting tunes, "Sleepy Serenade" and "Aurora" are already among the country's favorites! Leading bands the country over have been quick to capitalize on the skyrocketing popularity of these two numbers and a wealth of recordings are available. "Sleepy Serenade" has been recorded for Decca by Woody Herman and the Andrews Sisters; for Okeh Records by Claude Thornhill; for Victor by Sammy Kaye; for Columbia by Benny Goodman; for Bluebird by Glenn Miller. "Aurora" has been recorded for Decca by the Andrews Sisters, Jimmy Dorsey, Harry Harden, Carmen Miranda and Fernando Alvarez. Ted Lewis has recorded all of his most famous numbers for Decca Records. Keep these seat-selling tunes playing in your lobby over your p.a. system. Go after the windows and counters of the music and record shops for special displays! Make sure every radio station in town is using them!

★ **RADIO STATIONS**　Contact the announcers in charge of the record programs on local radio stations. Suggest a special Ted Lewis program in which all the recorded numbers of this grand music-master are played. Provide free tickets for them to use with their "quiz program." They'll get those picture plugs and reach the radio fans. "Sleepy Serenade" and "Aurora" will already be among their "request" favorites . . . do your best to get picture-crediting announcements whenever they are played.

★ **JUKE BOXES**　Those "Queens of the Music Machines," the Andrews Sisters, are back in "Hold That Ghost"! In addition, Ted (Is Everybody Happy?) Lewis plays, and has recorded, a number of his famous tunes in the picture. Contact your local juke box concessionaire and promote space on his machine for special display material. Capitalize especially on every machine playing "Sleepy Serenade" and "Aurora" . . . the two tunes that every big-name band in the country has recorded! If possible, promote use of one of the machines for your lobby so passersby can get a "sound preview" of the picture's music!

★ **Exploitation Record**

This special campaign record features excerpts from the picture's music, as sung by the Andrews Sisters and played by Ted Lewis and his band, together with seat-selling sales copy. It is a double-faced, 10-inch, 78 R.P.M. disc. Use it on your sound truck, on your p.a. system and play it on your "non-sync" between shows. Get music stores and record shops to use it as a special ballyhoo. Plant it on ASCAP licensed stations. Priced at only $1.00 each at Universal Branches.

Page Seven

## ★ LUMINOUS

Hand 'em a laugh right at the marquee stunt. Cut-out the scare from the 24-sheet and spot them be made of light-weight cloth dr work. Carry copy as indicated white floods underneath the te will give figure an eerie glow a ghost's eyes and keep 'em wink

## ★ 'TALK TO GHO

Sell 'em the laughs, gasps, gags That Ghost" with a "ghost-to-gh way to handle it will be to set rated sheet draped over a wire your lobby. A two way p.a. sy cealed usher. A sign invites pa Ask Joe Ghost about 'Hold That those two funatics . . . Bud Abb cealed usher responds to any qu also spiel the picture. His answe as possible. The Display Lines g

## ★ CONTEST FOR

Go after the photog fans with every one of the amateur lenser collection . . . either made acci them out by offering cash prize handled either through local new club. Set the stunt with a came of producing the "ghost" pics and absorbing one for them. G "co-sponsor" of the "Hold That and run pictures of the daily wi judged both for their humorous

## CO

Use
All
mor
whi
face
par
the
Mak
by
fran
on
over

# anship!

## GHOST!

...U COSTELLO
'GHOST"
...TED LEWIS and BAND

...start with this chuckle-winning
...d figures of Abbott and Costello
...s indicated. Giant ghost should
...ped over wood and wire frame-
...and spot a couple of green and
...t-like skirt of the ghost. Lights
... night. Mount green flashers in
...ing!

## ...)ST' LOBBY GAG

...and gloom-chasing plot of "Hold
...ost" hookup in your lobby! Best
...up a ghost (appropriately deco-
...and wood framework) right in
...stem connects "ghosts" to con-
...ssersby to: "Get the lowdown!
... Ghost' . . . latest riotous hit of
...ott and Lou Costello!" Your con-
...stions put to Joe Ghost and can
...rs should be as flip and frivolous
...ive you your copy slant!

## 'GHOST' PHOTOS

..."ghost-photo" contest! Almost
...s has some "ghost" shots in his
...dentally or intentionally. Bring
...s and guest tickets in a contest
...yspaper, camera shop or camera
...a club if possible. The problem
...ill probably prove an amusing
...et newspaper to cooperate as a
... Ghost—Ghost Photos Contest"
...nning entries. Entries should be
...and "ghostly" qualities.

## ★ ...MIC GHOSTS ★

...this ghost gag to sell the laughs!
...you need do is doll up one or
...e men in sheets, muslin or other
...e material . . . paint on the gay
...s and copy . . . and have them
...ide around town. A novelty on
...stunt is shown in illustration.
...e one ghost eight or ten feet tall
...aving bally man carry extension
...ework of ghost's head and arms
...is shoulders and draping sheet
... entire assembly.

## ★ 'JOE BONES' TIPS 'EM OFF!

This stunt should prove appropriate for both your advance or
current campaigns. On an unused or prop door in your lobby
urge your patrons to: "Open the door! Meet Joe Bones and
get the latest dope on a new kind of GHOST!" Behind door,
spot some bones and chain in a heap together with big ex-
planatory card reading: "I'm all broken up from laughing at
'HOLD THAT GHOST,' starring Bud Abbott and Lou Costello!
(Play dates, etc.)"

## ★ ISSUE DOUBLE CHALLENGE

For a publicity break, offer to stage a special showing for "the
bravest sour-puss in town"! Gag it, of course, letting them
know that it's all in fun. Your challenge should read:

*REWARD! For Blank City's bravest sour-puss! The
Blank Theatre will pay $5.00 to any person not affected
by the ghouls and gags, hilarity and howls, chuckles
and chills of "Hold That Ghost" . . . starring those
two funatics Bud Abbott and Lou Costello! No screaming, no trembling, no giggling, no guffawing allowed!
Candidates apply to Manager Blank Theatre.*

## ★ GHOSTS PICKET THEATRE

A chuckle-winning stunt for your theatre front would be a
parade of picketing ghosts. Costume problem is simple and the
ghosts need only carry picket placards bearing copy such as:

*"UNFAIR! 'HOLD THAT GHOST' unfair to serious
spooks. Do not stick around these hilarious haunts
unless you can take your chills with your laughs!
Ghosts Local No. 13."*

## ★ SCARED GHOSTS BALLY!

This ghost gag is easily accomplished and should sell both the
ghost thrills and the laughs! Dress up a group of youngsters
in ghostly raiment and send them around town in an open car.
Car is bannered with: *"We can't take it! We're getting out
of town! Bud Abbott and Lou Costello in 'HOLD THAT*

*GHOST' are
coming to the
Rivoli!(dates)."*
The youngsters,
of course, should
cavort as much
as possible at
every intersec-
tion.

## ★ TED LEWIS IMITATORS

That master music-maker, Ted (Is Everybody Happy?) Lewis
is a top favorite. His familiar singing style is an appropriate
basis for staging a "Ted Lewis Imitation Contest" at some
nearby nite spot, on the stage, or over the air. Stipulate that
entries sing either "Me and My Shadow" or "When My Baby
Smiles At Me" . . . his two most famous numbers, both of
which are in the picture. Tie-up with a local Music or Dramatic
School for prizes on the stunt.

## ★ GHOST BALLY PARADE

A "BUCK-GOB" BALLY . . . Don't let 'em forget that Abbott
and Costello are the boys who convulsed them in "Buck Privates" and "In the Navy" with a street bally designed to
emphasize these two hits in selling this film. Select two bally-
men . . . probably you've got a pair on your theatre staff . . .
one of whom resembles Abbott and the other Costello. Dress
one in a "Buck Privates" soldier uniform and the other in a
sailor suit. Soldier can be carrying a rifle with the gob swinging a mop. Sign on soldier reads: "I'm GUNNING For Spooks
in 'HOLD THAT GHOST' at the RIVOLI" signed Bud Abbott
(Lou Costello). Gob's card reads: " 'HOLD THAT GHOST' and
I'll MOP HIM UP!" signed Lou Costello (Bud Abbott).

## ★ GAG BUTTON GIVEAWAYS

Use this clever twist
on the familiar "but-
ton-giveaway" gag
to sell both the
hilarity and haunt
elements of the pic-
ture! Real buttons
(stuck to card with
glue) form the eyes
of the rollicking
ghost. Print them
up locally, using

A COUPLE OF SPARES!
...TO REPLACE THOSE BUTTONS
YOU LOSE FROM LAUGHING—
WHEN YOU
SEE.........
Bud ABBOTT & Lou COSTELLO in
HOLD THAT GHOST
RIVOLI Theatre now!

suggested copy and shooting your art from the illustration.

## ★ 'GHOST' TACK CARDS

Instead of just using plain formula tack cards and snipes, get a
large quantity of heavy cheesecloth or muslin. Cut it up into
fair-sized squares and have your house artist stencil them with
a gay ghost together with picture copy. The squares will make
unusual and striking sales items for fences, walls, telephone
posts and other postable locations. Use huge ones for any
appropriate spots. The ad section of this pressbook will provide
plenty of art for designing a stencil.

## ★ REMEMBER!
In every stunt, bally or display
in which a "ghost" is used . . . KEEP HIM SMILING! Take
your cue from the ads and posters and your "ghosts" will sell
the gags!

## ★ 'DANCING' GHOST SET-PIECE

Exploit the picture with this animated spook show in your
lobby. Make front of display out of flat compoboard, using the
cartoon art from the posters together with suggested copy.
Large ghost holding display is also
made of compoboard with green
flashers mounted in his eyes. The
"ghosts" in the
shadow box are
made of light
muslin, with toy
balloons form-
ing the heads,
and are hung
from top by
means of light
threads. Mount
electric fans
directly below
and keep them
going on and
off by means of
flasher buttons.
Fans will keep
the "ghosts"
dancing mer-
rily. Illuminate
interior of box
with dull green
lights.

A HAUNTING WE WILL
GO! Those FUNniest
their raciest, riotous
BEST! ... More
merrimenr
than "Buck
Privates"
and "In
the Navy"!
BUD LOU
ABBOTT-COSTELLO
HOLD
THAT GHOST
IN ANDREWS SISTERS
TED LEWIS

Page Eight

# Posters

**TWENTY-FOUR SHEET**

## COLOR DESCRIPTION

Bright, full color figures of Abbott and Costello, Andrews Sisters and Ted Lewis with eerie blue and green ghost in background. Title in red against white panel with billing in blue.

**THREE SHEET**

**SIX SHEET**

ACCESSORIES
SHOWN ON
PAGE NINE

**ONE SHEET**

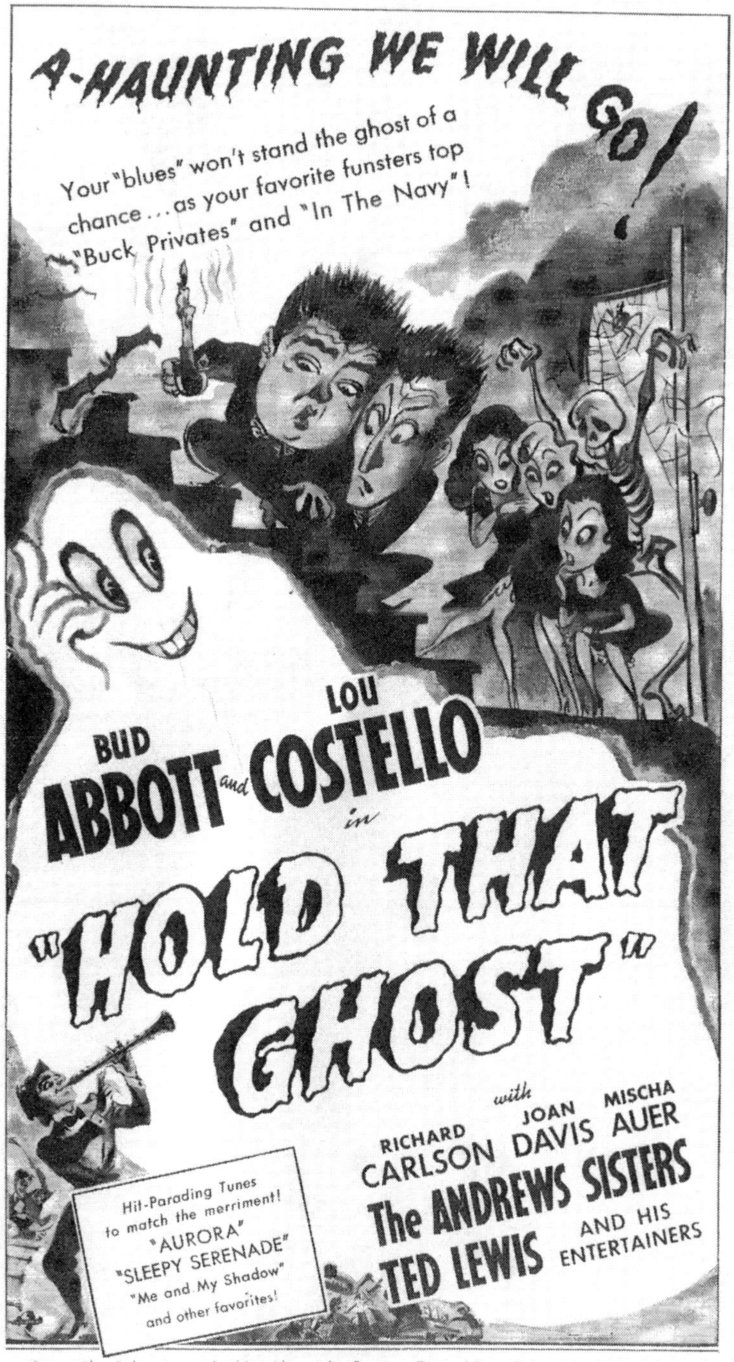


Screen Play, Robert Lees • Fred Rinaldo • John Grant Original Story, Robert Lees • Fred Rinaldo
Directed by Arthur Lubin Associate Producers: Burt Kelly • Glenn Tryon
A UNIVERSAL PICTURE

3B

Ad No. 3B—3 Col.—Mat 45c

A UNIVERSAL PICTURE

Ad No. 1E—1 Col.—Mat 15c

1E

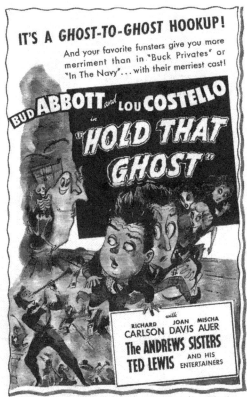

IT'S A GHOST-TO-GHOST HOOKUP!
And your favorite funsters give you more
merriment than in "Buck Privates" or
"In The Navy"... with their merriest cast!

BUD ABBOTT and LOU COSTELLO
in "HOLD THAT GHOST"

with
RICHARD JOAN MISCHA
CARLSON DAVIS AUER
The ANDREWS SISTERS
TED LEWIS AND HIS ENTERTAINERS

Screen Play, Robert Lees • Fred Rinaldo • John Grant   Original Story, Robert Lees
Fred Rinaldo   Associate Producers: Burt Kelly • Glenn Tryon
Directed by Arthur Lubin   A UNIVERSAL PICTURE

2C

Ad No. 2C—2 Col.—Mat 30c

HERE'S THAT ALL-AMERICAN *Laugh Team!*
They made things lighter
and brighter with "Buck
Privates" and "In The Navy!"
BUD LOU
ABBOTT-COSTELLO
in
"HOLD THAT GHOST"

with
RICHARD JOAN MISCHA
CARLSON DAVIS AUER
The ANDREWS SISTERS
TED LEWIS and his entertainers

Screen Play, Robert Lees • Fred Rinaldo • John Grant   Original Story, Robert Lees
Fred Rinaldo   Associate Producers: Burt Kelly • Glenn Tryon
Directed by Arthur Lubin   A UNIVERSAL PICTURE

2F

Ad No. 2F—2 Col.—Mat 30c

Ad No. 2E—2 Col.—Mat 30c

Ad No. 2B—2 Col.—Mat 30c

Ad No. 2D—2 Col.—Mat 30c

# Bibliography

Costello, Chris with Raymond Strait. *Lou's on First*. New York: St. Martin's Press, 1981.

Cullen, Frank with Florence Hackman and Donald McNeilly. *Vaudeville Old and New: An Encyclopedia of Variety Performers in America*. New York; London: Routledge, 2007.

Furia, Philip and Michael L. Lasser. *America's Songs: The Stories Behind the Songs of Broadway, Hollywood, and Tin Pan Alley*. New York; London: Routledge, 2006.

Furmanek, Bob and Ron Palumbo. *Abbott and Costello in Hollywood*. New York: Perigee, 1991.

Gordon, Mel. *Lazzi: The Comic Routines of the Commedia dell'Arte*. New York: Performing Arts Journal Publications, 1983.

Gomery, Douglas. "U.S. Film Exhibition: The Formation of a Big Business." *The American Film Industry*. Tino Balio, ed. Madison: The University of Wisconsin Press, 1985.

Izod, John. *Hollywood and the Box Office: 1895-1986*. New York: Columbia University Press, 1988.

Mank, Gregory William. *Women in Horror Films, 1940s*. Jefferson, NC: McFarland & Company, 1999.

McGilligan, Patrick and Paul Buhle. *Tender Comrades: A Backstory of the Hollywood Blacklist*. New York: St. Martin's Press, 1999.

McNamara, Brooks, ed., *American Popular Entertainments*. New York: Performing Arts Journal Publications, 1983.

Mulholland, Jim. *The Abbott and Costello Book*. New York: Popular Library, 1977.

Palumbo, Ron. *Buck Privates: The Original Screenplay*. Duncan, Okla.: Bear Manor Media, 2013.

Ruppli, Michael. *The Decca Labels: A Discography*. Westport, Conn.: Greenwood Press, 1996.

Server, Lee. "The Last Gangster: Marc Lawrence." *Film Comment*. Vol. 33, No. 3, 1997.

Slide, Anthony. *Actors on Red Alert: Career Interviews with Five Actors and Actresses Affected by the Blacklist*. Lanham, Md.: Scarecrow Press, 1999.

Thomas, Bob. *Bud & Lou*. New York: J.B. Lippincott, 1977.

Tucker, David C. *Joan Davis: America's Queen of Film, Radio and Television Comedy*. Jefferson, NC: McFarland & Company, 2014.

United States Congress. *Hearings Before the Committee on Un-American Activities, Eighty-second Congress, 1st and 2nd. Session, Volume 2*. Washington, D.C.: U.S. Government Printing Office, 1951.

Weaver, Tom and Michael Brunas and John Brunas. *Universal Horrors: The Studio's Classic Films, 1931-1946*. Jefferson, NC: McFarland & Company, 2007.

Made in the USA
Middletown, DE
11 July 2018